Irish
Educational Documents

Volume III

WITHDRAWN
FROM STOCK

A selection of extracts from documents
relating to the history of education
from 1922 to 1992
in Northern Ireland

EDITED By

Áine Hyland, Kenneth Milne, Gordon Byrne and John Dallat

C.I.C.E.

1995

ISBN 0 9509289 3 3

Text set in 10 and 11 pt Times.

Printed from camera-ready copy in the Republic of Ireland by the Leinster Leader, Naas, Co. Kildare.

Published by the Church of Ireland College of Education, Rathmines, Dublin 6, Ireland.

TABLE OF CONTENTS

IRISH EDUCATIONAL DOCUMENTS, VOLUME 3.

II ELEMENTARY/PRIMARY EDUCATION

III.16 Reorganisation of Secondary Education in Northern
Ireland, July 1976, HMSO.. 390
III.17 Education Reform in Northern Ireland — The Way
Forward, October 1988... 396
III.18 Education Reform (Northern Ireland) Order, 1989........ 401
III.19 The Curriculum for 14-19 Year Olds — A Framework
for Choice — DENI, March 1992................................... 407
III.20 Transfer from Primary to Secondary School —
1993/1994 and Beyond, DENI, October 1992................. 413

IV TECHNICAL AND FURTHER EDUCATION

IV.1 Interim Report of the Departmental Committee on the
Educational Services in Northern Ireland
(Lynn Committee), 1922, Cmd.6.................................... 417
IV.2 Education Act Northern Ireland 1923,
13 and 14 Geo.5, C.21... 421
IV.3 The Report of the Committee on the Financial
Relations between the State and Local Authorities —
August 1931, Cmd.131... 423
IV.4 Report of the Committee on the Scholarships System
in Northern Ireland — March 1938, Cmd.192............... 427
IV.5 Report of the Consultative Committee on Secondary
Education, October 1938, W.Spens (Chairman)............ 427
IV.6 Educational Reconstruction in Northern Ireland,
December 1944, Cmd.226.. 432
IV.7 Education Act (Northern Ireland) 1947, C.3................. 438
IV.8 Educational Development in Northern Ireland, 1964,
Cmd.470.. 440
IV.9 Higher Education in Northern Ireland, February 1965,
Chairman Sir John Lockwood, Cmd.475....................... 447
IV.10 Education (Amendment) Act (Northern Ireland),
1968, C.2.. 449
IV.11 Department of Education and Science Advisory
Council on Education for Industry and Commerce :
Report of the Committee on Technician Courses and
Examinations, HMSO, 1969,
Chairman, Dr. H.L. Haslegrave.................................... 450

V TEACHER EDUCATION 1922-1992

Acknowledgements

In 1984 the Church of Ireland College of Education celebrated its centenary. To mark the centenary, an exhibition of educational documents and materials was mounted by the college and a number of educational historians from university education departments and colleges of education came together to prepare a catalogue of the exhibition. In the course of that work it was agreed that it would be useful to publish extracts from some key educational documents and a committee was formed to carry out the task. Volume I of *Irish Educational Documents* which was published in 1987 contained a selection of extracts from documents relating to the history of Irish education from the earliest times to 1922. Volume II, which was published in 1992, contained extracts relating to education in the Irish Free State and the Republic of Ireland from 1922 to 1991. The current and final volume relates to education in Northern Ireland from 1922 to 1992.

This volume has been edited by Áine Hyland, Education Department, University College, Cork; Kenneth Milne, former principal of the Church of Ireland College of Education; Gordon Byrne, principal of Upper Bann Institute of Further and Higher Education and John Dallat, Education Department of the University of Ulster at Jordanstown. Section I was written by John Dallat and the late Canon Eric Elliott, rector of St. Thomas's Church, Belfast. Canon Elliott died in October 1990 while the work was in progress. We are indebted to George Boyd, formerly of Stranmillis College, Belfast, for

x

Section II. Sections III and IV are the work of Gordon Byrne
and Sections V and VI were contributed by Seán Farren of the
University of Ulster at Coleraine. Appendix I is the work of
Trevor Parkhill of the Public Record Office of Northern
Ireland while the bibliography was compiled by Kenneth
Milne. General editorial comment and advice was given by
John Coolahan, Education Department, St. Patrick's College,
Maynooth and by Susan Parkes, School of Education, Trinity
College, Dublin. The cover design is the work of Elizabeth
MacArthur O'Kelly, with help and advice from John Dallat
and Harold Hislop.

We would like to record our gratitude for the financial support
given towards the publication of this book by the Community
Relations Branch of the Department of Education of Northern
Ireland; by the Church of Ireland College of Education and by
the Faculty of Arts Research Committee of University College,
Cork. We would particularly like to thank Vivian McIver of
D.E.N.I. for his advice and help.

We are grateful to the staff of the libraries of Queen's
University, Belfast and the University of Ulster at Jordanstown
and Coleraine as well as the staff of the Public Record Office
of Northern Ireland. We are also grateful to the staff of the
Department of Education of Northern Ireland for their help in
locating relevant circulars and other documents. Our thanks to
Mrs. N. Poots of Upper Bann Institute of Further and Higher
Education for secretarial assistance in the preparation of
Sections III and IV.

Extracts from Crown Copyright documents are reproduced by
permission of the Controller of Her Majesty's Stationery
Office.

We would like to pay a special tribute to Monica Dowdall who typed the complete manuscript, often from poor quality originals and who patiently retyped some sections when the authors and editors introduced additions and amendments. She was also responsible for lay-out and for the preparation of camera-ready copy. Her commitment to the project was impressive and it was a pleasure to work with her.

Finally we would like to thank the Church of Ireland College of Education, and particularly its principal Sydney Blain, for the hospitality provided on the numerous occasions during the past decade when the editors and authors met in the college while work on the three volumes was going on. We would also like to thank Rosemary Bourne whose help in marketing and distributing all three volumes has been invaluable.

The editors are grateful for the co-operation and willing support to all those, north and south of the border, who contributed to this and the previous two volumes. The production of the three volumes of *Irish Educational Documents* has truly been a team effort.

ÁINE HYLAND AND KENNETH MILNE

INTRODUCTION

School Management and Administration

The management and administration of the educational services of Northern Ireland are dominated, in the earliest phases of their development occurring between 1922 and 1930, by three main themes: church-state confrontation, governmental capitulation and non-recognition.

The period 1922 to 1930 is a sensitive one in the history of Northern Ireland, given the fragile status of the new state, on the one hand, and the widening gulf that developed between the Northern Ireland government and mainstream churches, in the context of education, on the other. This gulf between church and state in education, had its origins in the age-old debate as to which authority, the former or the latter, church or state, should exercise the greater say in the governance of schools and religious and educational formation of the child.

From the outset in Northern Ireland, the state, represented by the Northern Ireland ministry of education, sought to administer educational services through a process of devolution aimed at involving local education bodies and their representatives in the management of schools to a much greater extent than had been the practice heretofore. Thus, for example, under the terms of the Education Act (Northern Ireland) 1923, teaching appointments, until this time the preserve of a school management committee, were henceforth to be made by newly appointed regional education committees, on which there was no in-built representation for existing managers of schools. On this issue of appointments alone, the ministry of education was confronted by all of the mainstream churches, though in a more orchestrated way by the Protestant denominations than the Catholic authorities.

Between 1924, in which year was founded the United Education Committee of the Protestant Churches with the aim of galvanising Protestant resistance to the 1923 Education Act, and 1930, which witnessed the introduction of a new act of education to replace the act of 1923, the state continually found its authority in educational affairs being undermined to a most serious degree. Only with the passing of a new act in 1930 were tensions eased, but at a political price to the government of the day; for in passing a new act to replace the existing act of 1923 it was considered, especially by Catholic authorities, that the state had capitulated under Protestant denominational pressure, exerted to ensure, among other things, protected representation of the managers of schools on regional committees, a provision which had not featured as part of government legislation in 1923.

The third theme, that of non-recognition, is reflected in a policy adopted specifically by Catholic authorities towards the new state of Northern Ireland, and was particularly prevalent in the field of education. As early as November 1921, for example, the Cardinal Primate, Cardinal Logue, on being invited by Lord Londonderry, first minister of education for Northern Ireland (1922-1926), to nominate Catholic representatives to a committee of inquiry which he was about to establish on the educational services of Northern Ireland, replied that he could not do so, for he believed that the committee was essentially being formed with a view to undermining the existing system of Catholic schools.

This stand-point of refusing to cooperate with the state in education was tenaciously adhered to by Catholic authorities for approximately another fifty years, as is clearly reflected in Catholic refusal to accept "4 and 2" committees, on which two members of the committee would be appointees of the state. Non-recognition by Catholic authorities must, however, also be seen and understood in a context wherein the state would not finance Catholic schools in equal proportion to schools run by the state itself. Catholic authorities were naturally resentful of this difference in treatment. The funding of Catholic and other voluntary schools is thus a central feature of management and administration throughout the first set of documentary extracts.

The theme of church-state confrontation is again to the fore, following the publication of a government White Paper, *Educational Reconstruction in Northern Ireland,* in 1944. On this occasion, the point of issue was a conscience clause for teachers, allowing them to elect not to give religious instruction, should they feel in conscience that they could not do so. However, unlike 1930, on this occasion the Unionist government refused to capitulate, and so the conscience clause became law in the Education Act (Northern Ireland) 1947.

This first set of documentary extracts is also concerned with the changing role, powers, composition and functions of school management committees, or as they are now called, Boards of Governors. There is also reference to local government reform where this has had significant practical implications for the management and administration of education.

Since 1986, and more especially since 1989, the education system of Northern Ireland has experienced momentous change as a result of government policy. The changes most pertinent to the focus of school management and administration are presented. They reflect the new powers given to schools in the context of, for example, delegated school budgets, as well as the new rights given to parents in respect of their children's education.

Primary Education

Although the main legislative and administrative thrust in education was concentrated on primary education, several major issues could not be solved simply by statutory regulations.

At local level there were two main issues during the inter-war years; the perennial debate about breadth and depth in the curriculum and the amalgamation of the numerous small denominational schools.

Amalgamation involved the control of schooling, so was bedevilled by political and denominational controversy. Added to this was the unwillingness of the Catholic community to countenance local control in the form of four and two committees. The rural nature of Northern Ireland, outside Belfast, and the religious divisions had caused this proliferation of small denominational schools which were often dilapidated and insanitary.

Thus from 1922 the ministry of education followed a policy of amalgamating small one and two-teacher schools, although this was always within denominational confines. Priority after the war was given to the removal of unnecessary schools in urban areas; only in the 1960s did the ministry pursue a general policy of rural amalgamation.

Curricular issues involved a fundamental analysis of the philosophical basis of education and, more prosaically the instrumental purpose of primary education.

For some years curricular attitudes remained staid and unvarying, being teacher and subject centred. Initially the inherited national school curriculum was little changed; grouping the children into standards was retained and children were still to be instructed. The first indication of a more child-centred approach came with the Robb report in 1931. The report also acknowledged the difficulty of catering for children from 5-14 in one school when it encouraged the development of senior schools for those over eleven.

The publication of the 1944 White Paper on educational reconstruction marked official acceptance of the 1926 Hadow Committee's proposal for a break between primary and secondary schooling. As a result the immediate post-war period was largely taken up with the organisation of secondary schooling. However, the White Paper enshrined the new curricular freedom when it suggested that:

> the primary school of the future should be far
> more than a building in which children receive
> instruction; it should be a community in which
> they learn to equip themselves with
> knowledge and experience suited to their ages
> and aptitudes; the three "Rs" will still be
> essential but they need not be dull.

The Doak report of 1955 encouraged a further loosening of curricular bonds, which was given impetus by the Primary Teachers' Guide in 1974. By the early eighties, in the eyes of the Conservative government, curricular freedom in primary schools had become curricular licence, and only a national, centrally directed curriculum could restore standards. Thus the 1989 Education Reform Order specified the curriculum for every grant-aided school, bringing the curriculum, in many respects, full-circle in seventy years.

Secondary Education

Until the 1940s the government paid little attention to secondary education. The grammar schools were left to themselves and only when some were in financial difficulties did they approach the local authorities for aid.

In the inter-war years secondary schooling was for the few; the few parents who could afford the fees. Some efforts were made to provide scholarships for those who could benefit but numbers were small and financial constraints prevented the government from implementing the 1926 Hadow proposals. The watershed was the second world war and the publication of the seminal White Paper, *Educational Reconstruction in Northern Ireland,* in December 1944.

Two concepts were dominant, secondary schooling for all and a break at 11+. These led to the establishment of junior secondary schools and the selection procedure. The latter would determine admission to the grammar schools for all but a limited number, and scholarships would be provided for those who qualified.

During the passage of the Education Bill in 1946-47 the government faced a renewal of Protestant agitation over the proposals for the management of the junior secondary schools and also over a new conscience clause for teachers teaching religious education. Giving way on the former the government held firm on the latter. Educational arguments were focused on whether the break with primary education should be at 11+ or 12+. Nevertheless the 1947 Act provided secondary schooling for all and set Northern Ireland on a new path of educational progress.

Post-war shortages, both financial and material, prevented the expansion of the grammar schools so that they could not accommodate all qualified pupils. Thus the 11+ became a competition and the bitterest and most divisive educational issue in Northern Ireland's educational history.

Grammar schools changed from Junior and Senior Certificate examinations in the 1960s to the General Certificate of Education ordinary and advanced levels. In the 1980s GCE "O" level was replaced by the General Certificate of Secondary Education (GCSE). The most radical curricular change was the introduction by the 1989 Education Reform Order of the national curriculum for all secondary schools.

Junior Secondary Schools, renamed Secondary Intermediate Schools and then High Schools, were built in large numbers during the late 1950s and early 1960s. In 1964 the ministry of education defined their position and charted their direction. Comprehensive education was ruled out so the High Schools would have to develop their own rationale and niche in the education system. The ministry encouraged them to develop academic streams and extended courses and later introduced the Certificate of Secondary Education (CSE).

Secondary schooling was not only divided into high schools nd grammar schools but also into controlled and voluntary; voluntary in turn split into Catholic and Protestant schools, the former called maintained since the 1968 Education Act. The main trend in the voluntary sector has been an increase in grant aid by the state in return for the establishment of governing bodies and local representation thereon.

Political changes in Great Britain impinge on Northern Ireland and comprehensive education seemed imminent after the Cowan Report in 1976 but the advent of a Conservative Government in 1979 led to its abandonment.

During the last five years Northern Ireland has adopted English legislation with little change, but faced with the intractable political problem, the government has been determined to encourage integrated education through the establishment of grant-maintained integrated schools.

Technical Education

Technical education had expanded rapidly under the impetus of the Agriculture and Technical Instruction (Ireland) Act of 1899 and most colleges in the, then, Northern part of Ireland were formed in the early 1900s with the support of enthusiastic local committees. Partnership between central and local government was one of the dominant educational ideas amongst unionists and so the technical sector was in harmony with government thinking. As a result technical education remained largely unchanged until after the second world war. It also remained the cinderella of the education service and expansion was curtailed by financial stringency, especially in the 1930s.

Although the technical sector had maintained links with its counterpart in the Irish Free State during the 1920s, these were sundered in the 1930s and technical education became increasingly influenced by developments in England and Wales.

The Spens Report had a major influence, particularly its recommendation for Technical High Schools. As Northern Ireland moved to full employment under the stimulus of a war economy, technical education increased dramatically to meet the demand for trained personnel.

However, educational thinking in Northern Ireland differed from the trilateralism encapsulated in the 1944 Education Act in England. The White Paper of December 1944 suggested a limited form of trilateralism with children from the new junior secondary schools being able to transfer to the junior technical schools at 13+. At the same time the Junior Commercial and Junior Domestic Science Schools were discontinued, their pupils being catered for in the new junior secondary schools.

Following the English precedent, proposals were made in the 1947 Education Act for further education for young people between the ages of 15-18 by day release, a system which never reached its full potential.

Once a network of junior secondary schools had been established by the mid-sixties, the interface between secondary and technical education became a crucial issue. The technical schools lost their 11+ streams, although still able to recruit students at 15+ from the secondary schools. Turning to new areas of work, mainly in the pre-vocational and further education fields, the system expanded rapidly in the late sixties and early seventies.

Influenced by the concept of regional colleges highlighted in the Lockwood report, the Department of Education encouraged the expansion of selected colleges through its control of course provision. Colleges were required to seek Department of Education approval before a full-time course could be established.

The 1970s were dominated by curricular changes, the most notable being the introduction of courses under the auspices of the Technician Education Council and Business Education Council which were to provide an alternative route to further and higher education for many young people.

The deteriorating employment situation for young unqualified school leavers led to the introduction of the Youth Opportunities Programme in 1978 which was replaced by the Youth Training Programme in 1982. These Northern Ireland schemes were forerunners of similar schemes in Great Britain.

The revolution in vocational training heralded by the introduction of National Vocational Qualifications in 1986 presaged an increasing ferment of change. The implications of the 1988 Education Act in England were worked out in a series of documents, legislated in the 1989 Order and culminated in the Stewart Report.

The 1990s will see the formation of a new pattern of further education with fewer but larger colleges, self-governing with increasing financial independence, and still coping with major curricular changes as National Vocational Qualifications and General National Vocational Qualifications become embedded in the system.

Teacher Education

Within higher education it was teacher education which was the first area to experience significant change following the establishment of Northern Ireland. The new curricula introduced in the southern colleges with their strong emphasis on Irish and on Gaelic culture generally proved unacceptable to the Ministry of Education in Belfast. Consequently, the Ministry refused to sanction the training courses in these colleges for students who would seek teaching posts in the North. In the absence of any teacher training facilities in Northern Ireland, apart from the Catholic female college, St. Mary's in Belfast, the Ministry had to move quickly to provide for this need and Stranmillis College was opened in 1922.

Stranmillis College was established as a mixed, non-denominational, Ministry controlled college, open to students from all denominational backgrounds. However, it proved unacceptable to the Catholic authorities as suitable for the training of Catholic male teachers, unless stringent guarantees were made regarding separate accommodation and religious instruction for such students. Despite attempts on the part of both the Ministry and the Church to reach a compromise, this did not prove possible. An agreement was eventually reached in 1924 whereby Catholic male students would be trained at St. Mary's College, Strawberry Hill, London. Separate facilities for Catholic male student teachers were provided in Northern Ireland when St. Joseph's College was opened in the late nineteen-fifties.

From the outset, therefore, teacher training came to reflect the same denominational divisions as did the school system in Northern Ireland. The controversy over representation for the Protestant churches on the board of management of Stranmillis College in the late nineteen-twenties and early thirties only served to reinforce this division.

As part of the reform of education in the immediate post World War Two years teacher education underwent a number of changes. These included an extended College course from two to three years, the introduction of concurrent courses for intending secondary teachers and a stronger emphasis on "practical" studies.

Further major changes in teacher education did not take place until expanding numbers of pupils at primary and secondary levels required a rapid expansion of teacher training facilities in the late nineteen-sixties. To help meet this need an Education Centre was included in the New University of Ulster, established at Coleraine in 1968, to train teachers for both levels. Not only did the Education Centre provide additional facilities for teacher education in Northern Ireland, but it did so in a way which bridged the denominational divide in a significant manner.

Declining school rolls in the late seventies obliged a review of teacher education facilities which resulted in considerable controversy when it was recommended that the Catholic colleges amalgamate and relocate to the Stranmillis campus. A vigorous campaign of opposition to this recommendation led to it being virtually completely abandoned. The one major element in it to be implemented was the amalgamation of the two Catholic colleges, St. Mary's and St. Joseph's into a single male and female college, St. Mary's. Further rationalisation was to be achieved through closer cooperation in course provision between St. Mary's and Stranmillis.

The focus of development in teacher education moved to curricular reform following the Education Reform Order of 1989. As had already happened in Britain, competency based courses were recommended following the adoption of a working party's report in 1993. Commencing in 1995 all future teacher education courses will be required to adopt such a basis and do so in a context, which will place considerably greater emphasis on the school classroom as the location for that education than was the case in the past.

University Education

University structures in Ireland underwent major change in 1908 when the National University of Ireland and the Queen's University of Belfast were created to replace the Royal University of Ireland, in a major effort to address Catholic and Presbyterian grievances over the provision of higher education. This 'partitioning' of university education was particularly welcomed in the North which then acquired its own distinct and separate third level institution. The political partition of Ireland which followed in 1920-21 did not, therefore, herald any immediate further changes in university education, and for the next sixty years Queen's was to remain the only university in Northern Ireland.

Following the Government of Ireland Act, 1920, Queen's became the responsibility of the government of Northern Ireland. However, apart from a number of minor legislative measures affecting the university's funding and the rather curious arrangement whereby the Northern Ireland Ministry of Agriculture established and maintained Queen's Faculty of Agriculture, successive governments left university education unchanged until the *Lockwood Committee on Higher Education in Northern Ireland*, reported in 1965.

The Lockwood Committee's report unleashed one of the most controversial phases in the history of higher education in Northern Ireland. The report's recommendation that a new university be established not in Derry as many had expected, but at Coleraine, became an issue which, at one stage, threatened to bring down the government. Derry, Northern Ireland's second city, which already possessed a small third level institution, Magee College with links to the University of Dublin (Trinity College) and which had been expected to be the base from which the new university would grow, was seen as being unfairly deprived of this prospect. Protestants and Catholics, Unionists and Nationalists in Derry united to protest against the recommendation, but in vain. The government decided to act as Lockwood had recommended and Northern Ireland's second university was located at Coleraine.

Coinciding with the decision to establish a new university was that to develop higher technical education through the establishment of the Ulster College. This institution, which, to begin with, was an amalgamation of several existing institutions, later became known as the Ulster Polytechnic, and expanded quite rapidly. Compared with the latter's growth, the New University at Coleraine grew quite slowly and by the close of the nineteen seventies it was becoming clear that it was not likely to reach its target figures for student enrolment.

Recommendations from the *Higher Education Review Group,* set up in 1978 to examine the future of the New University, were set aside by the government in favour of the creation of a multi-campus university to be known as the University of Ulster. This university was to include the Ulster Polytechnic, the Ulster College of Art, the New University of Ulster and Magee College, and came into existence on the first of October 1984. Often referred to as a 'polyversity' because of its origins and because of its provision of non-traditional university courses, such as Higher National Diplomas, it quickly gained popular acceptance and expanded to over 12,000 students within a decade.

The arrival of the Open University to Northern Ireland, with the establishment of its regional office in Belfast in 1971, was another significant development in the provision of higher education in this period. Catering for older and 'second chance' students as well as for those whose occupations and circumstances prevent them from availing of full-time higher education, the Open University has been meeting an important need for many thousands of people.

I

SCHOOL MANAGEMENT AND ADMINISTRATION

I.1   Ministries of Northern Ireland Act, 1921 (Northern Ireland), 12 Geo. 5, C.6.

This was an Act of the greatest historical significance, in that it provided for the establishment of five new ministries to administer the affairs of the newly created state of Northern Ireland, including educational.

The new minister of education was the seventh marquess of Londonderry, whose family owned a large country estate at Mount Stewart, situated on the shores of Strangford Lough, approximately six miles from the County Down town of Newtownards.

A soldier by training, Lord Londonderry saw military action in the trenches of France, during World War I. In 1917, however, he was recalled from active service, to Ireland, on being nominated a member of the Irish Convention. The purpose of this Convention was to discuss peace in Ireland and draw up a constitution for the country's future government.

Lord Londonderry was not an elected member of the Northern Ireland Parliament, rather he was invited to join the Northern Ireland cabinet by the prime minister, Sir James Craig. At the time, Londonderry was a member of the British government, his portfolio being that of under secretary of state for air.

On assuming office in the new cabinet, Lord Londonderry wasted little time in tackling his task. One of his first initiatives was the establishment of a committee of inquiry on education, chaired by the Unionist Member of Parliament for West Belfast, Robert Lynn. Lynn was also editor of the Unionist daily newspaper, the 'Northern Whig.' Anxious to involve all interested groups in the work of the committee, Londonderry requested Cardinal Logue to nominate representatives on behalf of Roman Catholic authorities but the request, much to Londonderry's disappointment, was refused. The Cardinal argued that the committee had merely been established to launch an attack on Catholic education. Since this was its 'raison d'etre,' reasoned the Cardinal, there was no point in joining it.

The relevant sections of the Ministries of Northern Ireland Act, 1921, are as follows. It was described as:-

An Act to provide for the administration of certain public services in Northern Ireland by the Departments established by the Lord Lieutenant, and for purposes connected therewith. (14th December, 1921).

2.   The following provisions shall have effect with respect to each Ministry ... that is to say:—

(1)   The Ministry shall be a body corporate with a capacity to acquire and hold land for the purpose of the powers or duties of the Ministry, and shall be styled by the name set forth in the first column of the schedule to this Act, and may sue or be sued by that name.

(2)   The Ministry shall have an official seal which shall be officially and judicially noticed, and that seal shall be authenticated by the signature of the Minister or of a secretary or assistant secretary of the Ministry.

(3)   In the execution or performance of its powers or duties the Ministry shall adopt and use the style and seal of the Ministry:

> Provided that the Minister may authorise the use of a special designation by any officer, officers or committee to whom any specified powers or duties have been assigned by him under this Act.

(4)   Subject to the provisions of this Act, any power or duty of the Ministry may be exercised or performed by the Minister or by a secretary or assistant secretary of the Ministry.

(5)   The provisions of this Act with respect to a secretary or assistant secretary of the Ministry shall apply to—

(a)   any officer of the Ministry who is appointed to be secretary or assistant secretary thereof; and

(b)   any parliamentary secretary or assistant parliamentary secretary of the Ministry.

SCHEDULE — Section 1.	
(1) Name of Ministry	(2) Branches of Ministry
4. The Ministry of Education for Northern Ireland	Commissioners of National Education in Northern Ireland. 4. {Intermediate Education (Board for Northern Ireland. {Commissioners for Endowed { Schools in Northern Ireland.

I.2   Interim Report of the Departmental Committee on the Educational Services in Northern Ireland, September 1921, Cmd.6.

This Interim Report, also known as the Lynn Report, is a most valuable source of information on educational provision at the time. Not only does it provide a comprehensive historical overview of the period from 1831 to 1920, but draws attention to difficulties and problems within the education system in the wake of partition.

The Committee of Inquiry was especially strong in its advocation of local community involvement in education, which it believed should be given the fullest possible expression and application by the new education ministry. The Committee was of the view that the management and administration of education in Ireland had become too centralised, too bureaucratic, and as a consequence local needs had been neglected. The Committee recommended many practical examples as to how local involvement could be achieved.

On the issue of the refusal of Roman Catholic authorities to participate in its work, the Committee expressed its regret that this was so, adding that it hoped that Catholic interests had not been overlooked as a result.

In the historical overview, reference is made to what were perceived as problematic aspects of elementary, secondary and technical education, as well as the vicissitudes associated with being a teacher in the Irish educational system at the time. The main responsibilities of the new education ministry are also explained, as is its administrative format, for example, a minister, parliamentary secretary and such similar personnel.

A major recommendation, much in keeping with the philosophy of decentralisation, was the creation of an Advisory Council, whose function would be to advise the minister of education on educational issues.

A most significant section of the Report is that dealing with the sensitive issue of grant aid to schools, and how this aid should be apportioned in the unlikelihood of all managers of schools transferring their premises to local authority control, as was then being advocated as part of the whole decentralisation process. In a recommendation which subsequently failed to gain widespread approval from the school managers, it was recommended that grants be determined in accordance with the degree and extent of local involvement each manager and school committee was prepared to allow. On this basis, the Committee recommended the creation of three classes of schools, Class I, Class II and Class III. The first would be schools managed by the new Local Committees of Primary Education, the second by School Management Committees and two representatives of the new Local Committees, and the third by managers who wished to remain entirely independent of local authority control.

The functions, duties and responsibilities of the new Local Committees are explained in detail.

1.—INTRODUCTORY

9.   The Government of Ireland Act, 1920, which established two autonomous areas, Northern and Southern Ireland, was accepted in Northern Ireland with reluctance by that section of the population which had up till then supported the legislative union with Great Britain.   It was, however, felt that with the responsibility of self-government there had come an opportunity to effect a much needed re-organisation of public education.

10.   Up to the present, education in Ireland has been administered by central boards, and, being central, these boards tended to overlook to some extent varying local needs. The highly industrialised North-East had naturally developed ideas on educational administration peculiar to its own necessities. It was not easy for these ideas to find expression so long as primary and secondary education throughout the country was under the control of the central boards in Dublin ...   In the appointment of this Committee there is implied a determination to take the fullest advantage of this opportunity

to reform the whole system from the elementary school to the University, and to place within the reach of the children of our province the best possible educational facilities.

11.   It is greatly to be regretted that on this Committee, reflecting as it does almost every other shade of opinion in the six counties, Roman Catholic interests have not been directly represented.   We understand, however, that the responsibility for this circumstance rests entirely with the Roman Catholics themselves, as invitations to serve on the Committee were issued to representatives of the Roman Catholic Church and were in every case refused ... We hope that notwithstanding the disadvantage at which we were placed by this action it will be found that Roman Catholic interests have not suffered.   We have throughout been careful to keep in mind and to make allowance for the particular points of view of Roman Catholics in regard to education, so far as known to us, and it has been our desire to refrain as far as we could from recommending any course which might be thought to be contrary to their wishes ...

II.—HISTORICAL

PRIMARY EDUCATION

16.   Primary Schools in Northern Ireland are of two kinds — private elementary schools and National schools.   The private elementary schools are either kindergarten establishments for infants and children up to about ten years of age, or preparatory secondary schools: they are attended by children whose parents do not desire to send them to the National schools, and they are all schools in which fees are charged.

19.   The existing system of National Education was established in 1831.   At the time of its inception the object of the system was "to afford combined literary and moral, and separate religious instruction, to children of all persuasions, as far as possible, in the same school, upon the fundamental principle that no attempt shall be made to interfere with the peculiar religious tenets of any description of Christian pupils," and this still stands in the forefront of the fundamental principles of the National system as they are stated in the Rules and Regulations of the Commissioners, and as an integral part of the system.   The original intention that Protestant and Roman Catholic children should be together for secular instruction has been largely abandoned in practice: Roman Catholic children are now nearly everywhere accommodated in schools under exclusively Roman Catholic local management ... The desire, in many localities, of each denomination to have a school under its own control has led to a wholly unnecessary multiplication of small schools.

24.   National schools are divided into two classes, viz.:—

(1)   Vested schools, including:

    (a)   those vested in the Commissioners of National Education; and
    (b)   those vested in trustees, under deeds to which the Commissioners are a party, for the purpose of being maintained as national schools.

(2)   Non-vested schools, which include all other National schools.

Schools vested in trustees have been provided partly out of private funds raised locally, and partly out of State grants, and the duty of keeping the buildings in repair devolves upon the trustees.

Schools vested in the Commissioners have been similarly provided, but are kept in repair by the Board of Works.

26.   The local managers of ordinary National schools are generally, though not necessarily, clergymen.   The non-vested schools have usually been provided in close connection with churches and are often used outside school hours for church purposes.   Vested schools must be used exclusively for the education of the pupils attending them, except with the special approval of the Board, but, on Sundays, they may be utilised for Sunday Schools with the sanction of the patrons or managers, subject to the veto of the Board in cases leading to contention or abuse.

27.   This system of private or partially private ownership and control of the buildings in which National schools are conducted has an important relation to the problem which it is our duty to investigate. However suitable to the carrying on of a centralised bureaucratic control of education, it cannot be said to be readily adaptable to what we feel is desired by the majority of people of Northern Ireland, viz., a central Ministry working through responsible local agencies representative at once of local authorities, and of persons interested in educational affairs.

28.   There was in fact under the National School system no such local control as we have described. The only approximation to it was the existence and recognition in certain parts of Ireland, especially in Ulster, of school committees. These committees were locally elected, generally

by parents of children attending the schools concerned. When constituted and functioning on lines approved by the Board, these committees were recognised as patrons of the schools and had the ordinary powers and functions, i.e. the appointment and removal of the local manager ...

SECONDARY EDUCATION

30.   Up to the time of the transfer of the educational services to Northern Ireland, two Government Departments, the Intermediate Education Board and the Department of Agriculture and Technical Instruction made grants to and exercised some control over Secondary schools.

31.   The Intermediate Board was established by the Intermediate Education (Ireland) Act, 1878, and had imposed upon it the duty of "promoting intermediate secular education in Ireland."

34.   One important power conferred upon the Board by this Act was that of advancing money to Managers of schools upon approved security to enable them to provide proper equipment and appliances for the teaching of practical science, and for similar purposes to be approved by the Board.   These advances, in conjunction with the work of the Department of Agriculture and Technical Instruction to be referred to later, helped materially in the advancement of the teaching of science in the schools.

51.   Apart from the question of the nature of the system, secondary education has suffered from the insufficiency and inelasticity of the sums at the disposal of the Intermediate Board to meet the needs of the situation.   As has been already noted, the sums available for grants to the schools increased considerably in recent years, but they are still far

from sufficient to meet even the most pressing requirements of the schools.   The fact that all the sums placed at the disposal of the Board were fixed sums had the result that any increase in the number of schools or pupils implied a diminution in the amounts paid per pupil.

52.   Meantime the financial situation of the teachers had become so serious owing to the economic and social effects of the war that in 1918 a Vice-Regal Committee was appointed to report on "the Conditions of Service and Remuneration of Teachers in Intermediate Schools, and on the Distribution of Grants from Public Funds for Intermediate Education in Ireland."   This Committee, under the Chairmanship of Lord Chief Justice Molony, in their Report dated March, 1919, made recommendations both with regard to the salaries of teachers and with regard to the system administered by the Board.   These recommendations were to a large extent embodied in the Education (Ireland) Bill, 1920, but the Bill was, after some discussion, dropped by the Government.

54.   A secondary school so far as the system was concerned consisted solely of pupils between the ages of twelve and nineteen years.   No grants could be paid in respect of any others, nor were classes composed of other pupils subject to inspection.   It was of course the case that in most of the schools, if not in all, there existed preparatory classes composed of children under the age of twelve, but these classes came in no way within the scope of the Board's operations.   A very important part of the school was thus subject to no supervision by the State Department, and received neither advice nor aid from it.   In our opinion this constituted a serious fault in the system, as we believe that a school should be looked upon as a unit, and that the preparatory classes should be considered as part of an ordered whole ... These classes and schools differ from the National

schools in two respects. In the first place the pupils in them pay substantial school fees, and in the second place nearly all the pupils continue their education in secondary schools.

55. For both these reasons we are of opinion that such schools and classes can be better treated under the regulations governing secondary schools than under those dealing with the National schools, and we make recommendations to this effect later on in our Report.

56. The second point to which we would call attention deals with the management of the schools. In this respect the schools fall under three heads —

(1)   those owned and controlled by religious communities;

(2)   those under regularly constituted Boards of Governors; (some belonging to this category, such as the Royal Schools, are very old foundations, while others are of modern growth. A few of them have endowments, though these are in general quite inadequate to meet the needs of the school even when supplemented by the fees of the pupils);

(3)   those under private ownership and conducted for private profit.

57.   Of the secondary schools in Northern Ireland which have up to the present been in receipt of grants, about one-third belong to each of the three categories mentioned above. Of the girls' schools the great majority, apart from convent schools, come under the third class; of the boys' schools, on the other hand, the majority are controlled either by religious communities or by Boards of Governors. With regard to this question of management also we make recommendations in this Report.

TECHNICAL EDUCATION

68.   The main work of the schools has been done, up to
the present, in evening classes of a purely voluntary type.
The system has admittedly met with great success, but has
inherent defects. Regularity of attendance cannot be
sufficiently secured where work is in the nature of overtime.
Moreover, the good intentions of students when they join the
schools are wont to give way under the stress of work, and
too frequently also because of an incomplete groundwork of
elementary knowledge.   The result is that only a small
proportion of those who enter upon a four-year course of
study complete it.

IV. — THE CENTRAL ORGANISATION

THE MINISTRY — THE HEADS OF THE BRANCHES

83.   The new Ministry will be responsible for primary,
secondary and technical education throughout Northern
Ireland.   Though the control has been unified under a
Minister, a Parliamentary Secretary, and a permanent
Secretary, it will be necessary, we believe, for facility of
administration to establish separate branches within the
Ministry for primary, secondary and technical education, and
to that end we were at first disposed to recommend the
appointment of three assistant secretaries, one for each branch.
We believe that to be the best arrangement, and trust that
eventually it will be adopted, but in the present circumstances,
having regard to the need for economy in public expenditure
as well as to the intimate connection of secondary and
technical education, we suggest that while for primary
education an assistant secretary should be appointed, one

other assistant secretary might for the present suffice for secondary and technical education combined.   It will, however, be necessary, if this latter suggestion be adopted, to make special arrangements whereby, pending the appointment of an assistant secretary for technical instruction, the Ministry shall be kept in close touch with current industrial problems.

85.   We have ... come to the conclusion that an Advisory Council should be created in connection with the Ministry of Education, and that it should be the function of this Council to tender advice to the Minister at any time, or to make any representation which it may deem desirable.   The Minister, on his part, should be prepared at all times to consider such advice and representations, and to consult the Advisory Council as to the expediency of any changes in policy which he may have in view.

86.   The Advisory Council should meet at least twice a year.   Additional meetings may be convened by the Minister or on the requisition of ten members.   Members should hold office for three years.   The Minister, or any officer deputed by him, should have the right to attend meetings of the Advisory Council, and to speak, but not to vote, and it should be within the power of the Ministry to appoint any of its own officers to act as secretaries or other officers of the Advisory Council.

87.   We recommend that representation on the Council should be on the following lines:—

	MEMBERS
Local Committees for Primary Education (exclusive of Belfast).....................................	4
Local Committees for Technical Education (exclusive of Belfast).....................................	3
Belfast Education Committee...............................	3
(The above representatives to be elected by the Committees concerned under rules to be framed by the Ministry).	
Representatives of the following interests should be nominated by the Minister after consultation with the interests concerned:-	
Primary Teachers................................	2
Secondary Teachers............................	2
Technical Teachers.............................	2
Universities..	1
Labour..	1
Industry and Commerce......................	1
The Churches:-	
Roman Catholic..................................	2
Protestant Churches............................	3
Boards of Governors of Secondary Schools	2
Managers of National Schools....................	2
Representatives directly nominated by the Minister	5
Total......................................	33

V.— LOCAL ORGANISATION

91.   Our first impulse was to recommend the establishment of local administration on a county basis. It was a solution which naturally suggested itself. The system of education in England and Scotland had already evolved from one of small administrative areas to a broad county system.

96.   We are aware of the cogency of the argument that in England and Scotland sub-divisions of the county were formerly the units of administration, and that these have now been superseded by a body representing the county as a whole. The conditions in Great Britain are, however, so different from those obtaining here, that there is danger in concluding too hastily that what is suitable in the one country must be a correct policy in the other. It is, moreover, to be remembered that in England and Scotland the evolution of the county system was gradual: it was not attained at a single bound. It would, we think, be hazardous in Northern Ireland to attempt to overleap an important and perhaps indispensable stage in the development of local administration — that of the smaller unit. It may be that in the future with better travelling facilities and increasing interest and experience in public affairs, a system of county administration will be evolved in Northern Ireland. In the meantime, we think that the County Boroughs, Urban Districts and Rural Districts should be the units for local administration or public education.

97.   It is not intended that the Councils should have direct relations with the schools in their area. It will be their function to finance the schemes of local education committees who will administer the funds obtained from local rates, and grants in aid thereof made by the Ministry. It will be necessary to allow to the local authority an adequate representation on these committees, in order that the rate-payers may exercise such check upon the demands of the committees as may be desirable. Our recommendations therefore provide for a majority representation of the local authority, other members of the committee being nominated as prescribed later, from persons in the locality interested in education.

LOCAL COMMITTEES FOR PRIMARY EDUCATION

100.   In our opinion two or more local Councils should be empowered to combine for primary education, and the Ministry should have power to insist upon such combination where necessary in the interests of sound administration.

101.   It should also be possible for a Rural District to be divided into two or more smaller units for the purposes of primary education, subject to the consent of the Ministry.

102.   Each Council or combination of Councils should create a committee of fifteen for primary education, made up of eight members appointed by the Council or jointly by the Councils concerned, and seven nominated by the Ministry ...

104.   It is not to be expected that in the case of all primary schools we can proceed at one step from the present managerial system to a general system of local control, but we are hopeful that the management of many of them will be handed over to authorities directly representative of the ratepayers.   New schools built and equipped by these authorities will of course be managed by them.   Schools managed by Local Committees for Primary Education will be referred to throughout this Report as Class I. schools.

105.   It must, however, be recognised that the great majority of the school buildings are not the property of the State, but of the Churches or private parties, and that it would not be desirable or possible for the State to purchase the buildings outright.   Some managers will be unwilling to part with the full control of their schools, and provision must be made for such cases.   We think that many would be prepared to adopt at least a modified form of local administration, and we recommend that in such cases School Management

Committees be formed, composed of two representatives of the Local Committee, and four representatives of the patron or patrons of the school or group of schools ... These schools will be referred to as Class II. schools.

106.   There may remain a third class of school whose managers may desire to remain entirely independent of the local authority. These schools will be referred to as Class III. schools.

107.   We trust that the differentiation which we propose later as regards the amount of rate aid to the various classes of schools will be an inducement to managers to admit the principle of local administration either wholly or in a modified degree.

LOCAL COMMITTEES FOR TECHNICAL EDUCATION

108.   No radical change in the organisation of technical education appears to be necessary or desirable, but the evidence we have heard points to the fact that the Urban District Committees have been more successful than the County Committees.

113.   It is recommended that County Technical Instruction schemes as such should disappear, and be replaced by joint Urban and Rural schemes or joint Rural schemes on the lines indicated above.

LOCAL ADMINISTRATION OF SECONDARY EDUCATION

118.   It will be found in our recommendations regarding secondary schools that for the present it is not contemplated that many of these schools will be managed by committees of local Councils, but it is desirable that in certain cases such

committees should have power to take over the management of existing secondary schools, or to establish new schools of this kind.

119.   We think therefore that any Technical Committee might, if special circumstances rendered it desirable, and if the Ministry approved, take charge of one or more secondary schools in its area.   It should equally be open to the Local Committee for Primary Education to take charge of one or more secondary schools in its area, should that course be expedient and be approved by the Ministry.

FUNCTIONS OF LOCAL COMMITTEES FOR PRIMARY EDUCATION

121.   Those duties which apply to the whole area administered and are of a general character, such as the obligation to see that adequate accommodation is provided for all school children and that compulsory school attendance is enforced, should be the functions of the Local Committee. This Committee should act either directly or through subsidiary Committees as manager of all Class I. schools, and it should also appoint two representatives on each of the School Management Committees of Class II. schools.

122.   School Management Committees of Class II. schools should be responsible for those matters which deal with the internal organisation of the school or group of schools managed by them.

123.   The following are amongst the duties indispensable to management:— The appointment and removal of teachers, the regulation of time-tables and curricula, the checking of school statistics, correspondence, visitation of the schools and their maintenance, repair, furnishing, cleansing, heating and equipment.

125.   We think that if possible all schools should be under the local committee, and that inducements should be offered to bring this about.   It would be inequitable to afford out of public funds the same degree of aid to schools which adopt only a modified form of local control, or none at all, as to those which are completely handed over.

126.   We accordingly recommend that —
In the case of Class I. schools the Local Committee for Primary Education should as Managers provide for the maintenance, repair, furnishing and equipment, and all the cost of heating and cleansing.   In the case of both these classes of schools the Ministry should make a grant in aid to the Local Committee for heating and cleansing: in drawing up regulations for this grant the Ministry should aim at making it approximately half the cost.   In the case of Class III. schools the Ministry should make to the Manager a grant in aid for heating and cleansing at the same rate as in Classes I. and II. but such schools should receive no aid from local rates.

130.   ... The State must continue to play a leading part.   It will still be responsible for the salaries of the teachers and will give substantial aid in the provision of new school buildings, and in other directions; but it can never supply the vivifying influence that springs from healthy local interest. That influence aroused, the rest is easy ...

131.   We recommend that the Local Committees should have power to provide books and school requisites for necessitous children attending recognised schools in their area: they should have power to provide where necessary means of conveyance for children in rural districts who have to travel an inconvenient distance to recognised schools. They may provide for Class I. schools library facilities, and

plots of land, with equipment for recreation or instruction, and they should have power to establish and maintain Day or Evening Continuation Schools.

I.3   Final Report of the Departmental Committee on the Educational Services in Northern Ireland, Cmd.15.n.d.

Following the presentation of the aforementioned Interim Report to Lord Londonderry, June 1922, the Lynn Committee would meet on a further fourteen occasions in order to finalise its second and Final Report for the minister.

This Final Report contains a wide range of observations and insights not covered in the Interim Report, and, for this reason, they are important. The Final Report examines the state of the art in teacher training, curricula and the examinations system. Two further areas considered are inspection and coordination of the new system, each of which is of most relevance in this first section of the documents.

The Report tackles the question of the age at which schooling should begin, advocates the termination of infant education once a child has ended its eighth year of age, and puts forward sound educational and economic arguments for the amalgamation of small schools in close geographic proximity to each other.

The Report also stresses the desirability of extending a child's post-elementary education in already functioning Junior Technical Schools, rather than building new secondary schools, referred to in the Report as Central Schools. Yet, ironically, it called upon the Northern Ireland community to be more alert to the importance of post-elementary school experiences and provision for its children.

In the matter of school inspection, due recognition was given to the value and importance of inspection within the total administrative framework of the education system. The Report describes how teachers were rated at this time, as well as the process by which inspection was conducted in the schools. It also discusses the criticisms then being levelled against the inspectorate by teachers and their unions, concluding with some insightful recommendations as to how the whole inspectorial process could be improved, not least in regard to those teachers required to enhance their efficiency rating.

II. — THE CO-ORDINATION OF THE PROPOSED EDUCATIONAL SYSTEM

52.   One of the principal advantages to be derived from the unified control of the various branches of public education under a single Ministry is the attainment of an ideal which could not well have been realised under the former divided administration.   The co-ordination of primary, secondary and technical education signifies much more than mere economy in administration.   There ought to be and under favourable auspices there will be a constant necessary inter-relation between these elements, which only a common control can harmonise, and we hope that any tendency to perpetuate the system of administration in water-tight compartments will be resisted.

(I)   THE AGE OF ADMISSION OF PUPILS TO AN INFANTS' SCHOOL OR CLASS (PRIMARY OR PREPARATORY).

54.   In the consideration of the subject of co-ordination the question of the instruction of infants takes first place. The great majority of infant children receive their education in primary schools. The minimum age for admission has hitherto been three years.   Grants are paid on all children attending primary schools who are over three years of age. Educationists in general deprecate the formal instruction of children at such an early age: many would fix the minimum at six years, but it is to be observed that these conclusions are often based on considerations which do not take into account the external circumstances of the children.   It is found in

actual experience that if children of tender years are not at school neither are they always under supervision at home; many are to be found playing in the streets and are under no guidance or restraint. This is particularly the case in crowded urban areas, where it is often necessary for both parents to be employed during the day, and where it is, therefore, desirable to bring the children under some skilled supervision.

56.   Whatever may be said for the educational advantage to be derived from attendance at school by a child between the ages of four and six, there is little doubt that prior to the age of four it is mainly negative in character. We think we may reasonably recommend from motives of economy as well as on hygienic grounds that the age for admission to a primary school be raised from three to four. This would, moreover, have the effect of reducing overcrowding where school accommodation is limited.

(2)   THE PERIOD OF RETENTION OF PUPILS IN AN INFANTS'
       SCHOOL OR CLASS

62.   The existing rule on the subject of the age at which pupils must be removed from an infants' school or class is as follows:-

> All pupils both boys and girls, must be removed from infants' school and from infants' departments of schools, on the 1st July next following the completion of their eighth year.

63.   We find it necessary to recommend a modification of this rule. In Chapter III of this Report we recommend that there should be in the primary schools a qualifying examination for entrance to secondary schools suitable for children of from eleven to twelve years of age, and that the

examination should approximate to that of the fifth standard in primary schools. If the above regulation were allowed to stand the pupils would not as a rule have reached the fifth standard at the age of eleven.

The gradation would be as follows:-

8 - 9	years of age in	first	standard
9 - 10	years of age in	second	standard
10 - 11	years of age in	third	standard
11 - 12	years of age in	fourth	standard
12 - 13	years of age in	fifth	standard

64. It is necessary, therefore, to put this scale back by one year, so that at the age of eleven to twelve it will be possible for a child to pass an examination in the work of the fifth standard.

(3) THE AMALGAMATION OF PRIMARY SCHOOLS HELD IN THE SAME BUILDING

76. Our recommendations under this head are as follows:-
Separate infants' schools should be amalgamated with the adjoining senior school or schools under the control of one principal teacher, and the Minister should endeavour to put this policy into effect as soon as possible. Vested interests of existing teachers should in all cases be conserved. The infants' department in a school where the average attendance is sufficient for the purpose and circumstances warrant it should be in charge of a vice-principal specially qualified in infants' school work.

Where the existing separate boys' and girls' schools can be more efficiently conducted as one establishment, amalgamation should be insisted upon. If, however, the existing separate schools are large enough to have a teacher for each standard such amalgamation would not as a rule be desirable. Should it be found that the manager entertains strong objection on moral grounds to amalgamation, careful consideration should be given to his views before coming to a decision, but the loss of efficiency in teaching is so great in small schools that separate schools should not be permitted where the average attendance is insufficient to warrant the recognition of two fully-qualified teachers in each.

(4)   The Amalgamation of Preparatory and Secondary Schools

77.   Attention is called elsewhere in this Report to the fact that the Intermediate Board was bound to pay grants to any secondary school complying with certain formal requirements. It had no power to refuse these grants on the ground of unsuitability of premises or equipment, or because there was already in the locality an adequate number of efficient schools. This has undoubtedly resulted in an undue multiplication of small schools in certain localities, where in our opinion the work of secondary education could be more efficiently carried on if the schools were larger and less numerous. We are of opinion that here, as in the case of primary schools, amalgamation in certain districts would be beneficial, and we recommend that the Ministry should aim at securing amalgamation of schools where this would lead to greater efficiency. This should be done as far as possible without inflicting hardship on the teachers concerned.

(6) TRADES PREPARATORY AND DAY COMMERCIAL SCHOOLS

95.   There are at present, apart from the secondary schools, two classes of schools which give a type of continuation education up to about the age of sixteen. These are the Trades Preparatory and the Day Commercial schools. Both of these types, with the single exception of the Christian Brothers' Trades Preparatory school in Belfast, are held in technical schools, and the services of the full-time teachers of the technical schools are utilised in providing the necessary instruction.   They can, therefore, be conducted at a much smaller cost than would be possible if separate buildings and staffs had to be provided.

96.   *Trades Preparatory Schools.* * — There are at present six of these in Northern Ireland — two in Belfast, and one in each of the following towns:— Ballymena, Lisburn, Londonderry and Portadown.   In most of these schools the course of instruction lasts for two years: in the case of the Christian Brothers' school it extends over three years.

97.   The programme is the same in all the schools, and it distinctly aims at preparing boys for industrial pursuits.   It is, therefore, natural that all the schools should be found in large industrial centres.   From experience gained in other parts of Ireland, it is doubtful whether this type of school would meet with any great amount of success in smaller centres. Attempts have been made to establish them in certain centres of the kind outside Northern Ireland but with very poor results.

102.   *Day Commercial Schools.*— There are altogether twenty-two Day Commercial schools in Northern Ireland ...

---

* Otherwise known as Junior Technical Schools.

104.   Day Commercial schools are attended by pupils of both sexes, and we are of opinion that the curriculum might with great advantage be extended so as to include Domestic Economy for girls and Manual Instruction for boys. A suitable common programme should be drawn up for use in these schools as has been done with marked success in the Trades Preparatory schools.

(7)   Central Schools

110.   Taking the two large cities of Belfast and Londonderry, where if at all Central schools might seem to be required, it appears that there were only 69 and 132 such pupils in these cities respectively.   This does not indicate a very urgent demand for continued education, and the fact that in Belfast the number of candidates for admission each year to the Junior Technical school is less than 400 confirms the impression that the establishment of Central schools would be inadvisable at the present time.

111. We therefore report that —

> Having inquired into the question of the need for Central schools in Belfast and Londonderry for the continued education of children who have passed the seventh standard in primary schools, we are not satisfied that there is at the moment a great demand for this type of education.

> We think, however, that if there should arise a greatly increased demand for continued education, it could be catered for by the extension and development of existing institutions such as Junior Technical schools, etc.

Further, we feel that this demand ought to be much greater than it is, and that everything possible should be done to encourage children to continue their education beyond the primary school stage. It is to be hoped that there will be an early awakening of public interest in this important matter. The demand for further education should undoubtedly exist in any progressive and energetic community, but until it becomes much more apparent in Northern Ireland than at present, it would be useless to incur the expense of establishing Central schools.

(8)   HIGHER ELEMENTARY SCHOOLS AND CLASSES

112.   In the co-ordination of the educational system the problem of providing for the further education of primary school children beyond the sixth and seventh standards cannot be approached in rural areas in the same manner as in the cities and larger towns. In the urban districts the establishment of trades preparatory and day commercial schools has in large measure solved the difficulty, but these types of schools do not exist and could not economically be provided in the country. We are obliged, therefore, to seek another expedient. The best course and in our opinion that most likely to prove satisfactory is to make use of and develop in rural areas the existing primary school system.

114.   Our recommendations are as follows:—

In rural districts where it is impracticable for pupils to attend a secondary school or other establishment providing a higher education, the Ministry should recognise selected primary schools in which an education on trades preparatory, day commercial or higher elementary school lines (according to the needs of the locality) might be provided for pupils who remain in the school after passing the Leaving Certificate examination ...

V. — THE INSPECTION OF SCHOOLS

PRIMARY SCHOOLS

213.   The Six Counties are divided into five circuits, each in charge of a senior inspector. The two Belfast circuits have each three section inspectors, and the other three circuits have each two.   There is also a lady inspector in Belfast who works in both of the Belfast circuits, and there are two special inspectors — one responsible for the inspection of Irish as well as for ordinary work, and one for the inspection of science.   There are thus, apart from the Chief Inspector of primary schools, twenty inspectors engaged on primary work. In addition to the inspectors there are three organisers for Domestic Economy and two for Kindergarten work. Thirteen of the twenty inspectors have been National school teachers.

214.   A "general inspection" is held once in every school year, and at this inspection the inspector not only observes the methods of the teachers, but tests the proficiency of the pupils. The present method is, therefore, a combination of examination and inspection.   In addition to the annual visit the inspectors pay incidental visits to the schools.

216.   The general report on the school has two chief parts — one is the efficiency table which contains the marks assigned to the efficiency of the teaching in the various subjects; the other is the Minute or written report in which the condition of the school is summed up as a whole.   Both sections of the report are taken into consideration in estimating the efficiency of the teachers — each teacher

being marked as "Highly Efficient," "Efficient," or "Not Efficient."   The distinction attached to the mark "Highly Efficient" is very much prized by the teacher, and on the other hand the mark "Not Efficient" is looked upon as a reflection on the teacher's ability and zeal.

219.   Should a teacher be dissatisfied with the finding of the inspector he is at liberty to appeal direct to the Ministry. In ordinary cases, the senior inspector is then sent to furnish a fresh report.   If, however, the original inspection was by a senior inspector, the Chief Inspector is sent.   In either case the appeal is finally considered by the Ministry, which decides what action is to be taken.

220.   The criticisms directed against the inspection system appear to fall into four groups dealing with —

•   The method employed by inspectors.

•   The dependence of salary increments on inspectors' reports.

•   Ministerial interference with the standard of marking, in the interests of economy.

•   The grading of inspectors.

221.   *The method employed by inspectors.* — Perhaps the most serious criticism directed by the teachers' organisations against the present system is that the inspectors sometimes manifest a want of sympathy with the teachers and pupils, and further that they sometimes show too little regard for the difficulties under which the teachers labour.

The inspectors for their part deny the imputation.   We can only say that if the best educational results are to be obtained, inspectors and teachers must realise that they are co-workers whose objects are or should be the same.   Inspectors are entitled to assume that the teachers are making honest efforts to get the best work possible, at any rate until there is real reason to believe the contrary.   The manner adopted by an inspector in a school is of the greatest importance.   If it is harsh, unsympathetic, suspicious or unkindly, he will be unable to discover the real merits of the teaching, for to do so he must secure the interest and confidence of both teachers and children.   When the work of a school is good there is little difficulty in this respect, because a favourable impression is produced in the mind of the inspector, and this is reflected in his attitude. Even where the work is not up to the standard which the inspector might reasonably expect, he should not express any dissatisfaction or show impatience in the presence of the pupils, but should at the end of the inspection point out the defects to the teacher and make suggestions as to how these defects might be remedied. It is to be observed that repeated instructions on these lines were given to the inspectors by the Commissioners of National Education.

223.   Another criticism directed against the method of inspection is that too much stress is laid on examination.   A system which provides no means of testing the results attained would in our opinion be very unsatisfactory. We are informed that the present practice is to judge the work of teachers partly by inspection of the methods employed and partly by examination of the proficiency attained by their pupils.   We consider that examination is a necessary corollary to inspection.   If our recommendations for the holding of a "Leaving" examination are carried out, some assistance will be rendered to the inspector in assessing the value of the teacher's work, but we believe that a periodic

testing of the entire work of a school is indispensable, and that this cannot be done without a certain amount of examination, oral and written.

225.   It is stated on behalf of the teachers that under the existing system of a uniform school year considerable hardship is caused by the inspection of a certain proportion of the schools rather early in the year, when the pupils are unfamiliar with the work of their standards.   On the whole we think that the uniform school year should be retained, but that arrangements might be made by which this source of complaint would be removed.

226.   Our recommendations are as follows:-

Where full general inspections are held they should be held in the second half of the school year, and the pupils should be tested only on that part of the programme which has been completed.

Schools doing very satisfactory work need not as a rule have a full general inspection more than once in every two or three years.   If this system proves satisfactory the question of its extension to schools doing satisfactory work might be considered.

Where a school comes under the preceding recommendation it should be provided that if there be a staff of two or more assistants, the principal teacher should submit annually to the inspector a detailed report on the progress of the pupils and the work of each teacher.

Before the principal teacher furnishes such a report it should be submitted to each member of the staff so that any who desire to do so may attach a statement.

The rating of a teacher at the previous general inspection should be continued unless altered after a special inspection held as a result of a principal teacher's report or teacher's statement. It should always be open to the Ministry to order a general inspection of any school in any year should the circumstances render this course desirable.

In cases of schools in which no general inspection is held for two or three years as recommended above, care should be taken that any member of the teaching staff not originally registered as "highly efficient" should, notwithstanding the temporary suspension of annual inspections, have full credit for improved efficiency.

228.   Another cause of complaint which we think might easily be removed is that at a general inspection no discrimination is shown as a rule between pupils who have been for all or most of the school year in regular attendance and those newly enrolled or whose attendance has been irregular.   A teacher's work may thus be tested to some extent by the proficiency of pupils who have not been for a sufficient time under his instruction.   We do not think it expedient to recommend the absolute exclusion of newly enrolled pupils or irregular attenders, but special care should be taken in the examination that no unfavourable estimate of the results should be based on the answering of children who have been irregular in attendance or who are newly enrolled — less than fifty attendances in the previous six months to be the determining figure.   A similar regulation should apply in the case of pupils who are suffering from mental or physical defects.   A list of such children should be available for the inspector before he commences the examination.

231.   On the question of assisting teachers to reach a higher state of efficiency several suggestions have been made to us.   One is that the inspector before leaving the school should discuss with the teachers the methods employed by them and should also lay his views freely before the principal.   An inspector who has been chosen for his position presumably on account of his high qualifications and experience, and whose business it is to see many methods of teaching, should be in a highly favourable position for transmitting fresh ideas.   If he is to do this effectively, he should, however, not be too much engrossed with routine work or with the duty of assigning marks for the efficiency of the teaching of individual subjects.   The inspectors in their evidence informed us that discussions of the kind mentioned are very frequent.   We think they should be general.

I.4   The Education Act (Northern Ireland) 1923, 13 and 14 Geo.5, C.21.

The seeds of reform having thus been sown in the two aforementioned reports to the minister, the latter immediately set out to bring many of their recommendations to fruition, and in the process, create a new and better educational system for the children of Northern Ireland.

As both Reports had made abundantly clear, reform and innovation were needed in almost every aspect of educational provision.

The 1923 Act has been regarded as a landmark in Northern Ireland's education system.   This is so because it sought to establish a new educational framework that was both decentralised in its administrative functions, and non-denominational in application and ethos.   This latter feature will be seen particularly in the legislation on the appointment of teachers and religious education.   Its recommendations on decentralisation will be seen in the legislation dealing with local education committees and the creation of an Advisory Council.

The Act did however have many critics, especially among the clergy of the mainstream churches, embittered by what they saw as the Act's usurpation of their traditional role in education, and not least so in the appointment of teachers. Under the Act, such appointments would be made by new regional education committees and not, as heretofore had been the case, by the management committee of a school, or indeed the clerical manager of a school committee acting on his own.

Additional grievances perceived by the clergy were related to the fact that neither had they been guaranteed representation on the new local education committees, or indeed their own schools should they transfer them, nor given the right to require teachers to provide religious instruction. Moreover, the new local education authorities were required only to 'afford opportunities for catechetical instruction,' but not to make specific provision for this instruction on a compulsory basis.

The fact that these 'opportunities' referred only to 'catechetical instruction' was, for the Protestant clergy in particular, a major blow to their religious, as well as educational, aspirations, since they did not regard such instruction in the same light as Bible instruction, considered to be an integral and fundamental feature of Protestant education.

In defence of the legislation, however, Lord Londonderry would argue that the 1923 Education Act had to comply with Section 5 of the Government of Ireland Act (cited below) which forbade the new government of Northern Ireland to 'endow' a particular religion. Clearly he believed that denominational religious education would contravene this section of the Act.

It will also be noted below, that the new Act implemented the Lynn Committee's significant recommendation on the creation of three main types of grant aid for the province's schools. The implications of these forms of aid, for the type and structure of a school's management committee, were significant.

In Part III of the Act, a controversial definition is given of 'elementary education.' Controversial in that there is no reference to religious education as a compulsory feature of elementary instruction; instead, the emphasis is on moral education.

The Act defines the terms 'transferred' and 'provided' schools, as well as the administrative and management roles and responsibilities of the new local and regional education committees. Sections 26 and 66(3) of the Act were regarded by clergy of the mainstream churches as especially objectionable. To bring the Act down, the Protestant churches were to form themselves into a single body which they called the United Education Committee of the Protestant Churches, formed November 1924.

GOVERNMENT OF IRELAND ACT, 1920.
10 & 11 GEO 5.

PROHIBITION OF LAWS INTERFERING WITH RELIGIOUS EQUALITY, TAKING PROPERTY WITHOUT COMPENSATION, ETC.

5. — (1) In the exercise of their power to make laws under this Act neither the Parliament of Southern Ireland nor the Parliament of Northern Ireland shall make a law so as either directly or indirectly to establish or endow any religion, or prohibit or restrict the free exercise thereof, or give a preference, privilege, or advantage, or impose any disability or disadvantage, on account of religious belief or religious or ecclesiastical status, or make any religious belief or religious ceremony a condition of the validity of any marriage, or affect prejudicially the right of any child to attend a school receiving public money without attending the religious instruction at that school, or alter the constitution of any religious body except where the alteration is approved on behalf of the religious body by the governing body thereof, or divert from any religious denomination the fabric of cathedral churches, or, except for the purpose of roads, railways, lighting, water, or drainage works, or other works of public utility upon payment of compensation, any other property, or take any property without compensation.

Any law made in contravention of the restrictions imposed by this subsection shall, so far as it contravenes those restrictions, be void.

(2)   Any existing enactment by which any penalty, disadvantage, or disability is imposed on account of religious belief or on a member of any religious order as such shall, as from the appointed day, cease to have effect in Ireland.

CHAPTER 21

An Act to establish local authorities for education in Northern Ireland; to make better provision therein as respects education, school attendance, the employment of children and young persons, the health and welfare of school children and afflicted children, and the training and employment of school teachers; and for purposes connected therewith.   (22nd June, 1923).

PART I.

ADVISORY COUNCIL AND LOCAL AUTHORITIES AND COMMITTEES

1. — (1)   For the purpose of advising the Ministry of Education for Northern Ireland (in this Act referred to as "the Ministry") on educational matters, there shall be established an Advisory Council, whose members shall be appointed by the Minister of Education for Northern Ireland (in this Act referred to as "the Minister"), and the Ministry shall take into consideration any advice or representation submitted to it by the Advisory Council.

2. — (1)   For the purposes of this Act the council of each county and county borough shall be a local authority for education (in this Act referred to as an "education authority") and the county or county borough shall, for those purposes, form the education area of the education authority.

(2)   The powers and duties under this Act of an education authority ... shall ... be exercised and performed through an education committee of the council, consisting of twenty-one members appointed by the council either from the members of their own body or partly from those members and partly from other persons, as the council think fit ...

(3)   The powers and duties under this Act of an education authority, not being the council of a county borough, shall be exercised and performed through regional education committees to be established under schemes framed by the education authority and confirmed by orders made by the Ministry in accordance with the provisions hereinafter in this section contained: Provided that the education authority shall themselves exercise and perform all their powers and duties in relation to —

(a)   the raising of money by rate or loan;

(b)   the general control of expenditure to such extent as that control may be retained by the education authority themselves;

(c)   the acquisition, holding or disposal of land; and

(d)   any other matters specified in the schemes framed and confirmed as aforesaid with respect to any particular education authority, as being matters in relation to which that authority ought to retain executive powers.

3. — (1) The education authority shall make provision, according to their powers and duties under this Act, for the local management of schools, or groups of schools, within their education area, in such manner as may be approved by the Ministry, and may, if they think fit, make such provision by means of the appointment of committees (in this Act referred to as "school committees") to carry out, or arrange for, the lighting, heating, cleansing, repairs, sanitation, and general upkeep of school premises and grounds, subject to the directions of the education authority ...

(2)   The education authority shall, in providing for the appointment of a school committee —

(a)   in general, have regard to the desirability for the representation thereon of the parents of children attending the schools, and school teachers, and other persons interested in education, and, in the case of schools transferred to the education authority, for the representation thereon of the trustees or persons by whom the school was so transferred; and

(b)   comply with the special provisions of this Act with respect to the representatives to be appointed on the school committee, in any case in which the appointment of a school committee is made a necessary condition for the receipt of a contribution from the education authority as aforesaid.

PART III.

ELEMENTARY EDUCATION

7.   For the purposes of this Act, the expression "elementary education" means an education both literary and moral, based upon instruction in the reading and writing of the English language and in arithmetic, provided for pupils who are in general of an age below fourteen years, and the expression "public elementary school" means a school or department of a school in respect of which grants are paid out of moneys provided by Parliament, and in which elementary education is the principal part of the education provided.

14. — (2) It shall be lawful for the managers of any school, which at the appointed day is a national school or a school recognised by the ministry as providing efficient elementary education ... to make an arrangement under the Second Schedule to this Act for the transfer of the school, and any land, buildings or equipment held or used in connection therewith (including a teacher's residence), to the education authority, upon such terms and conditions as may be arranged between the parties concerned with the approval of the Ministry, and the provisions of the Second Schedule to this Act shall apply with respect to any such transfer.

A school transferred under this section is in this Act referred to as a "transferred school."

****

(4)   A transferred school shall ... be held, maintained and managed as a public elementary school upon such terms and conditions as may be agreed upon, and the trustees or persons transferring such school to the education

authority shall, as from the date of such transfer, be absolutely freed and discharged from all responsibility in connection therewith, whether under any deed of trust relating thereto or otherwise ...

15. — (1)   It shall be the duty of the education authority to consider the needs of any public elementary school within the education area which is not a provided school or a transferred school but which complies with the requirements of the Ministry in relation to public elementary schools (in this Act referred to as a "voluntary school"), and is certified by the Ministry as necessary for the education area.

(2)   If the managers or body controlling a voluntary school, not being a school vested in the Ministry —

(a)   satisfy the education authority that the school will be carried on for some stated period, not being less than eighteen months, as a public elementary school, free of any charge to the education authority over and above the contribution hereinafter provided for; and

(b)   submit to the education authority estimates of —

(i)   any proposed expenditure on the lighting, heating and cleansing of the school premises and grounds;
(ii) such proposed expenditure on equipment, repairs, renewals and general upkeep as should ordinarily be met from year to year,

it shall be the duty of the education authority, if they have approved of the estimates, to contribute a sum equal to one-half of the expenditure within such estimates:

Provided that if any demand is made by the managers or body controlling a voluntary school to which this sub-section applies for a contribution towards any expenditure within such estimates, other than expenditure on the lighting, heating and cleansing of the school premises and grounds, the education authority shall not make a contribution in accordance with such demand unless a school committee is appointed for the school, in accordance with a scheme framed under this Act, to consist of not more than two representatives of the education committee, and not more than four representatives of the managers or trustees, and to have power to associate with themselves, in an advisory capacity, representatives of the parents of children attending the school and representatives of the school teachers.

18.   It shall be lawful for an education authority to aid by means of scholarships the education of children between the ages of twelve and fourteen years in public elementary schools, whether under the management of the education authority or not.

PART V.

Religious Instruction in Public Elementary Schools

26.   It shall be the duty of the education authority to afford opportunities for catechetical instruction according to the tenets of the religious denomination of the parents of children attending any public elementary school, being a provided or transferred school, and for other religious instruction to which those parents do not object (in this Act referred to as "religious instruction"); and those clergymen or other persons (including teachers at the school) to whom those parents do not object shall have access to the children in the school for the purpose of giving them there religious

instruction, or of inspecting and examining the religious instruction there given, at times to be arranged in accordance with regulations of the Ministry: Provided that the education authority shall not provide religious instruction in any public elementary school as aforesaid.

28.   All religious instruction at every school recognised by the Ministry as a public elementary school must be arranged so that —

(a)   the school shall be open to children of all religious denominations for combined literary and moral instruction;

(b)   in respect of religious instruction due regard shall be had to parental right and authority, and accordingly no child shall receive or be present at any religious instruction of which its parents disapprove;

(c)   the times for giving religious instruction in the school shall be so arranged that no child shall be thereby in effect excluded, directly or indirectly, from the other advantages which the school affords; and

(d)   the times at which religious instruction is given shall not form part of the times during which any child is required by this Act, and any bye-law made thereunder, to attend school.

PART XI.

TEACHERS

66. — (1)   Every teacher appointed to teach in a school to or in respect of which grants are made out of moneys provided by Parliament shall have such qualifications as may be approved by the Ministry.

****

(3)   The power of appointing teachers for any provided or transferred school shall be exercised by the education authority and shall not be delegated by them to a school committee appointed under this Act, nor shall the education authority have power to require that the teachers appointed for or holding office in any provided or transferred school shall be teachers who belong to or profess the tenets of, or who do not belong to or profess the tenets of, any particular church or religious denomination.

68.   If, at any time within six weeks after a teacher in a school to or in respect of which grants are made out of moneys provided by Parliament has been notified of dismissal from the school, a petition is presented to the Ministry by the teacher praying for an inquiry into the reasons for his dismissal, the Ministry shall cause to be made such inquiry as it thinks fit; and if, as the result of such inquiry (at which the teacher may be represented) the Ministry is of opinion that the dismissal is not reasonably justifiable, the Ministry shall communicate such opinion to the education authority and to the teacher, or, in the case of a voluntary school, to the managers or school committee of such school and to the teacher, with a view to reconsideration of the decision, and, in the event of the education authority, managers or school committee not departing from their

decision, the Ministry may withhold or reduce any grant payable to or in respect of the school out of moneys provided by parliament, but the teacher affected may be paid a salary for a period not exceeding twelve months:

Provided that nothing in this section shall affect the power of the education authority, managers or school committee, as the case may be, summarily to suspend any teacher from the performance of duty.

I.5 The Education Act (Northern Ireland) 1925, 15 Geo. 5, C.1.

Though the campaign against the 1923 Act would prove active and influential, Lord Londonderry, as minister of education, refused to concede to the clergy the alterations they were demanding. Simply put, he believed that the Act provided a new vista of educational and social opportunities for the people of Northern Ireland which would be to the great benefit of the common good. He has been described as an ecumenist; and certainly there is evidence to this effect. However, as a keen constitutionalist, and experienced parliamentarian, the new minister would have been keenly aware of the enormous significance of the 1920 legislation contained in the Government of Ireland Act of that year.

While utterly opposed to amendments of any kind, as Lord Londonderry was, the same cannot however be said of his prime minister, Sir James Craig. For Craig, Protestant opposition to the 1923 Act was a major political embarrassment. Here was his government implementing an Act of Parliament which that very government's most influential supporters could not and would not accept. The division in Unionist-Protestant ranks was somehow all the more wounding to the government, in consideration of the fact that the Boundary Commission at the time, adjudicating on the future territorial status and position of Northern Ireland, was in the final stages of preparing its report for public consideration.

In the initial stages of the dispute, however, Craig was reluctant to go against the wishes of his respected minister of education. When, however, in March 1925, the influential Orange Order came out publicly in favour of the United Education Committee of the Protestant Churches, Craig caved in, thus paving the way for the most offending clauses of the Act, to Protestants, to be rescinded.

The new Act of 1925 was extremely brief, and whilst it may be said, on the surface, to have met Protestant clerical demands, in actuality this was not so. As will be seen in the legislation, certain clauses of the 1923 Act were merely deleted. Nothing, however, had been put in their place. Soon it would become evident that the 1925 Act was but a breathing space for the government; in that it gave the clergy nothing of substance, the case for amendment had not been won. Thus there ensued, between 1925 and 1930, yet another phase of bitter charge and counter-charge, between the Protestant clergy and the Unionist government. It was only with the passing of the 1930 Act (Northern Ireland), as will be seen, that Protestant demands were met, and Protestant fears of a secular system of education developing in Northern Ireland were much allayed.

CHAPTER 1.

An Act to amend the Education Act (Northern Ireland), 1923, for the purpose of removing doubts as to the provisions of the said Act with respect to voluntary religious instruction in provided and transferred schools. (13th March, 1925).

1. — (1)   Sub-section (3) of section three of the Education Act (Northern Ireland), 1923 (in this Act referred to as "the principal Act") shall have effect as if there were inserted therein after paragraph *(f)* the following new paragraph:—

   (ff) the appointment of teachers by the education authority;

   (2)   The proviso to section twenty-six of the principal Act, and the words in sub-section (3) of section sixty-six of the principal Act following the word "Act" in that sub-section at the end of the sub-section, are hereby repealed.

2.   This Act may be cited as the Education Act (Northern Ireland), 1925, and the principal Act and this Act may be cited together as the Education Acts (Northern Ireland), 1923 and 1925.

I.6   Statutory Rules and Orders of Northern Ireland 1928, No.41.   Regulations Governing the Staffing of Public Elementary Schools, and the Qualifications and Duties of Teachers.

Though locked in a most bitter dispute with the Protestant clergy, between 1925 and 1930, resulting in the latter's widespread refusal to transfer their schools, the ministry of education still found the time to draw up this most detailed set of Rules dealing with many crucial aspects of the administration and management of schools, for example: staffing arrangements as regards the balance to be struck between the appointment of male and female staff in the different types of schools (girls, boys, infants); and criteria governing appointments to the positions of principal, vice-principal and assistant teacher. The Rules also set forth ministerial expectations regarding a teacher's moral conduct, as well as what was expected in the context of his or her teaching obligations towards the pupils.

Censorial of tone, in parts, the Rules are particularly alert to the reality of teachers being involved in party politics — this is forbidden — and they are also sensitive to the social and religious repercussions likely to occur if a teacher were, for example, to own and run a public house.

In another vein, the importance of rating the efficiency of teachers is explicitly emphasised, as are the rules on sickness and non-attendance.

Certain rather prohibitive legislation is enacted on married women teachers in the event of their absence from school following the birth of a child. For a period of two months before and after the birth, they were required to provide qualified substitutes at their own expense.

9. — (a)   A master will not be recognised in a girls' school; nor will an assistant master be recognised in any school under a woman principal.

(b)   A mistress will not be recognised as principal of a boys' school unless the school is an infants' school.

10.   On the occurrence of a vacancy in a mixed school with an average attendance of under 35 pupils the teacher appointed must be a mistress unless the special sanction of the Ministry has been obtained for the appointment of a master.

11.— (a)   The staff of a mixed school will not be considered satisfactory unless it includes a woman teacher.

(b)   In mixed schools with four or more assistants the proportion of men teachers to the whole staff must be, as a rule, not less than 1 in 4.

13.   On the occurrence of a vacancy for an assistant in a boys' school staffed entirely by men teachers, and in which boys under 7 years of age are enrolled, a mistress must as a rule be appointed.

14.   Except in schools with an average attendance of less than 30 pupils, principalships are confined to trained teachers who have successfully completed the period of probation prescribed in rule 23.

15. — (a)   Where a principal teacher is not rated as at least efficient the Ministry may refuse to sanction his appointment as principal of a larger school.

(b)   No assistant teacher is eligible for appointment as principal of a school with an average attendance of 30 or more pupils unless his work as assistant is rated as efficient.

17. — (a)   In order to be eligible for appointment as principal of a school with an average attendance of 50 to 94 pupils a teacher shall have been rated as efficient for each of the last three years of his service, and

(1) — have had at least five years' service, or

(2) — have had at least four years' service inclusive of one year's highly efficient service.

(b)   In order to be eligible for appointment as principal of a school with an average attendance of 95 to 139 pupils a teacher shall have been rated as efficient for each of the last three years of his service, and

(1) — have had at least seven years' service, or

(2) — have had at least six years' service and have been rated as highly efficient for one of these years; or

(3) — have had at least five years' service and have been rated as highly efficient for two of these years.

(c)   In order to be eligible for appointment as principal of a school with an average attendance of 140 pupils and upwards a teacher shall have been rated as highly efficient for the last year of his service, and

(1) — have had at least ten years' service; or

(2) — have had at least nine years' service with highly efficient service for one of the first eight years; or

(3) — have had at least eight years' service with highly efficient service for two of the first seven years; or

(4) — have had at least seven years' service with highly efficient service for three of the first six years.

(d)   In the case of teachers who are graduates of a British or Irish University the period of five years mentioned in (a), of seven years mentioned in (b) and of ten years mentioned in (c) may be reduced to three years, five years and seven years, respectively.

(e)   No teacher recognised for the first time as principal or assistant in a public elementary school in Northern Ireland after 1st April, 1930, shall be eligible for appointment as principal of a school with an average attendance of 350 or above unless he is a graduate of a British or Irish University.

19.   The following are eligible for appointment as vice-principal:—

(a)   Trained teachers, or untrained principal or assistant teachers appointed for the first time on or before 1st April, 1905, who have given at least five years' recognised service as principal or assistant teacher provided that in the last report they are rated as "highly efficient."

(b)   Untrained principal or assistant teachers with at least twelve years' service and rated as "highly efficient" for the last three years.

21.   The following are eligible for appointment as assistant teacher ...

(a)   All teachers, trained or untrained, eligible for appointment as principal under rule 18.

(b)   Girl monitors and girl pupil-teachers who complete their periods of service satisfactorily and who, in their final year, pass the King's Scholarship examination in the first or the second division provided they qualify in practice of teaching...

(c)   Girl monitors and girl pupil-teachers who pass the King's Scholarship examination in third division and who, in a two years' course of training, pass the examination at the end of the first year of training.

(d)   Women graduates of a university on passing the test in practice of teaching provided they also pass in such subjects of the King's Scholarship programme as are not covered by their university degree courses.

(e)   Women who successfully complete their first year's course in a training college under the Ministry and pass in practice of teaching at the final year's examination.

****

(h)   Monks and nuns who are certified by the manager to be members of a religious order and who pass the King's Scholarship Examination in the first or second division and also the test in practice of teaching conducted by a senior inspector of the Ministry are eligible, respectively, as untrained teachers, for the position of assistant in a monastery or convent public elementary school, not paid by capitation, but not in an ordinary public elementary school.

27. — (a)   All teachers must, on first appointment, be over 18 and under 30 years of age; provided, however, that a person, otherwise qualified under the Ministry's rules, who is between the ages of 30 and 45 years, may be admitted to the service if the Ministry is satisfied that since he reached the age of 30 he has been continuously employed in educational institutions of appropriate standing ...

(b)   A teacher whose last service was unfavourably reported upon (e.g. rated below "efficient") and whose service has been interrupted for a period of six months may not be re-admitted for permanent recognition unless a favourable report in regard to his efficiency is received from the inspector.   In order that his efficiency may be tested by the inspector he may be temporarily recognised for a few months.   During such period of temporary recognition he will be paid at the minimum salary of the scale for untrained teachers; but should his re-entry be sanctioned, on receipt of a favourable report, payment at the appropriate rate will be allowed for such service ...

32.   No clergyman of any denomination will be recognised as a teacher in a public elementary school.

33.   No person will be recognised as a teacher who is the owner, in whole or in part, or liable for the rent of the school-house; nor can any person be so recognised in a school owned in whole or in part, or rented by, a near relative or by any person acting in his interest.

34.   Teachers are not permitted to carry on or engage in any business or occupation, or to be members of any association, or to undertake any office or function, tending to impair their usefulness as teachers.   A teacher is forbidden to keep, to act as assistant in keeping, or to have any interest in

a public house, or house for the sale of spirituous liquors, or
to live in any such house; nor may a teacher be the husband
(or wife) of the owner or part owner, manager, or occupier of
such house, or of an assistant therein, or of any other person
having any interest therein.

35.   Teachers may not accept office as county or district
councillors, poor law guardians, or town commissioners,
unless appointed as "additional councillors" under Section 3
(2) or 25(1)*(a)* of the Local Government (Ireland) Act, 1898,
or unless chosen by the council, board of guardians, or town
commissioners to fill a casual vacancy.

36.   Teachers who hold the Commission of the Peace may
discharge all duties devolving upon them as magistrates,
provided that there is no interference thereby with the
performance of their duties as teachers.   They are expected
to refrain from adjudicating in cases in which, as teachers
they might be exposed to any charge of prejudice.

37.   Where a voluntary school is under the patronship or
management of a school committee a member of the teaching
staff may not be a member of that committee or act as its
secretary.

38.   The attendance of teachers at meetings held for party
political purposes or the taking part by them in parliamentary
or local government elections, except by voting, is forbidden.

This rule does not prohibit the employment of teachers by the
sheriff or returning officer, as presiding officers or polling
clerks, in polling booths at parliamentary elections, or at
elections held under the Local Government (Ireland) Act,
1898, provided that there is no interference thereby with the
performance of their duties as teachers.

40. — (a)   The Ministry may, at any time, withdraw recognition from, reduce the salary of, or inflict any lesser penalty upon any teacher who has seriously declined in efficiency or whose conduct has been unsatisfactory, or who has violated any of these or other regulations of the Ministry.

(b)   Before serious action is taken in the case of any teacher he is afforded an opportunity of forwarding to the Ministry any statement he may desire to submit in his defence.

(c)   In no case is a teacher dismissed for inefficiency before he has had ample opportunity of remedying the defects in his teaching which have been reported by the inspectors.

(d)   In no case shall a teacher be dismissed for inefficiency on the reports of a single inspector; before recognition is finally withdrawn his work shall be tested by means of a thorough inspection and an examination of all the standards for whose instruction he is responsible.   This inspection shall be conducted by a senior inspector, or by a chief inspector, as the Ministry may consider desirable.

(e)   Should it appear necessary to dismiss a teacher for inefficiency a formal statement of the grounds on which it is proposed to take action shall be furnished directly to the teacher.   Any representations or explanations which he may submit shall be carefully considered by the Ministry before final action is taken.

41.   Should a teacher have any well-grounded cause of complaint against the manager or the inspector he may submit his case in writing directly to the Ministry for its consideration.

42. — (c)   Should a teacher be absent from duty, through illness, for longer than 31 days in any calendar year no salary or other emoluments may be paid for the additional period of absence unless a qualified substitute approved by the manager is appointed.

(d)   Absence owing to illness shall not be sanctioned for more than six months continuously, or for more than six months in any calendar year.   For this purpose a period of absence includes any days of closing occurring therein.   Resumption of duty for periods of less than four weeks will not be regarded as interrupting the continuity of the six months absence ...

****

(f)   In the case of a teacher who is required to cease attendance at school owing to the occurrence of infectious disease in his home, leave of absence not exceeding one month may be allowed, without stoppage of salary, on the production of a medical certificate, but should he be absent from duty through this cause for longer than a month in any calendar year no salary or other emoluments may be paid for the additional period of absence unless a qualified substitute approved by the manager is appointed.

43. — (a)   When a school is closed in consequence of the absence of a teacher the fact must be at once notified by the teacher to the manager and to the senior and section inspectors, and to the school attendance officer.

(b)   In a school where more than one teacher is employed the absence of any teacher must be similarly notified to manager and inspectors, either by himself or by some person acting on his behalf.

(c)   When the school is closed on a day on which Domestic Economy is to be taught notice should also be sent to the organiser of instruction in these subjects.

45.   Recurring absences of a teacher on account of illness may render the teacher liable to withdrawal of recognition.

47.   A teacher absent on account of illness or owing to attendance at a training college shall be responsible for the salary of his substitute. Substitutes make their own terms with the teachers for whom they act as regards the remuneration for their services, and have no claim on the Ministry ...

49.   Married women teachers shall absent themselves from their schools for two months continuously during the period preceding and succeeding childbirth, and shall provide qualified substitutes at their own expense, for such portion of the two months as is not included in the ordinary vacation of the school. In exceptional cases, where it has been found impossible to obtain qualified substitutes for married women who are compelled to absent themselves from school under the provisions of this rule, the Ministry may sanction, with the approval of the manager, the employment of competent persons as substitutes, although not fully qualified under these regulations.*

59.   The strictest attention must be paid to the morals and general conduct of the pupils, and no opportunity should be omitted of inculcating the principles of honesty, temperance, thrift, unselfishness, politeness, and regard for property whether public or private. Teachers should impress upon the children the importance of cheerful obedience to duty, of consideration and respect for others, and of honour and

---

* This rule does not apply to teachers first appointed prior to 1st July, 1911

truthfulness in word and act.   They should cultivate kindly feelings among their pupils and discountenance quarrelling, cruelty to animals, and any tendency towards unseemly or improper behaviour.

61.   Teachers should treat their pupils with kindness, combined with firmness.   Good discipline must be maintained at all times and corporal punishment should be administered only for grave transgressions and never for mere failure in lessons.   It should be inflicted only by the principal teacher or under his supervision and in such a way as to avoid all risk of injury to pupils.

62.   Teachers shall exercise strict care over the pupils from the time of arrival in the morning until their departure at the end of the school day, save only during the luncheon interval in the case of pupils who are permitted to leave the school.   Arrangements should be made for necessary supervision during the luncheon interval, and this duty may be assigned to the members of the staff in rotation.   The necessity for orderly and rapid exit from the school, in case of fire, should be constantly borne in mind, and to this end the teachers of large schools are enjoined to hold fire drill at intervals.

67.   At the termination of his employment in a school a teacher must deliver to his successor or to the manager all school records, complete and in a satisfactory condition.

68.   Teachers seeking appointments in public elementary schools may have their names entered in a register kept in the Ministry for that purpose and known as the Employment Register.   The conditions of registration and other particulars may be had on application.

I.7   Education Act (Northern Ireland), 1930,
20 and 21 Geo.5, C.14.

After the Education Act, 1923, this Education Act of 1930 is undoubtedly the most significant until the passing of the Education Act, 1947, which will be dealt with separately.

This significance is evident in the fact that the 1930 Act not only reversed permanently those clauses of the 1923 Act which the mainstream churches in Northern Ireland regarded as contentious and offensive. (As we have seen the 1925 Amendment Act had failed to provide a permanent solution). It also laid down a new basis, at that time, for the administration and management of the majority of Northern Ireland schools, characteristics of which are still to be found in the present system, for example transferors' representatives on the Boards of Governors of controlled schools.

The 1930 Act provided the Protestant clergy with three main concessions. It legislated for the transferors of schools to be represented, as of right, on both (a) the management committees of the schools they transferred and (b) the local education authorities to which the transfers were made.

It empowered these local authorities to provide Bible instruction in all 'provided' and 'transferred' schools, and to require teachers to give this instruction.

Thirdly, in the matter of teaching appointments, it permitted the management committees of 'transferred' and 'provided' schools to submit to their local education authority the names of candidates they considered eligible for appointment. This had not been permitted under the 1923 legislation.

In essence, these three new enactments constituted a major reversal of the non-denominational principles which the 1923 Act had advocated and which the 1925 Act had failed to eradicate.

Needless to say, Roman Catholic authorities objected to the new enactment on Bible instruction, arguing that this form of instruction was fundamentally Protestant in nature, and as such, was discriminatory of their religious outlook. These authorities believed that the new Act contravened Section 5 of the Government of

Ireland Act, 1920. They also believed that the funding of Catholic schools should be on a par with the funding allocated to 'transferred' and 'provided' schools, that is 100%. This argument had as its basis the view that these schools were, in essence, Protestant, and so were as denominational in ethos and identity as their Catholic counterparts, for which funding was very much inferior.

CHAPTER 14

An Act to amend the Education Acts (Northern Ireland), 1923 and 1925, and for purposes connected therewith. (17th June, 1930).

PROVISIONS AS TO EDUCATION COMMITTEES AND COMMITTEES FOR SCHOOLS

1. — (1) The Minister of Education shall appoint, as members of an education committee for the purposes of the Education Act (Northern Ireland), 1923 (in this Act referred to as "the principal Act"), persons who, in his opinion, are representative of the transferors by whom any schools in the education area of such committee have been transferred to the education authority, and such appointments shall be made after consultation with the transferors (to such extent as may seem to the said Minister practicable and expedient) and with the education authority concerned.   In determining the number of representative persons to be so appointed as members of an education committee, the said Minister shall have regard to the number of schools transferred as aforesaid, and such members shall be additional to the members appointed under sub-section (2) or sub-section (4) of section two of the principal Act, but shall not in any case exceed in number one-fourth of the total number of members of the committee (including the members appointed by the said Minister), and the said sub-sections shall have effect as amended by this section.

(2)   In this Act and in the principal Act as amended by this Act, the expression "education committee" means the education committee of a county borough council or a regional education committee, and the expression "transferors" means any trustees, persons or body of persons by whom a school has been transferred to the education authority, and includes trustees appointed in place of such trustees, the representatives of such persons, and the successors of such body, as aforesaid.

2. — (1)   The following section shall be substituted for section three of the principal Act as amended by the Education Act (Northern Ireland), 1925:—

"3.— (1)   The education authority shall, as respects every public elementary school within their education area which is a provided school or a transferred school (as hereinafter in this Act defined), make provision for the local management of the school by means of a school management committee to be appointed by the education authority; but so that several such schools may be grouped under one school management committee, if the education authority so desire and the Ministry approves.

(2)   A school management committee appointed under the last preceding sub-section shall be so constituted that, so far as is practicable, not less than one-half of the members to be appointed thereto shall be representative of the following persons:—

(a)   the transferors of the transferred schools under the local management of the committee; and

(b)   the persons who were formerly managers of any public elementary schools which have been superseded by provided schools under the local management of the committee, or, if those persons were recognised by the Ministry as such managers by virtue of any office, then their successors in such office;

and the remaining members shall, to the extent of not more than one-fourth of the total number, be persons nominated by the parents of children attending the school or schools under the local management of the committee at a meeting held in accordance with regulations of the Ministry, and, except as last aforesaid, shall be persons nominated by the education authority.

The education authority shall nominate in addition, as respects each school management committee, one or more representatives of the school teachers employed at the school or schools under the local management of the school management committee, and such representative or representatives shall have the right to take part in meetings of the school management committee but shall not have the right to vote on any question regarding the selection of a teacher.

If any question arises as to the right of any person or body of persons under this sub-section to be represented on or nominate a member of a school management committee, that question shall stand referred to the Ministry, whose decision shall be final.

****

(4)   Whenever ... it is necessary that a teacher shall be appointed for a provided or transferred public elementary school under the local management of a school management committee, the education authority of the education area within which the school is situate shall, in the manner prescribed by the Ministry, issue advertisements inviting applications for the appointment and transmit the applications, with particulars of the candidates, to the school management committee, shall consider the applications for the appointment, and shall select therefrom and submit to the education authority, to be dealt with under the provisions of sub-section (3) of section sixty-six of this Act, the names of such of the candidates as are qualified for the time being under the regulations of the Ministry (in this Act referred to as "qualified candidates"), or, if there are more than three qualified candidates, the names of three of them, and shall take such further steps in relation to the appointment as may be required under the said provisions ...

(5)   A school management committee shall, if the education authority so desire and subject to their directions, exercise in relation to the provided or transferred school or schools which are under their local management all or any of the following functions:—

(a)   carrying out, or arranging for, the lighting, heating, cleansing, repairs, sanitation and general upkeep of school premises and grounds;

(b)   any other function of management assigned to the committee by the education authority;

(c)   the function of advising the education committee upon any matter arising in relation to any school under the local management of the school management committee, or upon the administration of this Act in the locality where such school is situate.

The members of the school management committee shall have the right to visit the school or schools which are under their local management.

(6)   The school management committee of any provided or transferred school or schools shall not appoint any officers or servants without the consent of the education authority, and no expenditure may be incurred by them unless such consent has been previously signified."

3.   The following sub-section shall be substituted for sub-section (3) of section sixty-six of the principal Act as amended by the Education Act (Northern Ireland), 1925:—

"(3)   The power of appointing teachers for any public elementary school being a provided or transferred school shall, in any case to which sub-section (4) of section three of this Act applies, be exercised by the education authority in accordance with the following provisions:—

(a)   The education authority shall take into consideration the qualified candidates for appointment whose names are submitted to them by the school management committee under sub-section (4) of section three of this Act;

(b) If the education authority are not satisfied to appoint some one or other of the said qualified candidates, the matter shall stand referred to the Ministry, and the Ministry may —

(i) direct that the matter shall be referred back to the school management committee for the selection and submission to the education authority of such number of other qualified candidates (not exceeding three) as the Ministry may require; or

(ii) direct the appointment of one of the qualified candidates whose names were submitted by the school management committee to the education authority; or

(iii) direct the appointment to be again advertised and dealt with under subsection (4) of section three of this Act;

(c) The decision of the Ministry under the last preceding paragraph shall be final, and it shall be the duty of the education authority to take all necessary steps for the due appointment as .teacher of a qualified candidate whose appointment is directed by the Ministry under the said paragraph;

(d) The foregoing provisions of this sub-section shall apply in a case where, in pursuance of a direction given under sub-division (i) of paragraph (b) thereof, the school management committee submit to the education authority the names of qualified candidates, and also in the case of any subsequent submission of such names in pursuance of a direction so given.

The power of appointing a teacher for a school provided by or transferred to the education authority, except in a case to which sub-section (4) of section three of this Act applies, shall be exercised by the education authority and shall not be delegated to a school management committee, and, in a case to which the said sub-section (4) applies, shall not be so delegated except to the extent mentioned in the foregoing provisions of this sub-section."

Provisions as to Bible instruction.

4. — (1)   If Bible instruction is not provided by the education authority in any public elementary school, being a provided school or transferred school, it shall be the duty of the education authority to provide Bible instruction, should the parents of not less than ten children who are in regular attendance at such school make application to the education authority for that purpose in the prescribed manner: Provided that the obligation under this sub-section shall not arise or continue where there is another public elementary school in which Bible instruction is given and which in the opinion of the Ministry such children can conveniently attend.

(2)   All Bible instruction provided by the education authority in a provided or transferred school must be arranged so that —

(a)   the school shall be open to children of all religious denominations for combined literary and moral instruction;

(b)   in respect of Bible instruction due regard shall be had to parental right and authority, and accordingly no child shall receive or be present at any Bible instruction of which the child's parents disapprove;

(c)   the times for giving Bible instruction shall be so arranged that no child shall be thereby in effect excluded, directly or indirectly, from the other advantages which the school affords; and

(d)   the times at which Bible instruction is given shall not form part of the times during which any child is required by the principal Act, and any bye-law made thereunder, to attend school.

(3)   Where the education authority makes arrangements for Bible instruction in a provided or transferred school it shall be the duty of the teachers of the school to give such instruction, if so required by the education authority:

Provided that —

(i)   the freedom of a teacher to give religious instruction under and in accordance with Part V. of the principal Act shall not be restricted by such arrangements, nor shall such arrangements be taken to impose upon any teacher an obligation to give religious instruction as aforesaid; and

(ii) a teacher who has given Bible instruction in a bona fide manner, in accordance with the programme of Bible instruction adopted by the education authority, shall not be liable to dismissal on grounds connected with the efficiency of the work of such teacher in giving Bible instruction.

(4)   The Ministry shall make such regulations as it may consider necessary for securing that the provisions of this section are complied with.

(5)   For the purposes of this section the expression "Bible instruction" means instruction based upon the Holy Scriptures according to some authoritative version or versions thereof, but excluding instruction as to any tenet which is distinctive of any particular religious denomination.

5.   No teacher in any school provided by or transferred to an education authority may be required, as a condition of appointment or holding office, to teach any religious catechism or religious formulary which is distinctive of any particular religious denomination.

10. — (1)   If the Ministry is satisfied that sufficient and suitable provision for the elementary education of any children of school age resident in an education area is required, and cannot otherwise be made, then the Ministry may pay to any person, for the purpose of the provision or equipment of a new voluntary school, or the alteration, enlargement, reconstruction or equipment of an existing voluntary school, one-half of the expenditure incurred for such purpose, and such payment shall be subject to the following conditions, that is to say:—

(a)   the school shall be vested in trustees appointed with the approval of the Ministry for the purpose of maintaining and carrying on the school;

(b)   the school shall be maintained and carried on as a public elementary school;

(c)   if, within a period of fifty years from the completion of the works for the purpose of which the payment was made by the Ministry, the school ceases to be maintained and carried on as a public elementary school, the said payment shall, unless the Ministry otherwise determines, be recoverable from any person in whom is vested for the time being the estate or interest in the school premises which was formerly held for the purposes thereof ...

I.8   Statutory Rules and Orders of Northern Ireland, 1934, No. 40: Regulations for Public Elementary Schools.

These 1934 Rules and Regulations cover a wide range of educational issues, ranging from the display of religious and political emblems and symbols, purposes other than educational to which school premises might be put, to ministerial policy on the teaching of Irish.

The Rules and Regulations set out the conditions acceptable to the ministry of education regarding a school's warrant of recognition, and the duties and responsibilities expected of managers of schools concerning the upkeep of the school premises and the employment of teachers.

Part III deals with the organisation of the school year, and it is here that the teaching of Irish is specifically referred to in a paragraph forbidding schools to make this subject compulsory.

The procedural aspects involved in teacher dismissal, and the powers and responsibilities of inspectors, not least in the ratings of teachers, are expounded. The Rules and Regulations are of an essentially pragmatic orientation. They provide valuable insights into the educational policy and thinking of the period.

PART 1

5. — (a)   A school shall not be conducted in a place of worship, save with the special sanction of the Ministry in order to meet a purely temporary emergency.

(b)   The inscription "Public Elementary school" must appear in plain and legible characters in a conspicuous position on the exterior of the school premises.

(c)   No inscription which contains the name of any religious denomination, nor any emblems or symbols of a denominational character shall be exhibited on the exterior of any schoolhouse or premises, nor shall any emblems or symbols of a denominational character be exhibited in the schoolrooms at any time other than that devoted to religious instruction.

(d)   No emblems or symbols of a political nature may at any time be exhibited in the schoolrooms or affixed to the exterior of the buildings; nor may any placards whatsoever, except such as refer to the legitimate business of the school, be affixed thereto or exhibited therein.

6. — (a)   The control over the use of school premises when not required for school purposes shall rest with the manager, subject to the provisions of sub-sections (b), (c) and (d) of this Article, and to the determination of the Ministry in cases that in its opinion might lead to contention or abuse.

(b)   No political meetings may be held in any school premises nor may any political business whatsoever be transacted therein. Schools may not be used for any purpose directly or indirectly connected with parliamentary or local government elections, except as polling booths on the requisition of the Sheriff or Returning Officer in accordance with the statutes regulating such elections.

(c)   The use of transferred schools shall be subject to any reservation embodied in the documents of transfer.

(d)   Voluntary schools vested in the Ministry or in trustees under deeds to which the Ministry is a party and schools built, altered, enlarged, re-constructed or equipped with the aid of a grant under Section 16 of the Education Act (Northern Ireland), 1923, as amended by Section 9 of the Education Act (Northern Ireland), 1930, from a local Education Authority subsequent to the passing of the Education Act (Northern Ireland), 1930, shall not be used for any purpose other than the education of the pupils attending them except with the special approval of the Ministry, previously obtained; *provided,* however, that on Sundays they may be employed for Sunday schools, with the sanction of the managers, and *provided further* that managers of such schools may allow their schools to be used outside school hours for instruction in technical or other courses approved by the Ministry (subject in the case of schools vested in trustees to the consent also of the trustees); but the Ministry will require managers to secure that any damage done to the schoolhouse, premises or equipment during or arising out of such use shall be made good either by the parties conducting the classes or from other local sources.

8.   In order to warrant the recognition or continued recognition of a school the Ministry must be satisfied that, so far as is reasonably practicable, the premises are —

(a)   suitably situated, planned and lighted; and also provided with a convenient supply of pure water;

(b)   provided with satisfactory cloakroom, lavatory and sanitary accommodation;

(c)   adequately furnished and equipped, and in good repair;

(d)   provided with facilities for safe and speedy exit in case of fire;

(e)   systematically and thoroughly ventilated, regularly cleansed, and adequately heated;

(f)   provided with proper facilities for the recreation of the pupils.

13.   Grants to separate schools for boys and girls or for infants and senior pupils may be withdrawn if, in the opinion of the Ministry, these schools can be more efficiently or more economically conducted as one establishment: *provided* always that where the average daily attendance of pupils at one of the schools for the preceding calendar year has been less than 50 amalgamation shall take place on the occurrence of a vacancy in the staff of either school unless for special reasons it shall be otherwise directed by the Ministry.

14. — (a)   Where the Ministry is satisfied that two or more neighbouring schools can be amalgamated with advantage for reasons of educational efficiency or economy it may give notice that after such date as the Ministry may determine no new appointment of a teacher may be made except in a temporary capacity until the question of the need for separate schools has been decided by the Ministry.

(b)   No new teacher shall be recognised, except in a temporary capacity, in any school with an average daily attendance of under 50 pupils and within three miles distance of one or more other schools until a re-arrangement of the schools in the district has been considered and until the Ministry has given a decision thereon.

(c)   The Ministry reserves the right to withdraw grants from any school in which the average daily attendance of pupils is less than 20.

PART II

PATRONAGE AND MANAGEMENT

20.   Managers of voluntary schools should visit their schools at frequent intervals and should check and certify the accuracy of returns furnished to the Ministry, and they should see that the school is conducted in accordance with the Regulations of the Ministry.

Where joint managers are recognised all returns and salary claims should be signed by each of them unless they agree that one of their number or some other person nominated by them shall act as correspondent and sign such returns on their behalf.   In case of disagreement between joint managers the matter in dispute shall be determined by the Ministry, whose decision shall be final.

21. — (a)   The manager shall be responsible for the maintenance of the school in accordance with the requirements of the Ministry and no financial responsibility may be allowed to fall upon the teachers; but teachers are expected to render all reasonable assistance in seeing that work connected with the cleansing and care of the premises is adequately performed ...

****

22.   Managers should arrange to have repairs to the school premises carried out, as far as possible, during vacation periods, so as to avoid unnecessary interruption of the work of the school.

23.   The manager shall enter into an agreement with each teacher on one of the forms approved by the Ministry and the execution of such agreement shall be a necessary condition for the payment of salary to the teacher; *Provided* that in temporary and exceptional circumstances the Ministry may relax this rule, and that the rule shall not apply to temporary assistants in 'large schools' (as defined in Part IV hereof) or to locum tenons teachers appointed in accordance with the same Regulations.

PART III

ORGANISATION

28. — (a)   The school year shall commence on the first day of July and end on the last day of June.   School programmes and time tables should date from the beginning of the school year.

(b)   All schools must be in full operation on every day of the year, exclusive of Saturdays and Sundays and the days of closing allowed under (c) and (d) of this Article.

****

(e)   When the school has not been kept in operation as required, the salaries and other emoluments of the teachers for the days of excess closing may be disallowed.

29. — (a) ... the programme to be followed in each school shall be determined by the manager after consulting the principal teacher.

(b)   The programme must be in accordance with the general programme issued by the Ministry, and the modifications provided for therein.

(c)   When Irish is taught in any school the instruction in this subject must not be made obligatory upon any pupil, and in cases where parents object to their children receiving instruction in this subject during the ordinary school hours the school time table must clearly indicate the alternative subject in which instruction is provided for such pupils at the time when Irish is being taught to the other pupils of the school.

30.   Work must be carried on in accordance with a time table prepared by the principal teacher with the approval of the manager and subject to modification if required by the Ministry.

31. — (a)   No child under four years of age may be enrolled as a pupil.

(b)   A child who is not enrolled in the school shall not be permitted to be present in the schoolroom during the ordinary school hours, except in accordance with special arrangements approved by the Ministry.

34.   Not less than four hours a day shall be provided on the time table after morning roll call for secular instruction on five days in the week.   The secular instruction period shall consist of two meetings separated by an interval of not less than half-an-hour and not exceeding one hour and a half.   In

large urban centres where arrangements are in operation for providing free meals the interval shall be at least one hour, and in other cases it shall not exceed one hour if serious inconvenience would result.

35.   For Grant purposes and the staffing of schools an "attendance" shall mean presence at secular instruction for not less than four hours; and a "half-attendance" shall mean presence at secular instruction for not less than two hours during a meeting ...

37. — (a)   The morning "attendance" shall begin not later than 10.30 a.m.   The school shall, however, be in operation from 10 a.m. at latest.

(b)   The attendance of the pupils must be recorded in the books supplied for the purpose in strict accordance with the instructions issued from time to time by the Ministry.

(c)   When, owing to the severity of the weather or other exceptional cause, the number of pupils in attendance on any day or days is under one-third of the average daily attendance for the whole month in which the day or days occur, the attendance on such day or days may be excluded from the calculation of the quarterly and annual averages.

DISMISSAL OF TEACHERS

83. — (a)   The Ministry may, at any time, withdraw recognition from, reduce the salary of, or inflict any lesser penalty upon any teacher who has seriously declined in efficiency or whose conduct has been unsatisfactory, or who has violated any of the Regulations of the Ministry.

(b)   Before serious action is taken in the case of any teacher he shall be afforded an opportunity of forwarding to the Ministry any statement he may desire to submit in his defence.

(c)   In no case shall a teacher be dismissed for inefficiency before he has had ample opportunity of remedying the defects in his teaching which have been reported by the inspectors.

(d)   In no case shall a teacher be dismissed for inefficiency on the reports of a single inspector; before recognition is finally withdrawn his work shall be tested by means of a thorough inspection and an examination of all the standards for whose instruction he is responsible.   This inspection shall be conducted by a senior inspector, or by a chief inspector, as the Ministry may consider desirable.

(e)   Should it appear necessary to dismiss a teacher for inefficiency a formal statement of the grounds on which it is proposed to take action shall be furnished directly to the teacher.   Any representations or explanations which he may submit shall be carefully considered by the Ministry before final action is taken.

84.   Should a teacher have any well-grounded cause of complaint against the manager or the inspector he may submit his case in writing directly to the Ministry for its consideration.

PART V.

INSPECTION

113. — (a)   Inspectors and other officers of the Ministry appointed for the purpose shall visit schools as often as may be convenient, with or without notice, and report on the condition and suitability of the premises, the adequacy of the teaching staff, the character, quality and suitability of the instruction given, the observance of the Ministry's Regulations and such other matters as may require attention.

(b)   They shall call the attention of manager and teachers to any defects observed and make suggestions for their removal, but they are not invested with authority to decide questions affecting the schools or the business of the Ministry.

114.   General inspections shall be held triennially, biennially or annually, and for this purpose the schools may be divided into three classes in accordance with instructions issued by the Ministry on the subject.

115.   At each general inspection a rating is assigned to show the merit of the work of each teacher and these ratings are continued until the next general inspection unless altered as the result of a special inspection held in the meantime.

116.   Extracts from general reports showing the efficiency of the teaching staff, the progress of the school and its value as an educational institution and any other matters calling for notice are furnished to managers and principal teachers; and each member of the teaching staff is informed of the official estimate of his efficiency as a teacher.   When it is considered necessary, extracts from incidental reports also are sent to the managers and teachers for their information.

117.   Should the manager or teacher be dissatisfied with an inspector's report an appeal may be made to the Ministry. This appeal must be lodged within fourteen days of the receipt of the report by the manager and the teacher, and a duplicate of the appeal must, at the same time, be forwarded to the inspector ...

I.9   Statutory Rules and Orders of Northern Ireland, 1936, No.159.   Public Elementary Schools Regulations, 1934. Amending Regulations No.2, 1936.

Article 35 and Clause 2 of Article 37, quoted previously, are among certain Articles of the 1934 Order amended by this legislation in 1936.

1.   The following clause is hereby added to Article 35 of the Principal Regulations:-

35. — (e) in schools in which an annual examination in the religious or bible instruction of the pupils is held, the minimum time constituting an "attendance" may, on the day of the examination, be reduced from four hours to three and one half hours, and the minimum time constituting a "half attendance" may be reduced from two hours to one and one half hours. This proviso may be availed of on only one day in any school year.

2.   Clause (c) of Article 37 of the Principal Regulations is hereby repealed and the following clause substituted therefor;-

37. — (c) When owing to the severity of the weather or other exceptional cause, the number of pupils in attendance on any day or days is under one-half of the

```

average daily attendance for the whole month in which the day or days occur, the attendance on each day or days may be excluded from the calculation of the quarterly and annual averages.

**I.10  Statutory Rules and Orders of Northern Ireland, 1937, No.17.**

Still further Amendments to the 1934 Regulations are made in this document. The following, quoted previously, are among those amended: Article 28 and Article 116.

PUBLIC ELEMENTARY SCHOOLS REGULATIONS, 1934.
AMENDING REGULATIONS, No.4, 1937.

1.    The following sub-section is hereby added to Article 28 of the Principal Regulations:—

"28. — (f)   Where a manager is satisfied that an annual examination in religious or Bible instruction cannot conveniently be held in a school without reducing the period of secular instruction on the day of the examination below the minimum of $3^1/2$ hours allowed by Article 35 (e) on such day, the said day need not be counted as one of the fifty school days referred to in sub-section (c) of this Article: Provided that the provisions of this sub-section may be availed of only if the provisions of sub-section (e) of Article 35 are not being availed of in the same school year and only on one school day in that year."

10.    Article 116 of the Principal Regulations is hereby repealed and the following Article substituted therefor:—
```

"116.   Extracts from annual reports showing the progress of the school and its value as an educational institution and any other matters calling for notice are furnished to managers and principal teachers. When it is considered necessary, extracts from incidental and other reports also are sent to the managers and teachers for their information."

I.11   Educational Reconstruction in Northern Ireland, 1944, Cmd. 226.

In the period between 1938 and 1944, there is little of significance to note in the contexts of school administration and management. With the publication of the 1944 White Paper, however, a new era of debate on the future shape of education in Northern Ireland was inevitably inaugurated.

The overall aim of the White Paper was that of stimulating discussion on and of the best and most appropriate means of securing a system of education which would give every child in Northern Ireland '... equality of opportunity to develop his abilities to the full ...' (par.29). In this regard, the effective management and adequate provision of both primary and secondary schools had to be a paramount consideration.

It is in this particular context of supply and demand, that the Paper makes reference to the financial difficulties likely to be experienced by voluntary authorities, if and when they were required by law to provide secondary education. The Paper makes it clear, however, that financial assistance to the voluntary sector would remain contingent upon the authorities within that sector accepting the principle of public representation on their school management committees.

The White Paper also draws attention to: (i) daily collective worship in schools; (ii) the matter of teachers exercising liberty of conscience in respect of the giving of religious instruction; and (iii) the issue of 'four and two' committees.

PART II

The Future

29.   ... The object of the proposals contained in this paper is to produce an educational system which will give every child in Northern Ireland equality of opportunity to develop his abilities to the full and which will at the same time be acceptable to all the different interests which have given service to the cause of education in the past and which must be allowed to play their part in the future. The prosperity of Northern Ireland no less than that of any other part of the United Kingdom depends on the quality of its individual citizens, and the aim of the Government is that no child shall be denied the type of education best suited to his needs and abilities, wherever his home may be situated and whatever his family circumstances may be. The schools must accept an increasing responsibility for preparing the children of to-day to become the skilled and contented citizens of to-morrow and must adapt itself to changing circumstances. The school, however, does not bear the sole responsibility; there must be a close partnership between home, church and school as the three great influences on the growing child and unless the citizen of to-morrow has a high sense of values the mere possession of greater skill and knowledge may be more a menace than a benefit ...

LIMITS OF COMPULSORY ATTENDANCE

30.   At the present time children between the ages of 6 and 14 are compelled by law to attend school, or to receive efficient elementary education otherwise than by attendance at school. It is now proposed that the lower age limit should be reduced to 5 and the upper limit raised to 15 ...   The raising of the school leaving age to 15 is closely connected

with the reorganisation of the entire educational system proposed later in this Paper.   This reorganisation will be achieved more easily in the larger towns than elsewhere, and it may be thought expedient that the raising of the school-leaving age should not necessarily take place in all areas on the same appointed day ...

NURSERY SCHOOLS AND CLASSES

32.   The Government propose to make it a duty of the education authorities to provide nursery schools or classes for children of 2 years of age to 5 where in the opinion of the Ministry of Education, after consultation with the authority, such provision is required.   Facilities will also be available for voluntary agencies to obtain from the Ministry building grants towards the cost of nursery accommodation in those cases where the parents of the children for whom it is proposed to provide the facilities may not wish them to attend schools or classes provided by the education authority ...

REORGANISATION : THE "BREAK" AT 11+

33.   In 1928 the Consultative Committee of the Board of Education* under the Chairmanship of Sir Henry Hadow presented to the President of the Board a report entitled "The Education of the Adolescent," which is now commonly referred to as the Hadow Report.   Its chief recommendation was that the "all-age" elementary schools catering for the great bulk of the children of compulsory school age should cease to exist and should be replaced by junior or primary schools for those under the age of 11+ and by senior schools for children

* Under the Education Act, 1944, the Board of Education has been renamed the Ministry of Education and the President of the Board has become the Minister of Education; to avoid confusion the old titles have been retained in this Paper.

between 11+ and 14.   This recommendation was adopted by the Board of Education and has been the cornerstone of English educational policy for the past 18 years ...

35.   ... the fundamental change in the new English educational system, namely that full-time education after the age of 11+ should in future be regarded as secondary education, is inherent in the recommendations of the Hadow Report.   It therefore becomes essential to consider whether the public elementary school system of Northern Ireland should be replaced by a system of primary schools for children under 11 years of age and secondary schools for children over that age.   The policy of effecting a break in the child's school life roughly at the age of 11+ has become so much a part of the English educational system that it was possible for the President of the Board of Education to say in the White Paper on which the new Act is based: "The principle of reorganisation is advocated in the Hadow Report, i.e., the provision of separate schools for all children over 11, is accepted as an educational axiom ..."   Apart from its limited application in a modified form by the Belfast Education Committee, which has built several new junior and senior schools, the principle is comparatively new in Northern Ireland ...

RELIGIOUS EDUCATION

54.   In paragraphs 18 to 21 a brief account was given of the provision made in the Education Act of 1923 and in subsequent amending legislation with regard to religious instruction.   It was pointed out that religion has always had a place in the time-table of almost all elementary and secondary schools, although (except for Bible instruction in the elementary schools under the education authorities)

provision for the subject has at no time been made the statutory duty of those responsible for school management. The Government are in no doubt as to the widespread desire of the people of Northern Ireland that, in the future, greater prominence should be given to religious education in the schools, and they now propose to emphasise its paramount importance by including in the forthcoming Bill a definite requirement that religious instruction shall be given in every primary and secondary school and that the school day shall begin with collective worship on the part of the pupils. Exceptions will of course be allowed for individual children whose parents desire that they should be excused, and where the school premises render a single act of worship impracticable, suitable modifications will be permitted.

55.   These important proposals are in general similar to the provisions contained in the recent English Education Act. Another feature common to both countries will be that in schools under the management of education authorities the collective worship and the instruction which are obligatory shall not be distinctive of the tenets of any particular denomination, while in voluntary schools the type of worship and instruction to be provided will be determined by the managers or governing bodies.   The detailed proposals for Northern Ireland will, however, go further than their English counterpart.   A notable divergence is that in Northern Ireland clergymen and other persons will, subject to certain limitations, be granted reasonable access to pupils in schools for the purpose of giving denominational or undenominational instruction.   Hitherto this "right of access" has been in force in all the elementary schools under the education authorities and in some of those under voluntary management; it is proposed that in future it should be extended to all schools, both primary and secondary, except that it will not apply to existing voluntary schools which have not previously been

obliged to grant it, unless the managers or governing bodies give their consent.   Where such consent is not forthcoming, however, the school concerned must, as an alternative, give facilities for the withdrawal from its premises of pupils whose parents wish them to receive suitable instruction elsewhere.

56.   The "right of access" enjoyed by clergymen to give religious instruction in elementary schools under the management of education authorities has also carried with it the right to examine or inspect religious instruction given by the teachers in these schools. It is proposed to continue this arrangement, which is well established in Northern Ireland ... The position of the voluntary schools, also, will remain unchanged; the managers or governing bodies will make such arrangements for inspection as they deem fit, save that where "right of access" applies clergymen will be able to examine or inspect the religious instruction which is given by reason of that right.

57.   The Government are fully assured that teachers as a body will, as in the past, be only too glad to exercise the high privilege of promoting the spiritual welfare of their pupils. They are satisfied, however, that it is proper that the right of individual conscience should be respected; it is also incumbent upon the Parliament of Northern Ireland to have strict regard to the prohibition contained in the Government of Ireland Act, 1920, against passing a law which would, directly or indirectly, impose a disadvantage on account of religious belief.   It is accordingly proposed that the liberty of conscience of an individual teacher in a school under the management of an education authority should be appropriately safeguarded in respect of the giving of religious instruction.

THE MANAGEMENT AND PROVISION OF SCHOOLS

59.   The subject of management and provision is difficult and complicated; it must be treated at some length, for considerations of importance are involved. Among the problems that arise are the management and finance of the new primary and junior secondary schools which will replace the existing voluntary elementary schools, the management of the new schools which similarly will replace the existing elementary schools under the control of education committees, and the source from which the voluntary senior secondary schools will derive the financial assistance required for the provision of extensions to accommodate increased numbers of pupils. The nursery school and the day technical school present no difficulties which do not arise more acutely in the consideration of the primary and secondary schools, and it will not be necessary to make reference to them here.

VOLUNTARY PRIMARY AND JUNIOR SECONDARY SCHOOLS

60.   The manager of a voluntary elementary school receives substantial grants from public funds; the salaries of the teachers are paid by the State, 50 per cent of the annual cost of heating, cleaning and lighting, within approved estimates, is defrayed by the education committee and 50 per cent of the cost of new building or reconstruction (including equipment) is paid by the State. Thus it remains for the voluntary manager who is unwilling to transfer his school to the education authority to find from the parents or elsewhere the balance of the money necessary for the operation of the school — half the annual cost of keeping the school warm, clean, and properly lighted and (unless the school is placed under the management of a "four-and-two" committee) the whole cost of maintaining the fabric of the building in good repair, and half the capital sum needed for building a new

school or reconstructing an old one.   This is the sacrifice he makes for the voluntary principle and sufficient has been said ... to show that often the principle is maintained at the expense of the well-being of the pupils.   It is obvious that when a scheme of reorganisation is being prepared which involves a considerable amount of new building at a time when costs are likely to be high, the question must be asked whether the voluntary manager can play his proper part in the new scheme with the financial assistance at present available from public funds, and if he cannot, what increased assistance should be given and from what source.

62.   The Government are satisfied that in Northern Ireland, as in England and Wales, it will be necessary to provide increased financial assistance to the voluntary manager; they are equally satisfied that where additional assistance is given the principle of representation must be observed.   It is proposed, therefore, that if those responsible for the conduct of a voluntary primary or junior secondary school are prepared to agree to the establishment of a "four-and-two" committee of management, and if at the same time they agree to certain restrictions upon the use of the school after school hours, the education authority should be required to accept full responsibility for the cost of the heating, cleaning, lighting and internal repairs; under similar conditions capital grants of 65 per cent for building, reconstruction, and equipment will be made available from the Exchequer.   If the principle of representation is not admitted the school will not be eligible for grants from either the authority or the Exchequer, other than those (50 per cent for heating, cleaning and lighting and 50 per cent for capital expenditure) which can now be obtained under the Education Acts of 1923 and 1930; it is proposed, however, that, whether the education authority is represented or not, all junior secondary schools should be under the control of boards of management.

Primary and Junior Secondary Schools under the
Management of Education Authorities

63.   In schools under the education authorities the problem
of management, while not complicated by considerations of
finance, is not without difficulty.   The elementary school,
with its school management committee established under the
precise terms of the Education Act of 1930, will now
disappear and its place will be taken by the primary school
and the junior secondary school, the latter drawing its pupils
from one or more primary schools which were formerly
elementary schools under the control of either the education
committee or voluntary managers.   For the management of
the primary schools the Government have no desire to vary in
any essentials the balance of representation of interests, which
is embodied in present legislation, but attach importance to
two considerations which, indeed, will apply also in the case
of the management of the new junior secondary school; the
management committee should be given the statutory right of
advising the education committee on the upkeep and welfare
of the school or schools concerned, and the existing two-fold
system of selection of teachers (first by the school
management committee and secondly by the education
committee from the short list of three submitted by the
management committee), should be reviewed, for it is well
known that it has led to widespread abuses.   It is not out of
place here to refer to the necessity of devising some scheme
which will facilitate the transfer from one school to another of
teachers serving in schools under the control of an education
committee, for only in this way can real security of tenure, to
which they are entitled, be achieved.

I.12 Education Bill (Northern Ireland) : Explanatory and Financial Management, 1946. Cmd. 242.

The object of this Bill was to give effect to the proposals for educational reconstruction outlined in the White Paper on Educational Reconstruction in Northern Ireland issued in December 1944. This Bill also contained some modifications of, and certain additions to, those proposals. Except for a few sections, the Bill repealed all existing Education Acts.

The following extracts cover the Local Administration of the three stages of the statutory system and the provision of primary and secondary schools suited to ' ... the ages, abilities and aptitudes of the pupils in attendance.' The distinction was made between county and voluntary schools. Each local education authority was required to submit to the ministry of education (Northern Ireland) a 'development scheme.' Systems of management for county primary and secondary schools were laid down. Provision was made for the management of voluntary primary and secondary intermediate schools in accordance with a scheme approved by the ministry. Provision was also made for the Appointment and Dismissal of teachers and for Religious Education in County and Voluntary Schools. This included a 'Conscience Clause' for teachers in county schools. Much controversy was subsequently to be focused on this clause. It is important to note the fact that while the 1930 Act required that teachers must teach Bible instruction, in this Education Bill and the 1947 Education Act which followed it, teachers had the option to elect not to teach undenominational religious instruction. Moreover, they were not to be penalised for having made this decision.

PRIMARY AND SECONDARY EDUCATION

Provision of Primary and Secondary Schools (Clauses 4 to 11)

5.   It will be the duty of every local education authority to ensure that there are in its area sufficient primary and secondary schools and that these are so equipped as to afford education suited to the "ages, abilities and aptitudes" of the

pupils in attendance.   In fulfilling their general duties for primary and secondary education, the authorities are directed to have special regard to the need for providing primary and secondary education in separate schools, to the need for nursery schools or classes for children under five years of age, to the need for making special provision for pupils "who suffer from any disability of mind or body," and to the expediency of securing the provision of boarding accommodation for primary and secondary school pupils.

Management of Primary and Secondary Schools
(Clauses 12 to 17)

10.   County primary schools are to be managed by school management committees constituted, except for what follows, in exactly the same way as was provided in the Education Act of 1930 for the management of provided and transferred public elementary schools; the only change is that the representative of the teachers must be the principal of the school concerned or one of the principals if more than one primary school is managed by the same management committee.   Nursery schools established by local education authorities are to be managed by committees appointed by the authority in accordance with a scheme framed by the authority and approved by the Ministry.

Appointment and Dismissal of Teachers (Clauses 18 and 19)

14.   The Bill provides that management committees of county primary and intermediate schools (other than technical intermediate schools) will have the right to select one qualified applicant and that, in normal circumstances, the local education authority will be required to appoint that person.   Teachers in all recognised schools and grant-aided educational institutions (e.g. technical colleges and training

colleges) will retain the rights for appeal against dismissal which they already enjoy under existing legislation.   The procedure whereby the Ministry will consider such appeals has been clarified.

Religious Education in County and Voluntary Schools
(Clauses 20 to 26)

15.   As forecast in the White Paper religious instruction and collective daily worship are made compulsory for every county and voluntary school, whether primary or secondary. The only requirement under the present Education Acts as to the giving of religious instruction in schools is that Bible instruction must be given in provided and transferred public elementary schools at the request of parents; there is no statutory requirement for the giving of religious instruction in any voluntary school or in any secondary school, whether voluntary or controlled by a local education authority.   No school of any kind has hitherto been required to hold collective worship.

16.   The religious instruction which must be given in county schools is to be undenominational ...

17.   It is made clear that it will be the duty of teachers in county schools to attend or conduct collective worship and to give undenominational religious instruction, if they are required to do so by the local education authority.   A teacher may, however, request to be excused from either or both of these duties, and if he also furnishes a statutory declaration that his request to be excused is made solely on grounds of religious belief he will be excused, and must not be penalised ...

Compulsory Attendance at Primary and Secondary Schools (Clauses 33 and 38)

22.   The upper age limit of compulsory school attendance is to be raised from 14 to 15, and the lower limit reduced from 6 to 5. A local education authority is, however, empowered to raise the lower limit from 5 to $5^1/2$ or 6 by bye-law either in part or the whole of the areas under its control. Provision is also made for the upper limit of compulsory attendance to be raised to 16 by Order in Council as soon as the Ministry is satisfied that this is practicable and Parliament has approved the draft of the Order. Parents are required to cause their children to receive "efficient full-time education" suitable to their ages, abilities and aptitudes, either by attendance at school or otherwise, so long as they are of compulsory school age.

26.   The Ministry of Health and Local Government is the department responsible for the supervision of the school medical services; after consultation with the Ministry of Education that department will draw up any necessary regulations and will give such directions as are necessary to local education authorities. Every authority is required to arrange for the medical inspection of, and to provide, except where otherwise provided, free medical treatment for, all pupils in attendance at grant-aided schools, that is to say all schools, whether primary or secondary, within the statutory system.   Parents must submit their children for medical inspection, but are not obliged to take advantage of any facilities for medical treatment.   The governing body of a voluntary grammar school may make their own arrangements for the medical inspection and treatment of the pupils at the school, if they wish to do so, but the arrangement must be in keeping with the prescribed standards, and the school must furnish returns to the local education authority.

27.   Local education authorities will be required by regulations to provide milk and meals for all pupils attending primary and intermediate schools, whether county or voluntary, and a similar duty will be placed on the governing bodies of grammar schools. Teachers may not be required to undertake any duties connected with the provision of milk and meals during school holidays, nor may they be required to undertake any duties connected with school meals other than supervision of the pupils. Local education authorities are empowered to arrange for the boarding outside the school of any pupil attending a primary or intermediate school or for a scholarship holder attending a grammar school, if this is considered necessary; they may also provide clothing for such pupils where necessary. The cost of boarding or clothing may be recovered from parents who are able to pay without hardship.

28.   Free books and other school requisites are to be provided by local education authorities for the use of all pupils attending primary and intermediate schools; this duty does not extend to pupils attending grammar schools but the cost of books for scholarship holders will be included, where necessary, in the value of the scholarships. The governing bodies of all grammar schools will be required by regulations to make available the necessary number of places for the holders of scholarships awarded by local education authorities.

I.13 Education Act (Northern Ireland), 1947, C.3.

The extracts from this major Education Act deal with the management of county primary and secondary intermediate schools, the provision for parents' representatives on school management committees, the management of county grammar schools, the management of voluntary schools, the appointment and dismissal of Teachers, Religious Education in county and voluntary schools, and the "Conscience Clause."

Liberty of conscience, in the matter of the giving of religious instruction, with which the Conscience Clause was concerned, was not, of course, for understandable reasons, an option for teachers which the mainstream churches were prepared to accept with any great warmth of commitment.

In their concern over this clause, the Protestant churches sought to negotiate with the government a form of wording with their clerical influence apparent in it, and which they felt they could tolerate in the longer term. This the Protestant churches believed they had secured at a meeting with representatives of the Northern Ireland government on 1 June 1945.

However, when the Education Bill was published on 28 September 1946, it contained a different Conscience Clause which was subsequently included in the 1947 Act.

As Professor Donald H. Akenson points out, in *Education and Enmity*, "Whereas the clause which the churches believed had been agreed to allowed the school management committee to decide if a teacher's conscientious objection claim was *bona fide*, the government's clause left them no discretion in the matter." (P.174)

This 1947 Act was a landmark in that it provided free secondary education for all school children. This aspect of the legislation is often obscured by the controversy that surrounded the Conscience Clause.

CONSCIENCE CLAUSE, 1 JUNE, 1945

"Where a teacher who has been appointed to give Bible Instruction finds himself unable on grounds of religious belief to continue to give Bible Instruction conscientiously and makes application, in writing, to the appointing body that he be excused from doing so, the appointing body if satisfied

that the application is bona fide shall not refuse the
application nor shall a teacher so excused be prejudiced in
any way thereby provided always that that part of the
teacher's duty shall be discharged by a qualified member of
the teaching staff of the same school, or if this is not
practicable by another qualified teacher.   Where a teacher
had not been appointed to give Bible Instruction he shall not
be required to give such instruction."

To meet the wishes of the Government and help to overcome
an objection from Secondary Teachers and the Attorney
General the Churches agreed subsequently to accept "a
statutory declaration" from a teacher as proof that this request
for exemption was a *"bona fide"* one.

THE CONSCIENCE CLAUSE (24[3] OF THE 1947 ACT) READ AS
FOLLOWS:

24. — (3) If a teacher in a county school who has been
required by the local education authority to conduct or attend
collective worship in the school or to give undenominational
religious instruction in the school, requests the school
management committee that he be wholly or partly excused
from conducting or attending such worship, or from giving
such instruction, or both from conducting and attending such
worship and from giving such instruction and, at the same
time, furnishes to the committee, for submission to the local
education authority, a statutory declaration that his request to
be so excused is made solely on grounds of religious belief,
then, until the request is withdrawn, the teacher shall be
excused accordingly.

(4) A teacher in a county school who is excused
from conducting or attending collective worship or from
giving undenominational religious instruction shall not

receive any less emolument or be deprived of, or disqualified for, any promotion or other advantage by reason of the fact that he does not conduct or attend collective worship or give undenominational religious instruction.

THE THREE STAGES OF THE SYSTEM

4. The statutory system of public education shall be organised in three progressive stages to be known as primary education, secondary education, and further education; and it shall be the duty of the local education authority for every area, so far as their powers extend, to contribute towards the spiritual, moral, mental and physical development of the community by securing that efficient education throughout those stages shall be available to meet the needs of the population of their area.

PRIMARY AND SECONDARY EDUCATION

Provision of Primary and Secondary Schools

5. — (1)   It shall be the duty of every local education authority to secure that there shall be available for their area sufficient schools —

(a)   for providing primary education, that is to say, full-time education suitable to the requirements of junior pupils; and

(b)   for providing secondary education, that is to say, full-time education suitable to the requirements of senior pupils, other than such full-time education as may be provided for senior pupils in pursuance of a scheme made under the provisions of this Act relating to further education:

and the schools available for an area shall not be deemed to be sufficient unless they are sufficient in number, character, and equipment to afford for all pupils opportunities for education offering such variety of instruction and training as may be desirable in view of their different ages, abilities and aptitudes, and of the different periods for which they may be expected to remain at school, including practical instruction and training appropriate to their respective needs.

Management of Primary and Secondary Schools

14. — (1)   The local education authority shall make provision for the management of each county primary school within their education area by means of a school management committee to be appointed by the authority, but so that several such schools may be grouped under one school management committee, if the authority so desire and the Ministry approves; and a school management committee so appointed shall, in relation to the school or group of schools under their management, exercise such functions as may be conferred upon them by a scheme framed by the authority and approved by the Ministry.

(2)   A school management committee appointed under the last preceding sub-section shall be so constituted that, so far as is practicable —

(a)   not less than one-half of the members to be appointed thereto shall be persons representative of the transferors and superseded managers of any schools under the management of the committee;

(b)   not more than one-quarter of the said members shall be persons nominated by the parents of children attending the school or schools under the management of the committee at a meeting held in accordance with regulations made by the Ministry; and

(c)   the remaining members shall be persons chosen by the local education authority.

The local education authority shall nominate in addition, as respects each school management committee, the principal of the school, or, if there are more schools than one under the management of the committee, one of the principals, to represent the teachers employed at such school or schools, and the principal so appointed shall have the right to attend, and take part in, the meetings of the committee, but shall not be entitled to vote on any question.

15. — (1)   The local education authority shall make provision for the management of each county intermediate school within their education area by means of a school management committee to be appointed by the authority; and a school management committee so appointed shall, in relation to the school under their management, exercise such functions as may be conferred upon them by a scheme framed by the authority and approved by the Ministry.

(2)   A school management committee appointed under the last preceding sub-section shall be so constituted that, so far as is practicable —

(a)   not less than one-half of the members to be appointed thereto shall be persons nominated by the school management committees of the contributory schools, such nominations being made from among members of those committees other than members nominated or chosen by parents or by the local education authority;

(b)   not more than one-quarter of the said members shall be persons nominated by the parents of the children attending the county intermediate school at a meeting held in accordance with regulations made by the Ministry; and

(c)   the remaining members shall be persons chosen by the local education authority.

The principal for the time being of the school shall have the right to attend, and take part in, the meetings of the school management committee, but shall not be entitled to vote on any question.

****

(5)   In this Act the expression "intermediate school" means a secondary school providing free education for senior pupils; and the expression "technical intermediate school" means a county intermediate school conducted in association with an institution of further education.

18. — (1)   Each voluntary primary school ... shall be under the control and management of a person or body of persons approved by the Ministry.

(2)   For each voluntary secondary school ... there shall be a body of managers constituted in accordance with a scheme approved by the Ministry, and the managers shall, in relation to the school, exercise such functions as may be conferred upon them by the scheme.

(3)   If, in the case of any voluntary school, a school committee is appointed under sub-section (2) of section eighty-one of this Act, the school shall be under the control and management of that committee.

Appointment and Dismissal of Teachers

19. — (1)   Whenever, except in a case to which this subsection does not apply, it is necessary that a teacher shall be appointed for a county primary or county intermediate school ... the local education authority for the education area within which the school is situate shall, in the manner prescribed by the Ministry, issue advertisements inviting applications for the appointment and transmit the applications, with particulars of the candidates, to the school management committee.

The school management committee shall consider the applications for the appointment and shall select therefrom and submit to the local education authority, to be dealt with under the provisions of sub-section (2) of this section, the names of such of the candidates as are qualified for the time being under the regulations of the Ministry (in this Act referred to as "qualified candidates"), or if there are more than three qualified candidates, the names of three of them and shall take such further steps in relation to the appointment as may be required under the said provisions.

(2)   The power of appointing teachers shall, in any case to which sub-section (1) of this section applies, be exercised by the local education authority in accordance with the following provisions:-

(a)   if the local education authority are not satisfied to appoint some one or other of the said qualified candidates, the matter shall stand referred to the Ministry, and the Ministry may —

   (i)   direct that the matter shall be referred back to the school management committee for the selection and submission to the local education authority of the names of such number of other qualified candidates (not exceeding three) as the Ministry may require; or

(ii)   direct the appointment of one of the qualified candidates whose names were submitted by the school management committee to the local education authority; or

(iii)   direct that the appointment shall be again advertised and dealt with under sub-section (1) of this section;

(b)   the decision of the Ministry under the last preceding paragraph shall be final, and it shall be the duty of the local education authority to take all necessary steps for the due appointment as teacher of a qualified candidate whose appointment is directed by the Ministry under the said paragraph;

(c)   the foregoing provisions of this sub-section shall apply in a case where, in pursuance of a direction given under sub-division (i) of paragraph (a) thereof, the school management committee submit to the local education authority the names of qualified candidates, and also in the case of any subsequent submission of such names in pursuance of a direction so given.

20. — (1) Where a teacher in any grant-aided school or institution has received notice of dismissal from his position at the school or institution, and within six weeks after the receipt by the teacher of such notice a petition is presented to the Ministry by the teacher praying for an investigation into the reasons for such dismissal, the Ministry shall cause to be made such investigation as it thinks fit.

Religious Education in County and Voluntary Schools

21. — (1)   Subject to the provisions of this and the next following section, the school day in every county school and voluntary school shall begin with collective worship on the part of all pupils in attendance at the school, and the arrangements made therefor shall provide for a single act of worship attended by all such pupils unless in the opinion of the local education authority, or, in the case of a voluntary school, the managers thereof, the school premises are such as to make it impracticable to assemble them for that purpose.

(2)   Subject to the provisions of this and the next following section, religious instruction shall be given in every county school and voluntary school.

****

(5)   Ministers of religion and other suitable persons (including teachers of the school) to whom the parents do not object shall be granted reasonable access at convenient times to pupils in any county school or voluntary school for the purpose of giving religious instruction ...

****

(7)   Collective worship and religious instruction at every county school and voluntary school shall be so arranged that—

(a)   the school shall be open to pupils of all religious denominations for instruction other than religious instruction;

(b)   no pupil shall be excluded, directly or indirectly, from the other advantages which the school affords.

22. — (1)   Subject to the provisions of this section, the collective worship required by sub-section (1) of the last foregoing section shall not, in any county school, be distinctive of any particular religious denominational religious instruction, that is to say, instruction based upon the Holy Scriptures according to some authoritative version or versions thereof, but excluding instruction as to any tenet which is distinctive of any particular religious denomination.

****

81. — (1)   This section applies to voluntary primary schools and to voluntary intermediate schools.

(2)   If, in the case of a voluntary school to which this section applies, a school committee is appointed for the school in accordance with a scheme framed under this section, to consist, in the case of a primary school, of two persons nominated by the local education authority and four persons nominated by the managers or trustees, or, in the case of an intermediate school, of such number of persons as may be determined by the scheme, of whom one-third shall be persons nominated by the local education authority and two-thirds shall be persons nominated by the managers or trustees, then, subject to and in accordance with regulations made by the Ministry, the local education authority shall be responsible for the lighting, heating and cleaning of the school premises and for the carrying out of internal maintenance.

I.14 Statutory Rules and Orders of Northern Ireland, 1948. No. 59.

In accordance with Section 27 of the Education Act (Northern Ireland) 1947 the ministry of education on the 20 March 1948, published the following regulations which aimed at ensuring that those certain provisions of the 1947 Education Act relating to the teaching of religion in county and voluntary schools were complied with in full.

The regulations required that schools indicate explicitly on their timetables the times at which daily collective worship would be held, as well as the times during which religious instruction would be given.

Clearly the regulations reflect how anxious the ministry of education was that schools and teachers should remain mindful of their obligations in regard to religious education subsequent to the passing of the 1947 Act. They also indicate that, for some, non-compliance with the statutory obligations was always possible, in the absence of ministerial insistence.

2.   Subject to the provisions of the Act and of these Regulations, the arrangements for collective worship and religious instruction in any county school or voluntary school shall be under the control of the managers of the school.

3. — (1)   The time at which collective worship is held, and the time or times during which religious instruction is given, in any county school or voluntary school, shall be clearly shown on the time-table of the school.

(2)   The time or times during which religious instruction is given in any county school or voluntary school shall be so arranged as to cause as little inconvenience as possible to any pupils attending the school who, in pursuance of sub-section (3) of section 21 of the Act, have been excused from attendance at such religious instruction.

4.   There shall be set apart for the purpose of religious instruction —

(a)   in all county and voluntary primary schools, a period of at least one half-hour each school day or its equivalent within each week;

(b)   in all county and voluntary intermediate schools, at least two hours and a half within each week;

(c)   in all county and voluntary grammar schools, two periods of at least forty minutes each, or the equivalent, within each week;

5.   A local education authority shall, if so requested by the minister in charge of any church or other place of worship in the vicinity of any school under the control of the authority, communicate to him the names of any pupils attending the school who are, or are stated to be, of the same religious denomination as that minister.

I.15 Statutory Rules and Orders of Northern Ireland, 1948, No.96.   County Primary and Intermediate School Management Committees.   Regulations for Meetings of Parents.

These regulations which were cited as the "Meetings of Parents Regulations (County Primary and Intermediate Schools), 1948," required that every new education committee should summon, without delay, a meeting of parents in all county primary and intermediate schools in the education committee's jurisdiction, so as to receive from the parents of the children in attendance at such schools nominations to the school management committee.   The regulations for parents were written in accordance with sub-section (2) of Section 14 and sub-section (2) of Section 15 of the Education Act (Northern Ireland) 1947, which required that not more than one-quarter of the members of a school management committee for a County Primary or County Intermediate School should be persons nominated by the parents of children attending the school.

2.   Every Education Committee shall without avoidable delay upon the first or subsequent appointment of a school management committee summon a meeting of the parents of children in attendance at the school or schools which it is proposed to place under the local management of the said school management committee (hereinafter referred to as a "parents' meeting") for the purpose of nominating that portion of the total membership thereof assigned to such parents under the scheme for the constitution of school management committees made by the Education Committee and approved by the Ministry ...

4.   A parents' meeting shall be held at a time and place reasonably convenient to the parents aforesaid.

Notice of the time and place of such meeting shall, at least seven days before the date thereof, be given in such manner as the Education Committee, with the approval of the Ministry, may determine to be suitable and sufficient.

5.   Only one of the parents as herein defined of each family from which a child or children are attending the school for which a school management committee is being appointed shall be entitled to attend and vote at a parents' meeting, and each parent so attending shall be entitled to one vote only in respect of each person to be nominated at such meeting.

The quorum necessary for any parents' meeting shall be fifty, or one-fifth of the number of parents as herein defined entitled to attend and vote whichever number shall be the less.

6.   The parents present at a parents' meeting shall elect a chairman who shall have a casting as well as a deliberative vote.

7.   The parents present at a parents' meeting shall nominate by show of hands or otherwise as the Education Committee may direct such number of persons to be members of the said school management committee as is assigned to them under the approved scheme aforesaid.

8.   Where a parents' meeting, having been duly called, fails of effect for want of a quorum or for any other reason, or, being duly held, neglects or refuses to nominate any, or the required number of persons representing the parents on a school management committee then the Education Committee shall take such action as they are required to take in accordance with the provisions of Section 16 of the Act.

9.   The Education Committee shall take all necessary steps to exclude from a parents' meeting all unauthorised persons and to ensure that only persons duly entitled thereto shall exercise a vote at such meeting and that the voting is carried out in a proper manner; but nominations made at such meeting shall not be void necessarily by reason only of irregularities in the conduct of the meeting and may notwithstanding any irregularities as aforesaid be confirmed by the Education Committee with the approval of the Ministry.

**I.16   Statutory Rules and Orders of Northern Ireland, 1948
No.98.   School Management Committees,
Representatives of Transferors, Superseded Managers
and Contributory School Committees.**

This was the Order implementing Section 14 of the Education Act
(Northern Ireland) 1947, which had provided that the local
education authority should make provision for the management of
each county primary school by means of a school management
committee appointed by the authority. Not less than one-half of the
members to be appointed were to be persons representative of the
transferors and superseded managers of any schools under the
management of the local authority.

In Section 15 of the 1947 Act, the same provision is made for
county intermediate schools, except that, in the latter context, half
the membership of the school management committees of these
schools should be persons nominated by the management
committees of the contributory primary schools but chosen from
among the members of those committees who were transferors'
representatives.

Now THEREFORE the Ministry in exercise of the powers
aforesaid and of all other powers thereunto enabling hereby
makes the following regulations:

1.   In the exercise and performance of their powers and
duties of appointing to any school management committee of
a county primary school or schools (hereinafter called a
"primary school committee") persons representative of the
transferors and persons representative of the superseded
managers of any schools under the management of the
primary school committee, as in the Act provided, an
authority shall appoint such respective representatives only
from persons recommended for such appointment by the
aforesaid transferors and superseded managers respectively
after due and sufficient notice given by the said authority to

the said transferors and superseded managers respectively of
their intention to appoint such primary school committee and
of the number of members thereof to be appointed as
representatives of the said transferors and superseded
managers respectively ...

2.   In the exercise and performance of their powers and
duties of appointing to any school management committee of
a county intermediate school (hereinafter called an
"intermediate school committee") persons nominated by the
school management committees of the contributory schools
(hereinafter called "contributory school committees") as in
the Act provided, an authority shall give due and sufficient
notice to the contributory school committees of their
intention to appoint such intermediate school committees and
of the number of members thereof to be appointed on the
nomination of the said contributory school committees ...

**I.17 Scheme for the Constitution of School Committees Under
Section 81 of The Education Act (Northern Ireland) 1947,
County Borough of Londonderry Education Committee,
Londonderry, 1949, Voluntary Schools.**

The Scheme for County Londonderry, cited here, was similar to
that to be used by the other County Borough Education Committees
for the constitution of school committees in voluntary primary
schools, in pursuance of Section 81 of the Education Act (Northern
Ireland), 1947. The Scheme laid down regulations on the frequency
of meetings, the keeping of Minutes and, most importantly, the
actual format of the school committee itself. The emphasis given to
the 'four and two' principle, which had yet to win the confidence of
Roman Catholic authorities, is significant.

2.   A School Committee shall consist of two persons nominated by the Education Committee and four persons nominated by the Managers or Trustees of the voluntary primary school for which the School Committee is appointed: A School Committee may associate with themselves, in an advisory capacity, parents of children attending the school and representatives of the Teachers of the school.

7.   The members of a School Committee shall at their meeting elect two of their number to be respectively Chairman and Vice-Chairman until the first meeting after the next appointment of the Committee; and should the Chairman and Vice-Chairman be absent from any meeting of the Committee the members present shall appoint one of themselves to be Chairman of the meeting ...

8.   A School Committee shall meet at such times as the conduct of business may require not being less than four times in any year; the Chairman may at any time call a meeting of a School Committee.

14.   A School Committee shall exercise all the functions of management that would ordinarily devolve upon the manager of a voluntary school; including all duties connected with the heating, lighting, cleaning, repairs, sanitation and general upkeep of the school premises, and the appointment of teachers.

I.18 Educational Development in Northern Ireland, 1964, Cmd. 470.

In a Foreword to this Report the minister of education, Mr Ivan Neill, stated that it was opportune, he thought, to review the progress made in the development of the education system since 1948, and to consider the main problems that had arisen in the implementation of the Act of 1947. It was also time to set new targets for the years ahead.

In his Introduction the minister made two points clear. The Paper was not intended to cover all aspects of the educational scene and there had been no consultations with any statutory or voluntary body before publication. This would come later before final decisions were made.

In his Foreword the minister made no reference to nursery education, special educational treatment and the schools meals service. This was not because these fields were unimportant but because no particular problems had arisen in them.

No attempt was made to deal with the increasing use of mechanical aids to teaching, radio, television, record players, tape-recorders, projection apparatus, language laboratories and teaching machines.

The minister recognised that while a Paper of this kind tended to focus attention on matters of administration it did no more than touch on the real stuff of education — the content of the curriculum — at the various stages of the teacher-pupil relationship in the classroom.

Mention was made of overcrowding in the primary sector and inadequate buildings. In the section entitled "Secondary School Organisation," the merits and disadvantages of comprehensive education are discussed briefly. The minister emphasised that the facts of the educational system could not be ignored and in the debate over comprehensive education in particular it was expedient to note the existence of a fully-developed grammar school system in Northern Ireland.

FOREWORD

... In my opinion the time is opportune to review the progress that has been made in the development of our education system since 1948. I think, too, that the main problems which have arisen in the implementation of the Act of 1947 should be fully considered so that it may be decided what changes of policy or emphasis are now required. We should also, I consider, set new targets for the years ahead.   It is with these objects in view that I present this White Paper to Parliament.

In doing so I should make two points clear.   The Paper is not intended to cover all aspects of the educational scene.   It deals mainly with those on which there are, or have been, differences of opinion.   In some matters it reaffirms existing policy, in others changes of policy or practice are proposed.   The second point is that there have been no official consultations with any statutory or voluntary body before publication.   I shall, therefore, take into account views expressed by interested bodies before final decisions are taken on the matters dealt within the Paper ...

I : PRIMARY EDUCATION

2.   Marked progress has ... been made in the field of primary education.   Some blemishes, however, remain, the most serious of which are the continuance in use of many school buildings falling far short of modern standards and the persistence of over-size classes.

4.   The number of over-size classes has been greatly reduced since 1947, but there were nevertheless in January, 1963, 1,045 classes out of a total of 6,007 with more than 40 children on roll and of these 260 had more than 45 pupils. The existing regulations are so designed that, provided the full complement of staff is employed, the average number of pupils to each class-teacher should not exceed 40, and in the smaller schools it is substantially less.   But in some cases lack of accommodation prevents the employment of the full number of teachers authorised by the regulations, and even when the full complement of teachers is employed some classes may need to be in excess of 40 for reasons beyond the

control of the principal.   To eliminate all classes with more than 40 pupils is bound to mean amendment of the present staffing regulations and the employment of more teachers; it must also mean the efficient deployment of the teachers available.

6.   The main objectives in the field of primary education in the immediate future will be the elimination of excessively large classes and the closing of small schools which are outworn, unhygienic and ill-provided with modern amenities. In order that real progress may be made by 1970 the Ministry proposes to set on foot a five-year campaign starting in 1965. A second five-year plan to operate from 1970 to 1975 should complete the operation if the school authorities, both county and voluntary, tackle the task with vigour, the necessary additional teachers are forthcoming and the teaching force available is used to the best advantage.   Discussions to this end will be started at an early date with the local education authorities and voluntary bodies.

II : SECONDARY SCHOOL ORGANISATION

8.   Strong arguments are advanced in favour of the comprehensive type of secondary school to which all the children living in a specified catchment area automatically go on leaving the primary school. No formal selection procedure is needed since all the children in the catchment area proceed to the same secondary school; the pupils are freed from the stress and strain associated with selection and the primary schools are relieved from examination pressures. Selection in the sense of streaming within the comprehensive school may still be carried out to ensure that pupils follow courses suited to their abilities and aptitudes, but transfer from one stream or course to another within the same school is a simpler matter than transfer from one school to another.

Socially, also, a comprehensive secondary school should have a unifying influence on the district it serves.

9.   On the other hand, some educationalists maintain that there are serious objections to the comprehensive school. The first usually raised is on the score of size: it is held that to offer a full range of sixth form courses of the grammar school type for its abler pupils a comprehensive school needs to have an enrolment in the region of 2,000 and may in consequence become an institution rather than a school. It is argued too that the academically less gifted children are likely to be in a relatively less favourable position in a comprehensive school than in a secondary (intermediate) school ... A further consideration is that the full adoption of the comprehensive system is only possible if all the children within a given area are in effect directed to the same school and parental choice of school is denied.   It must be allowed, however, that in spite of this argument opinion generally in the United Kingdom appears to be moving steadily towards support for a comprehensive type of secondary school organisation.

10.   In Northern Ireland the facts of the situation as it now exists must be taken into account.   Here a fully developed grammar school system is already in being.   There are in fact eighty-one grammar schools.   Since 1948 completely new premises have been provided for twenty of them and major extensions have been carried out at a further fifty-two;* during this period the enrolment in their secondary departments has more than doubled and three-quarters of the grammar schools are voluntary schools — approximately half under Protestant and half under Roman Catholic management; they have played their part fully in meeting the

_____

* Excluding extensions to Group B voluntary grammar schools.

increased demand for grammar school places. There is no sign that the grammar schools are failing to meet the challenge of the times or that the public is losing faith in them.

13.   Given, therefore, the facts of the existing situation and the disruption, expense, restriction of parental choice and ill-feeling which would be caused by an imposed system of comprehensive schools, the Government is satisfied that it would be wrong to make a complete change in the pattern of secondary education established under the 1947 Act ...

XIV : SUMMARY OF PROPOSALS

(i)   To replace the many unsatisfactory primary school buildings still in use, most of which are small rural schools, and to concentrate primary school provision in rural areas;

(ii)   To reduce the size of classes in the larger primary schools and, as a first objective in this process, to aim at the elimination of all classes with over 40 pupils;

(iii)   To encourage experiments in secondary school organisation designed to reduce the importance of selection at 11+;

(iv)   To take steps to lessen the differences between secondary schools of different types by amendment of the relevant regulations and otherwise;

(v)   To abandon the use of the title "intermediate school" and to replace it by "secondary school;"

(vi)   To promote the development of academic streams and extended courses in secondary schools wherever conditions are favourable;

(vii) To set up a working party to consider the application of the Newsom Report proposals to secondary schools and the external examination needs of these schools;

****

(xii) To discontinue the Qualifying Examination after 1965 and to replace it by a different method of selection;

(xiii) To maintain the age of transfer from primary to secondary education at 11+;

(xiv) To reduce the number of school leaving dates from three to two and to adopt the same arrangements as apply in Great Britain.

I.19 Local Education Authorities and Voluntary Schools, 1967, Cmd.513.

This Paper records with satisfaction the development of a closer relationship between local education authorities and voluntary schools, in the twenty years elapsing since the passing of the Education Act (Northern Ireland) 1947. In the Introduction to the Paper it is acknowledged that the Ministry of Education had felt it desirable to re-assess its relationship with the voluntary sector, so as to ensure that proper provision was being made for pupils in that sector, and to ascertain "... whether changes were needed in order to broaden the basis of cooperation and to remove certain administrative obstacles which impeded it."

The Paper was a response to requests from the voluntary sector for more funding, at a time of significant change in educational provision within that sector, necessitated by the need to make provision for secondary education following the 1947 Act.

However, the government remained adamant that, from its standpoint, any increase in funding would continue to depend on the willingness of the voluntary sector to accept at least minority representation from the public sector. The Paper suggested some ways in which grant-aid could be increased to voluntary authorities. The nomenclature, "maintained schools," is officially mentioned for the first time. The main proposals contained in this Paper were legislated for in the Education (Amendment) Act (Northern Ireland), 1968.

4.   Voluntary school authorities have over a long period made representations that the burden of their contribution to the system of public education has proved to be much higher than was contemplated in 1947, and have asked for further assistance from public funds.   The Government accepts that the cost of providing education has become increasingly heavy.   On the other hand it has also had to take into account that, whereas in England and Wales a measure of public representation on the bodies responsible for the management or government of voluntary schools has long been a pre-requisite for the recognition of such schools, in Northern Ireland most grants under the Act of 1947 have not been subject to this requirement.   Since 1947 Ministers of Education have, on numerous occasions, made it clear that increased assistance from public funds could not be contemplated for schools on which a public authority had not at least minority representation.   The following proposals accordingly, set out ways in which additional aid would be given to voluntary schools provided that the appropriate measure of public representation is accepted.

FORMS OF MANAGEMENT

6.   At present the Act [1947] deals differently with school committees appointed for voluntary primary schools and those for other types of schools under voluntary management.

In the case of primary schools, it specifies that the school committee shall consist of four members representing the original manager and two representing the local education authority, whilst for other schools it merely requires two-thirds of the members to be nominated by the manager and one-third to be chosen by the authority, without limiting the number of members to six. There appears to be no need to maintain this distinction between primary and other voluntary schools, and it is proposed to assimilate the primary school rule to that applicable to other schools whilst requiring a minimum membership of six.

CHANGE OF FORM OF MANAGEMENT

7.   At present if a school is placed under a "four-and-two" committee the original managers may resume management of the school on giving two years' notice. It would be wrong for this power to remain in respect of schools which choose to obtain the increased benefits proposed in this paper, and the right would accordingly be abolished, except that managers of schools which are already under "four-and-two" committees at the date when the new provision becomes effective would be given a reasonable period to opt whether their school should remain permanently under the management of the school committee or should revert to purely voluntary management. No alteration would be made in the rule that the placing of a school under a school committee does not affect the ownership of the school premises.

MANAGEMENT OF NEW SCHOOLS

8.   It is proposed that in future no entirely new school should be recognised as a grant-aided school unless it is managed by a school committee constituted on the "four-and-

two" principle. This provision would apply to all types of schools under voluntary management except voluntary grammar schools ...

"Maintained schools"

9.   So far there has been no simple statutory name for voluntary schools placed under school committees on which the local education authority has representation.   For convenience, and in the light of the proposal contained in paragraph 13 that these schools should, so far as their day-to-day operation is concerned, be maintained by the local education authority, it is proposed to designate them "maintained schools" and it is under this name that they are referred to in the remainder of this Paper.

Building grants

12.   At present the Ministry may pay grant at the rate of 65 per cent of the expenditure incurred on the provision or alteration of a primary (including nursery), secondary (intermediate) or special school under voluntary management. It is proposed that so far as concerns expenditure incurred after 31st March 1968 the rate of building grant for a maintained school should be 80 per cent.   Although a school would have to be a maintained school before grant is paid, schools which become maintained schools within a period of six months of the date when the necessary legislation is passed would be eligible for 80 per cent grant on relevant expenditure incurred between 1st April 1968 and the date on which the school becomes a maintained school.

Maintenance and Equipment

13.   The present position is that in a maintained school the local education authority is responsible for the lighting, heating and cleaning of and the internal maintenance of the school premises, excluding any boarding accommodation. The Ministry is responsible for the payment of grant at the rate of 65 per cent towards the cost of providing equipment and of external maintenance. It is proposed that for the future the local education authority should be directly responsible for the internal maintenance, external maintenance and equipment of the school premises (again excluding any boarding department). Maintenance would be re-defined to include all the day-to-day running costs (other than the cost of teachers' salaries and related payments). The local education authority's existing duty to provide free books, stationery and materials for pupils would remain. The effect would be that, once a voluntary school building has been provided, the duty of furnishing it, of maintaining it both internally and externally, and of meeting all necessary day-to-day running costs other than the salaries of teachers and related payments, would fall directly upon the local education authority. The Government considers that by the unification of responsibility for the various items of school expenditure referred to, simpler and more efficient administration would be possible than at present, when three distinct bodies — the school managers, the Minister of Education and the local education authority — share the responsibility. Not only should the volume of official correspondence upon these items be greatly reduced but local education authorities should, by bulk buying, be able to make purchases on advantageous terms ...

14.   These proposals would result in the transfer of responsibility for meeting some items of expenditure (i.e. equipment and external maintenance) from school authorities and the Ministry to local education authorities.   Some net additional cost would be borne by authorities, the extent of the addition depending upon the number of schools which adopt the new maintained status ...

I.20   Education (Amendment) Act (Northern Ireland), 1968, C.2

This Act represents a significant development in the state's funding of voluntary, mainly Catholic, schools, in that it legislated for an increase in the amount of grant aid payable to these schools, to cover the cost of approved building and alteration work. The increase in funding was from 65% to 80%.

However, in order to qualify for this increase in funding, a school management committee in the voluntary sector had first to accept the 'four and two' principle.   In so doing, it would be seen as having accepted the principle of local authority representation in its management.

The growing willingness of Roman Catholic authorities to accept such representation, at this time, is explained by two principal factors: first, the high financial outlay anticipated in the building and upkeep of new secondary schools; and secondly, ongoing improvements in relations between the Unionist government of the day, led by Terence O'Neill, and Catholic authorities.

The most relevant clauses of the Amendment are Clauses 9 and 18. The status of 'maintained' is officially referred to in Section 9, sub-section 4.   The 80% grant legislated for here was subsequently increased to 85%, under the terms of the Education (Northern Ireland) Order, 1976, referred to later.

9. — (3) From the 1st April 1969, the responsibility of a local education authority for the maintenance of the premises of a maintained school and the defrayal of certain expenses of

carrying on the school shall be extended and accordingly as from that date for the words in section 81(2) of the principal Act from "for the lighting" to the end of the subsection there shall be substituted the words "for the maintenance of the school premises and for defraying all the expenses of carrying on the school (including the provision and replacement of equipment) except —

(a)   the cost of providing new, or altering existing, school premises;

(b)   the payment of the salaries of teachers in the school and of the employers' national insurance and superannuation contributions in respect of those teachers;

(c)   the payment of redundancy payments under the Contracts of Employment and Redundancy Payments Act (Northern Ireland) 1965 in respect of teachers ceasing to be employed in the school;

but such responsibility shall not extend to any part of the school premises used wholly or mainly for boarding purposes or to any expenses of carrying on such part."

(4)   "... (2E)Schools for which committees have been appointed pursuant to a scheme framed under this section shall be known as "maintained schools," primary and intermediate schools which are maintained schools shall be known as "maintained voluntary schools" and special and nursery schools which are maintained schools shall be known as "maintained special schools" and "maintained nursery schools' respectively."

(5)   In section 81(3) and (4) of the principal Act the word "voluntary" wherever it occurs shall be omitted.

****

18. — (1)   In its application to expenditure incurred on or after 1st April 1968 for the purpose of the provision of a new maintained school or the alteration of an existing maintained school, section 106(1) of the principal Act shall be amended as follows:-

(a)   for the words "primary, intermediate or special school" wherever they occur there shall be substituted the words "maintained school;" and

(b)   for the words "sixty-five per cent of the expenditure incurred for such purpose" there shall be substituted the words "eighty per cent of the approved expenditure incurred for such purpose on or after 1st April 1968."

I.21 Commissioner for Complaints Act (Northern Ireland) 1969.

The purpose of this Act was to make provision for the appointment and functions of a Commissioner to investigate complaints alleged to arise from administrative acts for which certain local or public bodies were responsible, including those concerned with the provision of education.

The function of the Commissioner was to investigate any written complaints made to him by a person who claimed that he had suffered injustice in consequence of maladministration in connection with administrative action taken by, or on behalf of, any district council, any harbour authority, any Health and Social Services Board, an Education and Library Board, the Housing Executive and most of the other public bodies financed from public funds.

Matters excluded from the investigations of the Commissioners were criminal proceedings, the disclosure or non-disclosure of pecuniary interests by councillors, the actions of doctors and ancillary professions in the care and treatment of a patient, and matters subject to investigation by the United Kingdom Parliamentary Commissioner for Administration, or by the Northern Ireland Parliamentary Commissioner for Administration. The Commissioners would not normally investigate any matter on which the aggrieved person could take proceedings in a court of law or appeal to a tribunal.

The Commissioner was required to report the results of an investigation and to give his reasons for not conducting an investigation.

1. — (1)   For the purposes of this Act there shall be appointed a Commissioner, to be known as the Northern Ireland Commissioner for Complaints.

5. — (1)   Subject to the provisions of this Act, the Commissioner may investigate any action taken by or on behalf of a local or public body to which this Act applies, being action taken in the exercise of the administrative functions of that body, where —

(a)   A complaint is made to the Commissioner in accordance with this Act by a person who claims to have sustained injustice in consequence of maladministration in connection with the action so taken with a request to conduct an investigation thereon; and

(b)   in such cases as may be prescribed, not being cases in which by virtue of subsection (2) payment of a fee is not required, the complaint is accompanied by a fee of such amount, not exceeding £3 as may be prescribed.

****

(3)   Except as hereinafter provided, the Commissioner shall not conduct an investigation under this Act in respect of any of the following matters, that is to say —

(a)   any action in respect of which the person aggrieved has or had a right of appeal,reference or review to or before a tribunal constituted under any statutory provision or otherwise; or

(b)   any action in respect of which the person aggrieved has or had a remedy by way of proceedings in a court of law;

so, however, that the Commissioner may conduct an investigation —

(i)   notwithstanding that the person aggrieved has or had such a right or remedy as is mentioned in paragraph (a) or paragraph (b), if the Commissioner is satisfied that in the particular circumstance it is not reasonable to expect him to resort or have resorted to it; or

(ii)   notwithstanding that the person aggrieved had exercised such a right as is mentioned in paragraph (a), if he complains that the injustice sustained by him remains unremedied thereby and the Commissioner is satisfied that there are reasonable grounds for that complaint.

7. — (1)   The purposes of the investigation by the Commissioners be —

(a)   to ascertain if the matters alleged in the complaint (i) properly warrant investigation by him under this Act, ... and (iii) disclose any maladministration by or on behalf of the body against whom the complaint is made; and where it appears to him to be desirable,

(b)   to effect a settlement of the matter complained of or, if that is not possible, to state what action should in his opinion be taken by the body against whom the complaint is made to effect a fair settlement thereof or by that body or by the person aggrieved to remove, or have removed, the cause of the complaint.

(2)   Where on an investigation made by him under this Act the Commissioner reports that a person aggrieved has sustained injustice in consequence of maladministration, the county court may on an application made to it by that person, in accordance with county court rules and upon notice to the body against whom the complaint investigated was made, by order award that person such damages as the court may think just in all the circumstances to compensate him for any loss or injury which he may have suffered on account of —

(a)   expenses reasonably incurred by him in connection with the subject matter of the maladministration on which this complaint was founded; and

(b)   his loss of opportunity of acquiring the benefit which he might reasonably be expected to have had but for such maladministration; subject, however, to the application of the same rule concerning the duty of a person to mitigate his loss as applies in relation to damages recoverable at common law.

I.22   Review Body on Local Government in Northern Ireland, 1970.

The work of the Review Body was described clearly in the Terms of Reference in the Warrant of Appointment. These were:

1.   To review existing published Government proposals for reshaping local government in Northern Ireland.

2.   To examine any further proposals which may be made to the Review Body.

3.   To examine the consequences of the decision on housing.

4.   To consider any implications of that decision for the health, welfare, child care, education and public library services at present discharged by local government.

5.   To advise on the most efficient distribution under the Parliament and Government of Northern Ireland — whether under local government or otherwise — of the functions dealt with in proposals under 1 or 2 above.

6.   To bear in mind the implications for elected local government of any courses of action which the Review Body may deem advisable.

7.   To recommend how local opinion can best be brought to bear on administration.

8.   To advise on the number of local government areas; and to submit interim reports if they think fit.

In their introduction to the Report the members of the Working Party noted the urgency of the task and recognised the differences between those who believed in the retention of the major functions by elected local authorities and those who believed in their centralisation. An influential factor in these considerations was the decision in 1969 to set up a central housing authority. The main reasons for some form of centralisation were summarised.

Inevitably any review of local government had to include an examination of the then system of local administration of the education service. The Report included an important summary of the thinking and work of the Review Body and this is of such importance for the future organisation and administration of education in Northern Ireland that it is given here in full (par.49). The selection of the Report's Conclusions and Recommendations includes those which have a direct bearing on the administration of education. It is important to notice how these recommendations could have led to an increase in the work of the House of Commons and that consideration could be given to an increase in the size of that House (par.81). One of the difficulties associated with the restructuring of local government has been the absence of a continuing House of Commons in Northern Ireland. This tier of government was an essential part of the restructuring and its absence has created real problems in the functioning of local government.

MINISTER'S ADDRESS

6.   What you said to us at our first meeting served to impress upon us the urgency of our task. We noted the emphasis that you placed upon the need to further the social and economic development of Northern Ireland, as well as the paramount importance of political stability, without which that development must inevitably be frustrated.

TERMS OF REFERENCE

7.   We studied our Terms of Reference with care. We observed in particular the emphasis placed upon the decision that the Government had already taken to establish a central housing authority. We noted too the emphasis that was placed upon local involvement. But we noted also that there was no reference, as there was in the Terms of Reference for the Royal Commission on Local Government both for England and for Scotland, to "the need to sustain a viable

system of local democracy;" we were not asked to meet any political requirements nor to advise upon boundary lines; we observed that we were not asked to assume that the present range of local government functions should continue; on the contrary, we were specifically and clearly asked to advise on the most *efficient* distribution of all the relevant functions "under the Parliament and Government of Northern Ireland — whether under local government or otherwise" ...

EDUCATION

49.   The memorandum from the Ministry of Education confirmed its Minister's statement in the House of Commons in July 1969, when he said that the present system of local administration of the education service, based on eight local education authorities (the county and county borough councils), had on the whole worked well and considered in isolation, presented no compelling need for fundamental changes in the system in the immediate future.   It was, however, recognised that if local government was to be re-shaped, the administration of the education service must be reviewed.   Assuming that the retention of the present system of administration by county and borough elected authorities was ruled out, the Ministry of Education considered the possibility of either a single independent board or the Ministry itself directly administering the service, but rejected both possibilities; instead it proposed a system of not more than five area boards which would have broadly the same functions for educational (including library) services as the existing local education authorities.   A reasonable proportion of the membership of the boards should be representative of the local electorate and there should also be representatives of the transferors of schools, the maintained school authorities, the teachers and other persons interested in education or the public library service.   "A system of Area Boards constituted

in this way," wrote the Ministry, "would be nearest to the present system, which as stated by the Minister has, on the whole, worked well; it would however have advantages over the present system, in that Boards would be responsible for viable administrative areas of broadly comparable size and importance from the point of view of population and financial resources. They would have a broadly based membership drawn from sections of the community most capable of making a worthwhile contribution to educational administration. A system such as this would facilitate the creation of well balanced Boards consisting of responsible and public-spirited persons, who on the one hand would owe their loyalty primarily to the Boards and on the other hand, because they would be in a position to interpret the views of the main sectional interests, might be expected to induce a spirit of confidence, cooperation and goodwill amongst those interests. This form of administration would not be open to the objection of remoteness, and it would maintain the tradition of local interest and be responsible to the special needs of the areas for which the individual Boards would be responsible. Moreover, it would afford a measure of flexibility — the Boards could appoint separate committees of equal status for the education service and for the library service."

SUMMARY OF CONCLUSIONS AND RECOMMENDATIONS

1. The functions under review are divided into two broad categories: *regional,* i.e. wide-area functions which require large units for administration and *district,* i.e. small-area or local services which can be efficiently administered in small units (par.70).

2. The regional functions are; education, public libraries; personal health, welfare and child care; planning; roads and traffic management; motor taxation; housing; water and major sewerage systems; food composition, standards and labelling; tourism; electoral arrangements; criminal injuries compensation; gas; electricity; transport; major harbours; fire (par.74).

3. Independent boards, i.e. central, appointed and specialised bodies with independent standing are rejected for functions which have a substantial social or political content (pars.76-77).

4. Such boards are only suitable for services with a mainly technical content (par.77).

5. The representative principle is preferred (par.78).

6. The two-tier concept of local councils is also rejected (pars.79-81).

7. The concept of Parliament and Government as one level and a number of elected district councils as the second level constitutes the main recommendation in the report (par.81).

8. Stormont, i.e. the regional Parliament, Government and the Ministries should administer the regional services (par.81).

****

13. In the case of education, the personal health, personal social services and child care, delegation to a system of area boards acting as agents of the Ministry seems advisable (par.87 [c] and [d]).

14. To the extent that area boards may be thought advisable for the day-to-day management of regional services, then all such areas ought to be co-terminus, ought not to cut across district boundaries; and four such areas ought to be enough for the whole province. The boards ought to be appointed by Ministers and ought clearly to be their agents; their membership ought to reflect the community they serve; the membership ought to include some district councillors (par.87 [c]).

****

19. An increase in the work of the House of Commons is foreseen and this could lead to consideration being given to an increase in the size of the House (par.91).

20. A development of the select committee system is also foreseen (par.92.)

21. It should be possible for some other Mayors or Chairmen of local authorities to have seats in the Senate as well as the Lord Mayor of Belfast and the Mayor of Londonderry (par.94).

****

27. Not more than 26 district councils should be created — each based on a main town or centre (pars.115-116).

28. No place will remain for county councils in the new structure (par.117).

29. The County Boroughs of Belfast and Londonderry will become district councils but retain their ancient civic dignities (par.118).

****

32. Representatives of district councils should be
     nominated to serve on area boards, probably to the
     extent of 30 per cent to 40 per cent but never
     exceeding 50 per cent (par.123).

33. District councils should be consulted by Government
     about local opinion on matters of general public policy
     (par.124).

34. District councils will also have many ceremonial
     functions; and it should be open to all to apply for the
     status of borough (par.125).

**I.23 The Education and Libraries (Northern Ireland)
Order, 1972.**

This Order was significant in terms of its providing for the
establishment of five Education and Library Boards in Northern
Ireland, to administer educational provision and development
throughout the province. An important new feature of educational
provision, at this time, was the creation, within each new Education
and Library Board, of a Teaching Appointments Committee to
regulate and monitor teaching appointments within the controlled
sector. See Part 1 of Schedule 3 below. Each Education and
Library Board was further charged with the responsibility of
organising educational provision in three stages, primary,
secondary and further, and to contribute, at each stage, to the
"spiritual, moral, mental and physical development" of pupils by
securing "efficient education" throughout the three stages of a
pupil's education.

Complementary duties included the securing of, within each area of
jurisdiction, sufficient schools to ensure that the needs of all pupils
were being met. Particular regard was to be had to the need to
provide nursery schools for those pupils who had not yet attained
the age of five years and special schools for children with special
educational needs. Specific provisions were also made for the
appointment of a school management committee for each controlled

school within each of the Boards. Significantly, the principal of each controlled school would be a non-voting member of the newly constituted school management committees. Regulations governing the management of voluntary schools were also incorporated in the Order. Regulations also provided for "Religious Education in Schools" (Section 16), and the duties of teachers in controlled schools as to collective worship and religious instruction (17[1] to 17[4]). In Schedule 2 provision was made for the appointment of new members to the new Boards, in Schedule 3 for the composition of a teaching appointments Committee, in Schedule 4 for membership of school management committees of controlled schools, while in Schedule 5 arrangements were made for the appointment of a school management committee in maintained schools.

The importance of this Order, as regards the constitution and functions of school management committees, not to mention the appointment of teachers in the controlled sector, was enormous.

EDUCATION AND LIBRARY BOARDS AND COMMITTEES THEREOF

Education and Library Boards

3. — (1) for the purposes of this Order, there shall be established five Education and Library Boards (in this order referred to as "boards") and each such board shall from 1st April 1973 be the local education authority and library authority for its area.

Committees

4. — (1)   Each board shall have a teaching appointments committee and a library committee and may appoint such other committees as it considers necessary.

(2)   A teaching appointments committee shall be constituted in accordance with the provisions of Part 1 of Schedule 3 and a library committee shall be constituted in accordance with Part II of that Schedule.

PART III

PROVISION OF EDUCATION
General

Stages and purposes of statutory system of education

5.   The statutory system of public education shall be organised in three stages as follows:

(a)   primary education, that is to say, full-time education suitable to the requirements of junior pupils;

(b)   secondary education, that is to say, full-time education suitable to the requirements of senior pupils other than full-time education provided in an institution of further education; and

(c)   further education, that is to say, full-time education other than secondary education provided for persons over compulsory school age or in an institution of further education for persons over fifteen years of age;

and it shall be the duty of each board, so far as its powers extend, to contribute towards the spiritual, moral, mental and physical development of the community by securing that efficient education throughout those stages is available to meet the needs of its area.

Provision, maintenance and management
of controlled schools by boards

7. — (1) for the purposes of fulfilling its duties under this Order, a board may provide primary, secondary and special schools whether within or outside its area and shall maintain and manage any such school provided by it or transferred to its management by paragraph (2) (in this Order referred to as "a controlled school").

****

8, — (5) Where only one controlled school is under the management of a school management committee, the principal of the school shall be entitled to attend and take part in meetings of the committee but not to vote on any question and, where there are two or more schools under the management of a committee, the principal of each school shall be entitled to attend and take part in meetings of the committee when a matter relating to the school of which he is principal, whether alone or together with any other school or schools under the management of the committee, is under consideration but not to vote on any question.

RELIGIOUS EDUCATION IN SCHOOLS

Religious education in controlled and voluntary schools
other than nursery and special schools

16. — (1) Subject to the provisions of this Article, religious instruction shall be given in every controlled and voluntary school other than a nursery or special school and the school day in every such school shall also include collective worship whether in one or more than one assembly on the part of the pupils in attendance at the school.

(2)   In a controlled school the religious instruction required by paragraph (1) shall be undenominational religious instruction, that is to say, instruction based upon the Holy Scriptures according to some authoritative version or versions thereof but excluding instruction as to any tenet distinctive of any particular religious denomination and the collective worship required by paragraph (1) in any such school shall not, in any controlled school, be distinctive of any particular religious denomination.

(3)   In a voluntary school the religious instruction and collective worship required by paragraph (1) shall be under the control of the managers of the school and such religious instruction shall be subject to such arrangements for inspection and examination as the managers think fit.

(4)   Religious instruction and collective worship required by paragraph (1) shall be so arranged that —

(a)   the school shall be open to pupils of all religious denominations for instruction other than religious instruction;
(b)   no pupil shall be excluded directly or indirectly from the other advantages which the school affords.

Duties of teachers in controlled schools as to collective worship and religious instruction

17. — (1)   Subject to the provisions of this Article, the teachers in every controlled school other than a nursery or special school, if so requested by the board which controls the school, shall conduct or attend collective worship in the school and give undenominational religious instruction in the school but a teacher in a controlled school shall not be required to give religious instruction other than undenominational religious instruction.

(2)   A teacher who has under paragraph (1), been required to conduct or attend collective worship or give undenominational religious instruction, may make a request to the management committee of the school in which he is serving to be wholly or partly excused from conducting or attending such worship or giving such instruction or both from conducting and attending such worship and giving such instruction and at the same time furnish to the committee for submission to the board which controls the school a statutory declaration that his request to be so excused is made solely on grounds of conscience.

Religious instruction not to be inspected,
but complaints to be investigated by Ministry

18. — (1) It shall not be a duty of inspectors or other officers of the Ministry to inspect or examine the religious education given in schools.

SCHEDULE 2
EDUCATION AND LIBRARY BOARDS

PART I
CONSTITUTION OF BOARDS

Appointment of Members

1. — (1) The maximum number of members to be appointed to a board shall from time to time be determined by the Ministry.

(2)   The Minister shall appoint to a board —

(a)   persons nominated in accordance with paragraph 2 by each district council in the area of the board from amongst members of that council;

(b)   persons appearing to the Minister —

     (i)   to represent the interests of transferors of schools in the area of the board

     (ii)   to represent the interests of trustees of maintained schools in the area of the board:

     (iii)   to be suitable for appointment by reason of their interest in the services for which the board is responsible.

Members nominated by district councils

2. — (1) The Ministry shall from time to time determine the total number of members to be nominated to a board by district councils in the area of the board and the number to be nominated by each such district council and, in determining that total number, the Ministry shall ensure that —

(a)   the total number is as nearly as possible equal to two-fifths of the maximum number of members of the board; and

(b)   each district council in the area of the board may nominate at least one member; and in determining the number of members to be nominated by a district council, the Ministry shall have regard to the population in the area of that district council.

Other Members

3.   The Ministry shall from time to time determine the total number of persons to be appointed to a board as representing the interests of transferors of schools and trustees of maintained schools in the area of the board and the number of such persons to be appointed —

(a)   to represent the interests of transferors of schools shall as nearly as possible bear the same proportion to one-quarter of the maximum number of members of the board as the number of pupils enrolled in controlled primary schools in the area of the board bears to the total number of pupils enrolled in all primary schools in that area;

(b)   to represent the trustees of maintained schools shall as nearly as possible bear the same proportion to three-sixteenths of the maximum number of members of the board as the number of pupils enrolled in maintained primary schools in the area of the board bears to the total number of pupils enrolled in all primary schools in that area.

SCHEDULE 3

CONSTITUTION OF TEACHING APPOINTMENTS COMMITTEES
AND LIBRARY COMMITTEES

PART I
TEACHING APPOINTMENTS COMMITTEES

1.   A teaching appointments committee shall consist of the following persons appointed by the board of which it is a committee —

(a)   two principals of controlled schools under the management of the board appointed in accordance with paragraph 2;

(b)   two persons who have been appointed to the board under paragraph 1(2)(b)(i) of Schedule 2 and nominated to the committee by a majority of the persons who have been so appointed;

(c)   two persons nominated by the Minister from amongst the persons appointed to the board by him under paragraph 1(2)(b)(iii) of Schedule 2;

(d)   two district councillors nominated by the board from amongst those members appointed to the board under paragraph 1(2)(a) of Schedule 2;

and the quorum of a teaching appointments committee shall be four persons.

2. — (1) The principals of controlled schools shall for the purposes of paragraph 1(a) be appointed as follows:—

(a) a board shall prepare a panel of principals serving in controlled schools under its management;

(b) two principals from that panel shall be appointed by the board to attend each meeting of the teaching appointments committee and different principals may be appointed to attend different meetings of the committee.

(2) If so authorised by a board, the chief education officer of the board or, in his absence, another officer of the board authorised by him for the purpose may, on behalf of the board, appoint the principals to the teaching appointments committee.

(3) The principals appointed to attend any meeting of a teaching appointments committee shall have the like right to speak and vote at that meeting as the other members of the committee.

3. — (1) Substitutes for members of a teaching appointments committee may be nominated and appointed or, as the case may be, appointed under sub-paragraphs (b), (c) and (d) paragraph 1 in like manner as the members are nominated and appointed or appointed.

(2) Where the chief education officer of the board which appointed the committee or, in his absence, another officer of the board duly authorised by him is informed that a member of the committee will be absent from a meeting of the committee or where a member is disqualified by interest or otherwise from taking part in proceedings at such a meeting, he shall authorise the attendance at that meeting of a substitute, being the substitute or one of the substitutes nominated and appointed or appointed, in like manner as the

member, and if that substitute attend, he shall have at that meeting all the functions of the member except that, if he attends a meeting as substitute for the member who is chairman of the committee, he shall not, unless the committee otherwise decides, be chairman at the meeting.

(3)   The chief education officer of the board or a person nominated by him shall attend as assessor at each meeting of the teaching appointments committee of that board.

PART II

LIBRARY COMMITTEES

4.   The library committee of a board shall consist of such persons as that board appoints thereto but shall include all members appointed to the board by reason of their interest in the public library service.

SCHEDULE 4

MEMBERSHIP OF SCHOOL MANAGEMENT COMMITTEES OF CONTROLLED SCHOOLS

1.   A scheme under Article 8(2) shall so far as it relates to the appointment of members of school management committees comply with the following provisions of this Schedule.

2.   A scheme relating to the school management committee of one or more than one controlled primary school other than a nursery school shall ensure that—

(a)   not less than one-half of the members of the committee shall be appointed in accordance with regulations made by the Ministry as persons representative of the transferors and superseded managers of the school or schools under its management.

****

(c)   the remaining members shall be chosen by the board responsible for the management of the school or schools concerned;

but, where it is not practicable to appoint to a school management committee persons representative of transferors or superseded managers because a school is not a transferred school or does not supersede any other school or schools, the board shall appoint in their place an equivalent number of persons appearing to the board to be representative of transferors and superseded managers in the area of the board as a whole and those persons shall, so far as possible, be persons resident in the locality served by the school or schools under the management of the committee.

3.   A scheme relating to the school management committee of one or more than one controlled intermediate school shall ensure that—

(a)   not less than one-half of the members of the committee shall be persons nominated, in the manner provided by regulations made by the Ministry, by the school management committees of contributory schools from amongst members of those committees who have been appointed to those committees as representatives of transferors or superseded managers;

(b)   not more than one-quarter of the members shall be persons nominated, at a meeting held in accordance with regulations made by the Ministry, by the parents of the children attending the school or schools under the management of the committee;

(c)   the remaining members shall be chosen by the board responsible for the management of the school or schools concerned.

SCHEDULE 5

MAINTAINED SCHOOLS COMMITTEES

PART I

APPOINTMENT OF MAINTAINED SCHOOLS COMMITTEES

1. — (1) Subject to sub-paragraph (4), a board shall, if requested by the managers or trustees of a voluntary school other than a voluntary grammar school, make provision in accordance with the provisions of this Schedule for the appointment of a committee (in this Order referred to as "a maintained school committee") for that school.

(2) A board may make provision for the appointment of one maintained school committee for two or more such schools where the trustees or managers of the schools so request.

2. — (2) One-third of the persons appointed as members of a maintained school committee of a school or schools shall be persons nominated by the board and two-thirds of those members shall be persons nominated, when appointments are

first made to the committee, by the managers or trustees of the school or schools and, on any subsequent appointment of members, by such persons (to be known as "nominating trustees") and in such manner as the scheme for the school or schools may provide.

(3)   The managers or trustees of a school or schools may, at any time before they have signified their agreement to a scheme framed under sub-paragraph (1) for the school or schools, withdraw their request for the appointment of a maintained school committee for the school or schools.

SCHEDULE 6

MEMBERSHIP OF GOVERNING BODIES OF VOLUNTARY GRAMMAR SCHOOLS

1. — (1)   The trustees or governing body of a voluntary grammar school shall, notwithstanding anything in any statute or scheme made thereunder or in any charter, deed, memorandum of association, articles of association or other document constituting the school or under which the land used for the school is vested or which otherwise relates to the school or land used for the school, have power to enter into—

(a)   an agreement with the Ministry conferring on the Minister the right to appoint members to the governing body of the school amounting to not more than one-third of the total number of members of the governing body (including the members appointed by the Minister);

(b)   an agreement, approved by the Ministry, with one or
       more than one board conferring on the board or boards
       the right to appoint members to the governing body of
       the school amounting to not more than one-third of the
       total number of members of the governing body
       (including the members appointed by the board or
       boards).

I.24   A Teaching Council for Northern Ireland : Report of the Working Party appointed by the Minister of Education in 1970, HMSO, 1975.

As is stated in the Foreword, by Roland Moyle, minister of
education, the Working Party had been set up '... to consider the
question of a Teaching Council for Northern Ireland.' The Report
raised '... important issues for the teaching profession as a whole
and, indeed, for all concerned with educational administration.' The
Report makes recommendations on the most appropriate and
feasible means by which the teaching profession of Northern
Ireland might go about forming its own self-governing body.

The Report recommends that the Teaching Council should keep a
register of qualified teachers, discipline members when necessary
and determine standards of qualification and training for admission
to the profession.

The most important proposal is that legislation should be
introduced to establish a Council to be known as 'The Teaching
Council for Northern Ireland.' The following extracts deal with the
Council's Constitution, its functions and Committees, the Register
itself, as well as probation and professional discipline. Nothing
would come of the proposals put forward.

SUMMARY OF RECOMMENDATIONS

We summarise our recommendations as follows:

Paragraph

17. Legislation should be introduced to establish a Council to deal with the registration of teachers, to be known as "The Teaching Council for Northern Ireland."

CONSTITUTION

23. The Council should consist of 30 members as follows: 19 elected members comprising—

    7 primary or special school teachers

    7 secondary (including grammar) school teachers

    3 institution of further education teachers

    2 teachers in institutions concerned with the education and training of teachers.

    9 members appointed by the Minister of Education being persons appearing to him to be representative of employers, colleges of education, universities, the Ulster College and the general public.

    2 other members appointed by the Minister being persons appearing to him to have contributions to make to the work of the Council.

24.   The Council should hold office for a period of four years. The Chairman should be appointed by the Council from among its members. A person elected to represent teachers in a category of school or institution should cease to be a member when he ceases to be employed as a full-time teacher in that type of school or institution.

Casual vacancies should be filled by the Minister or the Council as appropriate. Provision should be made for a review of the functions and constitution of the Council by the Minister.

25.   The Council should be empowered to make representations to the Minister if experience should show that it would be appropriate to ensure the inclusion of principals among the elected members.

Employing authorities and other bodies should not have direct representation on the Council.

Appointment of Teacher Members

27.   Teacher members should be elected to the Council.

Method of Election

29.   The election of teacher members should be conducted by proportional representation. The single transferable vote system should be used.

FUNCTIONS AND COMMITTEES

33.   The Council should exercise responsibility for:-

   (i)   the establishment and keeping of a register of
          teachers, the Council to be advised by a
          Registration and Probationary Service Committee;

   (ii)   the professional discipline of registered teachers,
          to be exercised by a Disciplinary Committee on
          behalf of and in the name of the Council, the
          Disciplinary Committee considering cases
          referred to it by an Investigating Committee; and

   (iii) making recommendations to the Minister on
          standards of qualification and training required
          for registration and on the supply of teachers,
          the Council to be advised by an Education
          Committee.

THE REGISTER

37.   The Council should maintain a Register containing the
      following details:

   (i)   Full name
   (ii)   Address
   (iii) Date of Birth
   (iv)   Type of institution in which presently serving
   (v)   Registration number
   (vi)   Date of registration
   (vii) Type of registration

A teacher's registration number should be his current reference number. Details of entries in the register should be made available to any person making a legitimate enquiry.

CATEGORIES OF TEACHERS REQUIRED TO REGISTER

45.   All full-time teachers in grant-aided schools should be required to register. All temporary and part-time teachers should be required to register from such date as the Council feels it expedient to introduce such a requirement.

PROFESSIONAL DISCIPLINE

86.   The Council should have power to deal with cases of misconduct.

In such cases power to withdraw registration from registered teachers or to refuse the registration or re-registration of a teacher should be vested in the Council and operated through the Investigating and Disciplinary Committees recommended in paragraph 33.

87.   The teacher should have the right to appeal to the High Court of Northern Ireland against a decision to withdraw registration.

The Department should retain power to forbid the employment of a teacher on the grounds of ill-health or physical incapacity for teaching.

I.25 The Sex Discrimination (NI) Order, 1976. No.1042 (NI.15).

This Order established the Equal Opportunities Commission for Northern Ireland to work towards the elimination of discrimination and the promotion of equality of opportunity between men and women. The Commission provides confidential advice to the public free of charge. It is also happy to provide advice on the implementation of non-discriminatory practices and equal opportunities programmes in workplaces.

The Order described five kinds of behaviour which could constitute discrimination in the employment field. These are:

1. Direct Sex Discrimination: This is treating a woman less favourably on the grounds of her sex.

2. Indirect Sex Discrimination: This means applying a condition to both sexes which in practice means that fewer women can comply with it.

3. Direct Marriage Discrimination: This means treating a married person less favourably than a single person of the same sex.

4. Indirect Marriage Discrimination: This occurs when a requirement discriminates against married people because single people of the same sex can comply with it. An example of this would be a refusal to recruit people who had children.

5. Victimisation: This occurs when a person is victimised because he or she asserted rights under the Sex Discrimination (Northern Ireland) Order or might be suspected of doing so.

The Commission can take action about individual complaints or initiate action itself relating to certain allegations. An entire section of the Order deals with discrimination in education.

PART IV

Discrimination in Other Fields
Education

Other discrimination by Education and Library Boards

25.   It is unlawful for an Education and Library Board, in carrying out such of its functions under the Education and Libraries (Northern Ireland) Order 1972 as do not fall under Article 24, to do any act which constitutes sex discrimination.

General duty in public sector of education

26. — (1) Without prejudice to its obligation to comply with any other provision of this order, the body to which this paragraph applies shall be under a general duty to secure that facilities for education provided by it, and any ancillary benefits or services, are provided without sex discrimination.

PART VIII

Enforcement
General

Restriction of proceedings for breach of order

62. — (1) Except as provided by this Order no proceedings, whether civil or criminal, shall lie against any person in respect of an act by reason that the act is unlawful by virtue of a provision of this Order.

(2) Paragraph (1) does not preclude the making of an order of *certiorari, mandamus* or prohibition.

Enforcement in employment field

Jurisdiction of industrial tribunals

63. — (1) A complaint by any person ("the complainant") that another person ("the respondent") —

(a)   has committed an act of discrimination against the complainant which is unlawful by virtue of Part III, or

(b)   is by virtue of Article 42 or 43 to be treated as having committed such an act of discrimination against the complainant,

may be presented to an industrial tribunal.

(2)   Paragraph (1) does not apply to a complaint under Article 16(1) of an act in respect of which an appeal, or proceedings in the nature of an appeal, may be brought under any statutory provision.

Enforcement of Part IV

Claims under Part IV

66. — (1) A claim by any person ("the claimant") that another person ("the respondent") —

(a)   has committed an act of discrimination against the claimant which is unlawful by virtue of Part IV, or

(b)   is by virtue of Article 42 or 43 to be treated as having committed such an act of discrimination against the claimant, may be made the subject of civil proceedings in like manner as any other claim in tort.

(2)   Proceedings under paragraph (1) shall be brought only in a county court, but all such remedies shall be obtainable in such proceedings as, apart from this paragraph and Article 62(1), would be obtainable in the High Court.

****

(4)   For the avoidance of doubt it is hereby declared that damages in respect of an unlawful act of discrimination may include compensation for injury to feelings whether or not they include compensation under any other head.

I.26 Fair Employment (Northern Ireland) Act 1976.

The purpose of this Act was to promote equality of opportunity in Northern Ireland between people of different religious beliefs. It made unlawful certain kinds of discrimination on the ground of religious belief or political opinion in connection with employment and occupations and established a Fair Employment Agency for Northern Ireland to promote equality of opportunity and secure remedies for unlawful discrimination. The Order was based on the Report and Recommendations of the Working Party on discrimination in the Private Sector of Employment (the Van Straubenzee Report). The Order however covered both the private and public sectors. Part V, on 'Exceptions,' is of the greatest significance for teachers. It prevented the application of Parts II and IV, of such crucial importance, from being applied to the teaching profession. This clearly reflects the strong denominational ethos of the school system of Northern Ireland.

PART II
EQUALITY OF OPPORTUNITY
General

3. — (1)   In this Act "equality of opportunity" means equality of opportunity between persons of different religious beliefs.

(2)   For the purposes of this Act a person of any religious belief has equality of opportunity with a person of any other religious belief if, being —

(a)   A person who is seeking employment or in employment, or

(b)   A person who is seeking to become engaged in, or is engaged in, any occupation ...

PART III
UNLAWFUL DISCRIMINATION
General

16. — (1)   In this Act "discrimination" means —

(a)   discrimination on the ground of religious belief or political opinion; or

(b)   discrimination by way of victimisation; and "discriminate" shall be construed accordingly.

(2)   For the purposes of this Act a person discriminates against another person on the ground of religious belief or political opinion, if on either of those grounds, he treats that other person less favourably in any circumstances than he treats or would treat any other person in those circumstances ...

PART IV
OTHER UNLAWFUL ACTS

33. — (1)   It shall be unlawful to publish in Northern Ireland, or cause to be published there, an advertisement which indicates, or could reasonably be understood as indicating, an intention by a person to do an act which is unlawful by virtue of Part III ...

PART V
EXCEPTIONS

34. — (1) Parts II to IV shall not apply —

(a)   to any employment or occupation as a clergyman or minister of a religious denomination;

(b)   to employment for the purposes of a private household; or

(c)   to employment as a teacher in a school.

(2)   Part II shall not apply to any employment or occupation, other than one mentioned in subsection (1), where the essential nature of the job requires it to be done by a person holding a particular religious belief.

(3)   Parts III and IV shall not apply to any employment or occupation, other than one mentioned in subsection (1), where the essential nature of the job requires it to be done by a person holding a particular religious belief; nor shall they apply to an employment or occupation where the essential nature of the job requires it to be done by a person holding a particular political opinion.

****

35. — (2) For the purpose of assisting it in the discharge of its duty under subsection (1), the Agency may conduct investigations —

(a) into the composition, by reference to religious beliefs, of the staff employed as teachers in schools generally, schools of any class or particular schools; and

(b) into practices —

(i) affecting the recruitment or access to benefits of, or the terms of employment applicable to, such staff, or

(ii) involving any detriment to such staff,

including practices discontinued before the time of the investigation so far as relevant for explaining the composition of the staff at that time.

(3) The Agency may from time to time, and shall whenever the Secretary of State so directs, report to the Secretary of State upon the exercise of its functions under this section; and a report under this subsection may make recommendations as to any action which the Agency considers ought to be taken to further equality of opportunity in the employment of teachers, or teachers of any class, in schools, or in schools of any class including action by way of the exercise of the power conferred by section 36 to remove or limit the exception contained in section 34(1)(c).

**I.27   Reorganisation of Secondary Education in Northern
Ireland. A Consultative Document Issued by the
Department of Education, July 1976.**

The Introduction to this document recognised major differences
between the organisation of secondary schooling in Great Britain and
Northern Ireland. Two of these differences had an important bearing
on the reorganising of secondary education on comprehensive lines.

First in Northern Ireland the role played by independent schools
was insignificant. It was recognised that any arrangements for
comprehensive schooling in Northern Ireland should seek to avoid
the creation of conditions which would lead to the development of
independent schools. Secondly, the majority of secondary schools
in Northern Ireland are voluntary; controlled schools are in a
minority. This meant that a system of comprehensive schooling in
Northern Ireland would be as much dependent upon the voluntary
schools as the present selective system.

The Introduction to the Consultative Document recognised that any
new system in Northern Ireland must fit in with local circumstances,
but added that the Labour Government was nationally committed to
comprehensive schooling and that it was fundamentally convinced
of the merits of the comprehensive principle.

Not since 1947 were the proposals for the reform of education in
Northern Ireland more radical. It was to be expected that the
introduction of Direct Rule in 1972 would lead to Northern Ireland
following more closely education policy in Great Britain. From the
outset, however, the new proposals were unlikely to win
widespread acceptance since they were an attempt to reorganise
without capital expenditure. But the defeat of Labour and the
return of the Conservatives to power in 1979 effectively ended the
comprehensive issue throughout the United Kingdom.

SECTION II

BACKGROUND

9.   Under present legislation there are 2 types of grant-aided secondary school — intermediate, including technical intermediate, defined as secondary schools providing free education, and grammar, defined as secondary schools not being intermediate schools (i.e. secondary schools which charge fees). There are 184 secondary (intermediate) schools and 80 secondary (grammar) schools.

10.   The majority of the children who enter the grammar schools at 11+ are in receipt of scholarships from the Education and Library Boards, awarded on the result of the selection procedure carried out each year: these are the children considered best able to profit from the academic education the grammar schools provide; in general, those children who do not qualify for the award of a scholarship enrol in an intermediate school.   The 184 intermediate schools include a number which cater for the entire range of educational need of the secondary school pupils in their areas.   For example, in 5 cases an amalgamation of the local intermediate school with the local grammar school has taken place and 2 intermediate schools, which are remote from the nearest grammar school, also provide for the educational needs at secondary level of all the children in their catchment areas.

11.   Originally, selection was based on the results of an external examination which consisted of papers in English and Arithmetic.   Over the years criticism of this method of selection mounted — largely because of the adverse effect it was having on the work of many primary schools and for the psychological effect it was claimed to have on some children

— and following the Report of the Fifth Advisory Council for Education in Northern Ireland in 1964 a revised method — in essence, the present method — was introduced. This uses a combination of verbal reasoning quotients and teachers' estimates.

SECTION II

MANAGEMENT

OBJECTIVE

14.   In a comprehensive system, there would be no difference between schools in the type of children for which each caters, so far as ability and social background are concerned.   Therefore, although differences in ownership, religious outlook and probably tradition would continue, it would be desirable to eliminate differences which might hinder schools from developing their future potential or which might serve to divide them into different categories with no purpose or relevance in a comprehensive system.   In the field of school management there are many differences which would be unnecessary, and possibly even detrimental, in a new system.

MANAGEMENT STRUCTURES

15.   The structure of management for controlled secondary intermediate schools differs substantially from that for controlled grammar schools;   At present these schools have different functions.   If in a new system their functions became identical, continued differences in management structure would be unnecessary and might provide the popular mind with a basis for ill-founded judgements of relative merit.

16.   On the voluntary side, some schools have committees and some have governing bodies. Here, too, by the uninformed some deductions about merit or quality may mistakenly be drawn. Moreover, some voluntary schools recruit for management purposes from persons of distinction in the local community, from parents and from former pupils, while others recruit from a much more narrow field and thereby unduly limit the service available from well wishers and detrimentally curtail opportunity for community/school relationships.

17.   If it is accepted that the form of management structure creates, or contributes to, a difference between one school and another, this is one of the differences that, in pursuit of the objective set out in paragraph 14, it would be desirable to eliminate as far as possible in a comprehensive system. In seeing how this might be done, it is necessary to recognise that there are effectively 2 school sectors in Northern Ireland — the Roman Catholic sector and the non-Roman Catholic sector.

18.   In the non-Roman Catholic sector, the contrast is between the powers and structure of management bodies of the Board controlled schools, and the powers and structure of management bodies of the voluntary grammar schools. The controlled schools are managed by the Boards, but they have management committees whose composition is statutorily laid down in the 1972 Education and Libraries Order. The powers of the management committee of a controlled school are limited, in that the function of the committee, both in regard to the appointment of staff and the maintenance of buildings and equipment, is merely to make recommendations to the Board. The voluntary grammar schools have boards of governors on which in the case of all but 9 out of the 58 schools there is public representation (see Appendix C). The

board of governors generally, under present arrangements, has full control of the management and finances of the school.   It could be that, following the line pursued in paragraphs 11 and 12 above, the relationship between the board of governors and the trustees or owners would change, but the essential role of the governors as regards management would remain.

19.   In the experience of the Department, management by its own board of governors is in general a much more vital thing than is management by an Education and Library Board and school management committee; there is greater efficiency, a greater interest in the school is taken by the governors, and there is a greater involvement of the community in the affairs of the school.   For these reasons, it is suggested that this is the type of management structure that should be adopted by all controlled schools.

20.   Because the controlled schools are owned and managed by the Boards, discussion must take place with them before even broad principles are determined for the establishment of boards of governors for controlled schools. Discussions will also be necessary with the Protestant Churches in their capacity of "transferors."   This is because representatives of transferors or superseded managers constitute not less than half the membership of the present management committees of controlled intermediate schools (but not controlled grammar schools).

21.   It can, however, generally be said that there will be a choice between empowering a Board, within the framework of agreed broad principles, to draw up a scheme of management for each controlled secondary school in its area, which would permit local circumstances to be taken into account, or specifying precisely in new legislation (in a

similar way as in the present legislation) the constitution of a board of governors to apply to all the controlled secondary schools.   It may also be said that, in line with current thinking on school management, the general aim should be to have as governors persons who will be positively concerned with the essential interests of the school, such as parents, former pupils and representatives of the local community.

MANAGEMENT OF FINANCE

23.   Another difference between schools in a comprehensive system, if the arrangements in the present system were carried forward, would be in the financial provisions.   At present, Boards manage all finance for controlled schools: boards of governors manage all finance for voluntary grammar schools: trustees manage capital expenditure for maintained schools, but Boards look after maintenance and equipment ...

24.   It is claimed that governors of voluntary grammar schools interest themselves in the schools particularly because of their responsibility for their financial management, and for this reason governors of "good quality" can be obtained. Accepting the truth of this, it would be desirable to put responsibility for financial management in all comprehensive schools on the same basis as for the voluntary grammar schools.

25.   On the capital side, all schools, except the controlled schools, are at present (with grant assistance) responsible for their own expenditure; and, under the new system, uniformity could be achieved if the Boards were to give capital grants to the new boards of governors, instead of themselves executing capital works.

26.   On the current side, a voluntary grammar school's income for the running of the school is derived almost, if not entirely, from:

(a)   grants from the Department towards the salaries and related expenditure of the teaching staff;

(b)   capitation grants from the Department (per capita sums related to the ages of the pupils); and

(c)   tuition fees, paid by the Board in the case of "qualified" pupils and by the parents in the case of "unqualified" pupils.

The tuition fee is subject to the approval of the Department and is determined so as to achieve a balance between income and expenditure on the current account.

If a comprehensive system were adopted opportunity could be taken to simplify the financial arrangements as follows:

(d)   instead of paying a salary grant to the voluntary grammar schools the Department should assume full responsibility for the salaries and related expenditure of the teachers, as it does for the teachers in all other schools;

(e)   instead of the capitation grant and tuition fee, each school should be given an annual grant to cover its running expenses;

the amount of the annual grant would be determined in the same way as is the tuition fee at present; there would thus (as there is at present) be a separate calculation made for each school, taking into account its different circumstances.

I.28   Education (Northern Ireland) Order, 1976.

By this Order, the 80% grant to the voluntary sector, legislated for in the Education Amendment Act, 1968, was increased to 85%.

INCREASE OF GRANTS FOR CERTAIN VOLUNTARY SCHOOLS

13. — (1) In Article 106 (1)(a)(i) and (b)(i) of the principal Order (grants by Department equal to eighty per cent of approved expenditure incurred for the provision or alteration of the premises of, or the provision or equipment for, certain voluntary schools) for the words "eighty per cent" there shall be substituted the words "eighty five per cent" ...

I.29   Report of the Working Party on the Management of Schools in Northern Ireland, 1981.

The Working Party which produced this important report was chaired by Professor A E Astin, pro-vice chancellor of the Queen's University, Belfast. The Working Party was set up in June 1977, "To consider the arrangements for the management of schools in Northern Ireland, with particular regard to the reorganisation of secondary education and the Government's wish to ensure that integration where it is desired should be facilitated and not impeded and to make recommendations."

The Report recommended adoption of the term 'Boards of Governors' for all governing bodies of schools. It advocated certain functions for all Boards of Governors, including discussion of "... any matter pertaining to the school ...", as well as a statutory role in the appointment of full-time permanent staff.

It also emphasised the need for a common code of practice in relation to teaching appointments, offering recommendations that might ease the tensions associated with this aspect of management. The related need for a grievance procedure was emphasised.

The involvement of parents and assistant teachers in school governance, with right of representation as full voting members, is also recommended, much in keeping with the English Taylor Report, 1977, "A New Partnership for Our Schools." The role of a school's principal, on a Board of Governors, as well as his or her rights as a non-voting member, are discussed and clarified.

The Astin Report is significant not alone for the practical and, some would argue, long-overdue recommendations it made. It is also significant as a stimulus to the formulation of new policies in education throughout the 1980s. Its influence on the practice of present-day school governance has been enormous.

SUMMARY OF RECOMMENDATIONS

(This Summary does not include several suggestions and preferences which are set out in the report but are not presented as formal recommendations).

Chapter 5 : Title

1.   A common title, "Board of Governors" should be adopted for the governing bodies of all schools and the members should be termed "Governors."

Chapter 6 : A Basic Role for Boards of Governors

2.   There should be Boards of Governors responsible for all grant-aided schools; as a general principle every school of whatever type or category should have a separate Board of Governors.   Exceptions to this norm should be strictly limited and carefully monitored in accordance with well-understood criteria.

3.   There should be a separately constituted Board of Governors for each secondary (including grammar) school, nursery school and special school without exception.

4.   As the norm each primary school should also have a separate Board of Governors and without exception there should be a separately constituted Board of Governors for each primary school with an entitlement to five or more full-time teachers (including the Principal).

****

8.   Only in the most exceptional and compelling circumstances should more than three primary schools, whether controlled or maintained, be placed under a single Board of Governors.

CHAPTER 7 : FUNCTIONS AND POWERS

11.   It should be within the competence of each Board of Governors, of whatever type of school, to discuss and comment upon any matter pertaining to the school for which it is responsible, including matters in respect of which it has no power to take decisions, and Boards of Governors should be actively encouraged to exercise this right freely and regularly.

12.   A Principal's report should be a stated item on the agenda of each stated meeting of every Board of Governors and the Principal's annual report (to be submitted in written form) should be a stated item of the agenda of one stated meeting each year.

13.   The Board of Governors of every grant-aided school should have a statutory role in the appointment of full-time permanent teachers to that school.

****

15.   So far as possible a common code of practice to govern the procedures for all teaching appointments should be negotiated, applicable to both the controlled and the voluntary sectors.

16.   It should be a requirement of the schemes of management for all schools that the Principal be consulted about all appointments to the staff of his school (except his own successor) and that he be entitled to be present at and to participate in all discussions of the Boards of Governors, and in the case of controlled schools also of the Teaching Appointments Committee of the Education and Library Board, about such appointments.

****

18.   If the Principal of a controlled school disagrees with the recommendation of the Board of Governors he should have the right to have his disagreement, supported by reason, recorded in the minutes for submission to the Teaching Appointments Committee of the Education and Library Board along with the Governors' recommendations.

19.   For appointments to "prescribed" posts in controlled schools (Vice-Principal, Senior Master and Senior Mistress) the Principal and one other member of the Board of Governors, normally the Chairman, should be in attendance (without vote) when the Teaching Appointments Committee of the Education and Library Board is selecting from the short-listed candidates; for the appointment of a Principal, two Governors, one of whom should normally be the Chairman, should be in attendance (without vote).

20.   In the case of maintained schools, a code of practice to govern procedures for the appointment of teachers, parallel to the code for Grievance Procedure, should be negotiated and so far as possible it should be aligned with a common code for all schools.

****

22.   For appointments to "prescribed" posts in maintained schools (Principal, Vice-Principal, Senior Master and Senior Mistress) arrangements should be made whereby two independent assessors who are teachers, of the same category as those who would act for corresponding appointments in controlled schools, should attend a Board of Governors engaged in the appointment and selection of staff in the designated categories, and such assessors should have the right to advise and to participate in discussion at all stages of the procedure.

23.   The statutory requirements regarding the advertising of teaching posts in controlled schools should be copied under other arrangements for maintained schools.

****

29.   The code of procedure should include provision for the effective notification of all vacancies for senior posts to staff within the school and a job description should be available in respect of each senior post (this is intended to include the "prescribed" posts of Principal, Vice-Principal, Senior Master and Senior Mistress).

30.   Applicants for senior posts should be interviewed by the Board of Governors, after short-listing if necessary, and Boards of Governors of larger schools should be given discretion to delegate to Appointments Panels the task of short-listing and interviewing applicants for senior posts

(except the "prescribed" posts), provided the Board itself remains fully responsible for the actions of such Panels and provided the Panels include non-teaching as well as teaching members.

31.   Negotiations for a code of procedure concerning internal promotions should deal also with the establishment of appropriate arbitration machinery.

****

34.   All Boards of Governors should be given discretionary power to delegate to a small committee (*not* to an individual) on either an occasional or a regular basis, the selection of non-teaching staff for recommendation to the Education and Library Board, and the submission of the recommendations to the Education and Library Board.   The exercise of these delegated functions should be subject to clearly defined conditions and limits, and to the submission of a full report to the next meeting of the Board of Governors.

****

36.   As a matter of urgency, discussions should be entered upon with a view to remedying the serious deficiency in the redeployment of teachers in both maintained and voluntary grammar schools.

37.   A statement of aims should be formulated and recorded for each school.

****

40.   Each Education and Library Board should prescribe in broad terms aims for each controlled school in its area and should formally communicate these aims in writing both to the Board of Governors and to the Principal.

41. For an individual school, the Board of Governors and the Principal, if they are in full agreement, should be entitled to propose to the Education and Library Board a more elaborate expression of the prescribed aims applicable to that school.

42. While the right of decision must rest with the Board of Governors in the case of voluntary schools, before overruling a Principal on a matter related to curriculum a Board of Governors should be required to seek an opinion from an appropriate outside body and this requirement should be written into the scheme of management.

43. The Principal's explicit and unqualified responsibility for implementation of the aims of the school should be included in schemes of management for voluntary schools in such a way as to encourage recognition of the distinction between unfettered discussion and influence on the one hand, and actual interference with the Principal's actions on the other.

****

46. Education and Library Boards should be required to consult both Boards of Governors and Principals on a regular basis throughout the initiation, planning and execution of a capital project for a controlled school.

****

51. Every Board of Governors should be required to carry out an annual inspection of school premises, to prepare an assessment of their condition and of needs, and to submit an annual report to the Chief Officer of the Education and Library Board. This annual inspection and the annual report should be stated items on the agenda of appropriate meetings of the Board of Governors.

52.   Schemes of management for maintained schools should specify that Boards of Governors are responsible, subject to the overriding authority of the trustees, for arrangements governing the use of school premises for purposes other than the education of the pupils.

****

57.   Procedures should be established to be followed in all cases in which consideration is given to the expulsion of a pupil from a particular school.   A decision on expulsion should be taken only after a period of suspension and consultation, which should always include consultation about the future provision of suitable education for the pupil in question.   Those involved in the consultation should always include the Principal of the school, the parents or guardians of the pupil, the Chief Officer of the Education and Library Board (whatever the category of the school, in virtue of the Board's statutory obligations) and the Chairman or another representative of the Board of Governors.

58.   Discussion should be opened with the appropriate authorities of the maintained schools with a view to working out a suitable procedure embracing the provisions for expulsions which are recommended in paragraph 7.76.

****

CHAPTER 8 : COMPOSITION OF BOARDS OF GOVERNORS

60.   There should be transferor representation as of right on the Boards of Governors of controlled primary and secondary schools and in most instances provision should be made for this on the Boards of Governors of such controlled secondary and grammar schools as are brought into a system

of secondary education reorganised along comprehensive lines (except sixth-form and tertiary colleges). It should be made permissible for a controlled grammar school, upon being brought into a system of secondary education reorganised along comprehensive lines, to be provided with an individual scheme of management which would take account of special circumstances and which would not necessarily include transferor representation. On each occasion when a decision is taken to bring a controlled grammar school into such a system, the Education and Library Board should consider whether an individual scheme of management would be desirable.

61.   There should continue to be provision for the trustees of maintained schools to nominate, as of right, representatives to serve on the Boards of Governors of such schools.

****

63.   Provision should be made for representatives of parents on the Boards of Governors for all grant-aided schools.

64.   In the scheme of management for every grant-aided school provision should be made for the representation of assistant teachers. Such representatives should be full voting members of the Board of Governors, subject to negotiation about a possible requirement to withdraw in certain defined circumstances; and where a legal obstacle to actual membership is found to exist efforts should be made to remove it but until this has been achieved arrangements should be made for representatives of assistant teachers to be in attendance at meetings of the Board of Governors.

65.   In every scheme of management for a grant-aided school provision should be made for the principal to be a member of the Board of Governors without vote; where a legal obstacle to actual membership is found to exist every effort should be made to remove that obstacle but until this has been achieved arrangements should be made for the Principal to receive the agenda and papers in the same way as actual members and for him to be invited to be in attendance throughout the meetings.

****

CHAPTER 9 : MISCELLANEOUS MATTERS

76.   Every Board of Governors of a grant-aided school should be required to meet on not less than three occasions during each school year.

77.   Reasonable and appropriate steps should be taken to make known the names of Governors, especially to parents of pupils in the school and to the teachers.

I.30 The Education and Libraries (Northern Ireland) Order 1986.

This is a document of the greatest significance. It has laid down the basis for ongoing forms of management and administration in the schools and colleges of Northern Ireland.

It reshaped central features of its earlier counterpart, The Education and Libraries (Northern Ireland) Order, 1972. It will prove interesting to compare sections of the two documents, for example those dealing with composition of the Teaching Appointments Committee for the controlled sector, and the membership composition of school governing bodies in both maintained and controlled schools. The election of a teacher governor, under the terms of the 1986 Order, is one of the most significant comparisons in this particular context of management.

Another difference may be found in nomenclature. For example, the term School Management Committee used in the 1972 Order becomes Board of Governors in the 1986 Order, no doubt in response to the relevant, corresponding recommendation in the Astin Report, 1981.

Schedule 14 deals with the appointment of teachers to controlled schools. It outlines the procedures that will come into operation should any disagreement arise between an Area Board and a Board of Governors in the matter of appointing a principal.

The procedural arrangements for the appointment of an assistant teacher, in the controlled sector, are set out in Part II of this Schedule.

PART II

EDUCATION AND LIBRARY BOARDS AND COMMITTEES THEREOF

Committees

4. — (1)   Each board shall have a teaching appointments committee and a library committee and may appoint such other committees as it considers necessary.

(2)   A teaching appointments committee shall be constituted in accordance with the provisions of Part I of Schedule 3 and a library committee shall be constituted in accordance with Part II of that Schedule.

PART III

Provision of Education

The Statutory System of Education

Stages and purposes of statutory system of Education

5.   The statutory system of public education shall be organised in three stages as follows:—

(a)   primary education, that is to say, full-time education suitable to the requirements of junior pupils;

(b)   secondary education, that is to say, full-time education suitable to the requirements of senior pupils other than full-time education at an institution or establishment providing further education; and

(c)   further education that is to say, full-time and part-time education other than secondary education provided for persons over compulsory school age;

and it shall be the duty of each board, so far as its powers extend to contribute towards the spiritual, moral, mental and physical development of the community by securing that efficient education throughout those stages is available to meet the needs of its area.

School Management

Management of controlled schools

10. — (3) The membership, procedure and functions of the Board of Governors of a controlled school or controlled schools shall, subject to the provisions of Schedule 4 as to membership and to the other provisions of this Order, be such as may be provided by a scheme prepared by the board and approved by the Department and such a scheme may provide for the carrying out by the Board of Governors in relation to the school or schools under its management of specified functions on behalf of, and in the name of, the board.

****

Management of voluntary schools

11. — (3) A voluntary school for which a Board of Governors is constituted in accordance with Part I of Schedule 5 (in this order referred to as "a maintained school") shall be under the control and management of that Board of Governors and may be withdrawn from the control and management of that Board of Governors in accordance with the provisions of Part II of that Schedule.

****

Appointment of teachers

68. The provisions of Parts I and II of Schedule 14 shall apply to the appointment of a teacher to a controlled school and the provisions of Part III of that Schedule shall apply to the appointment of a peripatetic teacher or a supply teacher.

****

PART II

PROCEEDINGS OF BOARDS

9. — (1) A board shall, at its first meeting after its appointment, elect one of its members to be chairman and one of its members to be vice-chairman who, unless the board otherwise determines, shall hold office until the next subsequent appointment of members of the board under paragraph 1(4) becomes effective.

(2)   Where, at any meeting of the board, the chairman is absent, the vice-chairman, if present, shall be chairman at that meeting and where, at any such meeting, both the chairman and vice-chairman are absent, the chairman at that meeting shall be such member of the board present as the members attending the meeting shall appoint.

(3)   The chairman at any meeting of the board shall, in addition to his right to vote as a member of the board, have a casting vote.

10. — (1) The quorum of the board shall be one-third of the total number of members of the board.

****

SCHEDULE 3 [Article 4(2)]

CONSTITUTION OF TEACHING APPOINTMENTS COMMITTEES AND LIBRARY COMMITTEES

PART I

TEACHING APPOINTMENTS COMMITTEES

1.   A teaching appointments committee shall consist of the following persons appointed by the board of which it is a committee —

(a)   two principals of controlled schools under the management of the board appointed in accordance with paragraph 2;

(b)   two persons who have been appointed to the board under paragraph 1(2)(b)(i) of Schedule 2 and nominated to the committee by a majority of the persons who have been so appointed;

(c)   two persons nominated by the Head of the Department from amongst the persons appointed to the board by him under paragraph 1(2)(b)(iii) of Schedule 2;

(d)   two district councillors nominated by the board from amongst those members appointed to the board under paragraph 1(2)(a) of Schedule 2;

and the quorum of a teaching appointments committee shall be four persons.

2. — (1)   The principals of controlled schools shall for the purposes of paragraph 1(a) be appointed as follows:-

(a)   a board shall prepare a panel of principals serving in controlled schools under its management;

(b)   two principals from that panel shall be appointed by the board to attend each meeting of the teaching appointments committee and different principals may be appointed to attend different meetings of the committee.

(2)   If so authorised by a board, the chief education officer of the board or, in his absence, another officer of the board authorised by him for the purpose may, on behalf of the board, appoint the principals to the teaching appointments committee.

(3)   The principals appointed to attend any meeting of a teaching appointments committee shall have the like right to speak and vote at that meeting as the other members of the committee.

3. — (1)   Substitutes for members of a teaching appointments committee may be nominated and appointed under sub-paragraphs (b), (c) and (d) of paragraph 1 in like manner as the members are nominated and appointed.

(2)   Where the chief education officer of the board which appointed the committee or, in his absence, another officer of the board duly authorised by him is informed that a member of the committee nominated and appointed under paragraph 1(b), (c) or (d) will be absent from a meeting of the committee or where such a member is disqualified by interest or otherwise from taking part in proceedings at such a

meeting, he shall authorise the attendance at that meeting of a substitute, being the substitute or one of the substitutes nominated and appointed in like manner as the member, and if that substitute attends, he shall have at that meeting all the functions of the member except that, if he attends a meeting as substitute for the member who is chairman of the committee, he shall not, unless the committee otherwise decides, be chairman at that meeting.

(3) The chief education officer of the board or a person nominated by him shall attend as assessor at each meeting of the teaching appointments committee of that board.

4. — (1) Where a meeting of the teaching appointments committee is to be held to exercise any of the functions conferred on the committee by Part I of Schedule 14 in relation to a post in a school, the committee shall invite representatives of the school to attend the meeting for the purpose of advising the committee generally on matters relating to the school and the nature of the post.

(2) Representatives of the school invited to attend a meeting of the committee under this paragraph shall be entitled to be present at the meeting only for the purpose mentioned in sub-paragraph (1) and shall not be present during the interview of any candidate for the post nor during any discussion or decision relating to the appointment of any particular candidate to the post.

****

SCHEDULE 4 [Article 10(3)]

Membership of Board of Governors
of Controlled Schools

*Controlled primary schools
(other than nursery or integrated schools)*

2. — (1) There shall be 9, 16 or 24 voting members appointed to the Board of Governors of one or more than one controlled primary school, other than a controlled nursery school or controlled integrated primary school.

(2) Subject to paragraph 6, where there are 9 voting members appointed to such a Board of Governors, then of those members —

(a) four shall be nominated by the transferors and superseded managers of the school or schools;

(b) two shall be elected by parents of pupils attending the school or schools from amongst the parents of such pupils;

(c) two shall be chosen by the board responsible for the management of the school or schools;

(d) one shall be elected by assistant teachers at the school or schools from amongst such assistant teachers.

(3) Where there are 16 or 24 voting members appointed to such a Board of Governors, sub-paragraph (2) shall apply as if for the numbers mentioned in heads (a), (b), (c) and (d) of that sub-paragraph there were substituted the fractions three-eighths, one-quarter, one quarter and one-eighth respectively.

*Controlled intermediate schools
(other than technical or integrated schools)*

3. — (1) There shall be 9, 16 or 24 voting members appointed to the Board of Governors of a controlled intermediate school, other than a technical intermediate school or a controlled integrated intermediate school.

(2)   Subject to paragraph 6, where there are 9 voting members appointed to such a Board of Governors, then of those members —

(a)   four shall be nominated by the Boards of Governors of contributory schools from amongst members of those Boards of Governors who have been nominated by the transferors and superseded managers of the contributory schools;

(b)   two shall be elected by parents of pupils attending the school from amongst parents of such pupils;

(c)   two shall be chosen by the board responsible for the management of the school;

(d)   one shall be elected by assistant teachers at the school from amongst such assistant teachers.

(3)   Where there are 16 or 24 voting members appointed to such a Board of Governors, sub-paragraph (2) shall apply as if for the numbers mentioned in heads (a), (b), (c) and (d) of that sub-paragraph there were substituted the fractions three-eighths, one-quarter, one-quarter and one-eighth respectively.

****

SCHEDULE 5 [Article 11(3)]

MAINTAINED SCHOOLS

PART I

CONSTITUTION OF BOARD OF GOVERNORS
FOR MAINTAINED SCHOOL

2. — (2)   The Board of Governors of one or more than one
maintained school shall consist of —

(a)   10, 18 or 27 persons (in this paragraph referred to as
        voting members); and

(b)   the principal of the school, or each of the schools, who,
        subject to sub-paragraph (5), shall be entitled to attend
        and take part in meetings of the Board of Governors
        but not to vote on any question.

        (3)   Where there are 10 voting members of the Board
of Governors of one or more than one maintained school,
then of those members —

(a)   six shall be nominated —

        (i)   when appointments are first made to the Board
                of Governors, by the managers or trustees of the
                school or schools,
        (ii)   on any subsequent appointment to the Board of
                Governors, by such persons (to be known as
                "nominating trustees") and in such manner as
                the scheme may provide,

at least one of whom shall, at the time of his appointment be a parent of a pupil attending the school or one of the schools;

(b) two shall be nominated by the board;

(c) one shall be elected by parents of pupils attending the school or schools from amongst the parents of such pupils;

(d) one shall be elected by assistant teachers at the school or schools from amongst such assistant teachers.

(4) Where there are 18 or 27 voting members of the Board of Governors of one or more than one maintained school, sub-paragraph (3) shall apply as if for the numbers mentioned in heads (a), (b), (c) and (d) of that sub-paragraph there were substituted the fractions five-ninths, two-ninths, one-ninth and one-ninth respectively.

(5) Where two or more schools are grouped under one Board of Governors, the principal of a school shall not be entitled to attend or take part in any meeting of the Board of Governors whenever a matter relating exclusively to one or more of the other schools is being discussed.

(6) The Board of Governors shall, with the approval of the Department, make arrangements for the election of persons under sub-paragraph (3)(c) and (d) and such arrangements shall ensure that any vote taken for the purpose of any such election shall be by secret ballot.

SCHEDULE 14 [Article 68]

Appointment of Teachers

PART I

Appointment of Principals and Certain other Teachers
in Controlled Schools

3. — (4)   Where a Board of Governors informs the board that it is not prepared to recommend any of the candidates and the board agrees that none of the candidates should be appointed, the board may again advertise the post in the prescribed manner and where it does so shall again comply with the provisions of this paragraph.

(5)   Where the board is not prepared to appoint the candidate or any of the candidates recommended by the Board of Governors or where the Board of Governors has informed the board that it is not prepared to recommend any of the candidates and the board is of opinion that one of the candidates should be appointed or the Board of Governors fails to comply with sub-paragraph (2), and if, after consultation with the Board of Governors, the board and the Board of Governors cannot agree either that one of the candidates should be appointed or that the post should be advertised again under sub-paragraph (1) and that this paragraph be again complied with, the board shall refer the matter to the Department.

(6)   Where a matter is referred to the Department under sub-paragraph (5) the Department shall, after making such inquiries, if any, as it considers necessary, either —

(a)   direct the appointment of one of the candidates; or

(b)   direct the board to advertise the post again in the prescribed manner and to comply again with the provisions of this paragraph;

and the board shall then forthwith take all necessary steps to comply with the Department's directions.

(7)   In this paragraph "provisionally qualified" in relation to a candidate for appointment to a teaching post means a person who may reasonably be expected to hold such qualifications as may be approved by the Department for appointment to such post before the date on which the appointment would take effect.

PART II

APPOINTMENT OF ASSISTANT TEACHERS
IN CONTROLLED SCHOOLS

7. — (1)   Where it is necessary for a board to appoint a person as an assistant teacher, other than a temporary or part-time assistant teacher, in a controlled school in the area of the board —

(a)   the board shall advertise the post in the prescribed manner;

(b)   applications for the post shall be made to the board on forms approved by the Department:

(c)   the board shall send to the Board of Governors of the school to which the appointment is to be made, the application forms from candidates for the appointment who appear to the board to be qualified or provisionally qualified for the post.

(2)   The Board of Governors shall, at a meeting or meetings duly convened for the purpose, consider all application forms sent to it under sub-paragraph (1)(c) and, after interviewing such number, if any, of the candidates as it considers necessary, shall either —

(a)   inform the board that in its opinion none of the candidates should be appointed; or

(b)   inform the board of the name of the candidate whom it proposes should be appointed and of the names of such other candidates, if any, as it proposes should be offered the appointment if the first-named candidate is for any reason not available for appointment, the names of such other candidates, if more than one, being placed in the order in which it considers that they should be offered the appointment.

(3)   Where a Board of Governors informs the board that in its opinion none of the candidates should be appointed and —

(a)   the board is satisfied that none of the candidates should be appointed, the board may again advertise the post in the prescribed manner and, where it does so, shall again comply with the provisions of this paragraph; or

(b)   the board is of opinion that one of the candidates should be appointed and if, after consultation with the Board of Governors, the board and the Board of Governors cannot agree either on the appointment of one of the candidates, or that the post should be advertised again under sub-paragraph (1) and that this paragraph be again complied with, the board shall refer the matter to the Department.

****

I.31 Education Reform in Northern Ireland : The Way Forward, October 1988.

This Conservative inspired document outlines the new thinking on government policy in education for the next century.

As Dr. Brian Mawhinney, minister of state for education in Northern Ireland at the time, was to explain at the outset, the new reforms were vital if the young people of Northern Ireland were ".. to be suitably prepared to meet the demands and challenges of the 21st century."

There is much emphasis on the value and importance of parental involvement in education, and of parents having the freedom to choose the schools they preferred their children to attend. This was in keeping with a market forces approach to the public sector which the Conservatives advocated as an essential criterion in the raising of standards and pursuit of excellence in all public sectors.

A unique concept for the management of education in Northern Ireland, was that of the financial delegation of budgets to the schools. It was claimed that this would make schools more autonomous in the management and deployment of resources.

Renewed importance was given in the document to the concept of grant maintained integrated schools, aimed specifically at the education together of Protestant and Catholic children. Dr. Mawhinney concedes, however, that the concept of grant maintained schools did not have widespread support in Northern Ireland.

The importance of this document may be related to the fact that it helped clear the decks for the legislative implementation of its essential recommendations.

3. OPEN ENROLMENT AND PARENTAL CHOICE

SCHOOL ENROLMENT

3.1   The Government is committed to ensuring that parents are given as much freedom as possible in choosing the schools their children should attend, unhindered by administrative constraints or quotas ... However, the Government also intends to incorporate in legislation the general principle that admissions to all primary and secondary schools should normally be constrained only by the existing capacity of their accommodation. With very limited exceptions, therefore, schools will have to admit all pupils applying for admission so long as there are places available. Schools will not be required to expand to meet demand, but it will, of course, continue to be necessary to take account of the demographic needs of individual areas and to provide additional places where this is seen to be necessary. By the same token, the Government also recognises the need to offer a measure of protection, in the form of additional teaching resources, to the curriculum of schools serving isolated communities and reaffirms its commitment to these schools.

3.2   Arrangements will be made for the Department to determine, in consultation with school authorities, the physical capacity of each school and, in light of the capacity approved, the number of pupils which the school must admit, subject to demand, each year. Parents will for the first time be given a statutory right to express a preference for the school they wish their children to attend. Although every effort will be made to meet this preference, account will have to be taken of the school's physical capacity and also of certain specified circumstances such as those outlined in paragraph 3.9 ...

3.3   All school authorities will be required to publish details of the admission arrangements for the schools under their control. The information to be published will include:

— the number of pupils which the school must admit, subject to demand, each year, as determined by the Department after consultation with the school authorities;

— an explanation of the respective roles of the Education and Library Board and the school Board of Governors in relation to admissions;

— a statement of the admissions criteria to be used by the school in deciding which children are to be admitted in circumstances where applications for admission exceed the number of places available.

The admission criteria will apply only where the school is oversubscribed. In order that schools can demonstrate fairness and objectivity in selecting pupils for admission, the criteria will need to express clearly and in order of priority the factors which the school proposes to take into account.

3.4 Provision will be made for parents whose preference is not met to appeal against the school's decision to an independent tribunal. The decision of the tribunal will be binding on the school authorities concerned.

4. FINANCIAL DELEGATION TO SCHOOLS

4.1 Respondents to the consultation paper expressed misgivings about the practicalities of the introduction of financial delegation, though in many cases this reflected unfamiliarity with the concept, or misunderstanding of the benefits and advantages which can accrue to schools from direct responsibility for their own resource deployment. The Government believes that the practical implementation issues can be resolved, and remains of the view that those who take the day-to-day decisions on the implementation of the curriculum, and on the organisation and general running of the school, are best placed to decide how the resources available to them should be deployed.

4.2   Accordingly the Government has decided to introduce financial delegation, initially to secondary schools, with a reserve power to extend this to other schools in the future. Details will be worked out in consultation with the Education and Library Boards, taking account of the experience gained in the pilot scheme currently operating in four Board areas.

4.3   For the same reasons of good management, and the involvement in financial decision-making of the managers within the school, the Government has further decided that other schools without full financial delegation should also have control over a part of their running costs, to include certain prescribed elements such as books and practice materials, stationery and small equipment.

4.4   The Government intends that financial delegation, initially to secondary schools, will include the capacity to manage the human resources — i.e. teaching and non-teaching staff — available to them, to the extent that schools should be able to increase their staffing complement or to decide that savings can be made in this area without detriment to the running of the school or the education of the pupils.   The normal procedures for appointment and dismissal will however be unchanged for the purposes of financial delegation.

4.5   Almost all respondents on the topic of financial delegation emphasised the need for training for principals and Governors in the administration and techniques involved. The Government fully accepts that training will be necessary, and will be considering further the form which this should take, based on the experience of the pilot project and discussions with Education and Library Boards.

5 GRANT-MAINTAINED SCHOOLS

5.1 The Consultation paper proposed new provision which would enable schools to apply to the Department of Education for grant-maintained status. The paper explained that grant-maintained schools would operate with a high degree of autonomy, funded directly by central Government, and that parents themselves would be able to initiate the procedures for the change of status.

5.2 The consultation paper indicated that the underlying principle was to offer new opportunities for greater parental influence and involvement. As a basis for consultation, arrangements were set out whereby schools might choose between grant-maintained status (GMS) and grant-maintained integrated status (GMIS). Specifically, GMIS was intended to encourage and assist those schools with a particular commitment to provide for the co-education of Protestant and Roman Catholic children. At the same time it was recognised that other schools might prefer to seek GMS as a step towards GMIS in the longer term.

5.3 However, the clear view has emerged during the consultation process that, in the particular circumstances of Northern Ireland, it would be of more direct relevance to the needs of the community to concentrate entirely on GMIS. Accordingly, the Government has decided not to proceed with the proposal for grant-maintained status, but to proceed with the introduction of legislation for grant-maintained *integrated* status, and to associate with it a range of additional measures in support of integrated education generally.

I.32   Education Reform (Northern Ireland) Order 1989.

The reforms signalled in the previous document were given legislative status in this 1989 Order.   They include financial delegation, parental preferences, open enrolment and the setting up of Grant-Maintained Integrated Schools.   The duties and expectations of Boards of Governors are explained and clarified.

Further to a recommendation in the Astin Report (1981) on the establishment of an 'upper layer' within the maintained sector, with responsibility to oversee the provision and management of education therein, a Council for Catholic Maintained Schools (CCMS) was established.   Provision was also made for an Annual Report from a school's Board of Governors and for an Annual Meeting of Parents.   The Order established a Schools Examinations and Assessment Council.   The legislation it contains has brought about radical change in the management and administration of education in Northern Ireland.

PART III

THE CURRICULUM

Preliminary

Duties with respect to the curriculum

4. — (1)   It shall be the duty of the Board of Governors and principal of every grant-aided school to exercise their functions as respects that school (including, in particular, the functions conferred on them by this Part) with a view to securing that the curriculum for the school satisfied the requirements of this Article.

(2)   The curriculum for a grant-aided school satisfies the requirements of this Article if it is a balanced and broadly based curriculum which —

(a) promotes the spiritual, moral, cultural, intellectual and physical development of pupils at the school and thereby of society; and

(b) prepares such pupils for the opportunities, responsibilities and experiences of adult life.

****

The Northern Ireland Schools Examinations and Assessment Council

20. — (1) There shall be established a body to be known as the Northern Ireland Schools Examinations and Assessment Council (in this Article and Articles 21 and 22 referred to as "the Council") which shall perform the functions conferred on it by Articles 21 and 22 ...

Duty to conduct examinations and assessments

21. — (1) The Northern Ireland Schools Examinations and Assessment Council shall, subject to the following provision of the Article, —

(a) conduct, and award the appropriate certificates for, the relevant examinations, in accordance with such rules as the Council may determine;

(b) conduct the relevant assessments, in accordance with such assessment arrangements as are specified under Article 7(1)(b);

(c) conduct the moderation of relevant examinations and relevant assessments;

(d)   seek to ensure that the standards of the relevant examinations and of the relevant assessments are recognised as equivalent to the standards of examinations and assessments conducted by other bodies or authorities exercising similar functions elsewhere in the United Kingdom.

****

Other functions of the Northern Ireland
Schools Examinations and Assessment Council

22. — (1) The Northern Ireland Schools Examinations and Assessment Council shall —

(a)   keep all aspects of examinations and assessment under review;

(b)   advise the Department on such matters concerned with examinations and assessment as the Department may refer to it or as it may see fit;

(c)   publish and disseminate, or assist in the publication and dissemination of, information relating to examinations and assessment;

(d)   advise the Department on the exercise of its powers under Article 9(1);

(e)   carry out such other activities as the Department may direct, being activities which the Department considers to be appropriate for the Council to carry out for the purpose of, or in connection with, the exercise of any of its functions under Article 21 of this Article ...

PART IV

ADMISSION OF CHILDREN TO GRANT-AIDED SCHOOLS

Parental preferences

36. — (1) Every board shall make arrangements for enabling the parent of a child resident in the area of the board to express a preference as to the school at which he wishes education to be provided for his child and to give reasons for his preference ...

Appeals against admission decisions

37. — (1) Every board shall make arrangements for enabling the parent of a child to appeal against any decision made by or on behalf of the Board of Governors of a grant-aided school situated in the area of the board refusing the child admission to the school ...

Criteria for admission to grant-aided schools

38. — (1) Subject to paragraphs (2) and (5), the Board of Governors of each grant-aided school shall draw up, and may from time to time amend, the criteria to be applied in selecting pupils for admission to the school.

(2) When drawing up or amending the criteria to be applied in selecting pupils for admission to —

(a)   a controlled school, the Board of Governors of the school shall consider any representations which are made to it regarding those criteria by the board responsible for the management of the school;

(b)   a Catholic maintained school, the Board of Governors of the school shall consider any representations which are made to it regarding those criteria by the Council for Catholic Maintained Schools.

****

(4)   The criteria to be applied in selecting pupils in the relevant age group for admission to a secondary school shall not include the performance of the pupils in any test or examination held by, or on behalf of, the Board of Governors of a secondary school.

(5)   A test or examination of an individual pupil held by a board at the request of the Board of Governors of a grammar school shall not be taken for the purposes of paragraph (4) to be a test or examination held by, or on behalf of, that Board of Governors.

(6)   Regulations may provide, in relation to any school or description of school, —

(a)   that the criteria to be drawn up under this Article shall include such matters or matters of such description as are specified in the regulations;

(b)   that those criteria shall not include such matters or matters of such description as may be so specified.

Restriction on number of registered pupils
at a grant-aided school

39. — (1)   Subject to paragraph (2), the Board of Governors of a grant-aided school shall not cause or permit the number of registered pupils at the school at any time to exceed the school's enrolment number.

(2)   In calculating for the purposes of paragraph (1) the number of registered pupils at a school at any time, no account shall be taken of any pupils registered at the school in compliance with the direction of an appeal tribunal or in compliance with a school attendance order.

****

PART V

FINANCING SCHOOLS

Financing of controlled and maintained schools

Schemes for financing controlled and maintained schools

46. — (1) It shall be the duty of every board to prepare a scheme in accordance with this Part and submit it for the approval of the Department in accordance with Article 47.

(2)   The scheme shall provide for —

(a)   the determination in respect of each financial year of the board, for each school required to be covered by the scheme in that year, of the share to be appropriated for that school in that year of the part of the general schools budget of the board for that year which is available for allocation to individual schools under the scheme (referred to in this Part, in relation to such a school, as the schools budget share);

(b)   the delegation by the board of the management of a school's budget share for any year to the Board of Governors of the school where such delegation is required or permitted by or under the scheme; and

(c)   the making available by the board to the Board of Governors of the school of a sum of money to be spent at its discretion, where the management of the school's budget share is not delegated to the Board of Governors.

****

49 — (3)   The allocation formula under a scheme —

(a)   shall include provision for taking into account, in the case of each school required to be covered by the scheme in any financial year, the number and ages of registered pupils at that school on such date or dates as may be determined by or under the scheme in relation to that year; and

(b)   may include provision for taking into account any other factors affecting the needs of individual schools which are subject to variation from school to school (including, in particular, the number of registered pupils at a school who have special educational needs and the nature of the special educational provision required to be made for them).

****

PART VI

INTEGRATED EDUCATION

CHAPTER 1

GENERAL FUNCTIONS OF DEPARTMENT AND BOARDS

*General functions of Department and boards
in relation to integrated education*

64. — (1)   It shall be the duty of the Department to encourage and facilitate the development of integrated education, that is to say the education together at school of Protestant and Roman Catholic pupils.

(2)   The Department may, subject to such conditions as it thinks fit, pay grants to any body appearing to the Department to have as an objective the encouragement or promotion of integrated education.

(3)   It shall be the duty of a board to provide free of charge to any person seeking it, advice and information about —

(a)   the procedures for acquisition by a school of controlled integrated status;

(b)   the implications for a school of the acquisition of that status.

CHAPTER II

GRANT-MAINTAINED INTEGRATED SCHOOLS

Management of grant-maintained integrated schools

Management of grant-maintained integrated schools

66. — (1)   Each grant-maintained integrated school shall be under the control and management of a Board of Governors constituted in accordance with the provisions of Schedule 5.

(2)   The scheme of management for a grant-maintained integrated school shall require the Board of Governors to use its best endeavours, in exercising its functions under the Education Orders, to ensure that the management, control and ethos of the school are such as are likely to attract to the school reasonable numbers of both Protestant and Roman Catholic pupils.

****

Initiation of procedure for acquisition of
grant-maintained integrated status by existing school

69. — (1)   Subject to paragraph (5), in the case of any controlled or voluntary school which is eligible for grant-maintained integrated status, a ballot of parents on the question of whether grant-maintained integrated status should be sought for the school shall be held in accordance with Article 70 ...

Ballot of parents

70. — (1) Where the Board of Governors of any school is under a duty by virtue of Article 69 to secure that a ballot is held in accordance with this Article, it shall secure that all necessary arrangements for the ballot are made by such body as may be prescribed ("the prescribed body").

(2)   The arrangements shall provide for a secret postal ballot.

CHAPTER III

CONTROLLED INTEGRATED SCHOOLS

Management of controlled integrated schools

88.   The scheme of management for a controlled integrated school shall require the Board of Governors to use its best endeavours, in exercising its functions under the Education orders, to ensure that the management, control and ethos of the school are such as are likely to attract to the school reasonable numbers of both Protestant and Roman Catholic pupils.

****

Constitution of Board of Governors for controlled integrated schools

89. 5. — (1) There shall be 14 or 21 voting members appointed to the Board of Governors of a controlled integrated school ...

(a)   two-sevenths shall be elected by parents of pupils attending the school from amongst the parents of such pupils;

(b)   two-sevenths shall be chosen by the board responsible for the management of the school;

(c)   one-seventh shall be nominated by the transferors and superseded managers of controlled schools (other than controlled integrated schools) in the area of the board responsible for the management of the school;

(d)   one-seventh shall be nominated by the nominating trustees of Catholic maintained schools in the area of the board responsible for the management of the school;

(e)   one-seventh shall be elected by assistant teachers at the school from amongst such assistant teachers.

****

Withdrawal of delegated powers

Withdrawal of delegated powers for mismanagement, etc.

117. — (1) Where it appears to a board, in the case of any institution in respect of which financial delegation is required for the current financial year under a scheme, that the governing body of the institution —

(a)   has been guilty of a substantial or persistent failure to comply with any requirements or conditions applicable under the scheme; or

(b)   is not managing the appropriation or expenditure of the sum put at its disposal for the purposes of the institution in a satisfactory manner, the board may take any action permitted by paragraph (2).

(2) The actions so permitted are —

(a) complete suspension of the governing body's right to a delegated budget;

(b) the limitation of that right to part only of the budget share of the institution concerned; and

(c) the restriction, in any manner that appears to the board to be appropriate in the circumstances, of the discretion of the governing body to spend any sum made available to it in respect of the institution's budget share or any part of it as the board thinks fit for the purposes of the institution.

****

PART VIII

SCHOOLS — GENERAL PROVISIONS

CHAPTER I

MANAGEMENT OF GRANT-AIDED SCHOOLS

Annual report of the Board of Governors

125. — (1) The scheme of management for every grant-aided school shall provide for it to be the duty of the Board of Governors to prepare, once in every school year, a report containing —

(a)   a summary of the steps taken by the Board of Governors in the discharge of its functions during the period since its last report ...

****

Annual parents' meeting

126. — (1) The scheme of management for every grant-aided school shall provide for it to be the duty of the Board of Governors to hold a meeting once in every school year ("the annual parents' meeting") which is open to —

(a)   all parents of registered pupils at the school; and

(b)   such other persons (including assistant teachers at the school) as the Board of Governors may invite.

****

PART IX

THE COUNCIL FOR CATHOLIC MAINTAINED SCHOOLS

The Council for Catholic Maintained Schools

141. — (1) There shall be established a body to be known as the Council for Catholic Maintained Schools (in this Part referred to as "the Council").

(2) The provisions of Schedule 8 shall apply in relation to the Council.

****

SCHEDULE 5 [Article 66(1)]

MEMBERSHIP OF BOARD OF GOVERNORS OF
GRANT-MAINTAINED INTEGRATED SCHOOLS

2. — (1) Of the voting members of the Board of Governors
of a grant-maintained integrated school —

(a)   three-eighths shall be foundation governors, at least
        one-third of whom shall, at the time of their
        appointment, be parents of pupils attending the school;

(b)   one-quarter shall be appointed by the Head of the
        Department;

(c)   one-quarter shall be elected by parents of pupils
        attending the school from amongst parents of such
        pupils;

(d)   one-eighth shall be elected by assistant teachers at the
        school from amongst such assistant teachers.

        (2) In this paragraph —

        "assistant teacher" means a teacher, other than the
principal or a temporary or part-time teacher, employed on
the staff of a school;

"foundation governors" means persons appointed —

        (a)   when appointments are first made to the Board
                of Governors, by the body or person by which or
                by whom the relevant proposal was submitted
                under Article 71(1) or (2);

(b)   on any subsequent appointment to the Board of Governors, by the persons holding office as foundation governors

being persons appearing to the body of persons appointing them to be persons committed to the good management and continuing viability of the school as a grant-maintained integrated school;

"relevant proposal," in relation to a grant-maintained integrated school, means the proposal approved by the Department for the acquisition of grant-maintained integrated status for the school as a grant-maintained integrated school.

****

SCHEDULE 8 [Article 141(2)]

THE COUNCIL FOR CATHOLIC MAINTAINED SCHOOLS

Constitution

1.   The Council shall be a body corporate to which, subject to the following provisions of this Schedule, section 19 of the Interpretation Act (Northern Ireland) 1954 shall apply.

2. — (1) The Council shall consist of —

(a)   the Archbishop of Armagh or a person nominated by him;

(b)   the Bishops of Clogher, Derry, Down and Connor, Dromore and Kilmore or, in each case, a person nominated by that Bishop;

(c)   14 persons appointed by the Archbishop and Bishops mentioned in heads (a) and (b) acting jointly;

(d)   8 persons appointed by the Head of the Department after consultation with the said Archbishop and Bishops;

(e)   4 parents appointed in accordance with sub-paragraphs (2) and (3) by the Council after consultation with the Head of the Department from amongst parents elected under paragraph 2(3) of Schedule 5 to the principal Order to the Boards of Governors of Catholic maintained schools;

(f)   4 assistant teachers appointed in accordance with sub-paragraphs (2) and (3) by the Council after consultation with the Head of the Department from amongst teachers elected under paragraph 2(3) of Schedule 5 to the principal Order to the Boards of Governors of Catholic maintained schools.

(2)   For the purposes of appointments to the Council under sub-paragraph (1)(e) and (f) 15 parents and 15 assistant teachers shall be nominated by diocesan education committees established under paragraph 3 as follows, namely—

(a)   3 parents and 3 assistant teachers shall be nominated by the diocesan education committee for the Archdiocese of Armagh;

(b)   2 parents and 2 assistant teachers shall be nominated by the diocesan education committee for the dioceses of Clogher and Kilmore;

(c)   3 parents and 3 assistant teachers shall be nominated by the diocesan education committee for the diocese of Derry;

(d)   5 parents and 5 assistant teachers shall be nominated by the diocesan education committee for the diocese of Down and Connor;

(e)   2 parents and 2 assistant teachers shall be nominated by the diocesan education committee for the diocese of Dromore,

and the persons nominated by each diocesan education committee shall, as equitably as possible, represent the interests of primary schools and of secondary schools within the area of that committee.

****

I.33 The Parents' Charter for Northern Ireland, Raising the Standard, 1992.

With this Charter, the rights of parents in education have been brought forward to a new phase in their development. They are intended to promote greater interest by parents in their children's education and hold schools more accountable for the education they provide.

In his Foreword, Jeremy Hanley, Conservative parliamentary under secretary of state for education in Northern Ireland at that time, describes the Charter as a document to be used by parents as "... a key to a fulfilling and constructive participation" in the education of their children.

The Charter points out to parents that they are entitled to receive information about their child's education, in the following areas: performance at school and how it is assessed; the educational performance of all schools and how this is assessed; the types of schools in an area and how educational services are organised therein.

The Charter also explains how parents can exercise their rights in relation to naming the school they would like their child to attend; how they might institute an appeal against decisions made about their child's education with which they do not agree, and influence or play a part in decisions affecting their child's education. The Charter is a significant landmark in the provision of parents' rights in education. It has created many implications for schools in terms of how they market themselves and how they publicise and clarify their entry and assessment procedures.

FOREWORD

... The Parents' Charter draws together in one document the most important information about both the existing and new rights and responsibilities of parents, to help them play an even more active role in supporting and shaping the work of schools. In commending this Charter to all parents, I hope that they will use it as a key to a fulfilling and constructive participation in an education service which links us all, and which can yield enormous benefit for their children and for the whole society of Northern Ireland.

****

CHOOSING A SCHOOL

The School's Admissions Criteria
The education and library board will give you a copy of a school's admissions criteria. These will show how the Board of Governors of that school decides which pupils to admit when the school has more applicants than places. For example, some primary and secondary schools may wish to give preference to those children who live near to the school, or to those who have a brother or sister already at the school. Only grammar schools may use academic ability as an admission criterion. The school's admissions criteria should

give you a better idea as to whether your child has a good chance of being admitted to the school of your choice.

Appeals Procedure

You will be informed by the education and library board of the school to which your child will be admitted. If you think that the admissions criteria were not correctly applied, you may appeal against the decision to an *independent* appeal tribunal arranged by, but not under the control of, the board. If you wish to make an appeal you should contact the Transfer Officer of the education and library board for your area.

... in particular you will be entitled to:—

* an annual report about your child's performance;

* an annual report about your child's school from the Board of Governors;

* a summary prepared by the Department of Education of the findings of any general inspection of your child's school;

* a prospectus about each individual school and college of further education;

* information on the performance of all schools, and

* a publication by each education and library board about the education in its area. Boards also publish booklets about the arrangements for admission of pupils to schools, and the arrangements for the provision of special education.

****

THE CURRICULUM :
WHAT YOUR CHILD WILL LEARN AT SCHOOL

As a parent, you have a right to know about the education which your child is entitled by law to receive at school. The Department of Education intends to publish a guide to the Northern Ireland Curriculum, including the assessment arrangements, by the end of this year.

****

Religious Education
All schools, except nursery and special schools, must provide religious education for all pupils as part of the curriculum, and must also give them the opportunity to take part in daily collective worship ...

EDUCATION FOR CHILDREN WITH SPECIAL NEEDS

****

The Board's Action
The board may then wish to carry out a formal assessment of your child's difficulties. This means that your child may have to be assessed by an educational psychologist or, if his or her learning difficulty may be physical in origin, by a doctor ...

The Statement
The statement will set out your child's special educational needs and the special educational provision the board proposes to make ...

HOW YOUR CHILD'S PERFORMANCE WILL BE ASSESSED

The performance of pupils will be continuously monitored by teachers. In addition, pupils will be formally assessed against specified attainment targets during year 4 (P4) and year 7 (P7) in primary school, and during year 10 (form 3) and year 12 (form 5) in secondary schools, including grammar schools. Pupils in special schools will also be assessed at the same stages except where their statement of needs ... indicates otherwise ...

AN ANNUAL REPORT
ON YOUR CHILD'S PERFORMANCE

From the 1991/92 school year you will receive an annual report on your child's progress. This report will tell you:—

* the teacher's assessment of what your child has achieved during the school year in English, Mathematics and Science;

* how your child is progressing in other subjects and school activities;

* your child's results in any assessment and public examination which he or she has undertaken during the year;

* how the principal or class teacher sees your child's general progress;

* his or her attendance record, and

* the name of a contact in the school with whom you can make arrangements to discuss the report with a teacher.

****

Timing
From the beginning of the 1992/93 school year schools will be inspected more frequently. Every school will have one major inspection every five years.

II

ELEMENTARY/PRIMARY EDUCATION

II.1 Public Education in Northern Ireland, Ministry of Education 1923.

In June 1921 the Ministry of Education became responsible for the administration of approximately two thousand national schools and their attendant problems. National schools were re-designated 'public elementary' in 1923 and in 1947 this description in turn was changed officially to 'primary.' The Ministry inherited some long-standing difficulties.

A system which operated effectively for ninety years in the highly charged atmosphere of Irish politics of the time clearly had its merits, but by 1921 reconstruction was long overdue. The unchecked growth of denominational schools had resulted in much overlapping and duplication in the field of primary education. The relative poverty of the country meant that many schools were provided as cheaply as possible and were badly designed and poorly equipped. The system often produced a hybrid type of building which had to serve as both school and church hall and was not well adapted to the purposes of either. Once a school had been erected it was difficult to secure its replacement, extension or repair; there were, in 1921, many obsolete buildings in use for the replacement or modernisation of which there was locally neither the urge nor the means.

**II.2 Report of the Ministry of Education for the Year
         1922-1923 Cmd.16.**

Education was transferred to the Ministry of Education against a
background of civil and political upheaval which added greatly to
the difficulty of inaugurating the new service.

4.   Pending the introduction of the necessary reforms the
Ministry devoted its energies to the task of providing for the
efficient working of the schools transferred to its
administration. The sudden change of government in Dublin,
which took place immediately prior to the date of transfer,
when the Provisional Government of the Irish Free State
came into existence, gave rise at first to many difficulties.
There was for some months a period during which the
Ministry found it impossible to secure the full cooperation of
the new authorities in Southern Ireland in giving effect to the
transfer of services. In a few cases the members of the
administrative staff were not readily released from their
duties in Dublin and sanction to transfer themselves to the
North was withheld. Avoidable delay also occurred in the
transfer of necessary files and documents. These and other
administrative difficulties, however, passed away and it is not
now necessary to dwell on the subject.

5.   The political unrest of the first six months of the year
1922 was reflected in the field of public education by the
enforced closing of certain elementary schools in the
disturbed areas for periods coincident with the local outbreak
of social disorder. Attacks were threatened against the
scholars and damage was done to school premises. In May,
1922, the Model Schools in Belfast, the property of the
Ministry, were totally destroyed by fire, but it is satisfactory
to record that, thanks to the kindness of the Belfast Technical
Committee, these schools were carried out with little

interruption in the College of Technology until the close of
the school year, when a new site was produced by the
Ministry. Here the work has been continued in temporary
premises, pending the erection of permanent school
buildings. Attendances generally suffered in the disturbed
areas where the schools were not closed, and the Ministry
looks for great improvement with the establishment of settled
conditions.

****

8.   Although the Ministry found a general willingness on
the part of the managers and teaching staffs of the schools to
fall in with the new arrangements, a considerable number
proved reluctant to submit to the authority of the new
Government.   The schools involved, to the number of some
270, represented about one-third of the elementary schools
under Roman Catholic management.   For some months these
managers and teachers refused to accept salaries from the
Ministry and to recognise its jurisdiction by admitting its
inspectors and complying with its regulations.   This state of
things continued until the end of October, 1922, when the
resistance ceased and the managers and teachers concerned
sought a renewal of the recognition of their schools from the
Ministry and offered to comply with its conditions for the
payment of grants.   After some negotiation the Ministry
agreed to restore recognition to the schools on receiving a
signed declaration from the managers and their teaching
staffs that they would, for the future, carry out the rules and
regulations of the Ministry.   No payments have been made in
respect of the period during which recognition was
withdrawn from the schools, but it was exceptionally
conceded to the teachers that they should not suffer any
disability in pension rights or increments of salary in
consequence of what had occurred.   Since the above date the

relations with the schools have been harmonious, and the Ministry gladly records that the undertakings given have been honourably observed.

II.3 Interim Report of the Departmental Committee on the Educational Services in Northern Ireland, Ministry of Education 1922, Cmd.6.

In September 1921, the Minister of Education, Lord Londonderry, instituted a Departmental Committee of Enquiry under the Chairmanship of Mr. R.J. Lynn, the Member of Parliament for the constituency of West Belfast. The Committee was requested to examine the existing organisation and administration of the services and to recommend any measures "considered necessary for the proper coordination and effective carrying out of these services." Those matters which were felt to require legislative authority were considered first and the findings and recommendations of the enquiry were presented in an Interim Report in June, 1922.   One difficulty faced by the enquiry was the refusal of Roman Catholic interests to either serve on the Committee or to provide evidence.

RELIGIOUS EDUCATION

136.   The original object of the system of National Education should be maintained. This object was "to afford combined literary and moral, and separate religious instruction, to children of all persuasions, as far as possible, in the same school, upon the fundamental principle that no attempt shall be made to interfere with the peculiar religious tenets of any description of Christian pupils."

137.   Strict care should be taken that the existing rules and regulations of the Commissioners of National Education with reference to religious instruction, except in so far as modified below, should be continued.

138.   In schools of Class I. such religious instruction as is approved by the parents or guardians of the children should be given for a period of, as a rule, at least half-an-hour in each school day, or its equivalent within each week.

139.   The Churches should prescribe the programme of religious instruction for their own children either separately or in agreement amongst themselves. It is hoped that a common Scripture programme will be agreed upon for the religious instruction of children belonging to all Protestant denominations.

140.   While it is expected that teachers will give religious instruction in schools of Class I., it should not be obligatory upon them to teach any part of the prescribed programme which requires catechetical or other instruction in the denominational tenets of any denomination, but a teacher may voluntarily give such instruction, if he has the approval of the authorities of the Church, and of the parents to whose children the instruction is given.

141.   The right of entry of the clergy or others, to whom the parents or guardians of the children do not object, to give Scriptural and denominational instruction at fixed and stated hours, with facilities for examination and inspection at other times, should be given in all schools of Classes I. and II. The persons entitled to right of entry to a school or group of schools should be those appointed thereto by the authorities of the Churches.

COMPULSORY ATTENDANCE

145.   We feel, therefore, that we are acting in accordance with the spirit of the times in recommending that the law relating to compulsory school attendance be made universal

in its application; that its procedure be greatly accelerated; and that the penalties attached to its non-observance be made so severe that it will no longer be profitable to treat it with contempt.

146.   Too much latitude has hitherto been allowed in regard to excuses for non-attendance, and it has been too easy for employers of child labour to offend against the spirit of the law while complying with the letter.

147.   We believe that the adoption of our recommendations will remedy these and other defects in the existing law.

148.   These recommendations are as follows:-

1.   Compulsory attendance should be enforced generally, and not restricted as at present to those places where the local authorities desire to adopt it.

2.   A Local Committee for Primary Education should have all the powers and duties of a local authority and of a school attendance committee under the Irish Education Act of 1892, and the powers and duties of every existing school attendance committee should be transferred to the Local Committee.

3.   The age limits for compulsory school attendance should be six and fourteen years.

AMALGAMATION OF SCHOOLS

164.   The problem of the distribution of primary schools in Northern Ireland is a two-fold one. There are areas, generally, though not exclusively rural, where there has been, owing chiefly to a spirit of denominationalism, an unnecessary

multiplication of small schools. This superfluity has to some extent been accentuated by a decline in the rural population. On the other hand, there are areas, notably the City of Belfast, where there is an alarming insufficiency of school accommodation. We have referred to the latter part of the problem in another chapter entitled "School Buildings." So far as those areas are concerned in which there are too many schools, we are strongly of the opinion that the Ministry should pursue a policy of amalgamation. These small schools have never been justifiable on educational or economic grounds. It became apparent during the course of our inquiry that there is a marked tendency towards unity among the Protestant denominations on the subject of religious instruction. In these circumstances, and having regard to the modification of the managerial system which will result from the introduction of local administration of education, we feel sure that the amalgamation of small schools, where the Ministry is satisfied that it is desirable in the interests of economy and efficiency, will be facilitated rather than resisted.

165.   Whilst we deplore the fact that children of all denominations have not been educated together in the same schools, and believe that this separation of the pupils has been productive of great injury to the community, we think that under existing conditions no attempt to amalgamate schools under Roman Catholic and Protestant management would meet with any measure of success.

166.   We recommend that it should be in the power of the Ministry to amalgamate primary schools where it is considered necessary, regard being had in all cases to the respective needs of the Roman Catholic and Protestant communities.

167.   In all cases of amalgamation the rights of the teachers affected should be carefully preserved, and as far as possible all hardship avoided.   Redundant teachers should be provided with employment elsewhere, and where the transfer has not been at the teacher's own instance, his removal expenses should be paid.

II.4 Final Report of the Departmental Committee on the Educational Services in Northern Ireland, Ministry of Education 1923, Cmd.15.

Three areas of the report are worthy of note.   The first deals with the proposal, by then practiced widely in England and Wales, that secondary education should be a pre-requisite for entry into first level teacher training. The second centres on the recommendation that there should be a two-tier examination system with one tier providing access to secondary schooling at the age of '11+' — a notion that was to be more fully exploited after the 1947 Education Act.   The third illustration is significant as it would appear to lend support to the belief that not every facet of the inherited system required major revision.

PRELIMINARY TRAINING OF TEACHERS

22.   We have ... been impressed with the truth of a complaint that is often made, viz., that candidates for admission to training colleges are in many cases deficient in general education to such an extent that a disproportionate amount of their time in training has necessarily to be spent in studying the ordinary school subjects instead of being given to that professional instruction which properly constitutes the work of a teachers' training college. This want of knowledge is felt all the more if the candidate desires to enter upon University studies.

23.   We determined, then, to suggest, that these defects in the existing system be remedied by the reduction of the period to be spent in actual teaching, and by making it necessary that apprentices to the teaching profession should secure during their course a good education of a secondary type. The distinction which has hitherto existed between monitors recruited entirely from amongst the pupils in National schools, and pupil teachers appointed on passing an Intermediate examination appears to us to be unsound and invidious. We think, therefore, that the term "monitor" should disappear, and that there should be two classes of pupil teacher — junior and senior — differing in manner of recruitment and in period of apprenticeship, but subject to the same requirements as regards secondary education and the practice of teaching.

24.   Our recommendations on the preliminary training of teachers of primary schools are as follows:-

(1)   Senior pupil teachers should be recruited from students who decide early to follow the profession of teacher in primary schools, and it should be laid down that such students should be required in the first instance, as a test of qualification, to pass the (junior) examination proposed to be set up in the new secondary school system.   Successful candidates should then spend two years at a secondary school. During both of these years they should be required to spend a certain limited time each week teaching in a primary school, viz., one school day or two half days per week.   At the end of the two years' course in a secondary school the students should be required to pass the "Leaving" (senior) examination of the secondary school, with special tests in certain subjects; they should also possess aptitude and temperament suitable to the teaching profession.

EXAMINATIONS

149.   Our recommendations as to primary school examinations are as follows:-

There should be an examination approximate to that of the fifth standard in primary schools consisting of English, Arithmetic, Elementary Geography and Drawing. This examination should be open to children from eleven to twelve years of age who desire to attend secondary schools.   It should be regarded as indicating the minimum standard of attainment for the admission of pupils of this age to secondary schools. This examination should be held annually by the Ministry, assisted by representatives of the teachers of secondary, preparatory and primary schools.   Scholarships should be given in connection with this examination, but for that purpose the examination should not be the sole test; there should be in addition a report from the principal teacher of the school that the pupil is one of promise likely to profit from a secondary education.

It will be necessary, at least for some time to come, to provide for the entrance to secondary schools of children who remain at primary schools beyond the age of thirteen years. At this stage also scholarships should be given, but to a more limited extent, as it is desirable to attract children at the earlier age.

The latter scholarships should be given on the results of the "Leaving" examination in the primary schools suitable for children over thirteen and up to fourteen years of age: this examination should be based on the work of the seventh standard and should be on the lines of the Higher Grade Certificate examination.   The subjects of the "Leaving" examination should be:-

Compulsory subjects —
Reading; Writing; Composition and Grammar; Arithmetic; Geography; Drawing.

Optional subjects —
Algebra; Geometry; Latin; French; or such other subjects as may be approved by the Ministry.

****

150. We have recommended that there should be two distinct stages at which pupils should leave the primary school, one at eleven to twelve years of age, when there should be a qualifying examination for admission to secondary schools, and the other at thirteen to fourteen years of age, when a "Leaving" examination should be held. This "Leaving" examination should serve as a qualifying examination for admission to day and evening technical schools and (with the addition of a foreign language) for admission to secondary schools. It is proposed that the "Leaving" examination should be compulsory in the case of pupils of thirteen to fourteen years of age seeking admission to secondary and technical schools, but there will be no obligation that a child leaving school at the age of fourteen, when the law of compulsory attendance will no longer apply to him, should continue his education in any manner whatever.

CURRICULA

168.   As the Ministry of Education for Northern Ireland is following as nearly as possible the programme laid down by the Commission of National Education, and as this programme is generally suitable, it did not seem necessary for us, in approaching the subject of curricula, to propose any fundamental departure from the present system. We

recognised that it would be sufficient for us to suggest what modifications, if any, were required, and what improvements we thought the Ministry should introduce.

169.   Two considerations were prominently before our minds, — first, that English and Arithmetic should form the basis of education in primary schools, and secondly, that however urgent might be the claims advanced by people who advocate the instruction of children in special subjects, there should be no overloading of curricula.

170.   We set ourselves to prepare a syllabus of the subjects which we thought should be taught in the various standards, adding in each case a number of optional subjects.   The following table does not differ materially from the school programme of the National Board; it is in fact rather an extension of it, as we have considered it advisable to recommend the introduction of Grammar as an optional subject in third standard, and that more attention be given to Domestic Economy, Woodwork, Horticulture, Kindness to Animals and Civics and Elementary Economics.

Obligatory Subjects	Optional Subjects
STANDARDS I & II Reading; Writing; Composition; Spelling; Object Lessons (including "Talks on Temperance"); Arithmetic; Singing; Physical Training; Drawing.	Educational Handwork; Needlework;
STANDARD III Reading; Writing; Spelling & Composition; Arithmetic; Geography; Drawing; Singing; Needlework (Girls); Physical Training; Temperance.	Grammar; History; Nature Study. At least one optional subject to be taken.
STANDARD IV As above; Grammar; Temperance.	History; Nature study. At least one optional subject to be taken.
STANDARD V AND HIGHER STANDARDS English — oral and written; Geography; Arithmetic; Singing; Hygiene, including Temperance; Physical Training; Needlework (girls); Domestic Economy (girls); Drawing, (schools with staff of three or more teachers).	History; Drawing, (schools with less than three teachers); Elementary Physical Science Nature or (Sic) Study; Algebra; Geometry and Mensuration; French; Latin; Irish.

In these standards at least one optional subject should be taken in every school with three or more teachers

**II.5 Education Act (Northern Ireland) 1923,
      13 & 14 Geo. 5, C.21.**

The general principles articulated in the 1922 Interim Lynn Report formed the essential framework of the Bill introduced into the Northern Ireland House of Commons by the Marquess of Londonderry, on 14 March, 1923.

Having passed through the Parliamentary process, the Bill received the Royal Assent on 22nd June, 1923 and became operative on 1st October of the same year.   This latter date, therefore, marks the final stage in the transfer of the education services, as since its inception the Ministry of Education had merely acted in succession to the former Dublin based central agencies.

During his introductory speech, Lord Londonderry noted that he had "certainly included in the Bill many proposals of a far-reaching character." In retrospect this comment may be regarded more as a prophecy than a mere observation, as many of the fundamental features of the current educational system of Northern Ireland were incorporated within the 1923 Act.

"ELEMENTARY" DEFINED

7.   For the purposes of this Act, the expression "elementary education" means an education, both literary and moral, based upon instruction in the reading and writing of the English language and in arithmetic, provided for pupils who are in general of an age below fourteen years, and the expression "public elementary school" means a school or department of a school in respect of which grants are paid out of moneys provided by Parliament, and in which elementary education is the principal part of the education provided.

SCHOOL CLOSURES

9.   If at any time it is determined by the Ministry that the continuance of a provided school or a public elementary

school transferred to an education authority is not necessary, no grants out of moneys provided by Parliament shall be payable by the Ministry to, or in respect of, such school, and steps shall be taken by the education authority for discontinuing any such school within such time as the Ministry may direct and for providing for the education of the children in attendance thereat by such other means as may be approved by the Ministry:

Provided always that, in the case of a school transferred to the education authority, the terms and conditions on which the transfer has been effected shall be duly complied with.

RELIGIOUS EDUCATION

26.   It shall be the duty of the education authority to afford opportunities for a catechetical instruction according to the tenets of the religious denomination of the parents of children attending any public elementary school, being a provided or transferred school, and for other religious instruction to which those parents do not object (in this Act referred as to "religious instruction"); and those clergymen or other persons (including teachers at the school) to whom those parents do not object shall have access to the children in the school for the purpose of giving them there religious instruction, or of inspecting and examining the religious instruction there given, at times to be arranged in accordance with regulations of the Ministry: Provided that the education authority shall not provide religious instruction in any such public elementary school as aforesaid.

27.   The managers or school committee, as the case may require, shall, as respects a public elementary school which is a voluntary school, determine whether any, and, if so, what religious instruction shall be given in the school and the persons by whom such instruction shall be given:

Provided that any such determination shall, as respects any such school to which Rule 25 or Rule 26 of the Rules and Regulations of the Commissioners of National Education in Ireland applied immediately before the first day of February, nineteen hundred and twenty-two, be in conformity with such Rule, or with any regulation which may be made in that behalf by the Ministry under this Part of this Act.

COMPULSORY ATTENDANCE

30. — (1) The parent of every child between the ages of six and fourteen or, if a by-law made by the education authority and confirmed in accordance with this Act so prescribes, between the ages of five and fourteen, shall cause the child to attend school during such number of days in the year, and for such time on each day of attendance, as are prescribed by regulations made by the Ministry, except in so far as —

(a)   The child being not less than twelve years of age has been exempted from school attendance by the education authority under the provisions of the Part of this Act relating to the employment of children and young persons; or

(b)   there is a reasonable excuse for the non-attendance of the child.

(2)   Any of the following reasons shall be a reasonable excuse for the purposes of this section and the by-laws made thereunder, namely:-

(a)   that the child has been prevented from attending school by sickness or any unavoidable cause;

(b)   that the child is receiving efficient elementary education in some other manner;

(c)   that there is not in the case of a child under ten years of age within two miles, or in the case of a child over that age within three miles, measured according to the nearest road or public path, any public elementary school or other school recognised by the Ministry as efficient at which the child can attend:

Provided that where the education authority provide suitable means of conveyance for a child between a reasonable distance of its home and a public elementary or other efficient school, it shall not be an excuse within the meaning of this section that there is no such school within the distances hereinbefore mentioned.

II.6(a)   Education Amendment Act 1925 (N.I.), 15 Geo.5, C.1.

During the Lynn deliberations and throughout the subsequent Parliamentary debates it had been anticipated that a local authority system would be accepted readily by Protestant school managers who would willingly transfer their former national schools to the statutory local authorities. However, while some Protestant communities took this course of action, the majority, like their Roman Catholic counterparts, continued to operate their elementary schools as voluntary units.

Essentially the Protestant agitation to amend the 1923 Act centred on three issues. In the first instance they believed that the Act, particularly Section 26, did not protect in the provided and transferred schools the teaching of their accepted interpretation of what constituted moral and religious instruction. Within this general objection they criticised not only the nature of the instruction but also its place within the overall curriculum and the apparent constraints placed on teachers, as local authority employees, on the provision of instruction. Secondly they resented the absence of church influence on teaching appointments within the individual school management structure. Finally, they took exception to the fact that former managers or their representatives had no statutory right to membership of county borough or regional local authority committees.

The Government compromised, introducing an amending statute and when this failed to satisfy the Protestant churches urged the Ministry of Education to reach a concordat with them. These measures together with the 1930 Education Act enabled the transfer of significant numbers of Protestant voluntary schools to the local authorities, although, even in 1947, several hundred Protestant managers still retained full local jurisdiction over their individual elementary schools.

An Act to amend the Education Act (Northern Ireland), 1923, for the purpose of removing doubts as to the provisions of the said Act with respect to voluntary religious instruction in provided transferred schools.

Be it enacted by the King's most Excellent Majesty, and the Senate and the House of Commons of Northern Ireland in this present Parliament assembled, and by the authority of the same, as follows:-

1.   (1)   Sub-section (3) of section three of the Education Act (Northern Ireland), 1923 (in this Act referred to as "the principal Act") shall have effect as if there were inserted therein after paragraph (f) the following new paragraph:-

(ff)   the appointment of teachers by the education authority;

(2)   The proviso to section twenty-six of the principal Act, and the words in sub-section (3) of section sixty-six of the principal Act following the word "Act" in that sub-section to the end of the sub-section, are hereby repealed.

2. This Act may be cited as the Education Act (Northern
    Ireland), 1925, and the principal Act and this Act may
    be cited together as the Education Acts (Northern
    Ireland), 1923 and 1925.

**II.6(b) Report of the Ministry of Education for the Year
1925-26, Government of Northern Ireland (HC No.107).**

In June 1925, the Minister was able to establish a concordat
which had the approval of all parties to the dispute. The
terms of the agreement were embodied in a letter addressed
to all local education authorities by the Secretary to the
Ministry, on July 4th, 1925, as follows:-

"I am directed by the Minister of Education to state that the
question of religious instruction in provided and transferred
schools has been under consideration by the Ministry, in
conjunction with representatives of the Churches and the
teachers in public elementary schools."

"The Ministry is advised that, notwithstanding the
amendment of Section 26 of the Education Act of 1923 by
the Education Act this year, it is not open to education
authorities to provide and pay for religious instruction, as
defined in Section 26 of the Act of 1923.   While the
education authorities are bound by that section of the Act to
afford opportunities for catechetical instruction according to
the tenets of the religious denominations, the Minister is
advised that an education authority may, if they so desire,
adopt a programme of simple Bible instruction, to be given
by the teachers in any or all of the provided and transferred
schools under their management, in the period set apart in the
Time Table of the school for the purpose of religious
instruction, under Regulation 16 of the Ministry's Regulations

in regard to Religious Instruction in Public Elementary Schools, provided that such programme shall not include instruction according to the tenets distinctive of any religious denomination."

"If any such programme of Bible instruction is adopted for any school or schools, it shall be regarded as part of the ordinary course of instruction in the school, although not within the hours of compulsory school attendance; and it shall be the duty of the teachers, if so required by the education authority, to give such instruction."

"Attention is drawn, in this connection, to the following important considerations:-

(1)   Any arrangement for undenominational religious instruction of the kind referred to does not restrict in any way the freedom of the teacher to give denominational instruction as provided in Section 26 of the Act.

(2)   Such arrangement imposes no obligation on the teacher to give denominational instruction.

(3)   Provided a teacher can show that he has given instruction, in a bona-fide manner, in accordance with the programme of Bible instruction adopted by the education authority, he shall not be liable to dismissal on grounds connected with the efficiency of his work in giving such instruction.

(4)   No pupil shall be under any obligation to attend school while the instruction so arranged is proceeding."

II.7 Report of the Departmental Committee of Enquiry on the Programme of Instruction in Public Elementary Schools 1931, Cmd.136.

It has already been suggested in Section II.4 above that the overall syllabus recommended for elementary schools in Northern Ireland resembled closely the areas of study that had been followed in the former national schools. From an examination of the guidance documents published at regular intervals by the Ministry of Education it is also apparent that most changes that were introduced were only in matters of detail. Thus, for example, Needlework was classed as an optional subject in the Final Lynn Report but in the 1924 syllabus it was in the obligatory category for girls; again in the 1927 list of subjects, a practical area became obligatory in all classes instead of being, as hitherto, regarded as optional. The overall approach to the implementation of the curriculum also tended to remain fairly formal and unvarying and two illustrations will suffice to justify this claim. In the first instance the grouping of children into 'standards' which had been introduced as a mode of classification to meet the attainment levels of the nineteenth century remained in operation throughout the period under examination and indeed up to the mid-1950s! Secondly, the fact that each Ministry guideline was entitled *Programme of Instruction for Public Elementary Schools* is indicative of a teacher and subject centred curricular attitude.

From time to time, however, there were indications of more enlightened approaches to the elementary curriculum and two of these are evident in the 1931 Report of the Departmental Committee of Inquiry on the Programme of Instruction in Public Elementary Schools (the Robb Report, — Mr. J.H. Robb was later to become Minister for Education).

CURRICULAR RELAXATION

10. — 11. We now proceed to consider the general question of a standard programme for schools. A point which has been raised in evidence in relation to the inspection system is that through fear of a lowering in rating a teacher is loth to depart from the rigid lines of the Programme and follow his

own initiative and that, as a result, his individuality is stifled to the detriment of his pupils and of their general proficiency. If this is true to any considerable extent it is a very serious matter. The real value gained from education depends largely on the personality of the teacher, and while a public system cannot be left entirely to individual inclinations, the importance of freedom within limits is well recognised. Indeed, there is even opened up the whole question whether the continuance of an official programme is advisable. In England the Board of Education, as the central authority, prescribes no standard syllabus and only publishes a general handbook of suggestions for the guidance of teachers; the head teachers are permitted to frame their own programme in accordance with generally understood principles. We are not certain, however, that this is found to be an entirely satisfactory solution, and in any case it does not follow that it would be the right course to pursue in the comparatively small area of Northern Ireland with its centralised system, so far as the oversight of the curriculum is concerned. We recommend that a standard programme should remain but that every encouragement should be given to principals of schools to submit for approval such modifications as they may consider desirable, either in the direction of omitting subjects or by curtailing the extent of the present courses, having regard to local conditions and their own considered opinions. This course is already open to them and they are invited to do so, but we understand that, for various reasons, very few avail themselves of the invitation. If it is through fear of what might happen to their rating, we trust that such fears can and will be removed. We suggest that inspectors should encourage the more progressive principals to lead the way in this respect. We would even go further and recommend that the inspector should be directed to confer with principal teachers as to the best programme for their schools, and that they should assist those who may be more nervous or unambitious to study their own local conditions and environment and to frame such modifications in the curriculum as are suitable. If this is carefully supervised, we have no fear that the trust will be abused.

SENIOR SCHOOLS

12. — 13. Another type of school calling for special notice is that known as the "senior" school, a classification which has recently been introduced into Northern Ireland with the practice which is being generally adopted in Great Britain as a result of the recommendations made by the Consultative Committee of the Board of Education and issued a few years ago under the title of "The Education of the Adolescent." Their Report recommended the re-organisation of what is commonly regarded as elementary education into two separate periods, the first being that up to the age of about 11 years, followed by a second stage with an age-range of from 11 to 15 years.   It is contemplated under the scheme that there should be a distinct "break" and, where possible, an actual transfer to a separate school, after reaching the age of 11 years, and that the subsequent courses should approximate to a form of secondary education.

In Belfast it has been experimentally arranged that some of the newly erected buildings should be organised as "senior" schools. We do not propose to discuss this important innovation except in regard to the curriculum, which naturally falls within our present enquiry. We are of opinion that, at this stage, it would be premature to indicate any hard and fast lines on which the programme for these schools should be framed. The principal teachers may be expected to be among the leaders in their profession and should be fully competent to draw up tentative courses for the present which would be based on the generally understood requirement of children at that stage of educational development, and they should receive every encouragement to do so.

****

19.   We have been naturally concerned in this enquiry with the curriculum which should be taught, and we realise that it is an important factor in determining the educational standards of the future generation in the province.   The importance of the official syllabus in the work of education can, however, be easily over-estimated.   It is, after all, only a guide to the competent teacher and inspector, and should be regarded as a servant rather than as a master; it can only supplement a broad and intelligent outlook on educational problems, and no amount of attention to the printed details can compensate for a lack of skill and personality on the part of those who give and those who test the instruction.

II.8 Public Elementary Schools Regulations 1934, S.R.& O., 1934 No.40.

Following the publication of the 1904 Dale Report on the state of primary education in Ireland, the Board of Commissioners for National Education embarked on an active policy of rationalisation to reduce the multiplicity of small educational units.   Despite this programme, the distribution of national schools transferred to the Northern Ireland Ministry of Education still bore the characteristics of the plurality much in evidence in the corresponding area at the turn of the century.   Thus while school accommodation in Belfast was grossly insufficient, the educational supply in all other districts was far in excess of the needs of the child population.   The determination of the Ministry to re-activate and pursue an amalgamation policy may be ascertained from the comments included in all annual reports published between 1923 and 1939. As a result of the consistent consolidation policy adopted by the Ministry, and later reinforced by the local education authorities, the total number of one, two and three-teacher elementary schools dropped by 19.5 per cent from 1,755 to 1,413 between December, 1924 and December 1938.   Within the regional committee areas the number decreased by 16.5 per cent from 1,655 to 1,382.

AMALGAMATION REGULATIONS

13.   Grants to separate schools for boys and girls or for infants and senior pupils may be withdrawn if, in the opinion of the Ministry, these schools can be more efficiently or more economically conducted as one establishment: provided always that where the average daily attendance of pupils at one of the schools for the preceding calendar year has been less than 50, amalgamation shall take place on the occurrence of a vacancy in the staff of either school unless for special reasons it shall be otherwise directed by the Ministry.

14.   — (a) Where the Ministry is satisfied that two or more neighbouring schools can be amalgamated with advantage for reasons of educational efficiency or economy it may give notice that after such date as the Ministry may determine no new appointment of a teacher may be made except in a temporary capacity until the question of the need for separate schools has been decided by the Ministry.

(b) No new teacher shall be recognised, except in a temporary capacity, in any school with an average daily attendance of under 50 pupils and within three miles distance of one or more other schools until a re-arrangement of the schools in the district has been considered and until the Ministry has given a decision thereon.

(c) The Ministry reserves the right to withdraw grants from any school in which the average daily attendance of pupils is less than 20.

15.   Before withdrawing grants from a school under Articles 13 and 14 hereof the Ministry shall consult with the managers of the schools affected and with the education authority.

16.   Where schools are amalgamated and the principal of any such school is retained as a privileged assistant in the amalgamated school such privileged assistant may continue to be recognised irrespective of the average attendance of pupils, and may receive (apart from any capitation grant to which he may be entitled under Part VI of these Regulations) such salary (inclusive of increments and additional emoluments for special qualifications) as in the opinion of the Ministry he would have received had he remained principal of the separate school.

17.   When two or more schools are amalgamated, re-organised or superseded in whole or in part by a new school the conditions of recognition of the staff of teachers appointed on re-organisation of the school provision shall be determined by the Ministry, full consideration being given to the reasonable claims of the existing teachers.   Should there be redundant teachers the Ministry shall prescribe the terms and limitation of recognition.

II.9 Report of the Ministry of Education 1945-46 Government of Northern Ireland (HC 783).

Throughout the 1930s elementary education in Northern Ireland suffered from the dual effects of economic depression and a falling birth rate.   As a result teachers' salaries were reduced, many teachers were declared redundant and initial teacher training and building programmes were curtailed.   The net effects of these and other difficulties led to the postponement of some of the provisions of the 1938 Education Act including the raising of the school leaving age to fifteen.

The general situation was understandably aggravated by the outbreak of war in 1939.   During the period of hostilities all aspects of education were affected including the publication of the annual report of the Ministry of Education.   When the publication was resumed in 1946 it contained a comprehensive account of developments in elementary education during the emergency years.

ELEMENTARY EDUCATION — EVACUATION

The Education (Evacuated Children) Act (Northern Ireland), 1939, which was passed in September, provided for the transfer of children from one education area to another in accordance with arrangements made by the Ministry of Home Affairs under the Civil Defence Act (Northern Ireland), 1939. It became the duty of the education authority in the reception area to make suitable provision for the elementary education of evacuated children and, under the Act, the authority had in relation to such children, the same powers and duties as for children normally resident in the area, except the duties in respect of higher education. The Act provided for the assignment of teachers from evacuating to receiving schools and safeguarded the position of a teacher while so assigned. Further, any additional expenditure properly incurred by a receiving authority or manager on account of evacuated children was recoverable from the local education authority of the evacuating area, which in its turn could receive a grant in respect of this expenditure from the Ministry.

****

The Act of 1939 was further amended in some respects by the Education (Emergency Provisions) Act (Northern Ireland), 1942. The Public Elementary Schools (Evacuated Children) Regulations made on 5th February, 1940, and amended from time to time by subsequent regulations, implemented these Acts. In particular they provided for the suspension of the ordinary regulations prescribing the average attendances required for appointment and the continuance of grants in the case of assigned teachers: also, they safeguarded the emoluments of assigned principal teachers in certain respects. "Double shifts" were permitted in receiving schools and some relaxation of the ordinary regulations relating to the length of the school day, etc., was allowed.

Arrangements were also made for the billeting of teachers or for the payment of Billeting Allowances to teachers on assignment and for the payment of certain other allowances.

The first official evacuation of school children took place from Belfast on the 7th and 8th July, 1940, and was followed by a further exodus on the 29th August, 1940; altogether on these occasions about 7,000 children left the city and there was no difficulty providing for their education in the reception areas. The main evacuation occurred during and after the air-raids on Belfast in April and May, 1941, when upwards of 30,000 children descended upon the rural areas. Some evacuation took place from Londonderry about the same time and later.

In most areas it was possible to arrange for the education of evacuees in the existing schools, though in some cases "double shifts" were necessary, but in a number of districts accommodation had to be supplemented by hired halls and equipment obtained on loan from Belfast.

The Belfast schools re-opened a short time after the raids and carried on as best they could, though, at first, the number of pupils in attendance was very small. However, in spite of strong official advice to the contrary, the children began to return to the city before the summer of 1941 was over and this drift back continued steadily until the end of the war. Thus the total of evacuated children on the rolls of receiving schools on 31st December, 1941, was 17,923. A year later this figure had dropped to 7,351 and the figures for the last days of 1943, 1944 and 1945 were 3,032 and 1,557 and 278 respectively. On the 31st December, 1946, 95 children were still classified as evacuees. A number of families settled permanently in the country. Altogether about 500 teachers were assigned to schools in reception areas, but all these have now returned to Belfast. High tribute must be paid to teachers and others concerned in the success of the evacuation schemes; these arrangements and the educational facilities provided did much to lighten the effects of war on the child population and to ensure that the schooling of the rising generation suffered as little as possible.

WAR SERVICE OF PUBLIC ELEMENTARY SCHOOL TEACHERS

In all 102 men teachers and 27 women teachers joined H.M. Forces during the war; of these 14 men were killed in action. The Public Elementary Schools (Teachers' War Service) Regulations, 1940, made under section 6 of the Teachers' Salaries and Superannuation (War Service) Act, 1939, and subsequent regulations issued from time to time made arrangements for the appointment of substitutes and contained provisions designed to safeguard the positions and the incremental, pension and other rights of teachers absent on war service.

TRAINING OF TEACHERS

At the outbreak of war it was decided to suspend for the duration of hostilities the training of men as elementary school teachers except for those who had already completed a year or more in a Training College, but since a number of trained teachers had undertaken war service, some men were admitted to training in 1940 on the results of the 1939 examinations. Apart from these, the training of men students was discontinued until 1943 when a limited recruitment was admitted: 19 were called to training in 1943 and 24 in 1944. In 1945 a much larger enrolment of men took place in the training colleges: 63 in Stranmillis, 50 in St. Mary's Belfast, and 6 in St. Mary's Strawberry Hill, Middlesex.

The training of women students, though reduced, was not interrupted. Early in 1940 Stranmillis Training College was taken over by the military authorities and the students and staff were transferred to temporary accommodation in Portrush, where the college operated, not without difficulty, until 1945 when it returned to its permanent quarters in Stranmillis.

Towards the end of hostilities, the Ministry, in view of the increased demand for trained teachers, initiated an emergency scheme to attract suitable men and women from the Services into the teaching profession, but this project was not realised until some months after the war had ended, when the Larkfield Training College was opened.

****

PLANTING AND HARVESTING OF CROPS

It has been customary for school children in the rural areas of the Province to help in the planting and harvesting of crops, and normally the vacations of country schools have been arranged to meet the farmers' needs.   In consequence of the increase in the area of land under cultivation during the war, the shortage of labour and the extreme urgency of farming operations, the Ministry urged managers and teachers to do what they could to facilitate farming operations by operating a flexible arrangement for vacations so that holidays might be taken when it was clear that the pupils' help would be immediately needed and by arranging that as many days as possible out of the maximum number allowed by the regulations should be set aside for inclusion in the "farming vacations."

"WAR AVERAGES" AND STAFFING

Because of the decline in school attendance caused by circumstances arising out of the war, the Ministry issued fresh regulations, operative from April 1st, 1941, allowing the calculation of average attendance for any month, quarter or year during the emergency to be based on the percentage of attendance to enrolment for the year 1939. Another concession was the continuance of the extension from two successive quarters to six successive quarters as the period of insufficient average attendance which might elapse before grants for an assistant teacher in a school were withdrawn.

Restricted facilities for training brought about a shortage of trained teachers; there were insufficient qualified substitutes to meet the demands and increasing difficulty was experienced in securing permanent teachers for schools in the more remote districts.   This situation was met, so far as substitutes were concerned, by granting exceptional recognition to persons who, though not trained teachers, possessed reasonable suitable qualifications, and in order to make available a wider selection of qualified women teachers the Ministry in 1943 reintroduced the grade of untrained junior assistant mistress.

WAR DAMAGE ACT

After the passage of the War Damage Act, 1941, the Ministry obtained the authority of the Ministry of Finance to recoup the managers of certain voluntary schools in respect of their contributions under Part I of the Act.

BUILDING AND MAINTENANCE OF SCHOOLS

On the outbreak of war new grants for the erection, etc., of voluntary schools under Section 10 of the Education Act, 1930, were suspended. Works of repair and maintenance were greatly curtailed, and, apart from the provision in some cases of huts as additional accommodation, school building ceased for the duration.

II.10 Educational Reconstruction in Northern Ireland, 1944, Cmd.226.

Within the transferred or devolved services one of the consistent aims of the Government of Northern Ireland was the achievement and maintenance of parity with the remainder of the United Kingdom. In the sphere of education the aim was frequently expressed in relation to England and Wales as, for example, when it was noted that the 1923 Act had brought to Northern Ireland some of the administrative features of the 1902 "Balfour" Act and the 1918 "Fisher" Act. During the war years the pursuit of educational parity was further emphasised by the publication in 1944 of the White Paper for Northern Ireland with the same short title and with similar essential proposals as the 1943 White Paper for England and Wales. The White Paper adopted the mainland principle of a two stage education system with a break at 11+ between the primary and secondary phases.

REORGANISATION : "THE BREAK" AT 11+

33.   In 1926 the Consultative Committee of the Board of Education under the Chairmanship of Sir Henry Hadow presented to the President of the Board a report entitled "The Education of the Adolescent," which is now commonly referred to as the Hadow Report. Its chief recommendation was that the "all-age" elementary schools catering for the great bulk of the children of compulsory school age should

cease to exist and should be replaced by junior or primary schools for those under the age of 11+ and by senior schools for children between 11+ and 14. This recommendation was adopted by the Board of Education and has been the cornerstone of English educational policy for the past 18 years. Many of the local education authorities in England undertook with vigour what became known as Hadow reorganisation and in some areas, principally urban areas, reorganisation of the elementary school accommodation had been completed, or was well on the way to completion by the outbreak of war in 1939. The senior schools, however, although running parallel to the junior forms of secondary schools were still staffed and administered as elementary schools. Under the new English Education Act Hadow reorganisation is now carried to its logical conclusion; primary education will cease at 11+ and full-time education for pupils over 11+, whether they leave school at the new leaving age of 15 or continue in attendance until 17 or 18, will be known as secondary education. The senior elementary schools of today will in the future become secondary schools and be staffed and administered as such.

34.   When the Hadow Report was published in 1926 the possibility of its application to Northern Ireland was naturally considered, but it was decided that the time was not ripe for such a radical reorganisation of the educational system. The local education authorities in England had been established for 24 years and by 1926 approximately half of the elementary schools, containing considerably more than half of the school population, were under their direct control The education authorities of Northern Ireland, on the other hand, had been in existence for less than three years, no new elementary schools had yet been provided by them and very few had been transferred to their control; moreover it was realised at the time that reorganisation would be much more

difficult in country districts than in the large centres of population. The position today is very different from what it was in 1926; the local administration of educational services through the education authorities is well established and 680 of the 1,667 elementary schools are now under their control. But the measure of their responsibility for elementary education is more accurately shown by the number of children in the different categories of elementary schools than by the number of schools; of the 185,542 children on the rolls of these schools on 31st December 1943, no fewer than 93,569 or 50.4 per cent of the total were in attendance at schools provided by, or transferred to the education authorities.

35.   As already indicated, the fundamental change in the new English educational system, namely that full-time education after the age of 11+ should in future be regarded as secondary education, is inherent in the recommendations of the Hadow Report.   It therefore becomes essential to consider whether the public elementary school system of Northern Ireland should be replaced by a system of primary schools for children under 11 years of age and secondary schools for children over that age.   The policy of effecting a break in the child's school life roughly at the age of 11+ has become so much a part of the English educational system that it was possible for the President of the Board of Education to say in the White Paper on which the new Act is based: "The principle of reorganisation is advocated in the Hadow Report, i.e., the provision of separate schools for all children over 11, is accepted as an educational axiom ..."   Apart from its limited application in a modified form by the Belfast Education Committee, which has built several junior and senior schools, the principle is comparatively new in Northern Ireland.   It is, therefore, thought advisable to indicate briefly the reasons which have led the Government of Northern Ireland to propose its adoption.

36.   Most of the elementary schools in the rural areas of Northern Ireland are small schools with not more than 40 to 60 children in attendance; no fewer than 247 are one-teacher schools and 961 have only two teachers. In the one-teacher schools all the pupils ranging in age from 4 to 14 have to be taught by a single teacher, while in the two-teacher schools one teacher is normally responsible for all the children from approximately 9 years of age upwards. Under these conditions it is almost impossible for the needs of the older children to be adequately met. This is particularly true of instruction in practical subjects and physical training, for the small schools cannot be provided individually with woodwork, metalwork and domestic science rooms, playing fields and gymnasium. Nor are many of the teachers qualified to deal with these vitally important aspects of education even if they were free to devote more time to them. In recent years something has been done to bring new life into the senior classes of the country elementary schools by the development of school gardens and the teaching of horticulture, but this in itself is not enough. It must be frankly admitted that the senior classes in the country elementary schools are not providing a really satisfying training at the present time; the academically gifted children are not being extended, and those less gifted academically are not receiving the opportunities for a more practical course which would give a new purpose and a new sense of reality to their education. This should not be interpreted as a reflection on the teachers who are faced with an impossible task, for within the limitations of the present system the great majority are doing good work and some teachers are exceptionally successful. The only solution in the country districts is to make arrangements whereby the older children can be gathered together in central schools serving larger areas. This will make it possible to provide the additional facilities so urgently required.

37.   The problem in the cities, towns and large villages is different; the need for reorganisation cannot be attributed in the main to the size of the schools, although there are still a considerable number of small schools in these centres in which one teacher is responsible for a group of classes covering a wide age range.   Nevertheless, there is an equal need in the cities and towns for a radical change in the elementary school system.   A certain deterioration is perceptible in the senior classes of many schools; there seems to be little sense of purpose in the work that is being done and an increasing lack of interest on the part of many of the pupils is evident.   This may be largely due to the lack of facilities for practical work and the consequent excessive stress on academic subjects in which many of the children have little interest.   Whatever the cause, there is no doubt of the need for a new approach to give life and purpose to the latter years of full-time education.   It is already the practice for some pupils to be transferred at this stage to the secondary schools and it is just as necessary that the remainder who form the bulk of the children at the age group should have a new start and not feel that they are being left behind as fitted only for an "elementary" education.

38.   At the age of 11 or 12 childhood is drawing to a close and adolescence lies ahead; by this time the average child has mastered the essential skills of reading, writing and number, and is equipped and ready to venture into new fields of knowledge and experience; the primary stage of his education has been completed and he is prepared to enter on the secondary stage.   There has, in fact, been a traditional change in the elementary school programme at the beginning of Standard V (which the average child enters at the age of 11), when new subjects such as domestic economy, woodwork and mathematics are introduced into the curriculum.   The term "elementary education" for children

over this age is a misnomer, for the elementary schools now overlap the secondary schools instead of leading up to them.

39.   It is for these reasons that it is proposed to recognise the principle of the break at 11+ and to reorganise the existing elementary school system, providing in its place primary schools for the younger children and secondary schools of different types for those over 11+. Thus in the new system there will be secondary education for all. But transfer from primary to secondary will not take place rigidly at that age irrespective of the individual child's progress through the primary school. Some may have completed the primary school course and be ready for transfer a year earlier; for others who are retarded it may be thought advisable to postpone transfer until after the 12th birthday; the general principle, however, will be for transfer to take place at 11+, i.e. at the end of the school year in which the child attains the age of 11. Some contend that the normal age of transfer should be 12+ but if this were adopted a considerable number of children, before reaching the new school-leaving age of 15, might have less than three full years in the secondary schools, a period too short for satisfactory courses to be planned.

THE PRIMARY SCHOOL

40.   Admissions to the primary schools will be allowed from the age of 4 and this age may be reduced where nursery classes are arranged, although no child will be required to attend school until the age of 5. Attendance at a nursery school may also be permitted over the age of 5, but it may be necessary to lay down a definite upper limit at which children must be transferred to primary schools. The primary school will, therefore, normally cater for children between the age of 4, 5 or 6 and 11+. Smaller classes should lead to a freer

atmosphere and a more natural approach than is often found in the junior classes of elementary schools today. The aim of the schools should be, not only to teach the essential skills — the three "Rs" of former days — but also to train the hand as well as the mind, to encourage grace and freedom of movement and to give full scope for the development of self-reliance and originality. The primary school of the future should be far more than a building in which children receive instruction; it should be a community in which they learn to equip themselves with knowledge and experience suited to their ages and aptitudes; the three "Rs" will still be essential but they need not be dull. In the junior classes of the most successful elementary schools these characteristics are already evident and the fact that they are not more common is due far more to the excessive size of classes than to the failure of the teachers to realise their desirability.

SUMMARY OF PROPOSALS

97.   The main proposals put forward in this Paper may be summarised as follows:

(i)   To reduce the lower limit of compulsory attendance from 6 to 5 but giving education committees power to raise it, with the approval of the Ministry of Education, to 5½ or 6, either in part or the whole of their areas;

(ii)   To raise the school-leaving age to 15 without exemptions and to take power to raise it subsequently to 16;

                    ****

(iv)   To discontinue the present public elementary school system and replace it by a system of primary schools for children up to 11+ and secondary schools of different types for the older children;

(v)   To establish a completely new system of free secondary schools — junior secondary schools — catering for children from 11+ to 15 or 16;

****

(vii) To arrange for a qualifying test, conducted by the Ministry, on which up to 80 per cent of the annual admissions to all senior secondary schools will be based, and to require the education committees to give financial assistance, where needed, to children who qualify for admission on this test, and to make arrangements for transfer at a later stage from one type of secondary school to another;

(viii) To reduce progressively the size of classes, especially in the infant divisions of primary schools;

(ix) To require education committees to supply free books and other school requisites for all primary and junior secondary (including junior technical) schools;

****

(xi) To make religious instruction and a collective act of worship compulsory in all primary and secondary (including junior technical) schools;

(xii) To increase to 65 per cent direct building grants from the Ministry to voluntary primary and junior secondary schools under the management of "four-and-two" committees, and to make education committees responsible for the internal maintenance of such voluntary schools so managed;

****

(xix) To require education committees to provide free medical and dental inspection and treatment for all children attending primary and secondary (including junior technical) schools (with possible alternative arrangements for senior secondary schools) and for young people under 18 in attendance at day technical courses and part-time continued education courses, and to require parents to present their children for inspection;

(xx) To require education committees to provide meals and milk in all primary and junior secondary (including junior technical) schools and in senior secondary schools under their management, and to give further consideration to the provision of meals and milk in voluntary senior secondary schools;

(xxi) To require education committees to make adequate provision for the education of all classes of children requiring special educational treatment;

****

(xxiv) To require the education authority for each county to carry out its duties through one education committee.

II.11(a) Education Bill (Northern Ireland) Explanatory Memorandum by the Minister of Education, 1946, Cmd.242.

An Education Bill based essentially on the White Paper's proposals was presented in the Northern Ireland House of Commons on 27 August, 1946, by Lieut. Colonel Hall-Thompson, the Minister of Education. Following a lengthy and, at times, stormy passage through Parliament, the Bill received the Royal Assent on 27 March, 1947.

When considering the implementation of the 1947 Act to first level education two difficulties are immediately apparent. In the first instance the term 'primary' was envisaged in the White Paper as the initial part of a two-stage process of compulsory education; however, until the new second level schools were provided, many 'junior' pupils who had "attained the age of eleven years and six months" (Sections 5 and 116 of the Act) were destined to pursue both stages of schooling in all-through or un-reorganised primary schools. Indeed in some of the more remote areas of Northern Ireland this transitional arrangement was operational for some two and a half decades. Secondly, unlike the 1923 Londonderry Act, which was centred on an all-age elementary system, many of the provisions in the 1947 Act were dual in that they applied equally to both primary and secondary schools and in the context of first cycle education they contain details that are not strictly relevant.

Although the publication of the Ministerial memorandum preceded the parliamentary deliberations, it remains one of the more straightforward descriptions of the intentions behind the proposed legislation, while it also identifies some of the changes in thinking that had taken place in, for example, terminology since the appearance of the White Paper. The selected extract is also useful in that it covers some of the aspects of the 1923 Act examined earlier, viz: local authority administration; management of individual schools; religious education and compulsory education.

EDUCATION BILL (NORTHERN IRELAND)
Explanatory and Financial Memorandum

OBJECT OF THE BILL

1.   The object of the Bill is to give effect to the proposals for educational reform outlined in the White Paper on Educational Reconstruction in Northern Ireland issued in December, 1944, but it contains a number of modifications of, and certain additions to, those proposals. It is a comprehensive measure reforming the whole educational system of Northern Ireland, and, with the exception of a few sections, repeals all existing Education Acts.

PART 1

STATUTORY SYSTEM OF EDUCATION
(Clauses 1 to 64) [Sections 2 to 65 of the Act]

2.   This Part of the Bill will come into operation on 1st April, 1948. It provides for the administration of the educational services through local education authorities, sets out the three stages of education (primary, secondary and further education), defines the powers and duties of the authorities in respect of each stage, and also deals, *inter alia,* with religious education, compulsory school attendance, ancillary services and certain miscellaneous provisions.

LOCAL ADMINISTRATION
AND THE THREE STAGES OF THE STATUTORY SYSTEM
(Clauses 1 to 3) [Sections 2 to 4]

3.   The council of each county and county borough becomes the local education authority for the area. In each area one education committee will exercise the functions of the local education authority, thus bringing to an end the regional education committees in Counties Antrim, Londonderry and Tyrone, though county committees may, with the approval of the Ministry of Education, delegate some functions to district committees.

4.   The present division of the educational system into elementary education and higher education, which covers secondary and technical education is abolished. In its place the statutory system will consist of three progressive stages, primary, secondary and further education. Further education includes technical education, youth welfare and all forms of adult education.

PRIMARY AND SECONDARY EDUCATION

PROVISION OF PRIMARY AND SECONDARY SCHOOLS
(Clauses 4 to 11) [Sections 5 to 12]

5.   It will be the duty of every local education authority to ensure that there are in its area sufficient primary and secondary schools and that these are so equipped as to afford education suited to the "ages, abilities and aptitudes" of the pupils in attendance.   In fulfilling their general duties for primary and secondary education, the authorities are directed to have special regard to the need for providing primary and secondary education in separate schools, to the need for nursery schools or classes for children under five years of age, to the need for making special provision for pupils "who suffer from any disability of mind or body," and to the expediency of securing the provision of boarding accommodation for primary and secondary school pupils.

6.   All primary and secondary schools, except nursery schools and special schools, under the control of local education authorities will be designated "county schools," whether they have been built by the authority or transferred to its control.   Primary and secondary schools not controlled by the local education authorities will be termed "voluntary schools," this expression has been in common use for elementary schools not controlled by local education authorities and will now be extended to include secondary schools not controlled by local authorities.   The Ministry will prescribe the standards to which both county and voluntary schools will be required to conform.

7.   Every local education authority will be required to submit to the Ministry a "development scheme" for its area within one year after Part I of the Act comes into operation, i.e., not later than 1st April, 1949.   The development scheme

will set out the authority's proposals for the provision of primary and secondary education in its area and will be drawn up after consideration of the extent to which, and the manner in which, the managers of voluntary schools are prepared to cooperate in the provision of the necessary schools. The managers of voluntary schools, for their part, will be required, before 1st October, 1948, to inform the local education authority whether they intend to transfer their schools to the authority and what steps they propose to take for the provision of voluntary secondary schools. Provision is also made for the consideration by the Ministry of objections to an authority's development scheme. After the scheme has been approved by the Ministry it will be the duty of the local education authority to put it into operation.

8.   Every local education authority will, therefore, be obliged to review the whole school provision of its area, to decide which of the existing elementary schools under its control are ultimately to be transformed into primary schools, which of them should become secondary schools and what new county primary and county secondary schools will be required. The managers of voluntary elementary schools must also decide whether they wish to continue their schools as primary schools, to transform them into secondary schools, to provide new voluntary primary or secondary schools, or whether they prefer to transfer all or some of their schools to the education authority, or to retain control of primary schools and allow the authority to provide the required secondary schools. It will clearly be necessary for voluntary managers to consult together particularly in regard to the provision of secondary schools. These clauses contain adequate safeguards to ensure that the interests of voluntary managers will not be disregarded; they are invited to cooperate to the fullest extent possible in the establishment of the new system.

9.   These clauses also lay down that proposals for the establishment or discontinuance of county or voluntary schools shall be submitted to the Ministry for approval, as must also the plans and specifications for new schools when their establishment has been approved. Voluntary schools, including nursery schools, may be transferred to a local education authority in accordance with the provisions of the first schedule to the Bill, which is similar to the corresponding schedule to the Education Act of 1923.

MANAGEMENT OF
PRIMARY AND SECONDARY SCHOOLS
(Clauses 12 to 17) [Sections 13 to 18]

10.   County primary schools are to be managed by school management committees constituted, except for what follows, in exactly the same way as was provided in the Education Act of 1930 for the management of provided and transferred public elementary schools; the only change is that the representative of the teachers must be the principal of the school concerned or one of the principals if more than one primary school is managed by the same management committee. Nursery schools established by local education authorities are to be managed by committees appointed by the authority in accordance with a scheme framed by the authority and approved by the Ministry.

RELIGIOUS EDUCATION
IN COUNTY AND VOLUNTARY SCHOOLS
(Clauses 20 to 26) [Sections 21 to 27]

15.   As forecast in the White Paper religious instruction and collective daily worship are made compulsory for every county and voluntary school, whether primary or secondary. The only requirement under the present Education Acts as to

the giving of religious instruction in schools is that Bible instruction must be given in provided and transferred public elementary schools at the request of parents; there is no statutory requirement for the giving of religious instruction in any voluntary school or in any secondary school, whether voluntary or controlled by a local education authority. No school of any kind has hitherto been required to hold collective worship.

16.   The religious instruction which must be given in county schools is to be undenominational. Undenominational religious instruction is defined as "instruction based upon the Holy Scriptures according to some authoritative version or versions thereof, but excluding instruction as to any tenet which is distinctive of any particular religious denomination." By reason of their right of access to all county schools clergymen may also give and examine the undenominational religious instruction, but may also give denominational instruction.   This right of access to schools controlled by the educational authorities, which was formerly restricted to public elementary schools alone, is now extended to county secondary schools of all types.   The nature of the religious instruction to be given in voluntary schools will be decided by those responsible for the management of the schools.

17.   It is made clear that it will be the duty of teachers in country schools to attend or conduct collective worship and to give undenominational religious instruction, if they are required to do so by the local educational authority.   A teacher may, however, request to be excused from either or both of these duties, and if he also furnishes a statutory declaration that his request to be excused is made solely on grounds of religious belief he will be excused, and must not be penalised.   The fact that a teacher in a county school has been excused from conducting collective worship or giving

religious instruction does not relieve the local education authority of its obligation to ensure that the religious education of the pupils is adequately provided for; if necessary the authority must appoint an additional teacher for the purpose. Provision is also made for dealing with complaints from parents in cases where the conductors of a school do not appear to be carrying out their obligations in regard to religious education, and the Ministry is empowered to make regulations for securing that the law relating to religious education is complied with in all schools. The duty of inspecting or examining religious education will not be placed on inspectors or other officers of the Ministry.

TRANSITIONAL PROVISIONS
AS TO COUNTY AND VOLUNTARY SCHOOLS
(Clause 27) Section [28]

18.   Almost all public elementary schools in Northern Ireland, being attended by both junior pupils (i.e. those under 11 years and 6 months) and senior pupils, are, in effect, providing both primary and secondary education; many of the existing secondary schools also contain a number of junior pupils.   When the Bill comes into operation it will be necessary to determine which schools are to be managed and conducted as primary schools and which as secondary schools. This Clause contains provisions necessary for the transitional period before the reorganisation of elementary schools into primary and secondary schools can be put into operation.

****

COMPULSORY ATTENDANCE
AT PRIMARY AND SECONDARY SCHOOLS
(Clauses 33 to 38) [Section 34 to 39]

22.   The upper age limit of compulsory school attendance is to be raised from 14 to 15, and the lower limit reduced from 6 to 5.   A local education authority is, however, empowered to raise the lower limit from 5 to $5^{1}/2$ or 6 by bye-law either in part or the whole of the areas under its control. Provision is also made for the upper limit of compulsory attendance to be raised to 16 by Order in Council as soon as the Ministry is satisfied that this is practicable and Parliament has approved the draft of the Order.   Parents are required to cause their children to receive "efficient full-time education" suitable to their ages, abilities and aptitudes, either by attendance at school or otherwise, so long as they are of compulsory school age.

II.11(b) Education Act (Northern Ireland)1947, C.3.

Several important amendments were incorporated into the Bill as it passed through Parliament.   One change that is worthy of note was the introduction, at the commencement of the Act, of a section relating to an Advisory Council for Education thus bringing the legislation for Northern Ireland further into line with England and Wales (1944) and Scotland (1945 and 1946).

ADVISORY COUNCIL FOR EDUCATION.

1. — (1)   There shall be an Advisory Council for Education and it shall be the duty of this Council to advise the Ministry of Education (in this Act referred to as "the Ministry") upon such matters connected with educational theory and practice as they think fit, and upon any questions referred to them by the Ministry.

(2)   The members of the Advisory Council shall be appointed by the Minister of Education (in this Act referred to as "the Minister") and the Minister shall appoint a member of the Council to be Chairman thereof and shall appoint an officer of the Ministry to be secretary thereto.

(3)   The Ministry shall by regulations make provision as to the term of office and conditions of retirement of the members of the Advisory Council and such regulations may provide for periodical or other meeting of the Council and as to the procedure thereof, but, subject to the provisions of any such regulations, the meetings and procedure of the Council shall be such as may be determined by them.

II.12   Report of the Committee on the Recruitment and Training of Teachers, 1947, Cmd.254.

Preparation of the implementation of the 1947 Act began shortly after the release of the1944 White Paper as it was realised that the new legislation would necessitate a marked increase in the supply of teachers and considerable changes in educational practice.   In 1945 the Minister appointed a committee under the Chairmanship of the Hon. Justice Black to consider the salaries and conditions of service of teachers and a further committee under Colonel W.D. Gibbon to report on the recruitment and training of teachers.

While the recommendations of the Black Report were undoubtedly important to both serving and potential teachers, it is to the Gibbon report that reference must be made to determine the type of training advocated for the young people preparing to teach in the proposed post-war primary schools.   It is interesting to observe that in Northern Ireland the first cohort of students entering the three year training course for primary teaching in 1948 preceded their counterparts in England and Wales by some twelve years. Meanwhile to alleviate immediate staffing shortages the Government instituted a temporary training scheme whereby 365 and 40 ex-servicemen and women respectively were trained between April 1946 and November 1949.

SUMMARY AND RECOMMENDATIONS

PRIMARY SCHOOL TEACHERS (CHAPTER VI)

LENGTH AND CONTENT OF COURSE

11.   The present two-year training college course should immediately be extended to three years.
12.   The maximum weekly timetable for the new course should not exceed 24 hours and a much smaller proportion of time should be devoted to lecture periods than at present.
13.   There should be opportunities for specialisation in the later stages of the new course.
14.   The number of subjects to be studied should be drastically reduced.
15.   Suitable provision should be made throughout the course for Religious Education and Physical Education.
16.   The study of English should occupy the foremost place in the curriculum throughout the primary training course.

TEACHING PRACTICE

17.   There should be a growing emphasis on teaching practice throughout the course leading up to a continuous period of full-time teaching practice of at least two months in the final year.
18.   As many students as possible should have opportunities for teaching practice in country schools and those who intend to seek their first posts in country schools should spend their continuous period of teaching practice in such a school.

PRINCIPLES OF EDUCATION

19. The approach to the study of Principles of Education should be informal and by way of problems which suggest themselves to the students after visits to the schools.

20. After a later stage the students should be introduced to a more systematic study of educational theory but this should be kept closely related to practical problems.

21. The course in Principles of Education should also include instruction in the use of objective intelligence and other tests of ability and aptitude, together with some account of the growth of the educational system and of the work of prominent educational pioneers.

SELECTION OF SUBJECTS, ETC.

22. The importance of practical subjects for primary school teachers should be fully recognised and the study of at least one practical subject should be maintained throughout the course.

23. The study of academic subjects in the second and third years of the course (apart from English and the subject selected for personal study) should be closely related to the teaching of these subjects in the schools.

24. The choice of the special subject for advanced personal study should be left as wide as possible.

25. In the final year of the course there should be some specialisation towards the teaching of the "under sevens" or the "under elevens:" (the "five to seven" infant group being common to both) and appropriate adjustments to the course should be made to this end.

26. More attention should be paid to the study of Health Education and School Hygiene.

27. There should be opportunities for practical sociological work in the final year of the course.

TRAINING OF GRADUATES

28.   The professional training of graduates who wish to be qualified to teach in primary schools could be undertaken by the training colleges.

29.   A one-year course of professional training for graduates should be provided.

30.   There should also be a concurrent four-year training college and university course for intending primary school teachers.

(Gibbon Report, pp73-74).

II.13   Report of the Ministry of Education, 1946-47, (HC 822).

Emergency Training Scheme.

The premises at Larkfield, Dunmurry, which has been acquired for the Emergency Training College were ready for occupation in May, 1946, and on 17th May the college was officially opened by Mr. D.R. Hardman, Parliamentary Secretary to the Ministry of Education for England and Wales.   The first "intake" consisted of 58 selected ex-service students; two further intakes of students were admitted to the college in September 1948 and February 1947, bringing the enrolment up to 211, of whom 19 were women.   The teaching staff increased with each intake of students, and early in 1947 numbered fourteen, some of whom were teachers seconded from schools.

Each applicant who was eligible for consideration under the Scheme was interviewed by a Selection Board which made recommendations to the Ministry on his/her suitability; some applicants were also required to take a short educational test. By the end of March, 1947, no fewer than 836 ex-servicemen and women had applied for admission to the college; of these 663 have been interviewed by the Selection Board and 432 accepted for admission.   Many of the applicants who were still serving in the Forces were interviewed during leave in

Northern Ireland and it was thus possible for those who were selected to take up training almost immediately after their release from the Forces.

Successful applicants were given the opportunity of spending some four weeks in an elementary school near their home before actually commencing their studies at the College, and a student's maintenance allowance was payable in full from the date on which he entered on this period of observation of teaching.

II.14   Report of the Primary Schools Programme Committee, Ministry of Education 1956, pp3-6.

Post-war Curricular Change

The Ministry reports of the late 1940s and early 1950s contain some positive curricular comments on the benefits conferred by the 1947 Act's free books and materials provision and on the gradual expansion in the application of school and class libraries, school broadcasting and other teaching aids.   Such advances were, however, achieved in an educational environment that was preoccupied with structural reorganisation and hampered by staff shortages, over-subscribed classes, outmoded furniture and obsolete buildings. Above all the curriculum was stifled by reliance upon a programme that, apart from some minor modifications, had been in operation since 1932.

The latter constraint was tackled in 1952 by the formation of a Primary Schools Programme Committee composed of equal members of teachers and inspectors under the chairmanship of Mr. W.B. Doak, the Chief Inspector.   The resultant report was furnished to the Minister in 1955 and with the accompanying revised programme was published the following year.   The extract has been abstracted from the Doak report and it indicates a further move towards the child-centred approach first detected in the 1931 Robb report.

The Committee invited written evidence from any interested bodies on aspects of the work of primary schools that came within the terms of reference, and a list of these bodies is given in an Appendix to our Report; we are much indebted to them for their helpful memoranda.

When we had completed a preliminary survey of our problems and formed a clear picture of the shape which the new Programme should take, we set up panels of teachers and inspectors to advise us on the individual subjects. The names of those who served on these panels are given in an Appendix; it will be noted that we enlisted the help of more than 40 teachers and 20 inspectors who were not members of the Committee. They were selected for their personal experience of the working conditions in either large or small schools, and for their knowledge of teaching methods and the day-to-day problems of teachers. To provide full opportunity for the exchange of information and views between the panels and the Committee, each panel included at least one inspector member and one teacher member of the Committee. The chapters dealing with the various subjects are largely the work of the panels; but since we found it necessary or expedient to make modifications, of greater or less significance, in the drafts submitted to us, we must emphasise that responsibility for the final form and content of the chapters rests solely with the Committee. The skill and industry of the panels were of immense assistance to us in our task, and we wish to record here our appreciation of their services.

The Programme we have drafted differs so widely from its predecessor in conception, form and syllabus content that we feel an explanation to be necessary. This can best be given in the shape of a history of the progress and developments in our educational system that have taken place since 1932, when the last Programme was constructed.

Previous to 1932, revisions of the Programme for primary schools were carried out every few years and any necessary alterations were made in order to keep it in accord with current educational theory and practice. Since 1932 there has been no general revision, but the Ministry dealt, as the occasion arose, with such matters as the need for a more definite programme for pupils who remained at the primary school after completing the work of Standard VII, the need for revision of the syllabuses in Arithmetic, Algebra and Geometry, and the advisability of having an alternative syllabus in needlework. The outbreak of war and, later, preoccupation with the task of educational reconstruction led to the postponement of any revision of the Programme as a whole. The piece-meal adjustments to which we have referred had been made within narrow limits and could take little account of the development of wider and more general trends in education. Defects became more pronounced and it is, in fact, true to say that the 1932 Programme has in several important directions now become obsolete and no longer serves as a reliable guide to the teachers.

With the subject content of the curriculum the Committee has found little reason to interfere; the traditional skills of reading, writing and arithmetic continue to be indispensable elements in the child's education and the other subjects which claimed a place in the curriculum of 1932 have in general firmly established their right to inclusion. But the detailed subject syllabuses which the 1932 Programme laid down have now a strangely inflexible appearance. They were based on the conception of a course in a series of more or less separate subjects taught in a succession of yearly assignments and give little recognition to what were then novel departures but are now accepted as commonplace — the close integration of all the constituents in the educational process, and the doctrine that the individual child progresses at his own pace and does not conform to a rigid pattern which dictates the amount of ground he will cover each year. Even when the need for a more liberal and enterprising attitude towards the Programme began to make itself felt, many teachers still showed reluctance in venturing away from the beaten track of tradition.

To explain this reluctance it is necessary to refer briefly to the machinery of inspection which the Ministry employed at that time. The more obtrusive side of school inspection was examination. The teacher's class was given an oral examination or a written examination, or both, in each subject he taught, and his work in each subject was assessed in terms of a scale of merit marks — Excellent, Very Good, Good, Fair, Middling, Bad. These merit marks were tabulated and issued to him in what was called the Efficiency Table. In addition he was assigned a general rating of Highly Efficient, Efficient, Fairly Efficient or Not Efficient based on the distribution of his merit marks and on the inspector's judgement of his all-round competence. The very direct connection which the teacher saw between the standard of the pupil's proficiency and the merit mark in each subject tended to divert his attention from the wider aspects of his function and concentrate his efforts on the narrow task of meeting the exigencies of subject examinations. It is not surprising that what was intended to be a teaching syllabus, capable of modification to suit differing circumstances, came to be regarded as an examination syllabus from which any deviation, however promising or desirable, was hazardous.

In 1936 a Conference between officers of the Ministry and representatives of one of the teachers' organisations recommended changes, which were put into operation in the following year. The Efficiency Table of merit marks was withdrawn and it was emphasised that in future the assessment of a teacher's merit should depend upon his efficiency in the widest sense. In the words of the Report issued by the Conference "the training of the pupils in character, address, good manners and intelligence, their due promotion in school from standard to standard, and the success of their general preparation for afterlife," were all matters to which due attention must be paid in assessing the value of the teacher's work for the community.

The effect of these changes on the teachers' outlook and on their attitude towards the Programme was not immediate. The new pattern of inspection was welcomed; but the Highly Efficient rating remained, and the close relationship between the teacher's rating and the pupils' performance under examination could not be lightly discounted. Nevertheless, an atmosphere conducive to greater freedom for experiment and initiative had been created.

We have indicated in this historical retrospect the conspicuous role played by the official Programme over the years, and the reason why many teachers, however great their professional zeal and their desire for more latitude, regarded it rather as a master than a servant. No assurances or encouragement given by inspectors could remove their misgivings. In 1947, the Highly Efficient rating was abolished and teachers were able to see in true perspective the faults of the official Programme and to take fuller notice of advances which had been made in educational theory in the last twenty-five years. Already the Programme had been widely recognised as obsolete and the more progressive teachers had struck out on enterprising and individual lines. Other and less adventurous teachers continued to follow uncritically the rigid pattern laid down in the syllabuses of the various subjects.

The task to which we addressed ourselves was to devise a Programme or guide which would reflect the present-day conception of a suitable training for primary school pupils and would stimulate teachers to use initiative in planning the details of the courses to meet the special needs of their own pupils and the environment of their own schools.   A radical change which we had to bring about was the shifting of emphasis from a "curriculum-centred" system to a "child-centred" system; we had to stress the need for thinking of the curriculum "less in terms of departments of knowledge to be taught, and more in terms of activities to be fostered and interests to be broadened."   It was clear that a Programme constructed on the principles of the existing one, with formal blocks of work assigned to each class subject by subject for each year could not give expression to this change of attitude. While we were willing, as a matter of convenience, to accept the division of the curriculum into "subjects," we were, nevertheless, conscious that no branch stands in isolation from other branches — that in modern practice there are many points of over-lap and intersection which tend to break down the barriers between the units. A more serious difficulty was the failure of the existing Programme to recognise that only in a subject where a simple and fairly straightforward progression from one operation to another is conceivable can positive and self-contained yearly assignments be suggested as a basis for the teacher's schemes; in most subjects the pattern is rather a concentric expansion of skills, the work done year by year being largely of the same nature as before but involving, as time goes on, greater intricacy and a growing degree of ability and proficiency.

These and other considerations led us to the conclusion that we should retain, for convenience, the traditional subject-divisions; and that within this framework we should present the material not in a series of yearly syllabuses but in the form of memoranda giving a broad picture of the standards of achievement a child should normally have attained in the various branches at perhaps two or three appropriate stages in his school course. Since the revised Programme would demand of many teachers a new outlook and a change of values, we decided to embody in the memoranda some guidance on points of teaching methods, and, in an Introductory chapter, when dealing with the school as a whole, to indicate some of the ways in which the application of the "child-centred" systems we were recommending was bound to affect the organisation of the work of both teachers and pupils.

The amount of guidance we have given on teaching methods varies from subject to subject according to the nature of the problem presented. In general, we have tended to limit ourselves to the statement of fundamental principles or to matters about which there could be little divergence of opinion. In Arithmetic, however, where a more precise assessment of the relative merits of different methods is possible than in perhaps any other branch, we have thought it desirable to enter into greater detail. The Programme we now recommend for approval differs widely from the existing Programme in form and content, and, not least, in its design for an organisation of the school work attuned to the Hadow principles which we quoted earlier. There is no doubt that many traditional methods will have to be examined afresh and modified or replaced, and that teachers will have to experiment till they find techniques which will translate into performance the ideals now set before them. We have borne in mind that every teacher has his own special difficulties and his own personal way of coping with them; he must, therefore, be given wide scope for moulding his teaching technique to suit his own requirements. The changes will call for the exercise of skill and resourcefulness, and vigilant care that there will be no misinterpretation of the aims of the new Programme, leading to a superficiality of approach or a lowering of standards of orderly, intellectual discipline.

There are still very many unreorganised primary schools in Northern Ireland, and though the provision of a new Programme for the senior classes of these schools does not come strictly within our terms of reference we had no doubt that you would wish us to suggest courses which might profitably be followed by pupils for whom intermediate school accommodation is not yet available. For these pupils, attending schools which lack, in greater or less degree, the ample provision of rooms for the practical subjects they would study in intermediate schools, we have planned as wide a course as is possible within the limits imposed by the restricted physical and staffing facilities. This course and the suggested subject syllabuses we have placed in an Appendix to the Programme.

II.15   Programme for Primary Schools, Ministry of Education 1956, Chap.1, pp14-15.

This brief extract taken from the actual programme for primary schools records the eventual disappearance of the nineteenth century class designations. A useful summary of the programme is given in the final chapter of the Ministry's Annual Report for 1955-56. (Cmd.368).

ARRANGEMENT OF THE PROGRAMME

The Programme is divided into two main sections. The first deals with pupils aged approximately from 5 to 11 years in all primary schools, and the second, the appendix, with senior classes in unreorganised schools.

In both parts and in the suggested time allocations given later in this chapter the work of the school has been considered in terms of the traditional subjects of the curriculum; but there are some changes in nomenclature with which teachers should make themselves familiar.

Nomenclature of classes: The traditional names for the various classes — Junior Infants, Senior Infants, Standard I, etc., — do not appear in the Programme. The omission is deliberate. It is felt that the traditional nomenclature might be taken to imply that a break occurs in the child's education at a point when he ceases to be an "Infant" and enters "Standard I" and that a fundamental change of attitude and method on the part of the teacher is then necessary. This is far from being so: the child's primary education must be regarded as a single and continuous process and any change of attitude and method must be a gradual one. Moreover, the term "Infant" is ambiguous, and the term "Standard" a survival of the days when a pupil's progress through the school was based strictly on his performance in an annual examination; this is no longer the case. A more logical and educationally speaking, less objectionable nomenclature has been introduced; the classes in the primary school are designated Primary 1 to 7 to correspond with the former Junior Infants to Standard V range, and the senior classes in unreorganised schools Primary 8 and 9.

Temperance and Hygiene: It is considered that the title Health and Habits more accurately reflects the widened scope of this subject. Reference has already been made to its treatment in the sections on Health Education and Citizenship.

Information and observations Lessons: It is felt that the name Information and Observation Lessons no longer indicates accurately the content and purpose of the lessons in elementary geography, history, nature study and hygiene given to pupils in the lower classes of primary schools, and it has been discarded. Instead, it is intended that in Primary 3 as much of that material as is suitable for children of the age should be included in the work covered by Sections (b) and (c) in the schedule of time allocations given below for that class (see pages 16 and 17); and from Primary 4 onwards Geography, History and Nature Study are included in the curriculum under their own names.

Science: In the curriculum for the senior classes in unreorganised schools this term has been introduced to describe what was formerly taught in Elementary Science, Nature Study and Horticulture.

**II.16   Report of the Ministry of Education 1956-57
            Cmd. 380, pp20-23.**

A cursory examination of the annual reports of the Ministry of Education is sufficient to confirm that the main issues dominating the primary sector in the years following the 1947 Act were the rate of 5-11+ re-organisation, the preponderance of oversize classes and the necessity to carry out an extensive primary school building programme. The provision of new and improved accommodation was considered to be imperative to cater for shifts in population, an ongoing bulge in the post-war birth-rate and a backlog of building that had accumulated since the war period. The extract from the 1956-57 report is representative of this type of recurring comment on primary school building while the results of the 1968 accommodation audit demonstrate that there was a considerable improvement programme to be carried out to eliminate the defects still to be found, especially in the older and smaller primary schools.

CHAPTER XII

SCHOOL BUILDING UNDER THE EDUCATION ACT
(NORTHERN IRELAND), 1947

In the 1930s the education authorities which have been set up under the Education Act (Northern Ireland), 1923, had entered upon a phase of building activity designed in the main to make good the deficiencies of the schools they had inherited. The outbreak of war in 1939 brought school building to a stop before the programme had approached completion, and also placed serious restrictions upon the amount of maintenance which could be carried out. In April, 1948, when the Education Act (Northern Ireland), 1947 came into operation the school accommodation problem which already existed before the war had been aggravated by almost nine years' enforced inactivity. In the interval further problems had arisen. The school population as a whole was about to increase rapidly as a result of the steep rise in the birth rate from 1941 onwards — 28,000 children attained the age of five years in 1948 compared with 22,000 in 1939 — and it was clear that for some time a continually increasing number of pupil places would be needed. Moreover, provision had to be made for the raising of the school leaving age. A further difficulty was that, particularly in the vicinity of Belfast and the larger towns, there had been considerable movement from older housing areas to the new estates which were beginning to spring up.

At the same time the 1947 Act called for a radical reorganisation of the school system. Public elementary schools, providing for pupils throughout the whole age-range of compulsory school attendance, were to be replaced by primary schools for pupils up to the age of eleven years and by secondary intermediate schools for those older pupils who were not to receive their secondary education in grammar or technical intermediate schools. It was clear that a large number of new secondary intermediate schools would have to be built to permit the reorganisation of the system to take place even if there had been no growth in the school going population. Although the number of grammar schools in existence was not far short of that required to meet foreseeable requirements, the number of places provided in these schools was seriously inadequate having regard to the increased demand for this type of secondary education which followed immediately upon the introduction of the new provisions for grammar school scholarships under the 1947 Act.

Nine year's wear and tear, aggravated by inadequate maintenance, had increased the long list of unsatisfactory old primary school buildings awaiting replacement, to which was added the demand of new primary schools in developing housing areas. There was also a growing need for a further forward movement in technical education which could clearly make its claim on building resources. The last major demand was that for the extension of the school meals service throughout the education system; this in itself called for heavy capital investment in new kitchens and dining rooms both for new and for existing schools.

The problem in short was one of making up for time lost and of providing for expansion and reorganisation at the same time.

The formidable programme of school building which the situation called for had to be begun at a time when the war-time scarcity of building materials of all kinds continued practically unabated. Shortages of cement, steel and soft wood, and at times even of bricks, very seriously restricted the amount of work which could be undertaken. The difficulty of planning new schools was increased by the fact that for nine years architects in Northern Ireland had virtually no experience of school building and that many of the younger architects had never had an opportunity of planning a school at all. To add to these difficulties, changing ideas in education demanded the reconsideration of standards not only in terms of floor-space and facilities for teaching purposes but of amenities outside the classroom.

In view of the urgency of the need for new accommodation it was impossible to allow the beginning of work on new schools or on extensions to existing schools to be deferred until a definitive long-term programme had been drawn up and a complete answer had been found to the new problems of school design to which the changing conditions had given rise. An immediate *ad hoc* solution had to be found for the more pressing short-term problems whilst simultaneous consideration of long-term requirements was undertaken.

The first step in carrying out the short-term policy was to determine which projects must receive prior attention. There was little difficulty in deciding that the most urgent need for additional school accommodation was in the new housing estates, where the proportion of children of school age was considerably above average, but where school places were often completely lacking. In these areas the number of young children was particularly high so that the need was clearly for primary school places. Secondly, in other areas some of the former public elementary schools were so grossly overcrowded as a result of the increased enrolments for which they had to provide that the need for extension was imperative. Thirdly, additional grammar school places had to be provided without delay if the new scholarship schemes were to be put into effect.

It was not overlooked that a radical solution could not be effected until secondary intermediate schools had been established and had taken away from the primary schools, pupils over the age of 11. In Belfast, Ballymena, Coleraine and Newtownards it was possible to adapt the premises of a few existing large primary schools to establish at short notice, although in conditions which fell far short of the ideal, a small number of secondary intermediate schools. To determine the location and enrolment of, and to prepare plans for, entirely new intermediate schools would, however, obviously require a considerable time, so that no immediate relief could be expected along these lines. In the first few years after the 1947 Act came into operation, therefore, new building work was almost exclusively restricted to primary and grammar schools.

An interim decision had to be reached upon the standards of accommodation which were to be called for in the new schools, since it was clear that there could be no question of merely adhering to the pre-war canons of design. Even the primary schools, with their relatively standardised curriculum, presented certain problems, such as, for instance, how the new statutory requirements regarding the provision of school meals were to be met. In addition, there had been a substantial change in the amount of teaching space specified for a given number of pupils. Up to 15 square feet of classroom space per pupil was now considered desirable instead of the 10 square feet which in pre-war days had been thought adequate. Revised schedules of accommodation for new primary schools took into account considerations of this nature. In the grammar schools it was largely a question of determining the additions required in each individual case, but particular attention had to be given to the provision of specialised rooms for the teaching of subjects such as Science, Art or Geography, in which the existing schools were in most cases deficient.   In Belfast the increased demand for grammar school places was such that the ministry approved the immediate provision of two entirely new county grammar schools.

Where these first new school buildings were to be erected in the traditional form of construction, the design had to be such as to call for the least possible amount of scarce building materials. In particular, softwood was not available for roofs and the amount of steel had to be reduced to the greatest possible extent. These shortages of materials inevitably imposed restrictions upon design.

In view of the urgency of the need in the first years of the operation of the 1947 Act reliance had largely to be placed upon non-traditional or pre-fabricated forms of construction which would enable schools to be erected more speedily. Entire schools or extensions in aluminium, concrete or wood were amongst the types built at this time. Although it was found that the mere adoption of a pre-fabricated method of building did not entirely eliminate planning delay, there is no doubt that a valuable saving in time was achieved.

Thus, during the school year 1949-50, it was possible to provide two new grammar schools in aluminium construction in Belfast. These non-traditional types of building again imposed new restrictions upon the architect, since he had to meet educational requirements within the limits of the modules imposed by most of the specialised forms of construction. Moreover, the systems which did not permit of multi-storey construction, although presenting no particular problem where a small new school or a small extension was concerned, led to an excessively extended layout of buildings for large schools.

In the meantime, attention was given to the assessment of the long-term need for school accommodation. Section 8 of the 1947 Act required every local education authority to estimate the requirements of their area for primary and secondary education taking into account both county and voluntary schools, and to publish their conclusions in the form of a Development Scheme. The managers of voluntary schools were required to assist the authority by furnishing information about their intentions as to the future of schools under their control. As required by the Act the Ministry prescribed the form which Schemes were to take and the particulars which they were to contain. The first County Development Scheme was submitted in May, 1949, but in view of the large amount of detailed work involved, it was necessary to allow a considerably extended time for the submission of most of the remaining Schemes, and the preparation of the last was not completed until 1954.

So far as primary schools were concerned, the first problem was to determine which of the existing schools would continue to be needed and what additional schools would have to be built. The eventual withdrawal of senior pupils to secondary intermediate schools provided for by the Act meant that in most cases the enrolments of existing primary schools would be considerably reduced, and in some cases in rural districts would be so low after reorganisation that serious consideration would have to be given to the possibility of closing the school, the remaining pupils being transferred to other schools. In other cases, the question arose whether the provision of a larger school to supersede two or more small primary schools situated close together would be advantageous.

After the permanent enrolments which might be expected at the existing schools had been estimated, locations had to be selected for the new primary schools which movements of population and the increased birth-rate had made necessary. In reviewing the adequacy of the total primary school provision proposed in a Development Scheme, the Ministry's policy was based on the principle that wherever possible a primary school should be situated within two miles of the homes of the pupils who might be expected to attend. Where the sparsity of population or other considerations made it necessary to depart from this standard, the choice of location for a new school was influenced by the actual or potential availability of public transport.

When the need for an existing school and its probable enrolment had been established, it was necessary to consider whether the school buildings were suitable for retention either in their present state or after such improvements as were reasonable in the circumstances had been carried out, or whether there was an immediate or eventual need to provide new premises. Local education authorities indicated their views on the suitability of existing school buildings in their Development Schemes, and when the latter had been published and submitted to the Ministry, it arranged for every primary school in Northern Ireland to be visited by an Inspector and provisionally assessed as to its suitability for retention under one of four classes, viz:

(a)   those which were considered wholly satisfactory;

(b)   those which, although not wholly satisfactory, were considered sufficiently satisfactory to form part of the permanent school provision of the area, subject in certain cases to the carrying out of improvements or extensions;

(c)   those which were considered unsatisfactory and which should therefore be ultimately replaced but which could nevertheless be continued in use for some time without major alterations; and

(d)   those which were considered so unsatisfactory as to necessitate replacement at the earliest opportunity.

In many cases there was no doubt about the suitability or unsuitability of a building for permanent retention. Schools which could not be regarded as fully adequate without considerable alterations or additions — Class B Schools — gave rise, however, to some difficulty since in individual cases, when detailed proposals were subsequently prepared for their improvement, it was found that the cost of the works involved would be so high as to raise doubts whether the provision of an entirely new school would not be preferable. The general classification of primary school buildings on the basis of the Development Scheme could not, therefore, be regarded as more than provisional. Nevertheless, it gave a broad picture of the situation.   When all the Development Schemes had been examined in the Ministry, the conclusion reached was that about 190 county and 340 voluntary primary schools were housed in premises which would have to be replaced if they could not be discontinued or amalgamated with other schools.

II.17   Revised Development Scheme for Primary Education County Londonderry Education Committee 1962, pp3-4.

Post-war Primary School Consolidation.

Reference has already been made to the pre-war elementary school amalgamation policy pursued by the Ministry of Education. Since the war the total number of operational primary schools has been further reduced by approximately seven hundred and, as before, the majority of these have been in the one-, two- and three-teacher categories. An analysis of the relevant statistics indicated that this post-war contraction falls into two distinct phases separated by the 1960 Northern Ireland Education Act.

Although the 1947 Act and its attendant Statutory Rules and Orders contained similar provisions to the inter-war main and subordinate legislation for the termination of redundant schools, there seems to have been little immediate urgency to re-activate a major programme of school rationalisation. This is borne out in the initial local authority development schemes prepared for the Ministry under Section 8 of the Act. These schemes were designed to assist the ranking of the issues involved in the re-structuring of Northern Ireland's educational system and, at that juncture, the rationalisation of primary school facilities occupied a low level of priority. Such amalgamation schemes as were proposed in the late 1940s and early 1950s where directed at the removal of unnecessary duplication in the school supply of the urban centres of population and, as a general principle, the combination of small, rural units was not emphasised.

By the late 1950s it had become apparent, from a Ministry amenity survey, that the greater part of the short-term urban building programme had been realised; consequently local authorities were in a position to re-direct resources towards the modernisation and replacement of those small schools that could not be discontinued or amalgamated with neighbouring establishments. Before the authorities could be asked to embark on full-scale reappraisal, it was necessary to amend Section 8 of the parent Act which related only to the submission of the first development schemes and subsequent necessary modifications. To this end a clause giving the Ministry power to require local authorities to revise their development schemes was inserted in an Education Bill laid before Parliament in May, 1960. The power thus provided was used the following February when all authorities were requested to revise those parts of their schemes pertaining to primary school supply and to concentrate on the possibility of reducing the numbers of one- and two-teacher schools in their areas.

As in the case of the original schemes, the revised plans were submitted over a period of some five years: the first being provided in October 1961 and the last in July 1966. An examination of the re-vamped schemes shows that the authorities were at that stage as determined to reduce the future numbers of small schools as they had been to avoid widespread consolidation in the earlier phase. The publication of the revised development schemes marks, therefore, the final stage in the adoption of a general policy of post-war rural amalgamation in Northern Ireland.

The Committee's Development Scheme for Primary and Secondary education prepared in accordance with Section 8 of the Education Act (N.I.) 1947, was published in 1951. The scheme was concerned primarily with the setting up of a system of County and Voluntary Secondary Intermediate schools and the allocation to each of its contributory Primary Schools.

****

Supplementary Schemes, amending certain proposals in the original Scheme, were issued in 1957 and in 1961 but the experience gained in the past 12 years in the administration of the 1947 Education Act has made a further general review of Primary School provision desirable. The large number of small one and two teacher schools in the Committee's administrative area has raised problems of staffing and transport which have been accentuated with the reduction of enrolment following the transfer of the older pupils to Intermediate Schools. The small one and two teacher school is relatively expensive to operate. Moreover, the insecurity of tenure of the teaching staff in these schools, where a small decline in numbers can reduce the staffing entitlement, is making it increasingly difficult to secure and retain the services of qualified teachers in such schools and this difficulty is likely to remain. On the grounds both of offering the best possible opportunities for Primary School pupils and of making the most effective use of teaching resources, and having regard also to the probable financial saving in both capital and running costs, it has become clear that consideration should be given to the possibility of reducing further the number of small Primary Schools.

The increased provision of school transport to serve the new Secondary Intermediate Schools will make it easier and relatively inexpensive to make the necessary arrangements for the transport of Primary School children when the local school is closed.

A change of policy in the school meals service is also relevant. Until 1959 the Ministry advocated the establishment of large central kitchens delivering meals to small schools. Experience has shown that because of the very high cost of transporting meals and because they are more satisfactory and appetising when cooked on the spot, it is desirable that each school should, as far as possible, have its own kitchen. For this reason too there is much to be said in favour of the closure or amalgamation of a number of the very small primary schools to reduce as far as possible a multiplicity of very small kitchens.

Finally, new standards for Primary School premises and accommodation, issued by the Ministry of Education 1959, have made conditions in many of the older Primary Schools no longer acceptable on a long term basis, and a new scheme was clearly necessary to formulate proposals either to bring these schools up to standard or, if this could not be done economically, to close the school and erect a new building or to transport the pupils to an adjacent school.

**II.18   Educational Development in Northern Ireland
Ministry of Education 1964, Cmd. 470, pp7-8.**

1.   The Education Act of 1947 laid down that a child's
primary education should terminate at 11+, at which age he
should enter on some form of secondary education.   The
reorganisation of primary schools which this requirement
entailed has proceeded apace, so that fewer than 15 per cent
of pupils over the age of 11+ are now taught in primary
schools.   Nevertheless, owing to the rise in the number of
births and a general lowering of the age at which children
begin school attendance, the total primary school enrolment
in 1963 was 189,486, more than 4,000 higher than in 1947.
The number of full-time teachers at 6,235 was 883 higher,
giving an overall improvement in staffing ratio from one
teacher to every 34 children to one teacher to every 30.
Between 1947 and the end of 1963, 247 new primary schools
were built and 207 major extensions were carried out,
together supplying more than 60,000 pupil places at a cost of
upwards of £10,000,000.

2.   Marked progress has thus been made in the field of
primary education.   Some blemishes, however, remain, the
most serious of which are the continuance in use of many
school buildings falling far short of modern standards and the
persistence of over-sized classes.

3.   In order to assess the magnitude of the building
problem the Ministry recently arranged for a survey of all
primary school premises to be undertaken. it was found that,
of the 1,482 primary schools in operation on 31st March,
1963 half were built before 1900; 302 schools were short of
one or more teaching rooms; of the 1,012 schools with three
or fewer teachers, 751 lacked an additional space for dining
and more than 300 schools had no piped water supply, more

than 850 no central heating, and more than 450 no form of artificial lighting; 80 had no playground. It is significant that the majority of the premises most patently lacking in essential facilities were those of small schools in rural areas; of the 323 schools with no piped water supply, 307 were in the one-, two-, or three-teacher category; of the 870 schools without central heating, 763; of the 483 with chemical or dry closets, 465.

4. The number of over-size classes has been greatly reduced since 1947, but there were nevertheless in January, 1963, 1,045 classes out of a total of 6,007 with more than 40 children on roll and of these 260 had more than 45 pupils. The existing regulations are so designed that, provided the full complement of staff is employed, the average number of pupils to each class-teacher should not exceed 40, and in the smaller schools it is substantially less. But in some cases lack of accommodation prevents the employment of the full number of teachers authorised by the regulations, and even when the full complement of teachers is employed some classes may need to be in excess of 40 for reasons beyond the control of the principal. To eliminate all classes with more than 40 pupils is bound to mean amendment of the present staffing regulations and the employment of more teachers; it must also mean the efficient deployment of the teachers available.

5. At present many teachers are relatively uneconomically employed in small one- and two-teacher schools in rural areas. At a recent date the 742 one- and two-teacher schools in Northern Ireland had an enrolment of 28,100 pupils and needed 1,360 teachers to staff them, giving a pupil/teacher ratio of approximately 20 : 1. The 160 primary schools with more than 325 pupils had a total enrolment of 82,600 and a teaching strength of 2,410 giving a

pupil/teacher ratio of 34 : 1.   The greater economy in teaching strength of the larger school is apparent, as is the saving in teaching power that would result from the merging of small schools in larger units.

6.   The main objectives in the field of primary education in the immediate future will be the elimination of excessively large classes and the closing of small schools which are outworn, unhygienic and ill-provided with modern amenities. In order that real progress may be made by 1970 the Ministry proposes to set on foot a five-year campaign starting in 1965. A second five-year plan to operate from 1970 to 1975 should complete the operation if the school authorities, both county and voluntary, tackle the task with vigour, the necessary additional teachers are forthcoming and the teaching force available is used to the best advantage.   Discussions to this end will be started at an early date with the local education authorities and voluntary bodies.

II.19   "Development Scheme for Primary Education" Tyrone County Education Committee, 1965.

Some two years ago the County Education Committee in compliance with the suggestion made by the Ministry of Education decided to take a fresh look at the primary school provision in the County, not from the standpoint of the future of individual schools but rather from the standpoint of districts.

As most of the primary schools in the countryside were built in the latter part of the nineteenth century to serve a population differently distributed from that of to-day, it will be appreciated that the number of pupils in many of these schools is low owing to rural depopulation and the establishment in the last ten years or so of secondary schools to which children over the age of 11 years have been transferred.

The educational disadvantages under which these small schools of necessity work are well understood. The number of boys and girls is so small that there are only three or four children in any age group and the two teachers to be found in a majority of these small schools have between them to cover the normal curricular requirements of the whole of the primary stage and each has to deal with a wide age range and an even wider range of ability. For them it is not easy, if at all possible, to organise anything in the way of satisfactory schemes of work in Music, Drama, Physical Education and Games, Science, or Social Studies, or to take advantage of schools broadcasts in such subjects because of the disparity of ages involved. The inevitably modest total of a small school's allowance for books and materials may furthermore, have restrictive consequences and no matter how efficient the Education Committee may be, it is doubtful whether modern teaching aids can effectively be deployed in a school of around thirty children. Furthermore, the professional isolation which the teachers serving in these small schools with their declining enrolments feel will be understood as will their preference for living in the larger villages or towns than in the vicinity of their schools.

The County Education Committee, aware of the problems of the small school since it drew up its development scheme for primary and secondary education in 1951, has in this new development scheme for primary education proposed the closing and amalgamation of many small rural schools, having no doubt that primary education in the countryside will be immeasurably strengthened and revivified as a result. There is, of course, the occasional small rural school which cannot for one reason or another become part of a larger unit and every case has been judged on its merits. It is certain, nevertheless, that over the greater part of the County primary reorganisation of the kind suggested must sooner or later be accepted. No one who has the best interests of country children at heart and who appreciates the hard facts of the situation can possibly deny the necessity for the reappraisal of educational planning which has resulted in the production of this new scheme.

II.20   Programme for Primary Schools Circular 1966/18 Ministry of Education 8 March, 1966.

The adoption of the more flexible approaches advocated in the revised programme was facilitated in the next decade by the alleviation of some of the earlier problems associated with unsuitable school design and adverse pupil/teacher ratios and an increase in the rate of primary school reorganisation. The abolition of the long standing Elementary School Certificate Examination after 1964 also afforded a degree of relief from the effects of curricular backwash in unreorganised schools, while all primary schools benefited in 1966 from the introduction of a new selection procedure for secondary education which employed verbal reasoning tests and teachers' estimates instead of a formal 'Qualifying Examination.' These developments, together with evidence of a growing receptivity to new ideas by primary teachers and their willingness to participate in fresh techniques and procedures, led the Ministry to relax the rigorous application of the revised programme.

To: Education Committees,   Ministry of Education,
       managers and Principals,   Dundonald House,
       of Primary Schools   BELFAST, 4.

Correspondence should be addressed   8th March 1966
to "The Secretary"

Programme for Primary Schools

1. The Programme for Primary Schools was first
    published in 1956. Many new ideas and methods have
    gained currency in primary education since then and
    much experimental work is at present in progress. For
    example, the increase in the number of four-year-old
    children in Northern Ireland primary schools has
    required a reconsideration of the type of activity best
    suited to young children; the introduction of
    "discovery" methods is bringing about a fundamental
    change in the approach to arithmetic and mathematics;
    and the Nuffield Science project, in which a number of
    Northern Ireland schools are participating, seems likely
    to lead to changes in the treatment of science and
    nature study.

2. Many of the new developments are still at an
    experimental stage, and no generally accepted body of
    practice has emerged. The Ministry, therefore, does
    not consider the time opportune for a general revision
    of the Programme for Primary Schools. Nevertheless,
    it wishes to make it clear that, pending such a revision,
    schools are encouraged to experiment with syllabuses,
    teaching methods and forms of school organisation
    which are not covered by the Programme, provided
    that, if significant departures from it are contemplated,
    the Inspector in charge of the District is consulted.

                           J.M. Benn — Secretary.

II.21 Northern Ireland Education Statistics Vol.7, Table 62, Ministry of Education, 1968.

Survey of Primary School Premises — April, 1968.

	County	Voluntary Maintained	Voluntary Not Maintained	Total
1. Number of Schools (1)	697	42	612	1,351
2. Sizes of Schools:				
Enrolment under 25	55	9	31	95
25 - 59	292	14	195	501
60 - 94	98	8	128	234
95 - 129	39	1	60	100
130 - 199	50	3	72	125
200 - 304	34	5	45	84
305 - 514	75	2	52	129
515 and over	54	—	29	83
3. Ages of Schools:				
Built before 1850	86	8	43	137
1850-1899	149	17	212	378
1900-1922	68	7	111	186
1923 -March 1948	191	9	55	255
1st April 1948-March 1958	82	—	52	134
Since 1st April 1958	121	1	139	261
4. Premises Last Extended or Improved:				
Never so far as is known	356	18	318	692
Before 1923	35	3	21	59
Between 1923 and march 1948	74	4	42	120
Between 1/4/48 - March 1958	86	5	85	176
Since 1st April 1958	146	12	146	304

Survey of Primary School Premises —April 1968 (Continued)

	County	Voluntary Maintained	Voluntary Not Maintained	Total
5. Deficiencies in Classroom Spaces				
No deficiencies	603	31	458	1,092
Deficiencies of one classroom	68	10	94	172
Deficiencies of two classrooms	17	1	32	50
Deficiencies of three classrooms	6	—	9	15
Deficiencies of four or more	3	—	19	22
6. Other Accommodation used for Classrooms:				
Temporary (hutted) classrooms within school grounds	117	3	71	191
Rented or other accommodation elsewhere (e.g. Church Hall)	35	6	51	92
7. Particulars of Additional Spaces and Assembly Halls:				
Schools below 95 places with				
additional space	190	6	109	305
without additional space	255	25	248	528
Schools of 95 and over with				
assembly hall	186	5	117	308
without assembly hall	66	6	138	210

**II.22   "Primary Education in Northern Ireland": A Report
of the Advisory Council for Education, 1968.**

Attention has already been drawn to the amendment inserted into
the 1946 Bill to provide for an Advisory Council for Education in
Northern Ireland.   The first Council was appointed in April 1948
and was thereafter renewed on a three-year basis.   The topics
referred to the Council in the ensuing two decades included rural
education (Cmd.300, 1952), special educational treatment
(Cmd.331, 1954), school attendance (Cmd.362, 1956) and the
thorny issue of the selection of pupils for different types of
secondary schooling (Cmd.301, 1952; Cmd.335, 1955; Cmd.419,
1960; Cmd.471, 1964; and Cmd.551, 1971).   The Burges report of
1968 has been chosen as an example of the Council's work and the
selected portion illustrates that the maintenance of parity with
England and Wales remained of paramount importance to the
Ministry.

CHAPTER 1

Introduction

1.   In March 1967 the Minister wrote to the Chairman of
the Advisory Council referring to the recent publication of
the Plowden report on Children and their Primary Schools in
England.   The Minister was aware that the Council in its
study of the question of homework had already been
considering some of the matters covered by the Plowden
report and he judged the time opportune for a careful review
of existing policies and practices in the field of primary
education in Northern Ireland.   Accordingly he invited the
Council to undertake the task.

2.   Whilst making it clear that he was not suggesting that
the Council should limit itself to assessing the relevance to
Northern Ireland of the recommendations contained in the

Plowden report, the Minister nevertheless considered it would be useful if the Council could express its views on such matters as the development of nursery education, the age for the commencement of compulsory school attendance, the organisation of the primary stage of education, the length of the school day for young children and the use of part-time teachers and teachers' aides.

****

4.   The Plowden report was published in January 1967, and this was followed a year later by the Gittins report dealing with primary education in Wales. Both the Plowden and Gittins Councils produced their reports after work extending over a period of years in each case. Both Councils had extensive resources to call upon, including provision for research. Such resources were not available to us and in any event there seemed little need to go over ground that had already been covered adequately. We have felt, rather, that we could be of most help by looking at those specific matters referred to by the Minister and also at some other problems. Certain differences are apparent in the Northern Ireland situation as compared with that existing across the water, and we have made reference to these differences where necessary through this report. We consider that the recommendations which we have made are relevant to the situation here, and we trust that they will be of value.

5.   The Plowden and Gittins reports were valuable contributions to the understanding of primary education in England and Wales respectively. We have been anxious to see that a lengthy period of time should not elapse before some statement of the position in relation to Northern Ireland should be made. The present report is not intended to be a comprehensive report, but deals rather with those matters

which might be described as affecting the structure of primary education. We have referred in the report to certain matters which we feel require further investigation. These are selection for and the age of transfer to secondary education, the question of remedial education and also the problem of the "slow learner." All these matters are complex and the investigation of each on its own could well occupy the full term of existence of any one Advisory Council. We consider, however, that these problems should not be overlooked, but should be referred either to specialist Working Parties or to future Councils for examination. Consideration might also be given in due course to the questions of Religious Education in the primary school and of corporal punishment. We have not been able to deal with these matters as to do so would have delayed submission of our report for too long a time.

6.   Special reference should, however, be made to the question of Religious Education. We feel that this matter would require detailed examination before any recommendations are made affecting the present position. We note with interest the recommendations contained on this subject in both the Plowden and Gittins reports but at this stage we would not wish either to accept or reject all of those recommendations in relation to Northern Ireland. It would appear that there remains a vital task to be undertaken in schools in relation to religious teaching and the indications are that on the whole the parents want the schools to carry out this task. The Religious Education Council came into existence in 1966 with a view to integrating the preparation of Religious Education syllabuses and handbooks for different age levels and types of education. We understand that this Council is at present engaged in producing a completely revised Religious Education syllabus for use in primary schools. We are pleased to note that this is so and

consider that when this syllabus is available the general question might then be reviewed.

CHAPTER 8

The Future Place of the Small Rural Primary School

CONCLUSION

144. It appears on balance that the system of small schools spread more or less evenly over sparsely populated rural areas may be regarded as a relic of a social order which no longer obtains. New housing policies favour the principle of concentration, either by way of extensions to existing towns or villages or at selected growth points where the necessary services and amenities are available or can be economically provided. We are of the opinion not only that the closure of small rural schools should continue, for compelling educational and economic reasons, but that it inevitably will continue for reasons beyond the control of the educational planners.

RECOMMENDATIONS

145. (1)   The present policy in regard to the closure and amalgamation of small rural primary schools, both county and voluntary, and their replacement by larger units should be continued. Where it is practical to do so, the superseding school should be located in a rural environment.

(2)   Local education authority advisers who could be in close contact with primary school teachers at frequent intervals should be appointed.

(3)   New primary schools in a rural environment should be built and equipped in such a way that they can offer educational facilities in no way inferior to those found in schools in larger centres of population. Since most of these new schools will still be classed as small schools, they should have the benefit of the special formula for staffing small schools as recommended in paragraph 86.

(4)   Shelters affording adequate protection should be provided at waiting points for children using transport to and from school.

(5)   Arrangements being made for transport to and from school should be carefully planned to avoid too early an arrival at school and to ensure that children get home in reasonable time.   Care should also be taken to see that bus timetables are strictly adhered to and that there is proper supervision of the children in the bus.

(6)   Where a new community school is being provided, and areas are losing their schools as a result, every effort should be made to ensure that the parents involved remain in close contact with the new school, thereby creating a wider community and building up a sense of belonging to the larger unit.

II.23   Primary Education Teachers' Guide, DENI, 1974, Chap.1, pp1-2.

In 1969, following an appropriate recommendation in the Burges report, a Primary Study Group was established to prepare a suitable replacement for the "Programme for Primary Schools." The resultant document was published in 1974 and marked a distinct break from the former prescriptive programmes of instruction.

CHAPTER 1

INTRODUCTION

GENERAL

This guide presents what in a period of rapid and widespread change appears to its authors to be a fruitful approach to the work of the primary school. It will be modified and supplemented from time to time in the light of developments in knowledge and as new practices are validated. Suggestions on books for further reading can be obtained from any of the teacher training centres in Northern Ireland or from the Inspectorate.

No attempt is made to lay down in precise detail what should be taught and how teachers should organise their work. Broad objectives have been stated and practical advice given where necessary, on how these objectives may be realised. But each teacher must evolve, within broad and generally understood limits and in compatibility with her staff colleagues, the curriculum, organisation and methods most suited to her own circumstances.

The greatest hope for sound progress lies neither in the slavish following of what is familiar, nor in uncritical acceptance of what is novel but in well informed and open minded assessment of both current practices and new proposals. To this end the work of the Schools Curriculum Committee and the growth of teachers' centres will facilitate the planning and evaluation of experimental approaches and the pooling of knowledge and experience.

CURRICULUM OBJECTIVES

In a complex and diversified society such as that in which we live it is not possible to formulate for primary schools a set of objectives which will command universal and complete acceptance. Various factors such as religious beliefs, the physical environment, the attitudes and interests of the staff, the size of the school, may all operate differently on individual schools and affect the content of the curriculum, the organisation evolved and the type of teaching pursued. Nevertheless there is a wide measure of agreement on valid curriculum objectives, although they may well differ in detail and emphasis from one school to another.

When a group of Northern Ireland primary school teachers were asked to provide examples of such objectives, the examples they gave could be categorised within a framework of four basic values:

(i)   personal values — religious and moral beliefs, respect for other people's opinions, personal pride, perseverance and physical health;

(ii)   social values — individual co-operation, group membership, living in a community, national and international interests;

(iii) vocational value — literacy and numeracy, mental and physical skills;

(iv) aesthetic values — appreciation of beauty and the enjoyment of leisure pursuits.

Such objectives are not of course peculiar to primary schools in Northern Ireland but are in general accord with the conclusions reached by surveys conducted elsewhere. There is, of course, considerable overlap of one category with another, but translated into curriculum terms these values suggest that schools ought to concern themselves at least with:

religious and moral education;
language and other forms of communication, mathematics;
the study of the environment, including geography, history and the physical sciences;
physical education and health education;
art, music and other interests and hobbies.

Evaluation must play an important part and care must be taken to ensure the validity of the techniques of evaluation used. In particular, quality of learning should be evaluated as well as quantity. Testing children's grasp of concepts is more essential than testing relatively superficial learning such as memorisation. There is the further point that the attitudes and interests which children derive from particular learning and teaching methods are also important and some evaluation of these is necessary. In addition, various aspects of school routine may be evaluated, for example, reward and punishment, contact between parent and teacher, the time children spend on various aspects of the curriculum, opportunities for children to use their own initiative, or the nature and quality of the tests which children are set. In this way not only the children but also the whole spectrum of a school's organisation, teaching practices and philosophy are being tested.

Through the Inspectorate each school periodically receives an external assessment of its work. In a more personal way, teachers, by talking about their teaching methods at courses and conferences, are also enabled to carry out some evaluation of their own teaching. This process could be made more systematic; for example, a school might invite representatives from one or two other schools to call in order to discuss and evaluate certain lines of development in that school, or similar informal discussions might be held at a teachers' centre.

II.24   "A Review of the Educational and Library Provision in the Board's Area," SEELB 1974, pp.i-iii.

In this report the South-Eastern Education and Library Board summarised the changes which had taken place in primary education since the former Down and Antrim Education Committees published their original development schemes in 1949.

Under the terms of the Education and Libraries (N.I.) Order 1972 the South Eastern Education and Library Board assumed responsibility for the provision of educational and library facilities and, jointly with the District Councils, for the provision of recreational facilities in the south eastern part of the province with effect from 1st October, 1973. This area contains the districts of Ards, North Down, Down, Castlereagh and Lisburn which in 1973 had a total population of 310,617 and a school population on 1st January, 1974 of 64,854.

****

Under Section 11 of the Education and Libraries (N.I.) Order, 1972, the Board adopted those development schemes or parts of schemes prepared by the former Down and Antrim County Education Committees which related to its area or part of its area and, subject to any revised scheme or amendment subsequently prepared and approved, has executed or shall continue to execute the relevant parts of these schemes not executed at the date of reorganisation. The Board also adopted the forward plans of the former Down County Education Committee as stated in its "Review of the State of School Provision" adopted in November, 1972 and revised in September, 1973.

****

PRIMARY EDUCATION

The Board has continued the policy of the former Down County Education Committee of endeavouring to maintain small primary schools in thinly populated areas, but because of staffing or enrolment problems or the substandard condition of old school buildings a substantial number of one and two teacher schools have been closed in rural areas over the last ten years. The Board's present policy in this matter is guided by the instruction given by a former Minister of Education in 1968 that "we should not in future, as a general rule, agree to the provision of a new primary school in a rural area or to the expenditure of substantial sums of money on the rehabilitation of an existing building unless there is very good reason to believe that the enrolment for the foreseeable future will support at least three teachers." In the light of this statement the Board's policy with regard to rural school provision is based on:

(a)   the desirability of providing education for primary school children in surroundings up to the standard of the late 20th century;

(b)   a recognition of the important role played by rural schools in the social and communal life of the area and the need to preserve such schools wherever practicable;

(c)   the requirement to provide efficient instruction by means of a suitably qualified permanent staff, a properly designed curriculum and the provision of modern materials and equipment;

(d)   the need to ensure the efficient use of public finance by effecting economies of scale wherever possible within the context of the above three objectives.

In endeavouring to meet these conditions the Board will continue the practice of establishing central rural schools by the amalgamation of a number of small outmoded schools into a larger and more viable unit at a central location outside the towns.

In urban areas the Board's policy is to establish medium size primary schools (300-500 pupils) serving individual neighbourhoods rather than allowing the unchecked growth of single central schools.

All the present primary schools in the Board's area retain children from the age of five to eleven years but proposals for certain of the developing medium size towns may involve the establishment of separate junior and infant schools where a single school serving the town would grow to excessive size and a suitable location for a second full primary school cannot be established.

A number of the new primary schools being established in the near future will be of open or semi-open plan design and the Board is anxious to encourage experiments in the internal organisation of primary schools aimed at fostering the development of the individual child.

II.25   "Schools and Demographic Trends — A Backcloth to Planning," DENI 1981, pp5-6.

Social, political, economic, educational and emotional factors were involved in the closure of small rural primary schools.   With an increasing emphasis on value for money the debate intensified in the 1980s as a perusal of local newspapers amply illustrates.   The Department of Education summarised the factors in 1981 in a well-balanced chapter in this planning document.

CHAPTER 2

PRIMARY SCHOOLS

5.   MINIMUM VIABLE SIZE OF PRIMARY SCHOOL

5.1   Although primary schools, with their emphasis on cross-curricular patterns of teaching do not require specialist teachers to the same extent as do secondary schools, there is a clear need for staff with particular skills and expertise in separate areas of the curriculum.   Only a teacher with exceptional flair and versatility will be able to give adequate attention to the central place of language and communication, as well as to the development of the children's abilities in environmental studies, mathematics, creative studies and physical education.   Such teachers do exist, and the quality of education in many small primary schools is high, but it is unreasonable to assume that all teachers should be expected to cover the whole curriculum equally well. The absence of particular skills and expertise in a small school may result in unbalanced curricular provision and certainly the loss of a teacher with particular skills is more likely to cause difficulties in small schools than in larger ones.

5.2   Although it may be difficult to sustain the argument frequently advanced that a minimum of 7 teachers (one for each age group in the primary school) is necessary to ensure that the curricular needs of primary schools pupils are fully met, it is obviously more likely that a broader range of expertise will be available in schools of that size than in those having fewer teachers.   During their progress through the primary school, it is to the benefit of children that they should encounter a variety of teaching styles and approaches, if only to assist the smooth transition from primary to secondary schools. In addition, there are significant benefits to the children's social education through contact with larger numbers of other children.

5.3   Most teachers believe that it is educationally more sound for them to have charge of a single age group at primary level.   There is a considerable psychological barrier to be faced by teachers when they are required to deal with multiple age groups in their classes for the first time.

5.4   So far as it is possible, certainly for schools in urban areas, it should be the goal to maintain schools with a minimum enrolment to justify the appointment of one teacher for each primary age group.   This would facilitate the allocation of subject responsibilities to staff with particular skills, who would support the work of other classroom teachers. In urban areas, a policy of closure or fundamental reorganisation, such as amalgamation, should be adopted if the school enrolment falls below 200.

5.5   For rural schools the goal of one teacher for each age group may not be realistic because this could involve children in long bus journeys to a large central school which could entail an unduly early start or late ending to the children's period of absence from home. Equally, the isolation of such schools from the community they serve is most undesirable. On the other hand it is recognised that the strains and constraints imposed on the 2 teacher school are very severe, and unless both teachers have expertise and skill in a wide range of subjects the educational experience of the children may be restricted. Socially and educationally, the children would receive a more balanced provision in schools of larger sizes. It would be reasonable and in keeping with the idea that each school staff should have as wide a range of expertise as possible, that the minimum acceptable staffing for schools should be 4 teachers (i.e. an enrolment of about 100). This size offers the minimum acceptable flexibility of arrangement, and the use of peripatetic or part-time teachers to supplement and enrich the curriculum should be seen as almost inevitable. On educational grounds such schools will certainly be viable, but careful attention needs to be given to ways of providing the necessary inservice training support for the teachers who are likely to feel the pressure of working in isolation.

5.6   There may well have to be exceptions to these general rules but the need for such exceptions should be carefully considered and when proposals for rationalisation are presented the case for such exceptions should be critically examined.

7.   SUMMARY OF FACTORS TO BE TAKEN INTO ACCOUNT

7.1   School authorities should now examine how they might rationalise primary school provision. There are a number of factors to be taken into account, but it would appear to the Department that the following are the most important criteria to be borne in mind when reaching decisions:

(a)   the concentration of pupils in suitably located schools of appropriate size to meet curricular needs;

(b)   the reduction or elimination of over-crowding in those schools where accommodation will continue to be under pressure;

(c)   the reduction or elimination of temporary accommodation;

(d)   the reduction and eventual elimination of the use of the least satisfactory permanent accommodation; and

(e)   the closure of schools where the accommodation is likely to continue to be under-used to a great extent.

II.26 NICED and Curriculum Change in the Eighties: Northern Ireland Council for Educational Development 1989, Chap.2, pp3-5.

In 1969, the Northern Ireland Schools Curriculum Committee was established in recognition of the increasing participation by local schools in national curriculum projects and, in particular, those sponsored by the Schools Council for the Curriculum and Examinations. A shift of emphasis was initiated in 1973 by the recently formed Department of Education (formerly the ministry); thereafter the committee became more and more concerned with locally based projects and on experimentation generated and implemented by Northern Ireland teachers including those in the primary sector. In November, 1980 the activities of NISCC, together with the functions of the Northern Ireland Committee for Educational Technology (NICET) were subsumed by the Northern Ireland Council for Educational Development (NICED).

Throughout the 1980s NICED was instrumental in promoting curriculum innovation across the whole spectrum of education; however, within the primary portion the work of NICED was synonymous with the production of "The Primary Guidelines" and the associated support papers. It would be impossible to select one guideline or one support paper as representative of the total range therefore, as an alternative, a brief descriptive section has been selected from the booklet published to mark the termination of the Council's activities. It is clear from the chosen passage that "The Primary Guidelines" initiative was generated by a request for assistance from within the teaching profession and that this, in turn, had been prompted by inspectorial criticism of the lack of system and progression that characterised many of the curricular plans drawn up by individual schools working within the latitude granted by the 1974 "Primary Education Teachers' Guide."

WHOLE CURRICULUM REVIEW (PRIMARY LEVEL)

The Primary Guidelines

In 1981 a report of a survey which had been undertaken by DENI Inspectorate into primary education in the Province stated that the majority of primary schools had not written policies on the curriculum. The survey commented that:

> "... even when they are available, the curriculum guidelines prepared by principals for their staffs tend to lack clarity and direction ... much more emphasis should be placed on the development of systematic guidelines within subject areas."

Following the publication of the survey report the teacher union representatives on the Standing Conference for Primary Education, having asked DENI to provide appropriate guidelines for primary education were advised to make an approach to NICED. In response to this approach NICED set up in early 1982 a Primary Programme Committee (PPC) which brought together a number of teachers who had been identified as good classroom practitioners along with a few advisers, college lecturers and members of the Inspectorate. The PPC was given the following terms of reference:

—   to hold in review the curriculum of primary schools;

—   in particular to produce guidelines for primary education in Northern Ireland;

—   to collaborate with other bodies in Northern Ireland concerned with primary education; and

—   to make known developments in primary education elsewhere in the United Kingdom.

WHOLE CURRICULUM REVIEW

Concurrently with the approach from the Standing Conference for Primary Education, NICED had established a small working group to consider issues regarding curriculum review raised in a Schools Council publication "The Practical Curriculum." The discussions arising from this publication influenced NICED thinking on the curriculum. A contemporary NICED strategy document indicated an awareness that new approaches to the curriculum were more likely to become embedded in the work of schools if they were in line with the needs and interests of pupils and teachers and that effective curriculum development might best be promoted through whole curriculum review.   As a result pilot work was undertaken in whole curriculum review through a number of projects at post primary level and the thinking of the PPC was also influenced by the publications and discussions on whole curriculum review.

DECISIONS ON FORMAT

Early discussions at PPC showed that members had a keen appreciation of the holistic approach normally adopted in the primary curriculum and there was considerable debate as to the most appropriate approach to the task of writing guidelines for such a curriculum.   While there was a general sympathy with the notion of a single guideline ranging across the whole curriculum this was felt to be an inappropriate format for two very practical reasons; firstly that such a document would be extremely bulky and off-putting to teachers and secondly that writing it would present a very difficult task to PPC members.   There was an ensuing discussion as to whether an approach through areas of experience might be appropriate (e.g. subsuming history, geography and science within environmental studies and music, art and design, physical education and drama within creative and aesthetic studies) but in the event a decision was made in favour of single subject guidelines with cross-curricular references being introduced in each, wherever possible.

Nine subjects for which guidelines would be produced were identified as follows:

- music;
- science;
- mathematics;
- health and social education;
- language and literacy;
- physical education;
- art and design;
- history; and
- geography.

The 9 Curricular Guidelines were intended to facilitate curriculum review by promoting staff discussion on each particular aspect of the curriculum along the following lines:

- What is meant by this aspect of the curriculum within the primary school/within our primary school?

- What benefits might accrue to an individual child in terms of the development of attitudes, values, concepts and qualities as well as knowledge and skills?

- How might it be taught?

- What resources and support are available to the teacher?

It was agreed that the guidelines would be addressed initially to principals and that an Introductory Booklet would be produced to support principals in working with whole staffs to institute review and to develop statements of school policy and aims.

II.27   Education Reform in Northern Ireland — The Way Forward, DENI, October 1988.

The publication of this document marked the end of a period of consultation with educational interests in Northern Ireland consequent on the preparation and introduction of the 1988 Education Act in England and Wales. The time-lag provided an opportunity to tailor this Act to the different circumstances in Northern Ireland. As with most educational legislation in the 1980s it was comprehensive in its content and had few clauses specifically aimed at the primary sector. Other general clauses are included in Section 3.

The emphasis, according to Dr. Brian Mawhinney, Education Minister (N.I.) at the time, would be on a curriculum which would be broad, balanced and coherent and to which all children would have equal access, irrespective of the type of school they attended or where they lived.

Here was a National Curriculum for Northern Ireland with associated testing in line with the government's "back to basics" policy.

2. CURRICULUM AND ASSESSMENT

****

2.2   The responses provided a great deal of constructive comment on various aspects of the curriculum proposals, and in particular emphasised the need to build on the valuable work already undertaken in Primary Guidelines and the 11-16 Programme, which have influenced curriculum thinking and approaches to curriculum organisation and design in many schools. Many responses, including those from schools and teachers, described the beneficial influence of these initiatives on curricular provision, and argued that the way forward in curriculum development in Northern Ireland should be founded in the concept of school based whole curriculum review and planning promoted by these initiatives. Some writers, indeed, put the view that a statutory common curriculum in Northern Ireland was unnecessary, as, if these initiatives were allowed to continue their course, they would eventually result in the emergence of a broad and balanced curriculum in all schools, in practice, a "common" curriculum.

****

2.6   The Government fully recognises the contribution of Primary Guidelines and the 11-16 Programme to the development of a coherent approach to curriculum organisation in primary and secondary schools respectively. The progress which these initiatives have made since their inception has contributed significantly to curriculum thinking in the participating schools, and in many this is already being reflected in the quality of their educational provision. But the Government considers that voluntary participation in curriculum review and development would not achieve the aim of raising standards in all schools and improving educational opportunities consistently, or of ensuring that improvements occurred within a reasonable timescale. Accordingly the Government has concluded that it is necessary to provide in law for a basic curriculum containing the components of a broad and balanced education, to which all pupils will be assured equality of access. These components, in the form of subjects which all pupils of compulsory school age must follow, will be prescribed in the new legislation.

****

Areas of Study and Contributory Subjects

2.8   The curriculum of all pupils of compulsory school age will therefore include, in addition to Religious Education, certain areas of study, which may comprise more than one subject; the subjects contributing to each area of study will also be listed in the legislation. The areas of study which will be prescribed are:

> English;
> Mathematics;
> Science and Technology;
> The Environment and Society;
> Creative and Expressive Studies;
> Language Studies (secondary schools only).

2.9   The main subjects which will contribute to the various areas of study at the relevant stages of compulsory schooling are indicted in Table 1 below.   This list is not exhaustive; other subjects, not listed, may also contribute to a particular area of study and may be offered by a school if it wishes. Centrally prescribed attainment targets (i.e. the main teaching and learning objectives of a subject) and programmes of study (i.e. outlines of the main activities and content associated with each subject) will be drawn up for all subjects listed.

2.10   Pupils will be required to study, for all or part of their period of compulsory schooling, certain of these main subjects (marked "*" in Table 1) in which, in addition, they will be formally assessed. (Formal assessment means the assessing and recording of each pupil's knowledge, understanding and ability to undertake tasks).   Pupils will also be required to follow certain other subjects (marked "**" in Table 1) at the stages indicated, but will not be formally assessed in these.

TABLE 1

Areas of Study and Contributory Subjects

To emphasise the integrity of the programmes of study,
the years of compulsory schooling are referred to as Years 1-12,
rather than P1-P7 and Forms 1-5.

Areas of Study	*Years 1-7*
English	English*
Mathematics	Mathematics*
Science and Technology	Science* Technology*
The Environment and Society	History* Geography* Local Studies
Creative and Expressive Studies **Expressive Studies**	Art and Design** Music** Drama PE**
Language Studies	Not Applicable

****

Cross-Curricular Themes

2.12   In addition, a number of important strands of learning have been identified which, although possessing their own individual cohesion, are normally taught as part of several other subjects. The legislation will, therefore, provide that the curriculum of every pupil must contain certain educational themes, as set out in Table 2 below.   These themes will normally be taught on a cross-curricular basis, and the objectives within each theme will be incorporated into the programmes of study of appropriate subjects. They may also, where considered appropriate, be supplemented by units of work provided by the school.

TABLE 2

CROSS-CURRICULAR THEMES

Years 1-7
Information Technology Education for Mutual Understanding Cultural Heritage Health Education

****

Flexibility of Provision

2.18   It is not intended to prescribe the proportion of time which schools should spend on individual subjects. It will be for schools themselves to determine what is necessary to ensure that the programmes of study are adequately covered, and that the curriculum for each pupil is broad, balanced and coherent. It will also be for schools to determine how they organise the curriculum and what teaching and learning approaches they wish to use. For example, in primary schools in the early years much of the children's experience in science and creative and expressive studies may be gained through well-planned and structured play activities; and in secondary schools work in certain aspects of technology may be organised on a modular framework. Such aspects will remain the responsibility of individual schools.

****

Need for Formal Assessment

2.24 Responses to consultation supported the Government's view that regular assessment of pupils' progress is an essential and integral part of ensuring that every child is receiving the maximum benefit from the educational opportunities on offer, and that any learning difficulties are identified early and remedial action taken. The Government has decided that in Northern Ireland there should be formal assessment of pupils' progress in the programmes of study at ages 8, 11, 14 and 16 (Years 4, 7, 10 and 12).

2.25 The need for any formal assessment in the primary school before the age of 11 was questioned by many respondents: they felt that this could put children under pressure too early and that any classification of children at this stage was undesirable. The Government takes the view, however, that some formal assessment in the course of the primary stage is necessary to allow schools to check on the progress of pupils in the programmes of study, to provide for parents an objective indication of their child's progress against specified criteria, and to monitor the performance of schools.   Age 8, which represents roughly the mid-point of primary schooling, has been chosen rather than age 7 largely to take account of differences between Northern Ireland and England and Wales in the organisation of primary education in the early and middle years, and in order to provide a clearer indication of what the school, as distinct from the home, has contributed to the education of each child.

2.26   This is not to suggest, however, that schools should wait until children are formally assessed before taking action to deal with identified weaknesses in performance; responses confirmed that regular informal classroom assessment is an integral part of good teaching practice; formal assessment should complement this.

Format of Assessment

2.27   In principle, the Government considers that the formal assessment at ages 8, 11, 14 and 16 should, as in England and Wales, be based on the approach recommended in the report by the Task Group on Assessment and Testing, whereby different levels of attainment and overall pupil progress would be registered on a ten-point scale covering all the years of compulsory schooling.   The Northern Ireland Schools Examinations Council (NISEC) will be asked to give advice to the Government on how this general format should be applied in Northern Ireland, and also on assessment criteria appropriate to each level of attainment.

2.28   In view of the concern expressed by many respondents, the Government wishes to emphasise that it is not intended that assessment will be based solely on pencil and paper tests.   Assessment will identify what pupils know, understand and are able to do at each stage.   It will at all stages include an assessment of pupils' project and other work in the classroom, and of their listening and speaking skills. The precise form may vary depending on the subject and the age of the pupils; at age 16 assessment for most pupils will be through GCSE.

2.29   All of the formal assessment, including the marking and grading of written work, will be the responsibility of teachers, but it will be necessary for NISEC to develop adequate moderation arrangements to ensure consistency of standards in both written work and teacher assessment across all schools and with other parts of the United Kingdom.

II.28   The Education Reform (Northern Ireland) Order 1989, No.2406 (NI.20), HMSO, 1989.

The 1989 Order put into legislative form many of the proposals in The Way Forward, article five, specifying the areas of study to be followed, while article six stated the requirement for assessment in each of the compulsory contributory subjects based on attainment targets to be set in place by the Department of Education (Art.7).

PART III

THE CURRICULUM

****

PRINCIPAL PROVISIONS

The Curriculum

5. — (1) The curriculum for every grant-aided school shall—

(a)   include provision for religious education for all registered pupils at the school; and

(b)   in so far as it relates to registered pupils at the school of compulsory school age, meet the requirements of this Article and Article 6.

(2)   The curriculum for a grant-aided school shall include the following areas of study —

(a)   English;

(b)   Mathematics;

(c)   Science and Technology;

(d)   The Environment and Society;

(e)   Creative and Expressive Studies;

(f)   Language Studies, in relation to —
    (i)   schools which are Irish speaking; and
    (ii)   the third and fourth key stages in other schools.

(3)   For the purposes of this Part the subjects which fall within each area of study listed in column 1 of Schedule 1 are—

(a)   the subjects listed against that area of study in column 2 of that Schedule; and

(b)   any other cognate subjects which appropriately fall to be taught within that area of study and the subjects falling within any area of study by virtue of sub-paragraph (a) or (b) are referred to in this Part as the contributory subjects within that area of study and the subjects falling within any area of study by virtue of sub-paragraph (a) are referred to in this Part as the listed contributory subjects within that area of study.

(4)   The curriculum for every grant-aided school shall, in relation to each listed contributory subject which is taught to pupils at the school —

(a)   include such attainment targets and programmes of study as are specified in relation to that subject and those pupils under Article 7 (1)(a); and

(b)   require that the content of the teaching of that subject is consistent with those programmes of study and with the attainment by those pupils of those attainment targets.

****

(8)   Nothing in paragraph (2)(f) shall be taken to preclude the inclusion of Language Studies as an area of study in the curriculum of a grant-aided school in relation to the first and second key stages.

(9)   In paragraphs (2) to (6) and Article 6 —

(a)   references to the curriculum for a grant-aided school are references to that curriculum so far as it relates to registered pupils at the school of compulsory school age; and

(b)   references to pupils at such a school are references to registered pupils at the school of compulsory school age.

Compulsory contributory subjects and compulsory assessment

6. — (1)   The curriculum for every grant-aided school shall require each pupil at the school to be taught within each area of study the contributory subjects which in accordance with paragraph (2) are compulsory contributory subjects in relation to that pupil.

(2)   The compulsory contributory subjects within each area of study specified in column 1 of Schedule 2 —

(a)   in relation to pupils in key stages 1 and 2, are those specified in column 2 of that Schedule;

(b)   in relation to pupils in key stage 3, are those specified in column 3 of that Schedule;

(c)   in relation to pupils in key stage 4, are those specified in column 4 of that Schedule.

(3)   Subject to paragraph (4), the curriculum for every grant-aided school shall require each pupil at the school to be assessed in each of his compulsory contributory subjects in accordance with such assessment arrangements as are specified in relation to that subject and that pupil under Article 7(1)(b).

(4)   Paragraph (3) does not apply to any compulsory contributory subjects which are within the area of study called Creative and Expressive Studies.

(5)   For ease of reference, in Schedule 2 an "(A)" is placed after each entry relating to a compulsory contributory subject in which pupils are required under paragraph (3) to be assessed.

(6)   The Department may by order amend Schedule 2.

Attainment targets, programmes of study and assessment arrangements

7. — (1)   The Department may by order specify —

(a)   in relation to a listed contributory subject —

    (i)   such attainment targets; and
    (ii)   such programmes of study,

    as it considers appropriate for that subject; and

(b)   in relation to a compulsory contributory subject in which pupils are required under Article 6(3) to be assessed, such assessment arrangements as it considers appropriate for that subject.

(2)   It shall be the duty of the Department so to exercise the powers conferred by paragraph (1) as —

(a)   to set in place as soon as is practicable —

    (i)   attainment targets and programmes of study in relation to all the compulsory contributory subjects;
    (ii)   assessment arrangements in relation to all the compulsory contributory subjects in which pupils re required under Article 6(3) to be assessed;

(b)   to revise any existing attainment targets, programmes of study or assessment arrangements whenever it considers it necessary or appropriate to do so.

(3)   In this Part —

(a)   "attainment targets" means the knowledge, skills and understanding which pupils of different abilities and maturities are expected to have by the end of each key stage;

(b)   "programmes of study" means the matters, skills and processes which are required to be taught to pupils of different abilities and maturities during each key stage;

(c)   "assessment arrangements" means the arrangements for assessing pupils at or near the end of each key stage for the purpose of ascertaining what they have achieved in relation to the attainment targets for that stage.

(4)   An order made under paragraph (1) may not require —

(a)   that any particular period or periods of time should be allocated during any key stage to the teaching of any programme of study or any matter, skill or process forming part of it; or

(b)   that provision of any particular kind should be made in school timetables for the periods to be allocated to such teaching during any such stage.

(5)   An order under paragraph (1) may, instead of containing the provisions to be made, refer to provisions in a document published by Her Majesty's Stationery Office and direct that those provisions shall have effect or, as the case may be, have effect as amended by the order.

(6)   An order under paragraph (1)(b) may authorise the making of such provisions giving full effect to or otherwise supplementing the provisions made by the order as appear to the Department to be expedient; and any provisions made under such an order shall, on being published by Her Majesty's Stationery Office, have effect for the purposes of this Part as if made by the order.

Educational themes

8. — (1)   The curriculum for a grant-aided school shall not, in so far as it relates to pupils of compulsory school age, be taken to satisfy the requirements of Article 4(2) unless it promotes, wholly or mainly through the teaching of the contributory subjects and religious education, the attainment of the objectives of the following educational themes, namely—

(a)   Information Technology;
(b)   Education for Mutual Understanding;
(c)   Cultural Heritage;
(d)   Health Education;

****

Article 6. SCHEDULE 2

COMPULSORY SUBJECTS

(1) Areas of Study	(2) Compulsory contributory subjects in key stages 1 and 2
English	English (A)
Mathematics	Mathematics (A)
Science and Technology	Science (A) Technology and Design (A)
The Environment and Society	History (A) Geography (A)
Creative and Expressive Studies	Art and Design Music Physical Education
Language Studies	Irish (in Irish speaking schools only) (A)

NOTE: An "(A)" placed after an entry signifies that the compulsory contributory subject to which that entry relates is one in which pupils are required under Article 6(3) to be assessed.

III

SECONDARY EDUCATION

III.1   Interim Report of the Departmental Committee on the Educational Services in Northern Ireland, Cmd.6.

In 1920 secondary schools in Northern Ireland were privately controlled. Catholic schools were under clerical management, while the boards of governors of Protestant schools were composed of both clergy and laity. In addition a few schools still existed for private profit. The secondary educational system was rigid and examination bound under the influence of the 1878 Education Act.

The most serious immediate problem was staffing. Increasing numbers of teachers were leaving the schools due to low pay and insecure tenure.

The new Unionist government was determined to recast the whole education system. While the emphasis would be on primary education, the secondary system would not remain untouched. Unionists had supported the abortive Education Bills in 1919 and 1920 and once in control established the Lynn Committee in September 1921 to review and recommend. The Committee had strong representation from the secondary schools, electing R M Jones, headmaster of the Royal Belfast Academical Institution, as vice-chairman.

While the Lynn Committee was sitting, Lord Londonderry and his officials in the Ministry of Education began work on a major education bill. Their work was deeply influenced by the Lynn Committee's interim report, published in June 1922. The reports main comments on the secondary schools were as follows:-

132. It is important that there should be as complete co-ordination as possible between the three branches of education. Pupils who are highly qualified to profit by advanced education should be encouraged to proceed from the primary to the secondary or technical school. We think, therefore, that local Committees should have power, in the case of pupils who have reached a standard prescribed by the Ministry — which standard should be a high one — to assist them to attend secondary or technical schools by the payment of travelling expenses, in whole or in part, and by giving assistance towards the payment of fees. In the latter case the assistance should not exceed fifty per cent of the fees. Any such scheme for assistance should be a general scheme applicable to all qualified pupils in the area under the control of the Committee who desire to avail themselves of it.

142.   While we are of opinion that religious instruction should form part of the education given in preparatory schools, preparatory departments of secondary schools, and secondary schools, nevertheless, in view of the constitution of such schools, the nature of their foundation, the purposes for which and the conditions under which they are governed and managed, we consider it injudicious to impose any system or rules as to religious instruction, and we leave the matter rather to the bodies of trustees and governors.

161. — (4) In the case of secondary schools under approved Boards of Governors, the money required for new school buildings, or for the enlargement or structural improvement

of existing secondary schools, may be provided by means of a loan through the Ministry to the Governors; two-thirds of the interest and sinking fund may be paid annually by the Ministry, the remainder being paid by the Governors.

180.   Defects of various kinds, many of them serious, can be remedied gradually as a result of State Control, but there are two radical defects in the existing system of preparatory and secondary schools the removal of which should be made a condition of State aid; these are the generally unsatisfactory conditions of employment of teachers, and the fact that some of the schools are conducted for private profit.

181.   It is now commonly accepted that aid from public funds should not be given to schools conducted for private profit, and with this view we are in agreement. The State when making grants should be satisfied that in all grant-aided schools the entire income from all sources is devoted solely to educational purposes.

265.   ...We estimate that the total State contribution to secondary education, exclusive of pensions and of any sums which may be expended on such objects as the training of teachers, will, if our recommendations are adopted, amount to between £125,000 and £130,000 per annum, of which from £65,000 to £70,000 would be a new charge on the Vote.

III.2   The Education Act Northern Ireland 1923, 13 and 14 Geo.5, C.21.

The 1923 Education Act although a milestone in Northern Ireland's educational history had little to say about secondary education. Many of its permissive clauses could equally apply to all educational sectors. The implementation of the Lynn Committee's recommendations was left to statutory rules and orders.

Repealing much existing legislation, the Act inaugurated a period of increased central control by the Ministry of Education while freeing the schools from some of the curricular rigidity. Provision was made for the newly created Regional Education Committees to assume control of secondary schools. Most were reluctant to do so but many gave financial aid to secondary schools which found themselves in financial difficulties. Nevertheless this provision left the gate open for future changes:-

21.   It shall be lawful for the owners or trustees of any school, which at the appointed day is an intermediate or secondary school recognised by the Ministry, notwithstanding any provision contained in any instrument regulating the trusts or management of such school, to transfer the school, and any land, buildings or equipment held or used in connection therewith, to the education authority upon such terms and conditions as may be arranged between the parties concerned with the approval of the Ministry. The provisions of the Second Schedule to this Act shall apply with respect to any such transfer, and on the completion of the transfer the school shall be conducted by the education authority as a public intermediate or secondary school, but subject to discontinuance upon such terms as may be approved by the Ministry.

III.3   Report of the Committee on the Scholarship System in Northern Ireland, Cmd.192.

Racked by religious controversies the Ministry of Education paid little attention (during the inter-war years) to secondary education which largely remained a private preserve. Financial limitations hindered the development of the system on English lines.

When the Hadow Report was published in 1926, Northern Ireland simply had not the money to implement its revolutionary proposals, and so throughout these years the secondary schools remained the preserve of the few, although an increasing few.

Access to secondary education was restricted by the means of the parents. Only those who could afford the fees were able to climb the ladder. However educational philosophy accepted that bright children should be given a chance to get on the ladder by means of competitive scholarships. Although the Regional Education Committees framed scholarship schemes the number of scholarships was hardly lavish.

In response to parliamentary criticism at the paucity of scholarship provision a committee of enquiry was chaired by J. H. Robb, parliamentary secretary to the Ministry of Education, which reported in 1938 that:-

8.   ... In 1924 the Belfast Authority awarded 52 scholarships to secondary schools and 4 to universities and the Londonderry Authority awarded 2 secondary school scholarships.

In 1925 Scholarships to Secondary Schools were:-

Co. Antrim	— 19 of value of £20 each
Co. Armagh	— 15 of value of £20 each
Co. Down	— 16 of value of £20 each
Co. Fermanagh	— 8 of value of £20 each
Co. Londonderry	— 12 of value of £20 each
Co. Tyrone	— 14 of varying values each

20.   It is on record that on the 31 December 1929 there were in attendance at secondary schools in Northern Ireland 516 pupils who had been awarded scholarships by the Committees, covering the cost of tuition, books and stationery, and, in some cases, travelling expenses.

37.   Of the conditions applicable to scholarships of all kinds that involving what has come to be known as the "Means Test" has occasioned the greatest difficulty of administration and has given rise to most criticism.

40.   In interpreting this condition (i.e. every applicant must satisfy the Committee that he is in need of financial assistance to enable him to attend the course of study for which the scholarship is awarded) committees have met with two great difficulties:-

(i)   that of verifying the statement of means made by the parent of an applicant; and

(ii)   that of deciding whether an applicant is in need of financial assistance.

43.   A competition open to all candidates, irrespective of means, would weed out those who were least fitted to follow higher courses and would ensure that awards were made only to students who were capable of acquiring the greatest profit from scholarships. On the other hand it would then be possible for children of well-to-do parents to secure that the whole cost of their education was defrayed from public funds. In our opinion the objections to the latter alternative outweigh the advantages which would be gained by the former. We, therefore, recommend that, while the competition should be open to all candidates the "means" qualification be retained in the scholarship schemes of Education Committees.

47.   ... we consider it to be of great importance that Education Committees should adopt sliding scales based upon parental income and the numbers of dependent children or dependents in determining whether an applicant should be

considered for a full scholarship and we set forth (below) details of scales which we recommend as generally suitable.

50.   We believe that the usefulness of a student to the community depends in large measure upon his ability and mental powers and we accept the principle that scholarships should be given only to the best candidates. We therefore recommend that all applicants should be admitted to the scholarship examinations in every area and that the decision as to their eligibility for financial assistance should be deferred until the results of the examinations have been ascertained. We recommend that the award of scholarships should then be made strictly in order of merit as determined by the examination results and that the Committee should fix the value of each scholarship after consideration of the means of the parents, awarding scholarships of no monetary value to those not in need of assistance.

58.   As far as the Scholarship Examination in the areas other than Belfast is concerned we are not satisfied that it is well adapted to its purpose. We have been concerned to note that only a very small proportion, between 2 and 3 per cent, of the pupils eligible by age in these areas enter in any year for the Examination and that they come from less than 300 of the 1600 public elementary schools.

Criticisms have been levelled against the test on the grounds that it favours pupils from the large schools where intending candidates can be segregated into special classes and that the extensive programme of subjects militates against the chances of pupils from small schools, especially in rural districts, where a more restricted programme of instruction is in operation. We think there is point in these criticisms.

59.   The object of the Examination is to test the intelligence and ability of candidates rather than to measure their acquired knowledge. This object can, in our opinion, be secured by an Examination in a limited range of subjects, provided that certain precautions are taken in setting the question papers. In point of fact an inspection of the marks obtained by candidates at the Scholarship Examination of one year showed that the order of merit would have been only slightly disturbed had the marks been reckoned in English, English Composition and Arithmetic, instead of in these and two other subjects. The proposed reduction in the number of subjects has the advantage that the whole Examination can be conducted in one day without undue strain upon the candidates.

We recommend, therefore, that the Examination should be confined to the three subjects named.

60.   In order that the proposed Examination may best serve its purpose every effort should be made to prevent the question papers from becoming stereotyped. This ideal can only be attained if changes in the form and type of the papers and of the questions are made from year to year.

66.   At the stage when a secondary school scholar has completed the courses leading to the Junior Certificate Examination he is, under the existing system, faced with a second competition in which he must be successful before he is enabled by means of a senior scholarship to follow the higher courses. At this stage he may be in competition not only with other junior scholars, but also with students who have been in attendance at secondary schools, but who have not held scholarships awarded by Education Committees.

67.   ... certain Committees do not accept applications for senior scholarships from students who have not held junior scholarships. Such an attitude is, in our opinion, unsatisfactory. Cases are bound to arise in which students, who for one reason or another were not awarded junior scholarships, should be allowed to complete for senior awards.

68.   ... existing procedure has not been altogether satisfactory in that, on occasions, junior scholars who have reached the standard at the Junior Certificate Examination qualifying for the award of senior scholarships have not been given scholarships. We are strongly of opinion that all junior scholars who reach the qualifying standard should be offered senior scholarships to enable them to complete their secondary school education.

III.4   Plans for Post-War Ulster, J.M. Andrews
(The Prime Minister) 30th July, 1942. House of
Commons Parliamentary Report Volume 25, C2452.

By 1939 Northern Ireland had made substantial progress in its education system but it still lagged far behind developments in England and Wales. New school building fell short of what was needed. School medical services were inadequate, scholarship awards niggardly. There was little help for needy children except in Belfast. The war had a detrimental effect on the educational system. Some schools were damaged in the bombing of Belfast and all suffered years of neglect and over use as wartime shortages increased. New building was suspended in early 1940 and attempts to raise the school leaving age postponed. Absenteeism increased. A teacher shortage developed when the Ministry of Education decided to stop training male teachers.

Despite all these disadvantages educational thinking changed dramatically during the war. Northern Ireland was deeply influenced by the British wartime experience. While the majority of the population were predisposed to look to England for a lead in most matters of social legislation, the Government was determined to establish a Northern Ireland dimension in social reform.

Thus in the darkest period of the war, J. M. Andrews, the Prime Minister claimed the right for Ulster to develop its own educational system tailored to the Province's requirement. His demands were ill-received in Westminster.

The question of the youth of the country has been largely exercising the minds of my colleagues and myself, for upon the youth will depend the future of this Imperial province. The problems of youth are, to a very large extent, dependent on health and education. We are anxious, as a Government, that no child shall suffer from malnutrition, and that all children of ability and intelligence will have equal opportunity in education.

(Hon Members: Hear, hear.)

Many more scholarships must be given, the school-leaving age must be raised, and we must have a considerable extension of technical and agricultural education from which our future citizens will get a training for those occupations in which they afterwards intend to serve. Schemes for the provision of good wholesome meals and milk to school-children must be developed, and increased facilities for physical training must be afforded. Much has already been done in this direction, but we, as a Government, are by no means satisfied and are determined to give the youth of Northern Ireland such a chance as they have never had before. (Hon Members: Hear, hear.) We must have in the future, as far as humanly possible, an A1 population, both as regards health and education.

... The post-war programme I have outlined is an ambitious
one. It is, however, largely our domestic concern, and it will
be for our own Government and Parliament, together with
our local authorities, assisted by our people generally, to
carry it out.

III.5 Educational Reconstruction in Northern Ireland, Cmd.226.

English educational reforms were articulated before the Northern
Ireland government turned its full attention to educational
reconstruction. The King's speech, opening the parliamentary
session of 1944-5, announced that a white paper dealing with
educational reconstruction was being prepared. Its formulation was
largely in the hands of R. S. Brownell and his senior colleagues in
the Ministry of Education. Liaising closely with the Ministries of
Finance and Home Affairs the Ministry also established working
parties to ascertain the views of the teachers and regional education
committees.

The White Paper was published in December 1944 and marked a
radical departure from the system introduced by Lord Londonderry
in 1923. From being on the periphery secondary education now
came to the fore. Secondary education for all was no longer to be a
slogan but a reality.

INTRODUCTION

Nor have all the education committees taken a liberal view of
the need for scholarships to secondary schools, the provision
of such scholarships has been uneven and has remained far
from adequate in many areas. In the year 1942, in fact, the
total number of scholarships to secondary schools (exclusive
of pupil teacherships granted by the Ministry and
scholarships awarded by Governing bodies) did not amount
to more than 213 in the whole Province, although over three
times that number of candidates who were eligible for

assistance reached the qualifying standard in the examination. It cannot be claimed therefore that a secondary education has been within reach of every able child whose parents could not afford to pay the fees demanded by the schools.

10.   ... In effect, of the 75 recognised secondary schools now in operation only 9 are managed by education committees. It may be thought that this indicates some reluctance on their part to undertake the provision of secondary education, but it was found that there were sufficient voluntary schools already in existence in most areas to meet the demand for secondary education. With the aid of building grants made under certain conditions by the education committees, several of these voluntary schools have been enabled to expand; there are still, however, many inadequate and unsatisfactory premises.

... a further indication of progress may be in the increasing number of pupils in attendance at secondary schools. In 1924 there were approximately 7,000 children in intermediate and senior departments, i.e. preparing for the Junior and Senior Certificate Examinations. By 1938 this number had increased steadily to over 11,500 and in the war years has risen to almost 13,800.

29.   ... the aim of the Government is that no child shall be denied the type of education best suited to his needs and abilities, wherever his home may be situated and whatever his family circumstances may be.

30.   ... There is general agreement that full-time schooling should no longer cease at the early age of 14; all children will, therefore, be required to remain at school until they are 15 and no exemptions will be allowed in the last year of attendance such as were provided in the 1938 Act.

... It would obviously be undesirable to postpone the raising of the leaving age until reorganisation has been entirely completed but it would be equally undesirable to oblige children to remain in attendance until the age of 15 at schools which cannot cater adequately for their needs. A balance must be struck between these two extremes when the time comes to fix the appointed day for the raising of the age in each area.

34.   When the Hadow Report was published in 1926 the possibility of its application to Northern Ireland was naturally considered, but it was decided that the time was not ripe for such a radical re-organisation of the educational system.

36.   ... It must be frankly admitted that the senior classes in the county elementary schools are not providing a really satisfactory training at the present time; the academically gifted children are not being sufficiently extended and those less gifted academically are not receiving the opportunities for a more practical course which would give a new purpose and a new sense of reality to their education.

37.   ... there is an equal need in the cities and towns for a radical change in the elementary school system. A certain deterioration is perceptible in the senior classes of many schools; there seems to be little sense of purpose in the work that is being done and an increasing lack of interest on the part of many of the pupils is evident. This may be largely due to the lack of facilities for practical work and the consequent excessive stress on academic subjects in which many of the children have little interest.

38.   At the age of 11 or 12 childhood is drawing to a close and adolescence lies ahead.

39.   It is for these reasons that it is proposed to recognise the principle of the break at 11+ and to reorganise the existing elementary school system providing in its place primary schools for the younger children and secondary schools of different types for those over 11. Thus in the new system there will be secondary education for all.

41.   In the new system for Northern Ireland there will be two main types of secondary school, recruiting their pupils at the age of 11+ from the primary schools. The first type will be the existing secondary schools providing full-time education up to the age of 17 or 18 ... in this paper they are described as senior secondary schools. All these children who, on completion of their primary education, do not proceed to senior secondary schools — that is, the main bulk of the school population — will be provided for in secondary schools of an entirely new type in which no fees will be charged... described as junior secondary schools. They will normally offer a four-year course as the majority of the pupils may be expected to leave soon after their 15th birthday. It is proposed that in these junior secondary schools there should be a general course during the first two years, although the pupils will be grouped together, as far as possible, according to ability and aptitude and there may well be considerable variation in the amount of time devoted to academic subjects by the academically more gifted children and by the less gifted. After the conclusion of the general course some degree of specialisation will be introduced. The extent to which this is possible will obviously depend on the size of the school; in a school with an annual intake of about 50 pupils it may not be practicable to offer more than two courses, but in a large school it may be possible to organise as many as five parallel courses. Thus in the last two years two or more courses might be offered, e.g. a literary course, a mathematics — science course, a course including some elementary

instruction in commercial subjects, a practical course, a rural course. In all junior secondary schools practical subjects and physical training should receive much more attention than has hitherto been possible in public elementary schools.

42.   In the past, "secondary" education has had a specialised meaning and has been associated with an academic curriculum in which the study of languages or of mathematics and science plays a prominent part. In the future, "secondary" will mean what its name implies — the stage following primary. It is an essential part of the reorganisation plan that the junior secondary school should be looked upon as the counterpart of the senior secondary school and be accorded an equal status; it follows that it must be staffed on similar lines. Although it is realised that the majority of the pupils may leave at 15 or soon after, no attempt will be made to set a limit to the development of these new schools, which will provide a free secondary education, where there is a demand for more senior work arrangements will be made accordingly. Nevertheless the prestige of a school depends ultimately upon the quality of the school itself and cannot be secured by Act of Parliament or official regulations. It will be for the new junior secondary schools to justify themselves in public esteem, to build up a reputation and to win the confidence of parents. As the new system takes shape and junior secondary schools are established throughout the country, both by education authorities and by voluntary boards of managers, teachers of ability and ambition will welcome the opportunity of serving in them as pioneers breaking new ground in the service of education.

45.   ... it is clear that the voluntary schools, (senior secondary schools), most of which have a long tradition of independence, would strenuously resist any attempt to bring them under the control of the education authorities. The result of such an attempt might well be that some, especially those which are largely boarding schools, would be disposed to sever their connection with the public system of education and assume completely independent status. This would be an unfortunate development, for Northern Ireland has hitherto been very free from class distinction in its secondary schools; there are not more than three independent schools providing a full secondary education and these are small. It is therefore proposed that in the senior secondary schools fees should not be entirely abolished.

46.   Nevertheless the Government are determined that no Ulster child who is deemed fitted to profit by attendance at a senior secondary school shall be denied access to such a school by reason of his parents' inability to defray the cost. To replace the present restricted provision of scholarships awarded on a competitive basis a radical change is proposed which will ensure that admission to the senior secondary schools of all but a limited number of pupils will be determined by a qualifying entrance test ... To ensure uniformity in all areas, the test will be required to admit all who reach the qualifying standard, the choice of school in each individual case being left as far as possible to the parents and the school concerned.

47.   ... It is essential that the monetary value of a scholarship awarded to a child whose parents are in poor circumstances should be sufficient to cover these additional expenses (books etc, travelling expenses) and should include the cost of boarding as well as tuition fees, where daily travel to a suitable school is impossible. The education committees

will therefore be required to adjust the value of the scholarship to the needs of the child in accordance with the financial circumstances of his parents. The Ministry of Education will lay down appropriate scales for the whole of Northern Ireland, after consultation with the education committees, so that these shall be no variation between comparable areas as there has been in the past ... The scholarships will be tenable for the whole school course, subject to satisfactory progress, ... By these means a senior secondary school education will be made available for all who are considered suitable to profit by it; no question of competition will arise, and the number and value of the scholarships awarded will be adjusted each year according to the needs of those who qualify.

48.   It is intended that the selection test should continue to be based on a written examination and that, if possible, intelligence tests should also be used ... The method of selection may, however, be changed as greater experience is gained ...

49.   However carefully selection at 11+ is made, it will be desirable that there should be arrangements whereby suitable pupils may be transferred from junior secondary to senior secondary schools at a later stage if their parents so wish. An appropriate time for such transfers would be at the end of the first two years of the junior secondary school course and it is proposed that the education committees should be required to award supplementary scholarships for this purpose. If the numbers are not too large it may be possible to make these supplementary awards on the basis of nomination by teachers without the application of another formal test.

51. ... It is therefore proposed that the education committees should in future be required to provide free books, stationery and consumable material for handwork, etc. for the use of all pupils in primary and junior secondary schools. The supply should be sufficiently liberal to enable permanent collections of reference books and standard works for general reading to be built up gradually in every school.

52. ... Grants to preparatory departments (of senior secondary schools) will therefore be continued but, in future, pupils attending them who wish to qualify for entrance to the secondary department of the same or another school will be required to pass the Ministry's test in the same way as pupils from primary schools.

55. ... The detailed proposals (for religious education) for Northern Ireland will, however, go further than their English counterpart. A notable divergence is that in Northern Ireland clergymen and other persons will, subject to certain limitations, be granted reasonable access to pupils in schools for the purpose of giving denominational or undenominational instruction. Hitherto this "right of access" has been in force in all the elementary schools under the education authorities and in some of those under voluntary management, it is proposed that in future it would be extended to all schools, both primary and secondary, except that it will not apply to existing voluntary schools which have not previously been obliged to grant it, unless the managers or governing bodies give their consent. Where such consent is not forthcoming, however, the school concerned must, as an alternative give facilities for the withdrawal from its premises of pupils whose parents wish them to receive suitable instruction elsewhere.

62. The Government are satisfied that in Northern Ireland, as in England and Wales, it will be necessary to provide increased financial assistance to the voluntary manager. They are equally satisfied that where additional assistance is given the principle of representation must be observed. It is proposed, therefore, that if those responsible for the conduct of a voluntary primary or junior secondary school are prepared to agree to the establishment of a "four-and-two" committee of management, and if at the same time they agree to certain restrictions upon the use of the school after school hours, the education authority should be required to accept full responsibility for the cost of the heating, cleaning, lighting and internal repairs; under similar conditions capital grants of 65 per cent for building, reconstruction, and equipment will be made available from the Exchequer. If the principle of representation is not admitted the school will not be eligible for grants from either the authority or the Exchequer, other than those (50 per cent for heating, cleaning and lighting and 50 per cent for capital expenditure) which can now be obtained under the Education Acts of 1923 and 1930, it is proposed, however, that, whether the education authority is represented or not, all junior secondary schools should be under the control of boards of management.

63. In schools under the education authorities the problem of management, while not complicated by considerations of finance, is not without difficulty.

64. It is difficult to see how the claims of all managers or former managers of the contributory primary schools to representation on the board of management of a provided junior secondary school could be satisfied without producing an unwieldy body; it may also be thought that the education committee should be represented to a greater degree than is

prescribed for the management committee of the elementary school under the Act of 1930, and that the principal teacher should be given a voice in the appointment of assistant teachers. These, however, are matters for further consideration and discussion with the interests concerned.

65. For senior secondary schools under the education authorities no change of management is proposed; they will continue to be controlled by boards of governors appointed directly by the education committee. The voluntary senior secondary school, however, must be specially considered for it will require a measure of financial assistance to enable it to provide places for an increased number of pupils, and such assistance must normally be sought from either the Exchequer or the local rates. Hitherto, the education authority has had the power to grant this assistance and in return has been accorded representation on the board of governors together with a guarantee of "free places" for scholars.

It is now proposed to make available to voluntary senior secondary schools grants from the Exchequer not exceeding 65 per cent of the cost of new buildings, necessary extensions, and alterations; this grant will be made only where the finances of the school justify it and will be subject to such conditions as may be prescribed. The education authority will be empowered to grant further financial assistance subject to such conditions as to representation on the governing body and reservation of free places as may be agreed with the governing body and approved by the Ministry.

III.6   Education Act (Northern Ireland) 1947, C.3.

Piloting the 1946 Education Bill which enshrined the White Paper's proposals through Parliament was a wearying and acrimonious process resurrecting as it did all the old battles over the control of schooling and the place of religious education in schools.

The main issues to be decided for secondary schools were whether the division between primary and secondary schooling should be at 11+ or 12+; the structure of management committees for the new junior secondary schools; and selection for and the financing of the voluntary grammar schools.

The Government held firm on 11+ as the age of transfer but capitulated to the Protestant churches over management committees which were to be the same as controlled primary schools. Provision for voluntary grammar schools led to an unsatisfactory split into two groups which stored up trouble for the future. For the next forty years the 1947 Act was the foundation on which Northern Ireland's Education system rested.

4.   The statutory system of public education shall be organised in three progressive stages to be known as primary education, secondary education and further education; and it shall be the duty of the local education authority for every area, so far as their powers extend, to contribute towards the spiritual, moral, mental and physical development of the community by securing that efficient education throughout those stages shall be available to meet the needs of the population of their area.

5. — (1)   It shall be the duty of every local education authority to secure that there shall be available for their area sufficient schools —

(b)   for providing secondary education, that is to say, full-time education suitable to the requirements of senior pupils, other than such full-time education as may be provided for senior pupils in pursuance of a scheme made under the provisions of this Act relating to further education.

(2)   In fulfilling their duties under this section, a local education authority shall in particular, have regard —

(a)   to the need for securing that primary and secondary education are provided in separate schools.

6. — (1) For the purpose of fulfilling their duties under this Act, a local education authority shall have power to establish primary schools and secondary schools and to manage such schools whether established by them or transferred to them under this Act or any enactment repealed by this Act.

8. — (3)   With a view to assisting the local education authority in the preparation of the development scheme for their area, the managers of each voluntary school in the area shall, within six months after the date of the commencement of this part of this Act or within such extended period as the Ministry may in any particular case allow, furnish to the local education authority a return showing —

(b)   if the school is a primary school and the managers do not intend to transfer it to the local education authority, what steps, if any, they propose to take, either alone or in conjunction with the managers of other voluntary schools, for the provision of a voluntary secondary school.

15. — (1)   The local education authority shall make provision for the management of each county intermediate school within their education area by means of a school management committee to be appointed by the authority; and

a school management committee so appointed shall, in relation to the school under their management, exercise such functions as may be conferred upon them by a scheme framed by the authority and approved by the Ministry.

(2)   A school management committee appointed under the last preceding sub-section shall be so constituted that, so far as is practicable —

(a)   not less than one-half of the members to be appointed thereto shall be persons nominated by the school management committees of the contributory schools, such nominations being made from among members of those committees other than members nominated or chosen by parents or by the local education authority;

(b)   Not more than one-quarter of the said members shall be persons nominated by the parents of the children attending the county intermediate school at a meeting held in accordance with regulations made by the Ministry: and

(c)   the remaining members shall be persons chosen by the local education authority.

The principal for the time being of the school shall have the right to attend, and take part in, the meetings of the school management committee, but shall not be entitled to vote on any question.

(3)   If any question arises as to the right of any person or body of persons under the last preceding subsection to nominate a member of a school management committee, that question shall stand referred to the Ministry, whose decision thereon shall be final.

(4)   For the purposes of this section the expression "contributory schools" means, in relation to a county intermediate school, the county primary schools from which, in the opinion of the authority, a substantial number of pupils proceed to the county intermediate school for the purpose of continuing their education thereat; and the expression "intermediate school" does not include an intermediate school which is conducted as a technical intermediate school.

(5)   In this Act the expression "intermediate school" means a secondary school providing free education for senior pupils; and the expression "technical intermediate school" means a county intermediate school conducted in association with an institution of further education.

17. — (1)   The local education authority shall make provision for the management of each county grammar school within their education area ... by means of a school management committee to be appointed by the authority in accordance with a scheme framed by the authority and approved by the Ministry.

21. — (1) ... the school day in every county school and voluntary school shall begin with collective worship on the part of all pupils in attendance at the school ...

(2)   ... religious instruction shall be given in every county school and voluntary school.

42. — (1)   Subject to the provisions of sub-section (6b) of this section, it shall be the duty of every local education authority, in accordance with regulations made under this section, to provide for the medical inspection at appropriate intervals of pupils in full-time attendance at any grant-aided school in their area.

****

(6)   Sub-sections (1) and (3) of this section shall not apply in the case of pupils in attendance at any voluntary grammar school the managers of which have, by means of a medical scheme framed by them and approved by the local education authority, made provision for the medical inspection and treatment of pupils in attendance at that school.

(7)   A local education authority shall not refuse to approve of any medical scheme framed by the managers of a voluntary grammar school for the purposes of this section if the scheme complies with the requirements in that behalf prescribed by regulations made under this section; and in relation to any such scheme the managers of the school shall keep, or cause to be kept, such records, and shall make such returns, as may be prescribed by the regulations. If the managers of any school are aggrieved by the refusal of the local education authority to approve of any such scheme as aforesaid they may appeal to the Ministry of Health and Local Government against such refusal, and the decision of that Ministry thereon shall be final.

48.   It shall be the duty of the managers of each grammar school, in accordance with regulations made by the Ministry for the purposes of this section, to make available, for pupils having the prescribed qualifications, such number of places as may be determined in accordance with these regulations.

58.   The managers of a grammar school may, with the approval of the Ministry, determine the fees to be charged in respect of pupils admitted to the school.

71.   ... in the exercise and performance of all powers and duties conferred and imposed on them by this Act the Ministry and local education authorities shall have regard to

the general principle that, so far as is compatible with the provision of efficient instruction and training and the avoidance of unreasonable public expenditure, pupils are to be educated in accordance with the wishes of their parents.

76. — (1) For the purpose of enabling pupils without hardship to themselves or their parents to attend grammar schools, or institutions providing further education, it shall be the duty of local education authorities subject to and in accordance with regulations made by the Ministry, to grant scholarships to or in respect of such pupils as comply with the prescribed conditions.

81. — (2) If, in the case of a voluntary school to which this section applies, a school committee is appointed for the school in accordance with a scheme framed under this section, to consist ... in the case of an intermediate school, of such number of persons as may be determined by the scheme, of whom one-third shall be persons nominated by the local education authority and two-thirds shall be persons nominated by the managers or trustees, then, subject to and in accordance with regulations made by the Ministry, the local education authority shall be responsible for the lighting, heating and cleaning of the school premises and for the carrying out of internal maintenance.

(3) If, in the case of a voluntary school to which this section applies, a school committee has not been appointed in accordance with a scheme framed under this section, then subject to and in accordance with regulations made by the Ministry, it shall be the duty of the local education authority to make to the managers or body controlling the school an annual contribution equal to sixty-five per cent of the approved expenditure incurred on the lighting, heating and cleaning of the school premises, and on the carrying out of internal maintenance.

(4)   ... it shall be the duty of the local education authority to make provision for the appointment of the committee.

82.   A local education authority may give financial assistance to the managers of any voluntary grammar school in their education area upon such terms and conditions as may be agreed between the authority and the managers of the school with the approval of the Ministry.

106. — (1) Subject to the provisions of this sub-section and of any regulations made for the purposes thereof by the Ministry, with the approval of the Ministry of Finance, the Ministry may pay to any person, for the purpose of the provision of a new primary, intermediate or special school, or the alteration of an existing primary, intermediate or special school, a sum equal to sixty-five per cent of the expenditure incurred for such purpose ...

(2)   The Ministry may ... pay to the managers of a primary, intermediate or special school, a sum equal to sixty-five per cent of the expenditure incurred in any year by such managers on the external maintenance of the school, or on the provision of equipment for the school.

(3)   The Ministry may ... pay to any person for the purpose of the provision and equipment of a new voluntary grammar school or the alteration and equipment of an existing voluntary grammar school, a sum equal to sixty-five per cent of the expenditure incurred for such purpose.

(4)   All sums payable by the Ministry under the foregoing provisions of this section shall be paid out of moneys provided by parliament.

**III.7(a) Statutory Rules and Orders of Northern Ireland, 1950,
No.217 : Grammar Schools (Admissions, Scholarships
and Special Allowances, School Year 1950-51)
S.R. and O. 1950, No.217, 15 December, 1950.**

The senior secondary schools (grammar schools) were vital to the successful implementation of the 1947 Education Act. Only they could provide the places for those children deemed to have passed the qualifying examination, which according to Hall-Thompson, the Minister of Education, was not to be a competitive examination. Ever jealous of their independence these schools were unwilling to accept dictation from the newly formed local education authorities which replaced the regional education committees. Under the 1947 Act, voluntary grammar schools could receive 65% of their capital expenditure costs if they made available 80% of their places for local authority pupils.

The schools had to find the other 35% themselves. When the Ministry of Education decided that the governors could not include capital costs in school fees, a major row broke out. Finally a compromise was struck whereby each grammar school was given the choice of entering one of two categories (A or B) of state aid and regulation. Group A schools were to receive 65% of all capital costs from the exchequer, Group B schools would receive no money for capital costs but were allowed to charge whatever fees they wished. By mid 1951, 31 had opted for Group A, 33 for Group B. The choice of Group B by more than half the schools represented a major setback for the ideas enshrined in the 1947 Act.

5. — (1)   The school authorities of every Group A voluntary school or county school shall reserve for qualified pupils not fewer than 80 per cent of the places available each school year for the admission of day pupils to the lower division of the secondary department of the school.

(2)   The school authorities of a group A voluntary school or county school shall not without the prior approval of the Ministry increase the number of places available in the school for boarding pupils in such a way as to reduce the number of places available for day pupils.

(3)   No qualified pupil shall be refused admission to a Group A voluntary school or county school on other than reasonable grounds.

Provided, however, that, where the numbers of qualified pupils seeking admission to the lower division of the secondary department of a Group A voluntary school or county school is greater than the number of places reserved for such pupils in accordance with the provisions of paragraph (1) of this regulation, the school authorities may select such of the qualified pupils as appear to them best fitted to profit by the education provided at the school.

6.   The school authorities of a Group B voluntary school may admit each year to the lower division of the secondary department of the school such and so many qualified pupils as they think fit.

III.7(b) S.R. and O. 1950, No.219, 15 December, 1950.

4.   After Regulation 5 of the existing Regulations there shall be inserted the following Regulation:-

5A. — (1) Where the managers of a voluntary school notify to the Ministry, in such manner and before such date as the Ministry may determine that they wish the school to be classified —

(a)   as a Group A voluntary school or
(b)   as a Group B voluntary school

(2)   The income in respect of any period after the 31 July 1951, of a Group A voluntary school produced by the tuition fees charged in respect of pupils in the secondary

department shall not, without the consent of the Ministry, be devoted to expenditure which in the opinion of the Ministry is capital expenditure nor to any purpose not related to the tuition of pupils in that department.

****

(4)   Where the school authorities incur or intend to incur capital expenditure they may for the purpose of meeting such expenditure, include in the scale of fees a fee of such amount as may be sanctioned by the Ministry. The amount of such fee shall not save in exceptional circumstances exceed £3 per annum.

III.8   Selection of Pupils for Secondary Schools — Third Paper : A Report of the Advisory Council for Education in Northern Ireland, October 1960, Cmd.419.

The longest lasting and bitterest controversy arising from the 1947 Act was over the Qualifying Examination for entry to the grammar schools. The promise had been that every child would receive secondary education in the type of school most suited to his/her ability. When, as early as 1948, it became apparent that the number of places in grammar schools was less than the number of qualified children, resentment mounted.

Forty years later the resentment and bitterness are still there. All the panaceas have failed to placate those parents who desire but fail to obtain a grammar school education for their children.

Efforts by the Ministry of Education to make the examination fairer and increase its predictive value failed to assuage its opponents, reinforced as they were by the movement towards comprehensive education in Great Britain.

2. — (1) ... All children who have been entered for the Examination, except under-age children, are given two Verbal Reasoning Tests, the first in December and the second in January, ... only those whose performance in one of these tests is satisfactory are permitted to proceed to the Attainment Tests in March. The Attainment Tests consist of two papers in English and one in Arithmetic, and a syllabus is prescribed for each subject.

The Attainment Tests marks are given statistical treatment to ensure as far as possible that each paper carries its appropriate weight. Next a system of age allowances is devised and the appropriate number of marks added to the Attainment Test scores of all except under-age candidates. Thus a final mark is reached for each child. An "absolute pass mark" is determined by the Ministry and all candidates with this mark or over are regarded as qualified. The Ministry also determines a second mark, below which candidates are deemed to be "not qualified." Candidates with marks between these limits are regarded as within the "border-zone," unless they are under-age candidates. ... Candidates in the border-zone are dealt with by the Education Committee in whose area they reside.

(2)   A Review Examination is conducted by all the Education Committees. Children who have not become qualified through the Qualifying Examination may qualify by reaching a satisfactory standard in the Review Examination. The age of entry to this examination is one year later than that for the Qualifying Examination, except in Londonderry County Borough, where the age-limits are between 12 and 14 years on 1 July 1960.

6.   ... It became clear to us early in our deliberations that we were bound to examine very carefully the implications for secondary intermediate schools of the selection procedure as well as to consider whether the arrangements for selection for grammar schools and junior technical schools were satisfactory.

8.   ...Teachers in grammar schools and in junior technical schools for the most part expressed approval of the selection arrangements while secondary intermediate school teachers, primary school teachers, parents' associations and most individual witnesses expressed dissatisfaction with some of the principles on which the selection procedure was based or with some of its effects on schools and on children.

11.   ... We see no reason for disputing their (our predecessors) conclusion that the Qualifying Examination is a reasonably accurate predictive instrument.

18.   We are less certain that the abler children in secondary intermediate schools are following the most suitable courses in all cases. 2,184 of the 8,666 children tested had a standardised score of between 101 and 114 and 336 scored 115 or more. It seems probable that a substantial number of these children might reasonably follow a course leading to an external examination, but hitherto few such children have had an opportunity to do so. We have been informed by several witnesses that parents feel that the allocation of their children to secondary intermediate school robs them of the opportunity of careers which are open only to those with one of the Ministry's Certificates and that this seriously affects the prestige and morale of the secondary intermediate schools.

21.   ... Very few of us however would welcome the outright abandonment of the existing selective system. It seems to us to be successful in allocating most children to suitable secondary schools ...

22.   ... We are certain that at this stage the total abandonment of the selective system for a comprehensive or other similar system would not be acceptable to the community if it were to affect adversely the grammar schools, which have proved themselves over a long span of years to be eminently suited to provide an academic type of education and have established themselves in the affections and esteem of the public.

24.   ... We certainly think that, whatever may be said for the exercise of parental choice, even with advice from teachers, it could not provide a satisfactory substitute as a means of selection.

29.   ... We make a firm recommendation that ... a selective system of secondary school organisation and a Qualifying Examination be retained.

31.   ... We have considered whether all children in the age-group should take the entire Examination, but we are of the opinion that the Verbal Reasoning Test scores would provide sufficient information to ensure that every suitable child is encouraged to enter the Qualifying Examination.

46.   ... We therefore recommend that, the border-zone procedure should be as nearly uniform as possible in all areas. Such action, we think, might also help to remove any suggestion that the number of grammar school places available in certain areas has a significant bearing on the number of pupils who eventually qualify in these areas.

72.   ... We therefore recommend that as a general principle secondary intermediate schools should be enabled, where circumstances justify it, to organise courses leading to the Grammar School Junior Certificate or other suitable examinations and that pupils who have successfully completed examination courses up to the appropriate stage should be given the opportunity to transfer to the upper division of a grammar school or to the Further Education department of a technical institution.

73.   Where overlapping courses of the kind we have envisaged can be provided in secondary intermediate schools we recommend that the transfer of pupils through the Review Examination from secondary intermediate schools to grammar schools should cease.

76.   ... We have decided by a narrow majority to recommend that the review procedure should be discontinued for unqualified fee-paying pupils in grammar schools.

III.9   Educational Development in Northern Ireland, 1964, Cmd.470.

In 1964 the Ministry of Education took stock of the education system as it had developed since the passage of the 1947 Act.

The controversy over the 11+ rumbled on but the grammar schools were to remain inviolate, while experiments would be encouraged for the 70% of children who attended secondary intermediate schools.

By the mid-sixties the junior secondary schools (intermediate schools) were well established, but still had difficulty in finding a role. Creamed of the brightest students, the original intention was that they should not enter students for academic examinations. This denied them any chance of establishing equality of status, and faced with the need to ensure their success the Ministry allowed the development of academic streams and extended courses in Intermediate Schools.

The introduction of the Certificate of Secondary Education in England and Wales offered another way forward with an examination specifically designed for these types of school.

7.   The most serious educational problem at the present time is that underlying the continuing criticism of the "Qualifying Examination." The question which lies at the root of this criticism is whether the existing system of secondary education should be continued or should be replaced by a new system based on some form of comprehensive school.

10.   ... here a fully developed grammar school system is already in being. There are in fact 81 grammar schools ... during this period (since 1948) the enrolment in their secondary departments has more than doubled and three-quarters of the grammar schools are voluntary schools — approximately half under Protestant and half under Roman Catholic management; they have played their part fully in meeting the increased demand for grammar school places. There is no sign that the grammar schools are failing to meet the challenge of the times or that the public is losing faith in them.

12.   Such a proposal (to introduce a comprehensive school system) would moreover be certain to arouse strong opposition. Some voluntary grammar schools might, indeed, claim the right to secede from the grant-aided educational system and to operate as independent schools wholly dependent on fees, which would of course have to be very much higher than they are now. This would set up a social cleavage within the Northern Ireland educational system such as it has never known before.

13.   Given, therefore, the facts of the existing situation and the disruption, expense, restriction of parental choice and ill-feeling which would be caused by an imposed system of comprehensive schools, the Government is satisfied that it would be wrong to make a complete change in the pattern of secondary education established under the 1947 Act.

15.   Another promising line of advance would be the introduction of schemes on the Leicestershire model, in which a number of comprehensive schools, called junior high schools, provide a basic secondary course and jointly feed into a single senior school at the end of the third year. It is hoped that local education authorities will consider arrangements of this kind and that the governors of some grammar schools may be prepared to agree that, with suitable transitional arrangements, their schools should become senior schools each serving a number of comprehensive junior schools acting as feeders.

19.   A further means of lessening the difference between the two types of secondary school would be the abandonment of the term intermediate.

20.   To sum up, therefore, the Government does not intend to reconstruct the whole secondary school system on comprehensive or quasi-comprehensive lines in order to dispense with external selection at 11+. Instead, developments in secondary school organisation designed to reduce the importance of selection will be actively encouraged. It will also be the Ministry's policy to promote the development of academic streams and extended courses in the secondary schools wherever circumstances are favourable and to reduce the differences between these schools and the grammar schools in staffing and other matters wherever it is practicable to do so.

24.   The differences between one secondary school and another are more likely to increase than to diminish as they advance to meet new needs. The extent to which individual schools should develop at the top is likely to remain a problem of some difficulty.

26.   The Ministry has, however, a duty to ensure that, while allowing for local variations, the general development of the secondary schools is in line with National policy. It takes the view that, in general, courses for pupils over the school leaving age which are predominantly vocational should continue to be provided as further education courses in technical institutions and that courses of an academic type beyond GCE 'O' levels should be provided in grammar schools. It is right, however, that there should be exceptions to these general rules. If the local technical institute is unable to make the required provisions, or if the distance to the technical institution is too great, then a secondary school may be permitted to introduce a commercial, agricultural, pre-nursing, or pre-apprenticeship type of course, if conditions are favourable. A secondary school may be allowed to arrange 'A' level GCE courses where it is not practicable to transfer the pupils concerned to a suitable grammar school or technical institution or if there are other special circumstances.

27.   While every encouragement must be given to secondary schools to present their older children for appropriate examinations and to arrange, where desirable, extended courses, it must never be overlooked that their fundamental task lies in raising the general educational level of the main mass of the secondary school population ... the needs of the less able — the lower 50 per cent — should also be fully met ...

29.   It is not the intention to advocate the indiscriminate introduction of vocational instruction into the curriculum of the secondary schools, but experiments will be encouraged in the leavening of the curriculum particularly for the less able pupils, along the lines suggested in the Newsom Report. To this end the Ministry proposes to set up a working party including representatives of teachers, school authorities and other interests to consider in some detail how best the Newsom approach could be fostered in our secondary schools.

31.   There remains to decide whether for the second ablest quarter of the secondary school population (the top 25 per cent or so in the secondary school which has no grammar school side) the existing lower public examinations in Northern Ireland, the Junior Grammar and Junior Technical Certificate examinations, are suitable objectives. A new examination, the Certificate of Secondary Education, is now coming into being on a regional basis in England and Wales to meet the needs of secondary modern schools. It does not necessarily follow that a similar examination is required in Northern Ireland ... The working party set up to consider the relevance of the Newsom Report will be asked to consider this question and make recommendations.

47.   The Government now proposes that the Qualifying Examination should be discontinued and replaced by some other method of selection which would not involve formal attainment tests such as those now held in English and Arithmetic. In accordance with this proposal the last Qualifying Examination would be held in 1965.

51.   The school leaving age was raised from 14 to 15 in Great Britain in 1947; the corresponding advance took place in Northern Ireland in 1957. The Government, determined

that there should not be a comparable time-lag on this occasion, has already announced that the age will be raised to 16 not later than 1970, that is to say, not later than the year in which the change is to be made in Great Britain.

52.   There are two main obstacles to be overcome: shortage of teachers and shortage of school accommodation.

70.   Group A (voluntary grammar) schools undertaking new building projects are allowed to charge parents a special annual fee, distinct from the tuition fee, which is not taken into account by the local education authority as part of the cost of a scholarship. The purpose of this arrangement was to make it possible for the governors of the schools, lacking the necessary financial resources from endowments or other sources, to provide themselves with a separate income sufficient to service the loan charges relating to their 35% share of the cost of new buildings. The relevant regulations provide that, except with the approval of the Ministry in special circumstances, this capital fee, as it has come to be known, should not exceed £3 per annum. (has now reached £12 10s 0d in one school)

73.   In the light of experience the Ministry's view now is that there should be a statutory limit to the capital fee so that this could not be exceeded without an amendment of the regulations, thus bringing the matter to the notice of Parliament if a further increase has to be made. It is proposed accordingly to amend the existing regulations so as to provide that the Ministry may approve such annual sum not exceeding £15 as it may consider appropriate in the circumstances.

75.   It is no part of the Government's purpose to create
circumstances which would force the governors of voluntary
grammar schools to transfer their schools to the local
education authorities. But the maintenance of the principle
that assistance from public funds in respect of capital
expenditure should not exceed the standard rate of 65%
without some measure of public representation on the
management of a voluntary school is also important. The
Ministry therefore proposes to consult with the local
education authorities and the governors of voluntary grammar
schools to try to find an acceptable solution to this problem:
the aim would be to make it possible for the capital fee
chargeable to parents to be discontinued in any case where its
retention would be an obstacle to the reorganisation of
secondary education in such a way as to dispense with the
need for selection.

**III.10   Secondary School Organisation and Selection
Procedure : Report of the Advisory Council for
Education, June, 1964, Cmd.471.**

At the same time the Advisory Council for Education supported the
Ministry's opposition to the introduction of comprehensive
education.

It also proposed a new type of selection procedure which while less
contentious still did nothing to solve the underlying issues.

10.   The Council does not think that the wholesale
replacement of our present selective secondary school system
by a non-selective system is possible. It has noted that it is
largely only maintained secondary schools which the local
education authorities in Great Britain have succeeded in
fitting into their non-selective systems: the independent and

direct grant grammar schools have stood aloof. It seems to the Council unlikely that in Northern Ireland the voluntary grammar schools, which form the majority of our grammar schools, would be any more willing than their counterparts in Great Britain to lose their identity in a non-selective system.

11.   ... the Council recommends that in areas of development and in other districts where conditions are favourable, the Ministry should be asked to encourage the local education authority and voluntary authorities to consider the possibly of dispensing with selection by providing, for example, common secondary schools which would offer a full secondary course to all children of the area, or campus schools or schools on a two-tier system like that established in Leicestershire ...

SELECTION PROCEDURE REPORT

11.   The Council considered written and oral evidence about selection from many sources in Northern Ireland and was concerned at the extent and degree of the dissatisfaction expressed with the Qualifying Examination...

14.   In the light of all this evidence the Council recommends that for a trial period beginning in1966 the Qualifying Examination as at present operated by the Ministry of Education should be discontinued and replaced by a selection procedure based on teachers' estimates scaled against verbal reasoning tests ...

III.11   The Curriculum of Secondary Schools : Report of a Working Party, 1967.

The terms of reference of this Working Party were:

> To consider the curriculum of the secondary (intermediate) schools in the light of the Government's policy as set out in the White Paper on Educational Development in Northern Ireland 1964.

In his foreword to the report the Minister of Education, W. J. Long, drew attention to the Working Party's particular concern for the needs of the additional age group if and when the school leaving age was raised to sixteen. The Minister welcomed the report for its significant contribution to thinking on all aspects of the curriculum in Secondary schools and its humanitarian approach. He invited other interested parties to predict their views.

In their Report the Working Party explained that they had chosen to write of the curriculum in terms of principles and general spirit rather than of subject content and detail. This was a deliberate choice and was made for a number of reasons. First, there was the overriding importance of a concern for pupils as young people with lives to make in a very difficult world. The central theme of the Report was personal development.

Secondly, most of what the Report suggested was already found in the schools. The Working Party believed that education had been developing in the right direction over the past twenty years and what was needed was the inspiration which would ensure that the aims were followed with energy, devotion and understanding.

Finally, the Working Party did not claim all the knowledge and experience needed for a detailed study of the curriculum in secondary schools. This work, it believed, was that left to practising teachers operating through subject panel and curriculum study groups.

Significantly, the Report recommended that 'narrow specialisation' should not be allowed to hinder a pupil's personal development; that secondary education should last for five years, not four; that there should be more experimentation of non-streaming; a looking

SECONDARY EDUCATION

outward in the pupil's final two years of secondary schooling, to the community; curriculum continuity, possibly through thematic linking; and an end to the religious instruction examination, in its existing form, in County schools. Extending the aim of closer contact between pupils and schools and the local community, the Report advocated the setting up of what were called "Educational Study Centres" or "Teachers' Centres", in geographically selected areas throughout Northern Ireland. Such centres would promote and encourage interest among teachers in curriculum development.

176. — (1)   We recommend that all future planning of secondary education should start with a professional concern for the personal development of the pupils and that at no stage should narrow specialisation be allowed to hinder this aim.

(2)   We recommend that all future planning of secondary education should be on the basis of a five-year course, whether or not the five years are spent in one school or in two.

(3)   We recommend that during the first three years of the secondary course there should be a common curriculum in which subject selection takes place only because of a need to cater for both boys and girls.

(4)   We recommend that much experiment in the internal organisation of secondary education should take place. Thus for example, we shall be glad to find more schools experimenting with non-streaming, with pupils choice of subjects in the final two years and with a greater variety in the grouping of pupils.

(5) We recommend much further experiment in teaching subjects in a new way, with a new content or to more pupils.

(a) We recommend that modern teaching aids should be made available to many more schools.

(b) We recommend that schools should be encouraged to teach a second language to their whole range of ability.

(c) We recommend that critical experiment with the "New Mathematics" and with the "Nuffield Science Projects" should be continued.

(6) We recommend that the final two years of the secondary course, while still stressing the priorities of personal development, should encourage an approach which caters for the post-school needs of the pupils and looks outward to the community in which they will live.

(7) We recommend that there should be a continued development, during the final two years, of courses having a vocational bias, and further experiment in courses offering work experience.

(8) We also recommend courses in which the significant bias is towards the use of leisure or the study of modern society.

(9) We recommend an expansion of careers guidance within the schools and believe that it should extend over the final two years of the course.

(10) We recommend the introduction of some new subjects and the wider adoption of others. Social studies and screen education, as defined in the Report, are examples to be tried.

(11)   We recommend that encouragement be given to schools who wish to seek ways of unifying the curriculum either through correlation, a thematic approach or other such device.

(12)   We recommend that sex education should become part of the curriculum of the secondary schools but we leave to local choice the form and content of this subject.

(13)   We recommend a more "open-ended" approach in the matters of religious education and spiritual guidance and advocate the end of the religious instruction examination in this present form in County schools.

(14)   We recommend an expansion of further education and an end to the examination for entry into full-time further education courses.

(15)   We recommend, a few of our members dissenting, that there should be no transfer to further education until the end of the year during which the pupil reaches school leaving age.

(16)   We recommend much closer co-operation among the staffs of primary schools, secondary schools and colleges of further education.

(17)   We recommend the continued expansion of school work and life into extra-curricular activities and strongly urge the provision of facilities to make this expansion possible.

(18)   We recommend consultation among teachers, administrators and architects in the planning of any building project.

(19)   We recommend a great reduction in the number of public examinations attempted by secondary schools but not in the number of pupils being presented as candidates.

(20)   We recommend the immediate establishment of a Northern Ireland CSE Board with an aim of holding the first examination about 1970.

(21)   We recommend that the Ministry should initiate and sustain publicity in an effort to persuade able young people to enter the teaching profession.

****

(23)   We recommend improved conditions of work and service in an effort to encourage this recruitment to the teaching profession.

(24)   We recommend that training should be an essential qualification for recognition as a teacher.

(25)   We recommend that the training of teachers should be undertaken in the light of the priorities and possibilities outlined in our Report.

(26)   We recommend a vast increase in the facilities for in-service training so that existing teachers may equip themselves for the many new professional demands now made upon them.

(27)   We recommend an increase in the number and variety of ancillary helpers available to schools and advocate an open-minded if critical approach to the question of auxiliary teachers.

(28)   We recommend the widespread establishment of curriculum study groups of teachers and others so that the main purposes of this Report may be pursued by those actively working in the many fields of secondary education.

177.   These recommendations are offered as a guide to discussion. A few of them are simple and specific; many are general and should be read in the context of the Report, but all of them await argument. They are not, by numbers, addressed to the Ministry of Education, the education committees or the teachers but each of these groups has much to do if these recommendations are to be implemented.

178.   On the one hand the Ministry and the education committees must accept the fact that continued expenditure is essential; that the building of new schools and the extension of old ones must proceed apace; that the education of this and future generations requires the provision of facilities for games and field studies for which there have previously been only marginal demands; that the technology of education leads from the radio to the television, from the tape-recorder to the language laboratory and that it is only by such developments that education will remain relevant to the needs and aspirations of a rapidly changing society.

179.   On the other hand the teachers, whose task it is to use the facilities and buildings provided, must accept the challenge of new ideas and new equipment without surrendering the essential human quality of their profession.

180.   On all sides there is a need for co-operation and for the widest discussion of educational problems. Discussion there is but, at present, it tends to take place within certain groups — teachers in a particular type of school; lecturers in colleges of education; administrators, for example — and there are not the opportunities or facilities to bring these

groups together. We believe it is vital that adequate facilities should be provided and hence we propose one final and major recommendation. We advocate the establishment of educational study centres.

EDUCATIONAL STUDY CENTRES

181. Study centres, development centres or teachers' centres, as they are variously called, are already established in some parts of Great Britain. They owe their origins to many factors: the need to bring teachers into active partnership in research sponsored by universities or by bodies such as the National Foundation for Educational Research, the rethinking of syllabuses for the CSE, the participation in schemes such as those organised by the Nuffield Trust and the stimulation provided by the publications of the Schools Council — all these and many more have been factors in an upsurge of interest in curriculum study and in the part the teachers should play in shaping future development. We are convinced of the advantages to be gained from study centres, and we ask that the Ministry of Education should give urgent and serious consideration to their introduction as new features of our educational system. In Great Britain, centres have been established by education committees and, in at least one case, by a university but in our small Province we believe that the task should be undertaken by the Government.

III.12 Local Education Authorities and Voluntary Schools, October, 1967, Cmd.513.

Relations between the Catholic Church authorities and the Unionist government had been in a state of tension since the foundation of Northern Ireland. The former believed that the state should not control or provide education but aid voluntary efforts. The latter held to the view that the amount of state aid should be in proportion to the share of public representation in the management of the schools. The government's favourite instrument was the four and two committee, i.e. four representatives of the voluntary managers and two local authority or Ministry representatives.

The expansion of secondary schooling in the decades following the 1947 Act placed great financial pressures on the Catholic sector of education. When the Westminster government raised the grants to voluntary schools in England and Wales to 80% in 1967 the Northern Ireland government would have to follow suit. Its White Paper proposed a new 'maintained' status for voluntary primary and intermediate schools which were prepared to accept four and two committees. In addition entirely new schools would be recognised for grant purposes only if they accepted 'maintained' status.

The initial Catholic reaction was hostile but calmer counsels prevailed. Cardinal Conway acknowledged the Government's good intentions and with minor modifications the 1968 Education Act was accepted by the voluntary sector.

1.   ... The need for co-operation between Local Education Authorities and voluntary schools is now particularly important at the secondary level in order both to ensure that a proper variety of courses is available for all pupils and to prevent costly and inefficient duplication of provision in more specialised fields ... These proposals also take account of the legislation enacted earlier this year at Westminster whereby the rate of capital grant to voluntary schools in England and Wales was raised to 80 per cent ...

4.   Voluntary school authorities have over a long period made representations that the burden of their contribution to the system of public education has proved to be much higher than was contemplated in 1947, and have asked for further assistance from public funds. The Government accepts that the cost of providing education has become increasingly heavy ...   Since 1947 Ministers of Education have on

numerous occasions made it clear that increased assistance from public funds could not be contemplated for schools on which a public authority had not at least minority representation. The following proposals accordingly set out ways in which additional aid would be given to voluntary schools provided that the appropriate measure of public representation is accepted.

8. It is proposed that in future no entirely new school should be recognised as a grant-aided school unless it is managed by a school committee constituted on the 'four-and-two' principle.

13. ... It is proposed that for the future the local education authority should be directly responsible for the internal maintenance, external maintenance and equipment of the school premises (again excluding any boarding department) ...

VOLUNTARY GRAMMAR SCHOOLS

16. ... the Government does not consider that, solely as a condition of obtaining an increased rate of building grant, the governors of a voluntary grammar school should be required to provide for some of their number to be directly nominated by the local education authority. Instead, it is proposed that the new rate of grant should be restricted to schools which provide for the Minister to appoint not more than one-third of their governing body. Legislative provision would be made enabling governing bodies to accept members nominated by the Minister even if their present constitution does not permit them to do so.

18.　In order to encourage further co-operation between voluntary grammar schools and local education authorities Section 5(3) of the Act, which empowers authorities to provide practical instruction and training for pupils of any primary or intermediate school, would be extended so as to permit arrangements to be made by local education authorities and voluntary managers and governors, so that pupils enrolled in county schools can use educational facilities in voluntary schools and vice-versa. The increased demand for specialised courses such as those for GCE 'A' Level has led to difficulties in many areas, since clearly every secondary school cannot be expected to provide for every subject which a pupil might reasonably wish to take, and the exchange of pupils between schools to take particular subjects or to carry on their education to a more advanced level, would be assisted by the change proposed in this and the foregoing paragraphs.

III.13　Education (Amendment) Act (Northern Ireland) 1968, C.2.

9. — (4)(2E)　Schools for which committees have been appointed pursuant to a scheme framed under this section shall be known as "maintained schools," primary and intermediate schools shall be known as "maintained voluntary schools."

11.　After section 81A of the principal Act (as inserted by section 10 of this Act) there shall be inserted the following section:-

81B — (1) The trustees or governing body of a voluntary grammar school shall, notwithstanding anything in any statute or scheme made thereunder or in any charter, deed, memorandum of association, articles of association or other document constituting the school or under which the land used for the school is vested or which otherwise relates to the school or the land used for the school, have power to enter into —

(a)   an agreement with the Ministry conferring on the Minister the right to appoint members to the governing body of the school amounting to not more than one-third of the total number of members of the governing body (including the members appointed by the Minister)

(b)   an agreement, approved by the Ministry, with one or more than one local education authority conferring on the authority or authorities the right to appoint members to the governing body of the school amounting to not more than one-third of the total number of members of the governing body (including the members appointed by the authority or authorities)

(2)   Subject to sub-section (3), where, in respect of the governing body of a school, an agreement has been entered into under sub-section (1) (a) and under sub-section (1) (b), the number of members appointed by the Minister and by the local education authority or authorities shall not together exceed one-third of the total number of members of that governing body (including the members appointed by the Minister and the authority or authorities).

12.   For section 82 of the principal Act there shall be substituted the following section:-

(82)   A local education authority, may with the approval of the Ministry:-

(a)   give assistance other than financial assistance; and

(b)   where the trustees or governing body of the school have entered into such an agreement with the authority as is referred to in section 81B (1) (b), give financial assistance;

to the managers of a voluntary grammar school upon such terms and conditions as may be agreed between the authority and the managers of the school.

18. — (1)   In its application to expenditure incurred on or after 1 April 1968 for alteration of an existing maintained school, section 106(1) of the principal Act shall be amended as follows:-

****

(b)   for the words "sixty-five per cent, of the expenditure incurred for such purpose" there shall be substituted the words "eighty per cent of the approved expenditure incurred for such purposes on or after 1 April 1968".

(2)   Sub-section (1) shall not apply to expenditure for the alteration of a school unless —

(a)   the school is a maintained school when the expenditure is incurred; or

(b)   within six months of the date of the passing of this Act the managers of the school apply to the local education authority for a school committee to be appointed for the school under section 81 of the principal Act and have within that period taken such further steps as the local education authority reasonably require them to take within that period in order to enable a school committee to be appointed.

****

(5)   For section 106 (3) of the principal Act (government grants for voluntary grammar schools) there shall be substituted the following sub-section:—

****

(3)   The Ministry may, subject to section 9 (3A) of this Act and subject to and in accordance with regulations made by it with the approval of the Ministry of Finance, pay to any person —

(a)   for the purpose of the provision of a new voluntary grammar school or the alteration of an existing voluntary grammar school;

(b)   for the purpose of providing equipment for a voluntary grammar school; a sum equal to sixty-five per cent or, where the trustees or governing body of the school have, before the expenditure is incurred or within six months of the date of the passing of the Education (Amendment) Act (Northern Ireland) 1968, entered into an agreement with the Ministry under section 81B (1) (a) of this Act, eighty per cent of the approved expenditure incurred for such purpose on or after 1 April 1968.

III.14   The Existing Selection Procedure for Secondary Education in Northern Ireland — January 1971, Cmd.551.

Throughout the 1960s moves towards comprehensive education had been kept at bay while efforts to make the selection procedure more acceptable continued apace. When the Advisory Council was asked to consider this in March 1969, it suggested minor changes in January 1971. However as Dr N. A. Burges, the Chairman, wrote "early in the course of our consideration we decided that recommendations concerning the age of transfer should be made only after the conclusion of a study into the application to Northern Ireland of various forms of school organisation."

The Council recommends:-

(1)   that normally all eligible pupils should be entered for the verbal reasoning tests (except handicapped pupils and those whose parents specifically object) on the grounds that the results of the tests are of value, irrespective of the kind of school pupils are to attend; and that this should be made clear to school authorities and principals in the Ministry's circular.

(2)   that, coincident with local government reorganisation or, if practicable, earlier, a new border-zone scheme be devised which would require the circumstances of each child in the border-zone to be considered and a decision made in accordance with principles laid down by the Ministry and common to all educational areas.

(3)   that the percentage of entrants qualifying automatically should be increased and the size of the border-zone correspondingly decreased.

(4)   that boys' and girls' verbal reasoning test scores should be standardised separately.

(5)   that parents and teachers should be asked to co-operate in confining practice and coaching to agreed limits of one practice test and three one-hour sessions of coaching before each of the two tests.

* * * * * * * * * *

(7)   that cases of exceptionally close correlation between the principal's order of suitability and the order produced by the official verbal reasoning test should continue to be investigated.

(8)   that cases of individual pupils whose positions in the principal's order of suitability and in the order produced by the official verbal reasoning tests are markedly different should invariably be investigated.

(9)   that under-age entrants should not be included in the principal's suitability lists; they should be dealt with by the local education authority as special cases.

* * * * * * * * * *

III.15   **Reorganisation of Secondary Education in Northern Ireland : A Report of the Advisory Council for Education in Northern Ireland — February, 1973 — Chairman Dr. N.A. Burges, Cmd.574.**

SECTION 1

3.   In the study of possible school systems suitable for Northern Ireland we decided to consider first of all the Middle School concept.

6.   ... One important principle underlying the recommendations which we made for restructuring of the educational system is that school structures should suit the needs and conditions of the different localities and make the most effective use of existing facilities.

SECTION 2

10.   ... But the impression of a widespread belief that comprehensive developments are needed is inescapable.

19.   In considering much that has been written about comprehensive schools and in evaluating the arguments put forward in favour of schools of this kind we have come to the conclusion that many of the benefits claimed to result from abolition of selection at 11+ and the provision of some form of comprehensive school would not follow automatically from these external changes, the internal structure of a school may well be more important that the type of school ...

20.   ... Very complicated arrangements of catchment areas may be necessary if each school is to contain a balanced representation of different social levels and experience in the USA and in England has shown that such arrangements can be highly unpopular with parents ...

21.   ... We consider that for both educational and social reasons a comprehensive school should be co-educational.

23.   ... It would be unrealistic to expect the introduction of integrated schools in the near future ... We recommend, too, that every encouragement be given to teaching within schools which can lead to better understanding of other religious beliefs ...

24.   ... The contribution made to the life of the country by voluntary grammar schools in the past has been of very great value; but it would be unfortunate if these schools were now to become an impediment to developments which seem likely to benefit the country as a whole ...

25.   It seems to us that it would be possible for a least a good number of the grammar schools to choose to become part of one or other of the structures we have described.

29.   Whatever system is adopted for the provision of secondary education at all levels we think it important that such education should be free ... If voluntary grammar schools are to be brought into a system of comprehensive education new methods of financing would have to be introduced and the concept of scholarships dropped ...

30.   ... we think that restructuring of the school system should be undertaken in the hope of providing better educational opportunity to all children. Such improvement in opportunity cannot be achieved if we continue to select children for different kinds of schooling at the age of 11+: consequently, to enable all children to benefit by a more flexible system and to let decisions about their later education be taken at a more mature stage of development, the selection procedure at 11+ must be dispensed with. The recommendations which we make for restructuring are necessarily general ... all changes must be preceded by consultation with the teachers, parents, authorities and schools affected by the change.

RECOMMENDATIONS

32. — (1) The Minister of State make now a declaration of intent to eliminate selection at 11+ as soon as possible through a restructuring of the educational system.

(2)   local education authorities be asked to prepare as a matter of urgency development schemes for non-selective secondary schools in their areas and for this purpose enter into consultation with voluntary school authorities to determine the part their schools can play in a non selective system.

A NOTE OF DISSENT

by Mr J. Frost, Professor W. Kirk,
Professor F. J. Lelievre and Mr A. J. Tulip

Our main reservations are:

(1)   The role of the voluntary grammar schools...It is clear that any not-selective scheme that is adapted will need, for some considerable time, to rely on the firm academic traditions established by such schools, and their continuing service to the community — and yet the report implies that they would need to divest themselves of their preparatory departments, severely to curtail their boarding facilities, to forego their control of entry and to lose much of their freedom of operation.

We are particularly concerned about the implications of the proposal in paragraph 29 of the report, viz. that all secondary education would be free. This principle we welcome in respect of tuition fees, the provision of books and materials and the meeting of similar charges. On the other hand being able to levy a small capital fee from parents, with the power to remit in suitable circumstances, for the purpose of assisting in the provision of new buildings and equipment, gives such schools a degree of independence that can encourage individual initiative, involve parents directly with school projects and allow variety in the provision of educational amenities.

(2) The problem of the establishment of a system of comprehensive schools in highly differentiated urban areas.

... In the large urban centres, however, and especially in Belfast, the concept of the neighbourhood comprehensive school faces grave difficulties. The problem is heightened by the social homogeneity of certain heavily populated neighbourhoods and sharply defined occupational/class areas.

(3) FEARS OF SELECTION PROCEDURES.

... We do not subscribe to the abolition of all forms of selection procedure.

... We believe that much parental disquiet with the 11+ selection procedure was not concerned with the examination itself but with the result this might have on the possibility of entry to higher education and suitable occupations via 'O' and 'A' level certificates. It seems to us that, providing such opportunities were available at secondary schools or that extended use was made of the existing, virtually continuous, transfer facilities, much of the fear would be removed from the process of selective assessment.

* * * * * * * * * *

It will be seen that implicit in the reservations we have expressed is the belief that in the special circumstances of Northern Ireland the province may best be served in the future by promoting a variety of educational institutions with extended and improved use of systems of transfer.

III.16 Reorganisation of Secondary Education in Northern Ireland, July 1976, HMSO.

The return of a Labour government in 1974 increased the political pressure for Northern Ireland to move towards a comprehensive system. Thus in February 1975 the Department of Education initiated a major survey to be undertaken by T. Cowan, the senior chief inspector and Mr E.N.V. Hedley, a staff inspector. The document proposed reorganisational schemes covering the entire country and involving all 184 intermediate schools and the 80 grammar schools. Its publication threw the whole educational system into ferment as numerous meetings and discussions followed. Although the process of consultation had begun little progress had been made before a change of government put the whole issue into cold storage.

INTRODUCTION

2.   ... The majority of existing secondary schools in Northern Ireland are voluntary schools: controlled (i.e."state") schools are in a minority. This is quite different from the position in Great Britain; it means that in Northern Ireland a system of comprehensive schooling would be as much dependent upon the voluntary schools as is the present selective system.

PART 2

SECTION 1

2.   Consideration is then given to the minimum size of school which can provide the width of choice in subject areas and levels of study required to satisfy this wide range of educational need, and it is concluded that, subject to provision of appropriate and adequate accommodation, a 2 form entry comprehensive school (enrolment about 300) is viable for the age range 11+ to 16+, but that to provide satisfactorily for the age range 11+ to 18+ a school of 6 form entry (enrolment about 900 aged 11+ to 16+ and about 90 aged 16+ to 18+) is barely large enough. On the basis of these 2 major conclusions, it is then suggested that Northern Ireland could have a viable system of comprehensive schools consisting very largely of groups of 11+ to 16+ schools linked with 11+ to 18+ schools (or in some cases with sixth-form colleges), to which pupils transfer at 16+, together with a few self-contained 11+ to 18+ schools, some 11+ to 18+ schools sharing facilities at sixth-form level, and a very few geographically isolated schools which are so small that in a comprehensive system they could exist only as out-stations of larger schools to which their pupils transfer after a 2 or a 3-year course.

SECTION 2

12.   For 3 reasons the sixth-form college has not been seen in this study as a suitable general provision though it may provide a particular solution in some cases. A considerable body of educational opinion is opposed to it. Even when the minimum number needed for the academic component of viable sixth-form college is pitched as low as 300, a figure far below that usually taken as necessary in

England, there is still not a sufficient number of pupils except in the larger centres of population. Where the number of pupils is large enough, there is not as a rule an existing building in which they can satisfactorily and economically be housed.

14.   The second part of the existing dual provision at 16+ would be largely unchanged. Though the mass movement at 16+ in England and Wales of pupils from schools to courses in technical colleges has not occurred in Northern Ireland, it is useful, nevertheless, to have provision, where it can economically be made, for such pupils as wish to leave, or have left, school and who, nevertheless, desire to study for school examinations. Moreover, it would be economic folly to duplicate in schools the expensive industrial commercial and similar courses of which the technical colleges are now the sole providers. The change which is desirable is not that technical colleges and schools should compete with or try to supplant each other, but that they should co-operate even more fully than at present by further development of linked courses and by local agreement on the location of GCE advanced level courses for which there is only minority demand.

25.   There remains a further general question of fundamental importance, the place of the voluntary grammar schools in a system reorganised on a non-selective basis. These schools provide 24.5% of the pupil places at secondary level. They, and the controlled grammar schools, have considerable academic prestige and experience and both can contribute massively to standards and values in a new system and to the place of such a system in public esteem. It is essential that both voluntary and controlled grammar schools continue to play a very substantial part in secondary education in Northern Ireland, but consideration of how best

the voluntary grammar schools may take their place in a comprehensive system involves close examination of a multiplicity of administrative, financial and possibly legislative matters, none of which come within the scope of this study.

SECTION 4

37.   In considering possible arrangements, 2 criteria must constantly be borne in mind. In each locality the schools must be so large, or must be so grouped, that without undue expenditure adequate provision can be made for the full age range 11+ to 18+. In each school, the accommodation must be such as to facilitate curricular provision for the full spectrum of educational need in the age range suggested for the school.

39.   Consideration of overall adequacy of provision in particular localities showed that while in a reorganised system some will have an abundance of places, others will suffer from major deficiencies. In these latter cases, adjustment of school catchment areas may alleviate the situation, but in many instances a solution depends on the provision of additional accommodation or of transport to schools where places are available. It is a matter of opinion whether it is better to build extensions or to provide transport, but, in some instances, it may be advisable to provide transport in the short term and to consider the provision of additional accommodation as a more lasting solution to be brought about when circumstances permit.

SECTION 5

107.   Subject to all these reservations and qualifications, the total capital cost of reorganisation would appear to lie between £3.25m and £3.75m. Under the present arrangements for grants to voluntary schools, 83% to 84% of this overall expenditure would fall to be met from public funds.

PART 3

SECTION 1

7.   Particular consideration would have to be given, however, to the position of the voluntary grammar schools. These schools are in private ownership. The financial position of each school is different, involving possibly the existence of trust funds, of loans and other financial arrangements which permit the capital requirements of the school to be met with the receipt of income from the capital fees. It is the preference of the Government that the arrangements for the schools to come within a comprehensive system should permit this position to continue because the Government accepts that it is part of the essence of the voluntary principle. The problem, therefore, is one of income essential to the continuation of the schools, which is presently derived from the capital fees paid by all pupils and paid as a condition of entry into the school. It is assumed that, while for some voluntary grammar schools it will be possible to replace this income from private sources, this will not be a possibility for a majority of them.

10.   Each Board, in acknowledgement of the provision by the owners of the grammar school of facilities that come within the comprehensive system, should make a payment of

£20 per pupil entering the school under the Board's arrangements (or some such other amount prescribed in the Regulations, and determined in accordance with the same principles applying at present to the determination of the capital fee). Such an arrangement raises the question whether the relationship between the voluntary grammar school and the public interest should change if this were done.

11. The present arrangement is for one-third of the governing body of each maintained intermediate school and all but 9 of the voluntary grammar schools to be nominated by the Department or by the Boards. This suggests the principle that the contribution from public funds to a school's approved capital expenditure should be related to the degree of public representation on its governing body. With the arrangement in paragraph 10 leading to an increase in this contribution from public funds (raising the total in some cases to as much as 100%) the question arises whether public representation on the governing body should be increased to near half or, say, two-thirds. The Government's preference is that the public representation on the governing body should be raised to two-thirds, having regard to the safeguards referred to in the succeeding paragraph.

SECTION 3

39. With a reorganised system of secondary education in which no tuition fees were charged, it would seem inappropriate that fee-paying should continue in this small segment of the primary sector. (Preparatory Department)

46. While the need for boarding facilities might diminish after reorganisation, there is no reason to believe that it would altogether disappear. There would also be cases where parents, including parents employed overseas, would

themselves wish to make arrangements for their children to attend boarding schools in Northern Ireland. It seems, therefore that boarding departments should continue provided that they remain financially viable without assistance from public funds, other than that provided by a Board in respect of any boarding pupils it "sponsors". It is considered that the relatively few boarders in Northern Ireland schools would have little effect on the overall ability mix in the school; if this is a factor in the future method of transfer of pupils, boarders might well be excluded from these transfer arrangements. In regard to future financial viability, it is relevant to point out that many of the existing boarding departments cater for preparatory pupils as well as secondary pupils, and that the closing of a preparatory department might have considerable effect on the boarding department.

III.17   Education Reform in Northern Ireland — The Way Forward, October 1988.

The suspension of devolved government in Northern Ireland and its replacement by direct rule from Westminster brought the two educational systems closer together.

However the proposals made in the consultative document "Reorganisation of Secondary Education in Northern Ireland" published in July 1976 for the introduction of a modified comprehensive system were quietly dropped. Following changes in England and Wales the GCSE examination replaced the GCE 'O' level examination in the mid-eighties.

Radical changes were introduced in England and Wales by the 1988 Educational Reform Act. Recognising the different educational evolution of Northern Ireland and the province's peculiar difficulties the Northern Ireland Department of Education issued a consultation paper in March 1988. The Government's response was made in October 1988 in "The Way Forward" which suggested further consultation. In turn this led to a draft Order in Council "The Education Reform (Northern Ireland) Order 1989."

1.2   The Government's central aim is to raise educational standards. The proposals in the consultation paper sought to achieve this through a range of measures, including:

— a common curriculum, with associated attainment targets and assessment arrangements, for all grant-aided schools, to ensure equal access to a broad and balanced education for all pupils of compulsory school age;

— greater involvement of parents in their children's education through better information about each child's progress, and through fuller participation in school governance;

— greater freedom for parents in choosing the school which their children should attend, and more information about the performance of schools;

— a greater degree of autonomy for schools and Further Education colleges in managing their budgets in line with their educational priorities.

In addition, the paper contained outline proposals for the creation of grant-maintained schools on similar lines to arrangements put forward in Great Britain, with the added feature in Northern Ireland of using parallel arrangements to facilitate further progress on the establishment of integrated schools (as grant-maintained integrated schools).

THE GOVERNMENT'S CONCLUSIONS

2.5   As was envisaged in the consultation paper, Religious Education will retain its central position in the curriculum in every grant-aided school. The Government has decided, in the light of the comments received, that the new legislation should reaffirm this by providing that the curriculum must include Religious Education together with other specified areas of study. At the same time, although all schools will be required to include Religious Education in the curriculum at all stages, the freedom of teachers and parents to exercise their rights of conscience will continue to be guaranteed in law.

AREAS OF STUDY AND CONTRIBUTORY SUBJECTS

2.8   The curriculum of all pupils of compulsory school age will therefore include, in addition to Religious Education, certain areas of study, which may comprise more than one subject; the subjects contributing to each area of study will also be listed in the legislation. The areas of study which will be prescribed are:

> English
> Mathematics
> Science and Technology
> The Environment and Society
> Creative and Expressive Studies
> Language Studies (secondary schools only)

NEED FOR FORMAL ASSESSMENT

2.24   Responses to consultation supported the Government's view that regular assessment of pupils' progress is an essential and integral part of ensuring that every child is receiving the maximum benefit from the educational opportunities on offer, and that any learning difficulties are identified early and remedial action taken. The Government has decided that in Northern Ireland there should be formal assessment of pupils' progress in the programmes of study at ages 8, 11, 14 and 16 (Years 4, 7, 10 and 12).

SCHOOL ENROLMENTS

3.1   The Government is committed to ensuring that parents are given as much freedom as possible in choosing the schools their children attend, unhindered by administrative constraints or quotas. A start has been made on this in the current school year (1988/89) with the removal of individual admissions limits on the majority of post-primary schools, in line with the policy decision announced in April 1987. However, the Government also intends to incorporate in legislation the general principle that admissions to all primary and secondary schools should normally be constrained only by the existing capacity of their accommodation. With very limited exceptions, therefore, schools will have to admit all pupils applying for admission so long as there are places available. Schools will not be required to expand to meet demand, but it will, of course, continue to be necessary to take account of the demographic needs of individual areas and to provide additional places where this is seen to be necessary. By the same token, the Government also recognises the need to offer a measure of protection, in the form of additional teaching resources, to the curriculum of schools serving isolated communities and reaffirms its commitment to these schools.

3.3   All school authorities will be required to publish details of the admission arrangements for the schools under their control. The information to be published will include:

—   the number of pupils which the school must admit, subject to demand, each year, as determined by the Department after consultation with the school authorities;

—   an explanation of the respective roles of the Education and Library Board and the school Board of Governors in relation to admissions;

—   a statement of the admissions criteria to be used by the school in deciding which children are to be admitted in circumstances where applications for admission exceed the number of places available.

The admissions criteria will only apply where the school is oversubscribed. In order that schools can demonstrate fairness and objectivity in selecting pupils for admission, the criteria will need to express clearly and in order of priority the factors which the school proposes to take into account.

3.6   The consensus of opinion among respondents was that the new form of assessment should be used in place of the present verbal reasoning tests at age 11, in order to avoid imposing a double set of tests on pupils. The Government accepts this view. This means that, after the new arrangements are introduced, the present Transfer Procedure with its centrally-administered attributable verbal reasoning tests and quotas will be abolished. Instead, the type of secondary school to which a pupil transfers will normally be a matter of choice by parents, after consultation with primary teachers, and based on the information contained in the pupil's record of achievement.

3.8   Under the present transfer arrangements pupils may gain admission to grammar schools as fee-payers even though, on the basis of the results of the verbal reasoning tests, an academically-orientated education would not be regarded as suitable for them. However, under the new arrangements pupils accepted for admission by a grammar school will be regarded by the school as suitable for the type of education it provides. Accordingly, there will no longer be any justification for the charging of tuition fees in the secondary departments of grammar schools, and this practice will therefore be discontinued.

4.4   The Government intends that financial delegation, initially to secondary schools, will include the capacity to manage the human resources i.e. teaching and non-teaching staff — available to them, to the extent that schools should be able to increase their staffing complement or to decide that savings can be made in this area without detriment to the running of the school or the education of the pupils. The normal procedures for appointment and dismissal will however be unchanged for the purposes of financial delegation.

5.3   However, the clear view has emerged during the consultation process that, in the particular circumstances of Northern Ireland, it would be of more direct relevance to the needs of the community to concentrate entirely on GMIS (Grant-Maintained Integrated Status). Accordingly, the Government has decided not to proceed with the proposal for grant-maintained status, but to proceed with the introduction of legislation for grant-maintained integrated status, and to associate with it a range of additional measures in support of integrated education generally.

III.18   Education Reform (Northern Ireland) Order, 1989.

THE CURRICULUM

4.— (2)   The curriculum for a grant-aided school satisfies the requirements of this Article if it is a balanced and broadly based curriculum which:—

(a)   promotes the spiritual, moral, cultural, intellectual and physical development of pupils at the school and thereby of society; and

(b)   prepares such pupils for the opportunities, responsibilities and experience of adult life.

5. — (6) For the purposes of this Part the key stages in relation to a pupil are as follows:—

(a)   the period beginning with his becoming of compulsory school age and ending at the same time as the fourth school year thereafter;

(b)   the period beginning at the same time as the next school year after the end of the first key stage and ending at the same time as the third school year thereafter;

(c)   the period beginning at the same time as the next school year after the end of the second key stage and ending at the same time as the third school year thereafter;

(d)   the period beginning at the same time as the next school year after the end of the third key stage and ending at the same time as he ceases to be of compulsory school age.

8. — (1) The curriculum for a grant-aided school shall not, in so far as it relates to pupils of compulsory school age, be taken to satisfy the requirements of Article 4(2) unless it promotes, wholly or mainly through the teaching of the contributory subjects and religious education, the attainment of the objectives of the following educational themes,

namely:—

(a)   Information Technology;
(b)   Education for Mutual Understanding;
(c)   Cultural Heritage;
(d)   Health Education;
(e)   in relation to the third and fourth key stages, Economic Awareness;
(f)   in relation to the third and fourth key stages, Careers Education.

10. — (1) The scheme of management for every grant-aided school shall provide for it to be the duty of the Board of Governors:—

(a)   to determine, and keep under review, its policy in relation to the curriculum for the school; and

(b)   to make, and keep up to date, a written statement of that policy.

ADMISSION OF CHILDREN
TO GRANT-AIDED SCHOOLS

36.— (1) Every board shall make arrangements for enabling the parent of a child resident in the area of the board to express a preference as to the school at which he wishes education to be provided for his child and to give reasons for his preference.

(2) It shall be the duty of the Board of Governors of a grant-aided school:—

(a)   to make arrangements for the admission of pupils to the school;

(b)   subject to paragraphs (3) and (4), to comply with any preference expressed in accordance with arrangements made under paragraph (1).

****

(4) The duty imposed by paragraph (2)(b) does not apply if —

(a)   the preferred school is a grammar school; and

(b)   compliance with the preference would be detrimental to the educational interests of the child concerned.

38. — (1) Subject to paragraphs (2) and (3), the Board of Governors of each grant-aided school shall draw up the criteria to be applied in selecting pupils for admission to the school.

39. — (1) Subject to paragraph (2), the Board of Governors of a grant-aided school shall not cause or permit the number of registered pupils at the school at any time to exceed the school's enrolment number.

FINANCING SCHOOLS

46. — (1) It shall be the duty of every board to prepare a scheme in accordance with this Part and submit it for the approval of the Department in accordance with Article 47.

(2) The scheme shall provide for:—

(a) the determination in respect of each financial year of the board, for each school required to be covered by the scheme in that year, of the share to be appropriated for that school in that year of the part of the general schools budget of the board for that year which is available for allocation to individual schools under the scheme (referred to in this Part, in relation to such a school, as the school's budget share);

(b) the delegation by the board of the management of a school's budget share for any year to the Board of Governors of the school where such delegation is required or permitted by or under the scheme; and

(c) the making available by the board to the Board of Governors of the school of a sum of money to be spent at its discretion, where the management of the school's budget share is not delegated to the Board of Governors.

49. — (1) The provision to be included in a scheme for determining the budget share for any financial year of each school required to be covered by the scheme in that year shall require that share to be determined (and from time to time revised) by the application of a formula laid down by the scheme for the purpose of dividing among all such schools the aggregated budget for that year of the board concerned.

61. — (1) Before the beginning of each financial year the Department shall prepare a statement of the financial provision it plans to make in that year for voluntary grammar schools.

INTEGRATED EDUCATION

64. — (1)   It shall be the duty of the Department to encourage and facilitate the development of integrated education, that is to say the education together at school of Protestant and Roman Catholic pupils.

(2)   The Department may, subject to such conditions as it thinks fit, pay grants to any body appearing to the Department to have as an objective the encouragement or promotion of integrated education.

66.— (2)   The scheme of management for a grant-maintained integrated school shall require the Board of Governors to use its best endeavours, in exercising its functions under the Education Orders, to ensure that the management and ethos of the school are such as are likely to attract to the school reasonable numbers of both Protestant and Roman Catholic pupils.

69. — (1)   Subject to paragraph (5), in the case of any controlled or voluntary school which is eligible for grant-maintained integrated status, a ballot of parents on the question of whether grant-maintained integrated status should be sought for the school shall be held in accordance with Article 70 if either-

(a)   the Board of Governors decides by a resolution passed at a meeting of that Board ("the first resolution") to hold such a ballot and confirms that decision by a resolution ("the second resolution") passed at a subsequent meeting of the Board of Governors held not less than fourteen nor more than twenty eight days after that at which the first resolution was passed; or

(b)   the Board of Governors receives a written request to hold such a ballot which meets the requirements of paragraph (2).

(2)   Those requirements are that the request must be signed, or otherwise endorsed in such manner as the Department may determine, by a number of parents of registered pupils at the school equal to at least twenty per cent of the number of registered pupils at the school on the date on which the request is received.

71. — (1)   Where in the case of any controlled or voluntary school which is eligible for grant-maintained integrated status the result of a ballot held in accordance with Article 70 shows a simple majority of votes cast in the ballot by persons eligible to vote in the ballot (within the meaning of that Article) in favour of seeking grant-maintained integrated status for the school, it shall be the duty of the Board of Governors of the school to submit a proposal for the acquisition of grant-maintained integrated status for the school to the relevant board.

III.19   The Curriculum for 14-19 Year Olds — A Framework for Choice — DENI, March 1992.

Although all children were to undertake the national curriculum, this still failed to solve the problem of those pupils who preferred a more vocationally based education. Many of the latter had benefited from link courses at their local colleges of further education. The Department of Education wanted education from 14-19 to be regarded as a whole without the break at 16+. Schools and Further Education colleges were encouraged to form partnerships and so provide a seamless cloak for students.

INTRODUCTION

1.3   In Northern Ireland there is a strong tradition of academic study in secondary education, with a particular emphasis on achievement at GCE A level. While this emphasis is appropriate for a number of pupils, greater recognition also needs to be given to the value of vocational routes to further and higher education, and to employment, if we are to enhance the education and training which can be offered to young people in the 14-19 age group.

1.4   As a first step, there needs to be broad acceptance of a number of key objectives, and a consensus as to how they might be achieved. The objectives might be identified as:

—   coherence, continuity, flexibility and progression in the curriculum;
—   parity of esteem for all nationally recognised qualifications;
—   a clear and unified system of National Vocational Qualifications which offers access to further and higher education and to employment, and which is well understood by industry, commerce and the general public;
—   a significant increase in the proportion of the age group who achieve success, and at higher level of attainment, in approved qualifications, including GCSE's, GCE A and AS levels, and National Vocational Qualifications;
—   a system of records of achievement which is accepted by young people, parents, employers, training organisations and admissions officers in institutions of further education;
—   clear advice on careers throughout the 14-19 period, to help young people select the most appropriate routes and to ensure progression.

THE PRESENT POSITION

2.11   Whether through lack of curricular choice or through inappropriate guidance at a crucial stage of a young person's educational development there is an unacceptable waste of individual potential, and a loss to our society of a range of potential skills and expertise. This weakness could be overcome by the development of, and agreement on, a broad framework for curricular provision for 14-19 year olds.

A CURRICULAR FRAMEWORK FOR 16-19 YEAR OLDS

4.5   The curriculum for all 16-19 year olds, whether in a school or further education college or training organisation, should build on the foundations laid in Key Stage 4, and should itself be a foundation for further study or training and, ultimately, employment. To this end, all young people in this age range who are in full-time education and training should undertake studies which:

—   have an appropriate degree of rigour and relevance;
—   allow them to acquire additional competences and qualifications appropriate to their chosen career paths;
—   provide further opportunities to develop the personal and social qualities which young people will need in adult and working life;
—   include well-informed and objective careers guidance.

4.9   DENI now considers that the aims outlined for 16-19 provision could appropriately be reflected in a curricular framework consisting of a number of components within which post-16 provision for all young people in full-time education in schools and colleges of further education might be made. These components are:-

MAIN STUDIES

ADDITIONAL STUDIES

CAREERS GUIDANCE

4.20   General National Vocational qualifications are designed primarily for young people in the 16-19 age group who are in full-time education. Initially, they will cover five broad vocational areas - business and administration, manufacturing technology, health and social care, leisure and tourism, and art and design. They will be pitched at NVQ levels 2 and 3. They are intended as an alternative to traditional post-16 courses such as GCE A level, while at the same time enabling those who pursue them to keep their options open by providing a pathway both to higher education and to employment.

EXTENDED COURSES POLICY

5.1   At present, all extended courses at all schools must be specifically approved by DENI against criteria described in Circular No 1983/17.

5.2   DENI has therefore reviewed its extended courses policy, and from the beginning of the academic year 1992/93, schools will be permitted to offer such 16+ provision at NVQ level 1-3 and GCE A/AS level as they consider appropriate. Colleges of further education will have the same opportunities in terms of provision up to NVQ level 3 or its equivalent and at GCE A/AS level. DENI would, however, expect schools and colleges to satisfy themselves that:

— the necessary range of staffing expertise and facilities would be available in the school or college, or can be provided by consortia or link arrangements;

— all post-16 pupils, students and trainees would be working towards a nationally recognised qualification;

— intended courses would be capable of attracting sufficient pupils or students to generate adequate finance under the LMS/LMC arrangements to ensure that a disproportionate share of the budget is not directed to the support and resourcing of courses and programmes for a very limited number of participants. In practice, teaching groups should normally consist of between 10 and 20 students;

— pupils, students and trainees would be able to choose from a wide range of subjects and/or programmes well matched to their level of attainment, ability and interests. Further, the various national examining/validating bodies should be satisfied that the school or college is capable of offering the courses.

5.4   Where post-16 provision is being offered schools and colleges should ensure that:

(a)   careful consideration has been given to providing courses through consortia arrangements, either with other schools or, particularly in the case of vocational courses, with further education colleges to ensure the most economical use of resources;

(b)   provision should be in line with the framework
        outlined in this paper; pupils or students should not be
        offered narrowly based options, notably Main Studies
        consisting of repeat GCSE courses;

(c)   an appropriate breadth of courses can be sustained; in
        particular,

—   where NVQ programmes at levels 1 or 2, or equivalent
        (including BTEC First Diplomas and General NVQs)
        are offered, the pupils should be able to select at least 3
        contrasting vocational areas: for example, business and
        finance, science, and leisure studies. (In order not to
        overburden themselves, schools and colleges should
        consider a phased introduction of the 3 programme
        areas over the next 3 years);

—   where GCE A/AS level courses are provided, at least
        10 subjects should be offered. These should reflect the
        pattern of entry of the most popular subjects in the
        NISEAC GCE A levels and be drawn from across the
        full range of Areas of Study. Colleges and schools
        should, where necessary, consider consortia
        arrangements in order to make this level of provision;

—   where NVQ level 3, or equivalent programmes
        (including General NVQs and BTEC National
        Diplomas) are offered, students should be able to
        choose from a minimum of 3 contrasting occupational
        areas; for example, construction, computer studies, and
        travel and tourism. These programmes should be
        delivered in further education colleges or through
        programmes shared between colleges and schools or
        through the franchising of programmes between
        schools and colleges. A phased introduction of the 3
        programme areas over the next 3 years should also be
        considered.

**III.20   Transfer from Primary to Secondary School —
1993/1994 and Beyond, DENI, October 1992.**

One of the main aims of the 1988 Education Act in England and
Wales had been to instill an element of competition into schooling,
with parents being able to select the school of their choice. This
concept clashed with the selective system in Northern Ireland; here
choice meant choice of high school, not any school. Once again
educational development conflicted with the selection procedure.
The Department of Education had a further problem; children in
Northern Ireland would have to undertake not only the national
tests but also the 11+. Once again the Department tried to square
the circle with a consultation paper.

INTRODUCTION

2.0   The Government's objective is to ensure that the
transfer system operates in a way which is fair to all
concerned and which has the confidence of schools, teachers
and parents.

4.0   Transfer will continue to be operated in the context
of open enrolment, which means that schools will still have to
admit up to their physical capacity and to draw up objective
criteria to decide which pupils should be admitted and apply
them when they are over-subscribed; currently grammar
schools are the only schools which may select pupils on the
basis of academic ability and this will also continue: all other
schools must include only non-academic criteria in their
admissions arrangements.

BACKGROUND

6.0   The Government therefore decided 2 years ago that the 1992/93 school year would be the last year in which the current verbal reasoning tests would be used. No decision was taken at that time about an alternative system for transfer because the detail of the assessment arrangements remained to be worked out. It was, however, made clear that, for pupils transferring in the summer of 1994 and in succeeding years, the outcomes of assessments at Key Stage 2 will be used in the process of deciding which pupils should be admitted to grammar schools.

7.0   It might be helpful to explain how the current Transfer Procedure operates. The Transfer Procedure is in effect a "competition" in which all pupils are ranked in accordance with their performance in the tests and then split into 4 grades: the top 25% of the transfer age group (grade 1), the next 10% (grade 2), the next 10% (grade 3) and the remainder (grade 4). Over-subscribed grammar schools selecting on ability must take applicants with a grade 1 before those with a grade 2, and those with a grade 2 before grades 3 and 4. Where over-subscribed grammar schools have to choose among pupils with the same grade, they must apply other, non-academic, admissions criteria, in the order in which those criteria are stated, until the last place is filled. Non-grammar schools which are over-subscribed select on the basis of their (non-academic) admissions criteria.

16.   Since the majority of pupils are expected to achieve level 4 in each subject, and only a relatively small proportion would be expected to reach level 5 or above, it can be foreseen that grammar schools would not normally be able to reach their approved admissions numbers by enrolling only the pupils who had achieved level 5. A method would therefore be required to enable schools to select the

remaining pupils from amongst the broad band of pupils who are expected to attain the same subject outcomes in assessment.

17.   ...The future arrangements for transfer hinge on the issue of whether it would be appropriate for grammar schools to select most of their pupils on the basis of non-academic criteria.

19.   Additional information about attainment could be achieved by schools using the results of assessment at attainment target level, or by the use of a further test to supplement the assessment outcomes. Such information could allow grammar schools to select entirely, or almost entirely, on academic criteria, but would reduce the flexibility for grammar schools to select on other grounds.

OPTION 1:

SUBJECT LEVELS AND NON-ACADEMIC CRITERIA

Over-subscribed grammar schools would use only subject levels as evidence of attainment; non-academic admissions criteria would be used to distinguish among pupils with the same subject levels.

OPTION 2:

SUBJECT LEVELS, ATTAINMENT TARGET LEVELS AND NON-ACADEMIC CRITERIA

Over-subscribed grammar schools would use the level of attainment in each subject (as in option 1) and the remaining places would be allocated on the basis of firstly, attainment target results in each of the 3 subjects and secondly, non-academic criteria.

OPTION 3:

SUBJECT LEVELS, SUPPLEMENTARY TEST AND NON-ACADEMIC CRITERIA

Over-subscribed grammar schools would use subject levels (as in Option 1), together with a supplementary test which would be used to enable grammar schools to select pupils for admission from amongst those pupils who are not distinguishable on the basis of assessment outcomes alone. If further differentiation is required non-academic criteria would be applied.

IV

TECHNICAL AND FURTHER EDUCATION

IV.1 Interim Report of the Departmental Committee on the Educational Services in Northern Ireland (Lynn Committee), 1922, Cmd.6.

Technical education was the only part of the Irish educational system to be handed over in good order to the newly formed Ministry of Education in February 1922. Controlled by the Department of Agriculture and Technical Instruction since 1899, the technical schools were managed by technical education committees which included members of locally elected bodies, whether rural and urban district councils or the two county boroughs. As the committees were compatible with the Unionist desire for public control of education, they were incorporated with little change into the new system and conducted on existing lines.

The development of technical education in the inter-war years was hindered by two main problems, the poor state of many technical school buildings and inadequate funding. The latter was to stunt the system during the 1930s. Although technical education had widespread support within the community, it could rarely exert the same pressure on the Government as the other two branches of education.

The Lynn Committee having highlighted current difficulties suggested simplifying funding and encouraging slow if steady growth when it described and recommended as follows:—

67.   The two Acts of Parliament on which the system of Technical Instruction is based, while providing funds for teaching, made no provision for school buildings. Nevertheless, school buildings have been erected in each of the two County Boroughs, and in eight other centres. This has been done by pledging the rate for the repayment of interest and sinking fund on a loan from the Board of Works. By remodelling existing buildings — town halls, churches, factories, etc. — eleven other satisfactory schools have been obtained, but the remaining schools are housed in unsatisfactory buildings. Since the war the excessive cost of construction, together, with the high rate of interest demanded, has stopped all building programmes, the amount which could be raised by loan on a two-penny rate being as a rule insufficient to provide more than one-fourth of the necessary cost.

68.   The main work of the schools has been done, up to the present, in evening classes of a purely voluntary type. The system has admittedly met with great success, but has inherent defects. Regularity of attendance cannot be sufficiently secured where work is in the nature of overtime. Moreover, the good intentions of students when they join the schools are wont to give way under the stress of work, and too frequently also because of an incomplete groundwork of elementary knowledge. The result is that only a small proportion of those who enter upon a four-year course of study complete it.

69.   Recognising this, Technical Instruction Committees have in recent years endeavoured to develop day instruction in their schools. Two types of school have resulted. One is the Trades Preparatory School, which aims at preparing for industrial careers students who have completed their course at a primary school. In these schools general education is

continued and special attention paid to mechanical drawing, science, woodwork and metalwork. There are five Trades Preparatory Schools in Northern Ireland. The other type is the Day Commercial School, which aims at preparing students for business. There are eighteen schools of this type held in technical schools in Northern Ireland. The grants available for the latter type of school are altogether inadequate, but with proper financial encouragement, these schools could be greatly strengthened. In the past there may have been overlapping in schools of this type with other schools, which will, no doubt, be avoided in future under the unified control of the Ministry.

108.   No radical change in the organisation of technical education appears to be necessary or desirable, but the evidence we have heard points to the fact that the Urban District Committees have been more successful than the County Committees.

109.   When the department of Agriculture and Technical Instruction was first set up, two methods of dealing with Rural Districts were ... recognised as possible. One was to organise the work in the Rural Districts and smaller Urban Districts under committees of the County Councils. This was the method generally adopted. The other possible method was to attach to an Urban District the surrounding Rural District or Districts. In sparsely populated areas, the county system is probably the only possible one, but in Northern Ireland, which contains thirty Urban Districts and thirty-four Rural Districts, it is a question whether the Urban-cum-Rural system would not be more suitable and efficient. The evidence we have heard has been strongly in favour of the latter system, and our recommendations have been made accordingly.

110.   Another matter which has engaged our attention is the limitation in regard to rating power imposed by existing legislation. This limitation has in recent years prevented the erection of necessary schools and the enlargement of existing premises. We have, therefore, recommended the withdrawal of the legal limitation, and have made proposals which should greatly facilitate the provision of suitable school buildings.

197. — (5) In Day Technical Schools the rates of attendance grant should be the same as the rates paid for corresponding evening classes, provided that the pupils on admission to such schools have reached a standard of education satisfactory to the Ministry.

The attendance grant for pupils in these Day Schools should be limited to £10 for the first, £12 for the second, £15 for the third, and £20 for the fourth year.

(6)   The number of Trade Scholarships given annually by the Ministry should be very considerably increased, as these provide the only satisfactory means by which trade apprentices in smaller towns and more remote districts can obtain the necessary training. We estimate that at least two hundred such scholarships would be required annually for Northern Ireland.

266.   Our estimate of the State charge for technical education has already been given as about £120,000 per annum, this being an increase of £20,000, as compared with the cost at the beginning of the present year (1922).

267. As regards local contributions ... two pence in County Boroughs and Urban Districts, and a rate of a penny in the pound in all Rural Districts. ... total local contribution would amount to rather less than £29,000. At present the amount raised from rates for the purpose is slightly over £20,000.

268. The salaries of teachers in technical schools were on a somewhat more satisfactory basis during the war period than those of other teachers in Ireland, owing to the fact that the British Treasury granted war bonuses on Civil Service terms to all full-time teachers. This will be seen from the fact that in February last the average salary (including war bonus) of full-time technical teachers in the six county area was £354. If we exclude Belfast, where a considerable proportion of highly qualified and experienced teachers is necessary, the average was £308. The fall in the war bonus which took place at the end of February has reduced these averages to about £319 and £276 respectively. Any further reduction would deplete the schools of competent teachers, and we consider that if efficient work is to be secured the averages of February last must be restored.

IV.2   Education Act (Northern Ireland) 1923, 13 and 14 Geo 5, C.21.

The 1923 Education Act paid scant attention to technical education and its one major provision continued its complicated management structures. The Act allowed the urban district councils to continue as education authorities for technical education and to strike a rate for it in their respective areas, while in rural areas the new regional education committees assumed control of both primary and technical instruction.

23.   The following provisions shall have effect with respect to the exercise and performance of the powers and duties of the council of an urban county district in relation to technical instruction, that is to say —

(1)   If the council have not before the appointed day appointed or joined in the appointment of a committee under section fourteen of the Agriculture and Technical Instruction (Ireland) Act, 1989, the powers of the council in relation to technical instruction shall cease to be exerciseable.

(2)   If the council have before the appointed day appointed or joined in the appointment of a committee under the said section, the council shall exercise and perform, as respects the urban county district, the powers and duties of an education authority under this Part of this Act in relation to the provision of technical instruction, and for that purpose shall have power —

(a)   to appoint a committee, constituted in like manner as a committee under the said section;

(b)   to defray their expenses out of any rate or fund applicable to the purposes of the Public Health (Ireland) Acts, 1878 to 1918;

(c)   to borrow money as if the said purpose were a purpose for which the council are authorised to borrow under the said Public Health (Ireland) Acts.

Provided that —

(i)   The Ministry by order may determine that the said powers and duties shall cease to be exercised and performed, and that the district shall become, for the purposes of technical

instruction, part of the education area of the
appropriate education authority, or may combine
the council with the council of any other urban
county district or with any education authority,
on such terms and conditions as may be
prescribed by the order, for the joint exercise
and performance of the powers and duties of the
councils, or of the council and the education
authority, in relation to technical instruction.

**IV.3   The Report of the Committee on the Financial Relations
between the State and Local Authorities — August 1931,
Cmd.131.**

As technical education was more directly funded and managed by
the local authorities it came under very close scrutiny by the
committee established to investigate the financial relationship
between central and local government in Northern Ireland. The
Government had been constantly criticised by Treasury officials in
London about the low proportion of expenditure on education and
policing borne by the rates in Northern Ireland. As the depression
deepened in the early 1930s, Northern Ireland found it increasingly
difficult to balance the budget.   Coupled with raids on reserves, the
Government pared expenditure on services including education.

It was against this background that the Committee reported in
August 1931 and the drastic cuts proposed for Technical Education
caused a furore especially the insensitive remark about 'evening
pastimes.' The Ministry of Education was inundated with
complaints from management committees, regional education
committees and local urban and rural district councils.

While the committee's financial proposals were not implemented,
the technical system grew very slowly in the 1930s and the
attendance grant declined from £42,000 in 1930 to £38,159 in 1937,
before recovering dramatically to £44,000 in 1938. Student
enrolment oscillated around the 23,000 mark but there was an
increasing trend towards full-time attendance, highlighted by an
increase in the incremental grant towards teachers' salaries from
£21,820 in 1930 to £32,702 in 1938.

16. — (6B) The former (attendance grants) consist of a fixed annual amount of £42,000, which is payable to the Committees (Regional Education Committees) in proportion to the number of hours of attendance of pupils, account being had to the varying importance of the different subjects.

67.   ... if, as we hold, the limit of taxable capacity has now been reached in Northern Ireland, the limit of rateable capacity is similarly not far off ... it would seem apparent that the State cannot expect to escape from the consequences of further central expenditure by attempting to transfer any appreciable portion of the existing State burdens to the ratepayers.

131.   Technical education, for a large number of those attending classes, cannot be regarded as a vital necessity. Although there is no doubt that it has in the past, and does still, serve a most useful purpose, this purpose is less a matter of National concern than one of importance to the locality and particular individuals in it. We, therefore recommend that the amount of the fixed grant of £42,000 be substantially reduced. We consider that the persons benefiting by technical education should be required to make some larger contribution, by way of fees, towards its cost, special concessions being made to those who have not adequate means and who may be expected to make proper use of the opportunities thus provided. Moreover, we have reason to think that investigation would disclose the possibility of economies by way of abolishing unnecessary classes, or classes that can only be regarded as in the Nature of evening pastimes.

* * * * * * * * *

TECHNICAL AND FURTHER EDUCATION   425

EDUCATION

160.   We recommend that the grant towards the
expenditure of the Education Committees should be made as
follows:-

No distinction should be made between the portions of the
grant applicable to Technical Education and to Elementary
Education, that is to say, the present grant of £42,000 to
Technical Education and the grants made by virtue of Section
76 of the Education Act 1923 (a sum not exceeding two-
thirds of the produce of a rate of one shilling in the pound on
the net annual valuation of the area of each authority) should
be amalgamated.

A single grant would thus be paid towards the annual
schemes of education authorities under Section 76 of the Act,
but the provision limiting the amount of this grant to the
equivalent of an 8d. rate would be removed. The single grant
would consist of two portions, viz:-

(i)   A unit portion, to be fixed on the basis of 8/- per "unit"
        of Technical Education plus 12/- per head of average
        attendance of pupils at Public Elementary Schools and

(ii)   a percentage-portion, consisting of 25% of the
        remaining approved net expenditure of the
        Committees.

161.   It will be remembered that we recommended that the
fixed Technical Instruction grant of £42,000 should be
substantially reduced, and we have given effect to this
recommendation by fixing the value of the unit at 8/-.

162. Translating this proposal into concrete figures, we find that the number of technical "units" during the year ended June, 1930 was about 58,000, and the average attendance of elementary pupils about 167,500. The unit-portion would, therefore, amount to 58,000 x 8/- + 167,500 x 12/- = £23,200 + £100,500 = £123,700.

RESERVATION BY MR. BONAPARTE WYSE

... I am strongly of opinion that the amount proposed as the "unit-grant" for technical education (8/- per "unit") is unduly low and calculated, therefore, not only to retard the work of the education authorities in general, but seriously to discourage the development of a branch of education which is of vital importance to the general welfare of the country ... and although the proposed system of payments allows for expansion, this expansion would necessarily be so slow that the loss to the authorities for some appreciable time would be in my opinion, unduly restrictive of educational work in all branches.

When it is remembered that substantial reductions have been made in the Education Vote in the present year through the effect of the "cut" in teachers' salaries, I think it will be agreed that the further sacrifices demanded from Education in the interests of economy by the adoption of the figures in the Report would be more than is reasonable.

In my opinion the lowest figure that should be fixed for technical education as a constituent of the new composite grant is 15/- per "unit." This figure represents a decrease amounting to approximately £13,000, compared with the present grant, and it is only because I am seriously impressed with the absolute importance of keeping down expenditure that I could assent to it.

IV.4   Report of the Committee on the Scholarships System in Northern Ireland — March 1938, Cmd.192.

While the Robb committee was more concerned with scholarships for grammar schools its report emphasised the difficulties facing the Technical Schools in persuading young people and their parents that technical education provided a viable alternative to the academic curriculum offered by the more prestigious grammar schools.

33.   The majority of the technical school scholarships have been tenable at the full-time junior technical and junior commercial schools and have varied in amount so as to cover either the amount of the tuition fee or the tuition fee and the cost of books and instruments and in some cases an additional allowance towards the cost of travelling to and from the school.

90.   There has apparently been created an impression that scholarships to junior technical and junior commercial schools are of little importance. We think it advisable that measures should be taken to remove such an impression.

106.   We recommend that definite provision should be made in scholarship schemes for the award of scholarships to assist needy students to attend technical schools where courses more suitable to their requirements can be followed.

IV.5   Report of the Consultative Committee on Secondary Education, October 1938, W. Spens (Chairman).

Although Technical education in Ireland had the same origins, the Northern Ireland system looked increasingly to trends in Great Britain rather than those in the Irish Free State.

Due to financial limitations Northern Ireland had not introduced the Hadow proposals for secondary education for all, with a break at 11+ between primary and secondary schooling. However with the economic recovery consequent on rearmament in the late 1930s, the Government was more receptive to the ideas in the Spens Report. Unfortunately all proposals for reform were put in cold storage at the outbreak of war.

107.   Since the word "Junior" in the expression Junior Technical School has rather misleading associations, we recommend that henceforth the expression "Technical School" be used as a general term to describe all Junior Technical Schools recruiting their pupils at the age of 13+ and providing courses which last for two or three years. The name "Technical School" will thus embrace both the specifically vocational schools hitherto known as Trade Schools, which prepare for definite occupations, and those schools which prepare for a range of related trades and occupations, viz, the Junior Technical Schools for boys, bearing on the engineering and building industries, the schools designed to prepare girls for home management, and the Junior Commercial Schools.

108.   We have come to the conclusion that the Junior Technical Schools for boys, associated with the engineering and building industries have succeeded in developing their curriculum on a broad scientific and realistic basis, and we are of opinion that for certain types of boy the education provided by this curriculum and the practical method of approach to various subjects, e.g. Science, Mathematics, and Engineering Drawing, best develop their capacities, and in consequence provide the course most appropriate for them whatever occupation they may eventually choose.

109.   We are convinced that it is of great importance to establish a new type of higher school of technical character quite distinct from the traditional academic Grammar School. As a first step to this end, we recommend that a number of existing Junior Technical Schools orientated towards the engineering and building industries and any other Technical Schools which may develop training of such a character as —

(a)   to provide a good intellectual discipline altogether apart from its technical value, and

(b)   to have a technical value in relation not to one particular occupation but to a group of occupations, should be converted into Technical High Schools, in the sense that they should be accorded in every respect equality of status with schools of the grammar school type. We recommend that such schools, which would recruit their pupils at the age of 11+ and provide a five-year course up to the age of 16+, should be called Technical High Schools to distinguish them from full-time Technical Schools of other types which provide courses for pupils beginning at the age of 13 or 14.

110.   We recommend that pupils should be recruited for Technical High School at the age of 11+ by means of the general selective examination by which pupils are at present recruited for the Grammar Schools.

111.   The curriculum for pupils between the ages of 11+ and 13+ in Technical High Schools should be broadly of the same character as the curriculum in other types of secondary school of equal status.

112.   For pupils above the age of 13 the curriculum should be designed so as to provide a liberal education with Science and its applications as the core and inspiration. The subject matter would be English, History, Geography, Mathematics, Science, Engineering Drawing, Practical Crafts in the workshops, Physical Education and the Aesthetic Subjects, together with continued study of a foreign language for those pupils who have shown that they are capable of profiting by it.

113.   We strongly recommend that, wherever possible, Technical High Schools should be housed in the premises of Technical Colleges or Technical Institutes. In cases where it is not possible to accommodate the Technical High School in a Technical College, we think that it is most desirable that its buildings should be linked with the college buildings in order to facilitate full use of the equipment and staff of the college.

114.   We consider that a Technical High school should be organised as a department of the Technical College and with the Head Master of the school as the Head of that Department. The ultimate control of the school would be vested in the Principal of the college, who could best secure that the technical equipment of the various Departments would be available for pupils of the school, and could most effectively secure and maintain the co-operation and interest of the Heads of the specialised Departments and their staffs in the life and work of the school.

117.   We recommend that a new type of leaving certificate should be established for pupils in Technical High Schools on the basis of internal examinations founded on the school curriculum, and subject to external assessment by assessors appointed or approved by the Board of Education in order to afford an adequate guarantee for a uniform minimum

standard of certification in Technical High Schools throughout the country. We recommend that the arrangements for this leaving certificate would be planned on lines similar to those in use for the existing examinations for National Certificates.

118.   We recommend that these certificates should be given an equal standing with School Certificates as fulfilling the first condition for matriculation.

119.   We recommend that close relations should exist between Grammar Schools and Technical High Schools, so that opportunity of transfer at about the age of 13 should exist for those pupils whose later development makes it clear that they would be better suited by an alternative form of education.

120.   We hope that employers and Trade Unions will see their way to reconsider the conditions of entry into and service in industry, with special reference to the age of admission and the period of apprenticeship required for boys who have taken a course in a Technical High School.

121.   While we fully recognise that valuable work is being done in Junior Commercial Schools, we recommend, that these schools should continue as at present to recruit their pupils at the age of 13 or 14.

122.   We consider that valuable work is being done in Home Training Schools for girls, and we recommend that these schools should continue as heretofore to recruit their pupils at the age of 13 or 14.

123.   We desire to reaffirm the view expressed in our Report on The Education of the Adolescent (1926) that the Trade Schools within their own province are doing valuable work and should be developed as far as is possible in accordance with the needs and requirements of certain local industries. We recommend that admission to these schools should not be obtained at an earlier age than 13+, and we would prefer 14+. We think that in areas where there is a steady demand for an entry of young people to permanent employment in established trades, schools of this type are justified.

124.   We think that, before a local education authority decides to add a Junior Art Department to its Art School, it should be satisfied that the necessary variety of teaching power in art subjects can be found only in the Art School, and that the probable future occupations of the pupils are of such a character that specific art teaching cannot be deferred till the age of 15 or 16.

IV.6   Educational Reconstruction in Northern Ireland, December 1944, Cmd.226.

The war energised the Technical School system. Growth was concentrated in evening classes for those engaged in the greatly expanded engineering industry. Courses were introduced for the armed forces in radio mechanics, aircraft technology, fire control etc. In 1945 there were 28,105 students in 102 centres.

While the 1944 White Paper was largely supportive of technical education, especially in encouraging a modified form of technical high schools, it proposed the absorption by the new junior secondary schools of the junior commercial and domestic science schools. Thus began a forty year trend, the slow erosion of the technical school base, as the concept of further education began to slowly replace that of technical education.

11.   The education committees may have had a comparatively minor share in the development of facilities for secondary education but they have been closely connected with the development of the technical schools. Of the 61 permanent technical schools and centres 58 are controlled by them, the remaining three being under voluntary management. There is scarcely a town in Ulster with a population of 3,000 inhabitants which has not its technical school and several are situated in villages with as few as 1,000 inhabitants. The Belfast College of Technology is recognised as one of the leading institutions of its kind in the United Kingdom and at present caters for more than 8,000 students. In addition to the permanent schools there are also many itinerant centres which carry the technical school system into the heart of the countryside and provide classes for adults, mainly in woodwork and domestic economy.

****

12.   Since 1923 eleven new technical schools have been built and many others have been extended or reconstructed. The total number of students has increased from 18,026 to 22,435 in 1943. Nor are the activities of the schools confined to the evening classes, for which they were originally intended. Most of the larger schools have developed junior day schools providing two or three year courses for pupils up to 15 or 16 years of age. In this category there are 15 junior technical schools attended by boys, 25 junior commercial schools attended mostly by girls but with a fair proportion of boys, and 8 junior domestic economy schools for girls; the total enrolment in these schools in 1943 was some 3,700. The marked development of these junior day courses during the past twenty years has, incidentally, enabled the schools to employ more of their teachers on a full-time basis. In addition to a flourishing junior technical and junior commercial

school, the Belfast College conducts advanced day classes, including a School of Art, and under a co-ordination scheme with Queen's University, Belfast, students enrolled in the Faculty of Applied Science and Technology (and in the evening classes of the Faculty of Commerce) take their courses in the College. Its Training Department for domestic economy teachers enjoys a reputation equal to that of the best known institutions in Great Britain. The credit for the successful expansion of the technical school system must be ascribed not only to the teachers but also to the education committees, who have taken such an active interest in the development of their schools.

43.   As was indicated in Paragraph 12, there are three types of day school operated within the technical schools — junior technical, junior commercial and junior domestic economy — the first normally recruiting its pupils for a two-year course from the public elementary schools at the age of 13 and the last two at the age of 14, on completion of the elementary school course. It is proposed that the junior secondary schools shall provide courses similar to those now given in the junior commercial and junior domestic economy schools which, after a transition period has allowed the technical schools to adjust themselves to the new system, should cease to exist as separate entities. But the junior technical schools have a special claim to a separate existence. Although a list of the subjects taught in these schools would not suggest that they differ greatly from the junior forms of many of the senior secondary schools, less time is devoted to languages and more to science, mathematics and mechanical drawing and the approach to those subjects is much more practical. Moreover, the well-equipped workshops of the technical schools are available for practical instruction of a kind particularly suitable for boys who wish to enter industry as apprentices. It may be added that the undoubted success of

these schools is due in large measure to the fact that many of the teachers have had practical experience of industrial work and through their evening classes maintain a direct contact with young people engaged in industry. It is therefore proposed that while the junior commercial and junior domestic economy schools will gradually become absorbed as separate and distinct entities, they will recruit their pupils at the age of 13+ mainly from the junior secondary schools on completion of the general two-year course in these schools and they will also admit pupils from the senior secondary school who at the age of 13 decide that they would prefer the more practical approach of the junior technical schools. Hitherto, small fees have been charged in these schools but the provision of scholarships by the education authorities has been liberal; it is now proposed that fees should be abolished. It is also proposed that the junior technical schools should provide a three-year course and boys who wish to attend will be expected to remain beyond the new leaving age of 15.

FURTHER EDUCATION

PART-TIME CONTINUED EDUCATION

66.   The new English Act makes part-time continued education compulsory for all between the ages of 15 and 18 who are not in full-time attendance at school.

67.   No one could doubt the benefits of such a scheme for Northern Ireland; as in Great Britain prosperity in the future will depend more on the health and skill of its workers than on any other single factor. But it will be obvious ... that there is a great deal of leeway to make up in the provision of full-time schooling, and, however desirable the introduction of a scheme of compulsory part-time education may be, the

reform of the full-time educational system must come first. Moreover, it is much more difficult to organise a scheme of compulsory part-time continued education in country districts than in large centres of population, and Northern Ireland is still predominantly rural. To reorganise the existing educational system and at the same time attempt to provide part-time continued education for some 60,000 young people would place too great a strain on the local administrative machine. For these reasons the Government have reluctantly formed the opinion that it would not be advisable to introduce a comprehensive compulsory scheme in the immediate future, although it is proposed to take the necessary powers in the new Bill for the introduction of such a scheme as soon as circumstances permit.

68.   There is no reason, however, why nothing should be done before a comprehensive compulsory scheme is introduced. Many enlightened employers already realise the advantages to be derived from facilitating the continued education of their young workers and the conviction is growing that encouragement to attend evening classes is not enough. After a full day's work the young worker is often too tired to apply himself to study in the evenings; only the most determined persist in their studies and for them the strain is frequently too heavy. The only solution lies in arrangements for day-time release. With these considerations in mind the Minister of Education has recently set up a joint committee of employers and trade union officials to advise him on the whole question of the training and education of young workers (and particularly of apprentices), and it is hoped to develop part-time continued education classes for those young workers for whom the provision of semi-vocational courses is feasible ...

TECHNICAL EDUCATION

69.   ... In the future technical education will, together with part-time continued education and adult education, be regarded as a form of Further Education, and it will not be necessary to draw a clear line of demarcation between technical education designed to meet the requirements of particular occupations and further general education not directly related to the students' means of livelihood.

71.   The technical schools vary greatly according to local conditions and this elasticity must be preserved.   The new Bill will require education committees to submit schemes for the development of further education, including technical education, each of which will be related to the needs of the area it is designed to serve. As part of these schemes the committees will be urged to consider the introduction of full-time day technical, commercial and domestic economy courses for young people of the ages of 15 or 16 to 18. The technical course should be specially planned for boys who have successfully completed the junior technical school course (or a similar course in a junior secondary school) and who wish to continue their full-time studies; similarly, the commercial and domestic economy courses should be primarily designed for boys and girls who have left the junior secondary schools and who wish to follow specialised full-time courses in these subjects. It may also be found that the technical schools can play a considerable part in organising semi-vocational courses for voluntary schemes of part-time continued education ... and also make a contribution to the provision of agricultural and adult education. But nothing must be allowed to obscure the primary function of the technical colleges and schools in the larger centres of population to assist, both by day and evening classes, in the training and education of the skilled workers, technicians and

higher executives so essential to the industrial prosperity of Northern Ireland. To this aspect of their work the Government attach the highest importance.

IV.7   Education Act (Northern Ireland) 1947, C.3.

The 1947 Act had little to say about the detailed provision of technical education, except for the phasing out of the junior commercial and junior domestic science schools. Planning was to replace the *ad hoc* approach and the LEAs were required to draw up plans for further education and submit the details for the Ministry's sanction. The Junior Technical schools were renamed Technical Intermediate schools.

17. — (2) The local education authority shall make provision for the management of each technical intermediate school within their education area by means of a school management committee to be appointed by the authority and approved by the Ministry, but so that several such schools may be grouped under one school management committee if the authority so desire and the Ministry approve.

39.   Subject as hereinafter provided, it shall be the duty of every local education authority to secure the provision for their area of adequate facilities for further education, that is to say:-

(a)   full-time and part-time education for persons over compulsory school age; and

(b)   leisure-time occupation, in such organised cultural training and recreative activities as are suited to their requirements, for any persons over compulsory school age who are able and willing to profit by the facilities provided for that purpose:

Provided that the provisions of this section shall not empower or require local education authorities to secure the provision of facilities for further education otherwise than in accordance with schemes of further education.

40. — (1)   Every local education authority shall, at such times and in such form as the Ministry may direct, prepare and submit to the Ministry schemes of further education for their area, giving particulars of the provisions which the authority propose to make for fulfilling such of their duties with respect to further education as may be specified in the direction.

(2)   Where a scheme of further education has been submitted to the Ministry by a local education authority, the Ministry may, after making in the scheme such modifications or alterations, if any, as after consultation with the authority it thinks expedient, approve the scheme, and thereupon it shall be the duty of the local education authority to take such measures as the Ministry may from time to time, after consultation with the authority, direct for the purpose of giving effect to the scheme.

(3)   A scheme of further education approved by the Ministry in accordance with the provisions of this section may be modified, supplemented or replaced by a further scheme prepared, submitted and approved in accordance with those provisions, and the Ministry may give directions revoking any scheme of further education, or any provision contained in such a scheme, as from such dates as may be specified in the directions, but without prejudice to the preparation, submission and approval of further schemes.

(4)   A local education authority shall, when preparing any scheme of further education, have regard to any facilities for further education provided for their area by other bodies, and shall consult any such bodies and the local education authorities for adjacent areas; and the scheme, as approved by the Ministry may include such provisions as to the co-operation of any such bodies or authorities as may have been agreed between them and the authority by whom the scheme was submitted.

41. — (1)   A local education authority may, with the approval of the Ministry, make contributions to any body providing facilities for further education in the area of the authority.

(2)   Until the date upon which a scheme of further education is first approved by the Ministry under the foregoing provisions of this Part of this Act a local education authority may make to any such body as aforesaid such contributions as the Ministry may approve, and may, in accordance with arrangements approved by the Ministry, provide such additional facilities for further education as appear to the authority to be expedient for meeting the needs of this area.

IV.8   Educational Development in Northern Ireland, 1964, Cmd.470.

Further Education expanded quietly and unhindered during the 1950s as the Ministry of Education devoted its energies to the establishment of a country-wide network of intermediate schools. In the mid-sixties the Ministry began to examine the overlapping provision for students under the school leaving age. Support for a trilateral system waned as that for a comprehensive system grew.

The refusal of the Belfast Education Authority to establish Technical Intermediate Schools weakened the argument for the retention of the 11+ stream, which had been introduced in 1956, in the other colleges throughout the province and so the White Paper suggested the phasing out of these classes.

The provision that young people in the Intermediate Schools could transfer to the Technical School at 13+ diminished any chance of students in the former schools sitting external examination. With the introduction of the Certificate of Secondary Education and the need to ensure the viability of the Intermediate Schools this option was withdrawn.

Faced with these moves, which drastically reduced their intake, the technical schools looked to other areas for expansion. The provision in the 1968 Education Act which allowed a student to transfer to a technical college at 15+ preserved their GCE "O" level classes and also led to a great expansion of pre-nursing, pre-catering and pre-apprentice type courses.

Difficulties with those students who were not sitting for external examinations in the Intermediate Schools led to the establishment of link classes with local Technical Colleges. Here the students were offered practical activities making use of the more advanced industrial and commercial equipment available in the colleges.

14.   ... In Belfast there are no technical intermediate (junior technical) schools, the division at 11+ being simply between grammar and intermediate schools.

28.   The distinction between secondary education and vocational instruction cannot be precisely drawn ... In the secondary schools biased courses have been encouraged after the first two years, but only in commercial courses has it been the practice to include instruction which could be regarded as predominantly vocational — in Shorthand and Typewriting — and then only to a strictly limited extent.

29.   It is not the intention to advocate the indiscriminate introduction of vocational instruction into the curriculum of the secondary schools, but experiments will be encouraged in the leavening of the curriculum, particularly for the less able pupils along the lines suggested in the Newsom Report ...

30.   The (proposed) working party will, in particular, be asked to consider the extent to which there could be active co-operation between secondary schools and the technical institutions in suitable subjects. An arrangement of this kind would not only help to give a vocational bias to the last year of compulsory schooling but would also serve as an introduction to further education. It is of the first importance that the last two years of secondary schooling for those whose full-time education is not likely to extend beyond the school leaving age should afford a suitable basis for subsequent part-time further education and vocational training. Indeed, the Ministry would like to see an overlap between secondary and further education for the 15/16 age group so that, where accommodation and staff are available, it would be possible for full-time attendance at a further education course (e.g. a pre-apprenticeship course) to take the place of attendance at a fifth year secondary course. This may require a change in legislation.

FURTHER EDUCATION

34.   In recent years a remarkable expansion (of technical education) has taken place. National Certificate courses have been greatly developed, together with City and Guilds of London Institute courses in a wide range of subjects. Full-time further education courses have multiplied and day release classes are playing an ever more important role.

35. Given the extremely high cost of providing well-equipped laboratories and workshops and the need to make the maximum use of this provision, given too the small numbers of students for many courses outside Belfast and the need to use limited teacher resources to the best advantage, greater concentration of facilities is now called for than was formerly necessary. The need is for a limited number of really worthwhile technical institutions selected as growing points for expansion in the future and in such a way as to fit in with the Government's economic plans. It should be recognised that to provide a separate technical college in every town is out of keeping with the needs of the times; what is required is a smaller number of larger institutions to serve wider areas. The creation of a new city in the Lurgan/Portadown area in implementation of the Matthew Report affords a welcome opportunity, which is being grasped by the County Armagh Education Committee, to re-plan technical education in the area along these lines. Where no such opportunity is afforded other means of achieving the same ends should be adopted when the opportunity arises, as for instance the amalgamation of two separate colleges into a combined institution under one principal and one governing body.

36. The Ministry has in mind therefore the selection of a small number of institutions outside Belfast for development under distinctive titles. These colleges alone would provide the more advanced courses such as those leading to National Certificates; the other colleges would, under such an arrangement be asked to concentrate on other courses of a more general nature ...

37. Hitherto it has been the Ministry's policy to uphold the existence of separate secondary technical schools — junior technical schools - associated with institutions of further education. It has done so partly on the ground that they offer a distinctive form of secondary education particularly suited to boys intending to enter industry as apprentices, and partly on the ground that in most technical institutions outside Belfast the continued existence of a junior technical school was necessary to enable the institutions to maintain an adequate full-time staff to cope with part-time classes. But times are changing and policies should change to meet new circumstances.

38. Within the past five years secondary schools in Belfast (where there are no separate junior technical schools) have shown that they can prepare classes of boys successfully for the Junior Technical Certificate examination; there is no reason to believe that what has been done in Belfast could not, in comparable circumstances, be achieved in secondary schools in other areas where numbers are sufficient for the provision of technical courses. On the other hand, the past five years have seen a remarkable growth in the number of students taking full-time further education classes in technical institutions outside Belfast: it has increased from just under 2,000 students in 1957/58 to almost 5,000 in 1962/63. With the further growth of full-time further education courses, the development of day release classes and the demands likely to be made on the technical institutions when the new arrangements for the training of apprentices take shape, there will not be the same need in the future as there was in the past — at least in the major centres — to maintain junior technical schools as a means of sustaining full-time staffs.

39.   Apart from these considerations there is much to be said for the view that the presence of children of eleven and twelve years of age in an institution whose prime purpose is to provide for students above compulsory school age is undesirable. Their presence is incompatible with the more adult atmosphere appropriate to such an institution and it can tend to divert attention from the further education work. Finally, it is of importance to build up for the future the best possible relations between the secondary schools and the institutions of further education. Such relations are more likely to be established if the institutions do not compete with the secondary schools for pupils within the 11 to 15 range.

40.   The Ministry, therefore, proposes to invite local education authorities to review the need for the continuance of junior technical schools. The timing of the discontinuance of any particular school would have to be determined in the light of all the relevant local factors. It would be essential to ensure not only that the secondary schools in the area were staffed and equipped to provide a similar course but also that the growth of the other day classes in the technical institution itself would be sufficient to sustain a well-balanced staff.

41.   ... In all the larger institutions discontinuance of the junior technical school, if not already effected, should be practicable when its loss can be compensated for by acceptance of responsibility for part of the 15/16 age group. It may be found however, that some of the smaller institutions should be allowed to retain their junior technical schools after 1970 as well as catering for part of the 15/16 age group.

42.   The Ministry will consult the local education authorities individually before final decisions are made. The consultations will take place on the basis of this policy.

(i)   that junior technical schools recruiting pupils at 11+ should be discontinued as soon as possible wherever this is practicable.

(ii)   that when the school leaving age has been raised to 16 the technical institutions should offer full-time courses for some of the 15/16 age group at least until such time as full-time courses for students beyond the new leaving age have been built up.

44.   The changes suggested imply a deliberate break with the past of a kind which is seldom easy, but which should be made if the technical institutions are to be ready and able to fulfil the role which will properly be theirs in the future. They must be ready to meet a new need in the training of apprentices; they must offer a wide range of full-time vocational courses; they must be able to cope with any foreseeable increase in day or block release; and while the tendency will be towards more and more day work, they must in addition continue to provide even more extensively for vocational and recreational classes in the evening. The period of transition will doubtless present its special difficulties but the future is not in doubt: every worthwhile technical institution which is ready to adapt itself to changing needs will certainly develop and grow when it has emerged as a fully-fledged institution of further education. The strength of the technical institutions in the past has lain in their adaptability. The same must be true in the future if they are to play a full part in the educational system and make their unique contribution to the industrial development of Northern Ireland. To this end the development of technical institutions must harmonise with the Government's economic plans as a whole and there must be close co-operation, not only between the technical institutions and the schools, but also between the technical institutions and the industrial and commercial interests of the areas they serve.

IV.9   Higher Education in Northern Ireland, February 1965, Chairman Sir John Lockwood, Cmd.475.

The Lockwood Report had the most decisive effect on higher education when it recommended the establishment of a second university and the formation of the Ulster College, which in reality became the Ulster Polytechnic. The implications of this latter proposal filtered down through the whole technical system, implying a hierarchy of colleges. Only the larger colleges were to have more advanced courses, the smaller local colleges feeding students into these area colleges. This reflected Ministry of Education thinking and led to disputes over course provision which have continued ever since.

THE FUTURE ORGANISATION OF TECHNICAL EDUCATION

266.   It is of fundamental importance to recognise that technical education must comprise not a number of watertight compartments but a spectrum of interrelated opportunities designed to satisfy the needs of the individual student at any given time and to afford a means of moving to higher levels of study in keeping with his developing abilities and interests. Below university level there must be a well co-ordinated organisation of technical education which, we consider, should comprise:—

(a)   a Regional College of Technology situated in Belfast providing Higher National Diploma and Higher National Certificate courses and the more advanced of the City and Guilds of London Institute technicians' courses relevant to all the branches of applied science and technology for which provision at degree level is made by Queen's University; and

(b)   a group of area colleges in Belfast and at other centres throughout Northern Ireland providing Ordinary National Diploma and Ordinary National Certificate courses, City and Guilds of London Institute technician, craft and operative courses and also, if there is a substantial and justifiable demand and the work of the Regional College of Technology would not in consequence suffer, Higher National Certificate courses in subjects directly relevant to the industry of the particular area.

The regional colleges in England and Wales are institutions of undoubted standing to which the Robbins Committee has paid tribute. We propose Belfast as the location for the Northern Ireland Regional College of Technology for the same reason that led us to conclude in Chapter VI that technological education must be located in Belfast. The area college, or colleges, in Belfast will provide facilities for Belfast students in the lower levels of work not covered in the Regional College.

267.   This concept is fully in accord with the view expressed by the Ministry of Education in its 1964 White Paper, where it was indicated that the Ministry had in mind the selection of a small number of institutions outside Belfast for development under distinctive titles. These colleges alone (which would be area colleges) would provide the more advanced courses such as those leading to National Certificates. The remaining technical colleges throughout Northern Ireland would be asked to concentrate on other courses of a more general nature and, presumably also, on elementary courses.

273. REGIONAL AND AREA COLLEGE RELATIONSHIPS

It will be equally important that students attending the area colleges should be offered every facility for transfer to the Regional College of Technology when their progress has reached a point where the area college can no longer efficiently and economically offer continuing educational facilities. The Ministry of Education White Paper proposes that technical institutions throughout Northern Ireland should send intending (Ordinary) National Certificate students to a selected small number of institutions outside Belfast — the area colleges. We propose that the area colleges should contribute intending Higher National Diploma and Certificate students to the Regional College in a similar way. Without a contributory arrangement of this kind ordinary National Diploma and Certificate students wishing to proceed to HND and HNC would, to a great extent, be denied an opportunity which would be beneficial both to themselves and the community. Such arrangements whereby students transfer from one college to another, in some cases from an environment of home to lodgings, need to be backed by adequate financial support for the individual student.

IV.10 Education (Amendment) Act (Northern Ireland) 1968, C.2.

7. After paragraph (B) of section 39 of the principal Act (which imposes a duty on local education authorities to provide adequate facilities for further education for persons over compulsory school age) there shall be added the words "and, where an Order-in-Council has been made under section 33(2) of this Act raising the upper limit of compulsory school age to sixteen, local education authorities may, without prejudice to the duty imposed on them by the foregoing provisions of this section, provide such facilities for further education for persons over fifteen years of age."

**IV.11 Department of Education and Science Advisory Council
on Education for Industry and Commerce : Report of the
Committee on Technician Courses and Examinations,
HMSO, 1969. Chairman Dr. H. L. Haslegrave.**

With the suspension of the Northern Ireland Parliament and the
substitution of direct rule from Westminster, educational legislation
in the last twenty years has mostly been a mirror-image of that
introduced in Great Britain. The limited opportunity for revision
consequent on legislating by Order in Council has resulted in very
little modification to suit local conditions in Northern Ireland.

During the 1970s changes in the technical system have been mainly
curricular, the most far reaching being those established by the
Technician Education Council and the Business Education Council.

We were appointed by the National Advisory Council in
September 1967 "to review the provision for courses suitable
for technicians at all levels (including corresponding grades
in non-technical occupations) and to consider what changes
are desirable in the present structure of courses and
examinations."

165.   ... we recommend that the Secretary of State for
Education and Science should set up as soon as possible a
Technician Education Council (TEC) and a Business
Education Council (BEC). We see these Councils as
independent executive bodies served by their own staffs ...

TECHNICIAN EDUCATION COUNCIL

166.   The functions we envisage for the TEC are summed
up in the following terms of reference:

"To plan, administer and keep under review the development of a unified national pattern of courses of technical education for technicians in industry; and in pursuance of this to devise or approve suitable courses, establish and assess standards of performance, and award certificates and diplomas as appropriate."

167. We see the TEC as a relatively small policy making and co-ordinating body of not more than 15 to 20 persons drawn from the education service, industry (including the Industrial Training Boards) and the technician and professional bodies ... we think that a TEC comprising some two-thirds "education" members and one-third "other" members would be appropriate.

168. The TEC would, as soon as possible after its appointment, assume policy and planning responsibility for examinations and qualifications in the whole of the technician field at present covered by the joint committees, the City and Guilds of London Institute and the Regional Examining Bodies. In due course, it would become responsible for syllabuses, assessment, and the award of educational qualifications.

BUSINESS EDUCATION COUNCIL

173.   We suggest the following terms of reference for the BEC:

"To plan, administer and keep under review the development of a unified national pattern of courses in the field of business and office studies at levels below that of first degree; and in pursuance of this to devise or approve suitable courses, establish and assess standards of performance, and award certificates and diplomas as appropriate."

175.　... We do not, however, envisage that the BEC's responsibility would extend to "office skills" courses and qualifications.

177.　The task facing the BEC would be markedly different in some respects from that which we foresee for the TEC. Although the BEC's function of administering courses and awarding qualifications would probably be on a much smaller scale, in terms of courses and students, than that of the TEC, its course-promoting and co-ordinating functions would be relatively greater. As we see it the BEC would not be so much preoccupied with introducing a new pattern of courses as encouraging more people to use existing courses, reinforcing these where needed, and introducing a much needed measure of rationalisation into the multiplicity of professional and quasi-professional courses provided in the colleges at present to meet the separate needs of a large number of such bodies active in the business and commercial fields.

181.　... we would expect the two independent Councils to forge strong consultative and operational links with each other.

189.　... we recommend that the City and Guilds of London Institute should be invited to undertake the administrative work of both the TEC and BEC.

191.　... As we envisage it, the two Councils would be independent bodies responsible for the making and directing of policy in their respective fields, with each drawing on the resources of the CGLI for all servicing and other administrative needs ...

FUTURE PATTERN OF COURSES

209. ... Training programmes will look after the needs of today; further education must look after the needs of today and tomorrow. To this end, we foresee that courses must increasingly become vehicles for developing the right attitude on the part of the student and for teaching him how to train and educate himself, and less exercises in imparting a wide range of information.

210. They should devise effective arrangements for keeping the subject matter and structure of courses under review.

211. They should give early attention to reducing the multiplicity of individual subject courses for technician and comparable personnel that exist at present.

255. The overall duration of technician and comparable courses, with what is basically a two-year stage between one level of qualification and another, is about right, and we do not recommend that there be any general change in this.

IV.12 Education Provision for Unemployed Young People. Circular No.1978/10, Department of Education, February 1978.

Many young people, disenchanted by their experience of secondary schooling were reluctant to continue full-time education at technical colleges. At the same time the labour market had little to offer unskilled and unqualified school leavers. The number of unemployed school leavers aged 16-19 rose by 93% between 1978 and 1981.

The Youth Opportunities Programme (YOP), soon renamed the Youth Training Programme (YTP), was the end result of numerous efforts in the previous decade to alleviate this problem of youth unemployment in Northern Ireland. The new programme would offer training and work experience to young people, thus laying the foundation for a skilled flexible workforce capable of adapting to a rapidly changing economy.

INTRODUCTION

A number of initiatives are being taken to help alleviate the problem of unemployment amongst young people. In Great Britain, the Holland Report, issued by the Manpower Services Commission, suggested the establishment of a comprehensive range of training, education and work experience opportunities for unemployed young persons. In parallel with these initiatives, existing and new provision is being developed in Northern Ireland under the Department of Manpower Services' Youth Opportunities Programme.

ROLE OF THE EDUCATION SERVICE

The Department of Education considers that the Education service has an important role to play in helping the unemployed, viz:-

(a)   to initiate full-time education courses which will be an integral part of the Youth Opportunities Programme;

(b)   to provide education support for the various schemes initiated by the Department of Manpower Services under the Youth Opportunities Programme;

(c)   generally to extend provision for unemployed young persons within the Education service in addition to the response initiated within the Youth Opportunities Programme.

The provision of additional education opportunities will be a matter for Education and Library Boards working through their Institutions of Further Education. The purpose of this circular is to give guidance as to how this might be done.

TYPES OF COURSES

Courses should be open to both boys and girls and carefully designed with the needs of the students in mind. Special emphasis should be placed on provision for those 16-19 year olds who appear to have derived least benefit from their years at school and who are, therefore, most in need of further personal and social development. This will involve the adoption of a new and more flexible approach to provision than has been required in the past.

The Department, without in any way setting limits on the types of response which individual Colleges might develop to meet the needs of their areas, suggests the following possibilities for consideration:-

(a)   Youthways Type Courses
These courses, based on the experimental Youthways projects, would cater for those young people in greatest need. They would include elements of basic social requirements, and seek to improve general levels of numeracy and literacy. They could also broaden and improve the young person's qualifications for employment, and increase their capacity for social and recreational participation.

(b)   Work Preparation Courses
These courses would be aimed at improving knowledge of the world of work generally and, in specific areas, developing skills associated with particular sectors of employment. They could also be used to allow young persons, who are anxious

to sample particular jobs to test their aptitude for the skills involved in them and their potential ability to master these skills.

(c)   Work Simulation Units
It is widely recognised that there is a great need for young people to be given experience of the working situation before they enter employment. It is particularly important that the young unemployed be given this experience, so that they will be better prepared for employment when the opportunity arises. Work Simulation Units could also be used to extend the Work Experience Schemes operated by schools, in conjunction with industry and commerce. The aim of the Units would be to give young people undergoing education courses a better understanding of the world of work, and an opportunity to apply practical skills in a purposeful way. The Units could be used to support Work Preparation and Youthways type courses.

(d)   Extension of Existing Provisions
Consideration should be given to extending existing provision within the Further Education sector, either through increasing enrolments in existing courses, through providing additional courses, or both — particularly in areas where demand for places has exceeded supply.

(e)   Three Day Per Week Courses
These allow young people to attend part-time courses while continuing to obtain supplementary benefit. These courses could be designed on the basis of the objectives outlined in the preceding paragraphs, and places could also be provided in some existing day-release courses. When such courses are being planned, the College should contact the local office of the Department of Health and Social Services to discuss supplementary benefit arrangements. Young persons attending

these courses must continue to register for employment, and must demonstrate that they are immediately available to accept suitable work.

(f)   Support for DMS Schemes
In addition to the possible developments outlined above, schemes falling within the Department of Manpower Services' Youth Opportunities Programme will require educational support. This support will vary greatly depending on the actual nature of the scheme and the needs of the individual young people involved. The Department of Manpower Services will arrange contacts between Colleges and scheme organisers and will provide Colleges with details of schemes in each College area. Where Colleges propose to contribute to these schemes they should inform the Department of Education through Education and Library Boards.

IV.13   Working Together — Education and Training, HMSO, 1986, Cmd.9823.

During the 1970s the Business and Technician Education Council (BTEC) joined the Royal Society of Arts (RSA) and the City and Guilds of London Institute (CGLI) as the main providers of vocational qualification. C&G and RSA were highly regarded and their qualifications looked upon as the benchmarks in hundreds of vocational areas. However this system lacked transferability and compatibility. In addition there was no overarching co-ordination.

Conscious of the low skills base of the UK workforce and progress towards the creation of a free internal labour market in the European Community, the government set out to reform this fragmented sector of education. This became apparent with the publication of 'A New Training Initiative — An agenda for Action' in 1981 and the process was accelerated by the establishment of the National Council for Vocational Qualifications (NCVQ) in 1986.

National Vocational Qualifications are based on units of competence derived from standards of performance required by industry and commerce. Assessment is criterion referenced and NVQs are awarded at five levels ranging from competence in the performance of routine and predictable tasks to that which involves the application of a significant range of fundamental principles and complex techniques across a wide and often unpredictable variety of contexts.

INTRODUCTION

1.8 This White Paper shows how education and training policies, especially for young people, are being developed in a complementary and coherent way and announces:

— a national extension of the Technical and Vocational Education Initiative beginning in autumn 1987, which will over time become available for all schools in Great Britain for young people of 14-18 (see Part 3); the White Paper relates it to the continuing development of good quality vocational education and training in schools, non-advanced further education and YTS, for all up to the age of 18 at least (see Parts 2 and 4);

— the creation of a new framework of National Vocational Qualifications in England, Wales and Northern Ireland, to be developed and supervised by a new National Council for Vocational Qualifications (see Part 5). This will allow people to demonstrate clearly what they can do as well as what they know; and to progress with ease to learning and acquiring more skills without going back over ground already covered.

PART 5

REFORMING THE STRUCTURE OF VOCATIONAL QUALIFICATIONS

5.2   A year ago, the Government established a Review of Vocational Qualifications in England and Wales under the chairmanship of Mr H. G. De Ville, CBE. The Group included representatives of employers, employees, examining and validating bodies, other training and education interests and some of the professions. The Group's terms of reference were:

—   to recommend a structure of vocational qualifications in England and Wales which

- is relevant to the needs of people with a wide range of abilities;

- is comprehensible to users;

- is easy to access;

- recognises competence and capability in the application of knowledge and skill;

- provides opportunities for progression, including progression to higher education and professional qualifications;

- allows for the certification of education, training and work experience within an integrated programme.

5.6   In its final report the Group recommended that:

—   vocational qualifications in England and Wales should be brought within a new national framework to be called the National Vocational Qualification (NVQ);

—   a new National Council for Vocational Qualifications (NCVQ) should be set up to secure necessary changes, to develop the NVQ framework and to ensure standards of competence are set.

5.7   The Government accepts these recommendations.

5.8   The Government accepts the recommendation that the new national framework should be called the National Vocational Qualification (NVQ) and that this framework should be designed to incorporate and embrace existing vocational qualifications up to and including higher levels of professional qualifications.

5.14   There are so many interests involved in rationalising the present structure that we need an engine of change independent of existing interests. The Government has therefore accepted the recommendation to establish a new National Council for Vocational Qualifications (NCVQ).

5.15   The Government is setting the National Council nine specific tasks. They are to:

—   identify and bring about the changes necessary to achieve the specification and implementation of standards of occupational competence to meet the needs of the full range of employment, including the needs of the self-employed;

— design, monitor and adapt as necessary the new NVQ framework;

— secure the implementation of that framework by accrediting the provision of approved certifying bodies;

— secure comprehensive provision of vocational qualifications by the certifying bodies;

— secure arrangements for quality assurance;

— maintain effective liaison with those bodies having responsibilities for qualifications which give entry to, and progression within and from, the system of vocational qualifications into higher education and the higher levels of professional qualifications;

— collect, analyse and make available information on vocational qualifications and secure the operation of an effective, comprehensive and dependable data base;

— undertake or arrange to be undertaken research and development where necessary to discharge these functions;

— promote the interests of vocational qualifications and to disseminate good practice.

PART 6

DEVELOPMENTS IN NORTHERN IRELAND

6.1   The aims and objectives stated in this White Paper apply in principle in Northern Ireland as they do to the rest of the United Kingdom. The new structure of vocational qualifications will apply directly to Northern Ireland, and account will be taken in the administration of the new structure of any adjustments which may be necessary to cater for the particular institutional and aorta arrangements which exist there. The Secretary of State for Northern Ireland will be a sponsor of the National Council for Vocational Qualifications.

6.5   It is the intention to build on this firm foundation of vocational preparation provided under the Youth Training Programme and to concentrate on:

—   the enhancement of quality, including staff development;

—   the promotion of the concept of open routes and clear progression;

—   the delivery of relevant training linked to opportunities to work for nationally recognised qualifications;

—   the expansion of training provision, particularly in the second year of the Programme, to enable the Government's objectives in regard to guarantees (to which reference is made in Part 4 of this White Paper) to be delivered in Northern Ireland.

**IV.14   Education Reform in Northern Ireland : The Way
Forward — DENI, October1988.**

The radical reforms proposed for Further Education in England and
Wales by the 1988 Education Act had their counterparts in
Northern Ireland. The Department of Education issued a
consultation paper and the Department's general reply to the
responses received was made in The Way Forward published in
October 1988. This was soon followed by a draft Order which in
1989 became the Order in Council.

The import of the new legislation was increased devolution to
colleges by entrusting governors with wider powers and one line
budgets which gave greater flexibility in financial management.

FURTHER EDUCATION

7.1   Responses to the consultation paper broadly endorsed
the proposals for the delegation by Education and Library
Boards of financial powers and responsibilities to individual
Further Education colleges. The Government is convinced
that implementation of these proposals will make for more
efficient management of the colleges as well as enabling
colleges to respond more quickly and positively to local
demands.

7.2   Some respondents stressed the need for colleges to
maintain a balanced provision of courses. The Government
agrees. The legislation will therefore require Boards to
prepare and submit to the Department for approval schemes
setting out the principles to be applied by the Boards in
planning the provision to be made by colleges under their
management. In considering such schemes the Department
will wish to ensure that they promote responsiveness by
colleges to the needs of employers, students and the local
community.

7.3   The Government has also taken account of comments made about the composition of college governing bodies, and of amendment to the England and Wales position. Accordingly it is proposed that the legislation should provide that governing bodies should contain a maximum of 25 members, with at least 50% coming from the professions, local business or industry or other fields of employment relevant to the activities of the college, together with co-opted members. A further 20% of members should be Education and Library Board representatives. The Chairman should be elected by the members, but will not have to belong to any particular grouping on the governing body. Provision for other membership groups will be included in each college's scheme of management, which will be subject to the Department's approval.

IV.15   Education Reform (Northern Ireland) Order 1989, No.2406 (NI.20).

DUTY OF BOARDS WITH RESPECT TO FURTHER AND HIGHER EDUCATION

100. — (2) Subject to the following provisions of this Article, in this Order "further education" means —

(a)   full-time and part-time education for persons over compulsory school age (including vocational, social, physical and recreational training); and

(b)   organised leisure-time occupation provided in connection with the provision of such education.

MANAGEMENT OF INSTITUTIONS OF FURTHER EDUCATION

102. — (9) The articles of government of an institution of further education —

(a)   shall provide for the functions of the governing body under the articles in relation to the appointment of teachers and other staff to be carried out on behalf of, and in the name of, the board;

(b)   may provide for the carrying out by the governing body in relation to the institution of other specified functions on behalf of, and in the name of, the board.

PROVISIONS REQUIRED IN INSTRUMENT OF GOVERNMENT

103. — (1) The instrument of government of an institution of further education shall provide for the governing body to consist of not more than twenty-five members, of whom —

(a)   not less than one-half shall be   persons selected from among persons appearing to the person or persons selecting them to be, or to have been, engaged or employed in business industry or any profession;

(b)   not more than one-fifth shall be persons selected and appointed by the board, of whom not more than one-half shall be members of district councils;

(c)   not more than one-tenth shall be elected by teachers at that institution from amongst such teachers;

(d)   at least one shall be co-opted by the other members of the governing body.

****

(8)   In the case of the initial members within the category mentioned in paragraph (1)(a), the board shall appoint persons nominated by bodies determined by the board in accordance with paragraph (9).

(9)   In determining the bodies who are to be entitled to nominate such persons for appointment, the board shall consult —

(a)   the management committee constituted for the institution under Article 28 of the principal Order;

(b)   such bodies representing business or industrial interests, the professions or trade unions as the board considers appropriate.

PROVISIONS REQUIRED IN ARTICLES OF GOVERNMENT

104. — (3) The articles of government of an institution of further education shall provide for it to be the duty of the governing body —

(a)   to determine, and keep under review, its policy in relation to the courses of study to be provided by or on behalf of the institution and, when so doing, to take account of the plan drawn up under Article 105 by the board and of the scheme made under Article 106 by the board;

(b)   to make, and keep up to date, a written statement of that policy.

PLANNING OF, AND PUBLICATION OF INFORMATION WITH RESPECT
TO EDUCATIONAL PROVISION IN INSTITUTIONS OF FURTHER
EDUCATION

105. — (1)   Each board shall draw up and may from time to
time amend a plan for the educational provision to be made
by institutions of further education situated in its area.

****

(6)   The Department may make regulations
requiring every board to publish, in relation to each
institution of further education under its management —

(a)   such information as may be prescribed with respect
to —

(i)   the educational provision made by the institution
for students at the institution; and

(ii)   the educational achievements of students at the
institution (including the results of
examinations, tests and other assessments of
those students); and

(b)   such copies of any written statement made by the
governing body under Article 104(3)(b) as may be
prescribed.

SCHEMES FOR FINANCING BY BOARDS OF FURTHER AND HIGHER
EDUCATION

106. — (1)   It shall be the duty of every board to prepare a
scheme in accordance with this Part and submit it for the
approval of the Department in accordance with Article 107.

(2)   The scheme shall provide for —

(a)   the determination in respect of each financial year of the board, for each institution of further education situated in the area of the board, of the share to be appropriated for that institution in that year of the further and higher education budget of the board for that year (referred to in this Part, in relation to such an institution, as the institution's budget share); and

(b)   the delegation by the board of the management of an institution's budget share for any year to the governing body of the institution.

(3)   The scheme shall also set out the principles and procedures to be applied by the board in planning the educational provision to be made by institutions of further education situated in the area of the board (in this Part referred to as institutions covered by the scheme).

DELEGATION TO GOVERNING BODY OF MANAGEMENT OF
INSTITUTION'S BUDGET SHARE

109. — (2)   Subject to Article 117(6), it shall be the duty of the board in the case of each such institution to put at the disposal of the governing body of the institution in respect of each financial year a sum equal to the institution's budget share for that year to be spent for the purposes of the institution.

FURTHER AND HIGHER EDUCATION FUNDING SCHEMES:
DETERMINATION OF BUDGET SHARES

110.— (1)   The provision to be included in a scheme for determining the budget share for any financial year of each institution of further education covered by the scheme in that year shall require that share to be determined (and from time to time revised) by the application of a formula laid down by the scheme for the purpose of dividing among all such institutions so much of the board's further and higher education budget for that year as is appropriated by the board for allocation in accordance with the scheme among those institutions.

DELEGATION OF CERTAIN POWERS AS TO STAFF

114. — (2)   A scheme may include provision with respect to the complement and the dismissal of staff at any institution to which this Article for the time being applies and (without prejudice to the inclusion of other provisions as to staff and other cost to be met from the budget share of any such institution) with respect to costs incurred by the board in respect of the dismissal or premature retirement, or for the purpose of securing the resignation, of any member of the staff.

(3)   Subject to any provision of the relevant scheme or the articles of government of the institution, in the case of any institution to which this Article for the time being applies it shall be for the governing body of the institution to determine what staff (both full-time and part-time) are for the time being required for the purposes of the institution.

(4)   Subject to any provision of the relevant scheme or the articles of government of the institution, where the governing body of an institution to which this Article for the time being applies notifies the board concerned in writing that it has determined that any person employed to work at the institution under a particular contract of employment should cease to work there under that contract—

(a)   if the person concerned is employed under the contract of employment in question to work solely at the institution, the board shall, before the end of the period of one month beginning with the date on which the notification is given in relation to him, either —

   (i)   give him such notice terminating that contract of employment with the board as is required under that contract; or

   (ii)   terminate that contract without notice if the circumstances are such that the board is entitled to do so by reason of his conduct; and

(b)   in any other case, the board shall require the person concerned to cease to work at the institution.

(5)   The articles of government of an institution to which this Article for the time being applies shall provide for it to be the duty of the governing body to consult the chief education officer of the board concerned before making any determination which would have the effect of removing senior staff from work at the institution.

COSTS OF DISMISSAL, PREMATURE RETIREMENT OR VOLUNTARY
SEVERANCE

115. — (4) Subject to any provision of the relevant scheme
or the articles of government of the institution, costs incurred
by the board concerned in respect of the dismissal or
premature retirement, or for the purpose of securing the
resignation of any member of the staff of any such institution
shall not be met from the institution's budget share for any
financial year except in so far as the board has good reason
for deducting those costs, or any part of those costs, from that
share.

WITHDRAWAL OF DELEGATED POWERS FOR MISMANAGEMENT, ETC.

117. — (1) Where it appears to a board, in the case of any
institution in respect of which financial delegation is required
for the current financial year under a scheme, that the
governing body of the institution —

(a)   has been guilty of a substantial or persistent failure to
        comply with any requirements or conditions applicable
        under the scheme; or

(b)   is not managing the appropriation or expenditure of the
        sum put at its disposal for the purposes of the
        institution in a satisfactory manner, the board may take
        any action permitted by paragraph (2).

        (2) The actions so permitted are —

(a)   complete suspension of the governing body's right to a
        delegated budget;

(b)   the limitation of that right to part only of the budget share of the institution concerned; and

(c)   the restriction, in any manner that appears to the board to be appropriate in the circumstances, of the discretion of the governing body to spend any sum made available to it in respect of the institution's budget share or any part of it as the board thinks fit for the purposes of the institution.

****

(6)   During any period when a governing body's right to a delegated budget is subject to any suspension or limitation imposed under this Article the duty of the board concerned under Article 109(2) shall not apply in relation to that governing body or (as the case may require) shall apply only in relation to such part of the budget share of the institution concerned as is not subject to the limitation.

IV.16   Signposts for the Nineties, DENI, June 1990.

The 1989 Order had made structural rather than curricular changes. Deeply influenced by the introduction of the national curriculum for secondary schools and determined to have an integrated curricular framework from 14-19 the Department of Education mapped its holistic approach in the consultative paper, "Signposts for the Nineties" in June 1990.

THE CURRICULUM

CURRICULAR FRAMEWORK 16-19

4.2   The new curricular framework might have four closely related elements.

Main Studies:
Academic or vocational courses (ideally brought closer together through the provision of common units). Examples would include the A level courses referred to elsewhere in this paper and existing work-related Diplomas and Certificates. These studies should ensure high standards of attainment and reasonable degrees of specialisation.

Complementary Studies:
Areas of study similar to those included in the pre-16 school curriculum but not included within Main Studies or Core Competences. A student on a BTEC National Diploma in Business Studies could, for example, include short units on scientific and technological understanding, and aesthetic and creative studies in his or her curriculum; an engineering student might include units on the environment.

Educational Themes:
These themes would be similar in concept to cross-curricular themes in the pre-16 school curriculum and would permeate the courses in both Main Studies and Complementary Studies. The following themes are suggested:

Enterprise Education
Understanding Society
Education for Mutual Understanding
Health Education
Guidance and Counselling

Core Competences:
These competences are those which all young people require if they are to respond positively to the demands imposed by change. For the most part, these competences would be demonstrated within Main Studies. They would, however, have to be capable of separate assessment and reporting to

enable a profile of achievement to be produced. The following are suggested:

Communication
Analytical Skills/Problem Solving
Personal Skills
Mathematical Understanding
Information Technology
Modern Languages

The first three are to some extent present in all programmes; the final three are course-dependent and would require an extension to many syllabuses.

THE ADULT UNEMPLOYED

4.23   Many people in Northern Ireland have no qualifications and, with the establishment of the Training and Employment Agency, the time is right for the further education sector to collaborate fully with the Agency in tackling this problem. Colleges should develop new outreach strategies to help unemployed adults, with particular emphasis on women who wish to re-enter the workforce following absences owing to family and home responsibilities. They will also wish to review their provision for guidance and counselling of the unemployed.

ADULTS WITH LEARNING DIFFICULTIES

4.30   The Education Reform Order now requires Boards, when planning their further education provision, to have regard to the requirements of persons over compulsory school age who have learning difficulties. Existing provision in colleges for such persons is very limited. Boards and colleges will, therefore, have to examine ways in which the special educational needs of these adults can be met.

HIGHER EDUCATION

5.2   At present, most non-degree higher education (i.e. mainly HNDs) takes place in the University of Ulster. However, the high level of demand is putting pressure on provision and many of the HND courses provided by the University are heavily over-subscribed. This has resulted in increased provision being made in the FE colleges, either on a collaborative basis with the University, or by colleges taking on full responsibility for such courses. Another factor which has to be taken into account is the large number of Northern Ireland students who pursue their HND studies in other parts of the United Kingdom. Experience shows that substantial proportions of such young people do not return to the Province. While the opportunities for young people to broaden their horizons by studying outside Northern Ireland must be retained, there is little doubt that many of those who leave would prefer to remain here if appropriate provision were available. As indicated above, it is precisely this type of person, who will develop technical and middle-management skills, which local companies need if they are to become more competitive.

5.3   If there is to be more extensive provision for non-degree higher education courses outside the University of Ulster, there is a need to consider the most effective means of organising such provision, both on educational grounds and in terms of the most economic use of resources. For example, the dispersal of higher level students across a relatively large number of colleges is educationally undesirable. In such an arrangement, students have little contact with other higher level students within similar or different disciplines and it is not possible to establish a higher education ethos given the small percentage of each college's work at this level.

5.5   Possible options for future provision of these courses would appear to include the following:

(i)   the identification and development of a small number of existing colleges in appropriate locations which would contain all the non-degree higher education other than that provided in the University of Ulster; these colleges would also retain their lower level provision and might be called Colleges of Further and Higher Education; or

(ii)   the establishment of a single Regional College of Further and Higher Education which would provide all the full-time non-degree higher education other than that provided in the University of Ulster.

Such rationalisation of provision, which might be accompanied by increased capacity at this level, would have significant advantages in both educational and economic terms. In particular, it would be more likely to counter the flow of able young people to HND courses in Great Britain, thereby increasing the numbers of highly trained technicians and middle-management personnel available to meet the needs of local companies.

IV.17   The Road Ahead, DENI, June 1991.

Further education has always been highly vocational. The DENI has been striving for a broader based curriculum particularly for full-time students. This conflicted with the competency based National Vocational Qualifications (NVQs).

The dangers of this dichotomy have been recognised and the recent introduction of General National Vocational Qualifications (GNVQs) in broad vocational areas is an attempt to provide a core curriculum with vocational relevance.

The Signposts document provoked a wide response from further education college staffs, governing bodies, education and library boards and other providers. The government's vision of the future of further education and how this vision should be realised was encapsulated in *The Road Ahead*.

THE GOVERNMENT'S AIMS

1.1   This chapter sets out the Government's general aims for further education in Northern Ireland. These are:

- To increase participation in vocational education particularly by adults;

- To improve the quality of such provision;

- To enhance standards of attainment of those in further education;

- To develop the outreach of the sector to the business community and to schools;

- To ensure that the provision made is cost effective; and

- To ensure that further education programmes impact equitably on the different parts of the community.

OBJECTIVES

2.5   It is important that we achieve the objective of increasing the proportion of young people undertaking education and/or training, whether school-leavers at 16 or beyond. Not only does this benefit the individual, it can strengthen the ability of firms to become more efficient, more competitive and to respond more effectively to challenges.

Further education has an important role to play in encouraging young people to participate by providing programmes of study designed to meet their needs.

2.6   ... a basic objective must be to increase the proportion of adults undertaking professional updating or refresher courses. Colleges and employers must work together to create the necessary circumstances to achieve this.

2.8   Equally important are the needs of those without employment. It may not be fully recognised that unemployment, whether temporary or longer-term, offers an opportunity for adults to follow more continuous programmes of education or training. Colleges must take steps to provide access to appropriate programmes which will attract the unemployed and, in due course, provide them with skills and qualifications which will help to make them more employable.

2.11   The NCVQ framework will provide an increasingly wide range of National Vocational Qualifications (NVQ's) which have recognition throughout the United Kingdom and Europe. It is essential that young people and adults alike should have the opportunity of choosing the education or training options and routes to qualifications which suit them best. In particular, they should be encouraged to aim for higher levels of achievement. To make the right choices, both young people and adults need to have access to an effective careers guidance and counselling service.

2.16   It is unlikely that the improvements in cost-effectiveness which are necessary can be achieved without some rationalisation of the existing college structure and the present spread of course provision. This argues for a more co-ordinated approach to the planning, which must take account of both social and economic factors.

QUALIFICATIONS AND THE CURRICULUM

4.2   NCVQ is engaged in creating a clear framework for vocational qualifications and in establishing their relevance to employment. NVQ's are based on up-to-date standards, set by employers, which define the knowledge and skills that people need in the workplace. They are a guarantee of competence to do a job, not just in theory but in practice. NVQ's are set in a framework of 5 levels which allows people to plan their career paths on a clear and nationally recognised route to higher qualifications. They are free of artificial requirements about the pace, place or method of learning and are accessible to all ages from school right through to the end of a career.

4.6   The Government has asked NCVQ to develop criteria for accrediting more general vocational qualifications. General NVQ's will cover broad occupational qualifications and offer a general preparation for employment as well as being an accepted route to higher education. It will be important that as these new NVQ's come on stream they should be as freely available in Northern Ireland as elsewhere in the United Kingdom.

PLANNING AND COST-EFFECTIVENESS

5.8   Within the overall planning context, there is a need for a more rational and co-ordinated pattern of higher level provision and its development. It is important that the colleges which provide these courses should be able to marshal the resources, material, physical and teaching, to provide learning experiences of high quality, to allow high standards to be achieved, and also to ensure that learning takes place within an appropriate environment. An important ingredient in this provision is the opportunity for students following any particular higher level course in a college to have contact with as wide a range as possible of students in similar and different disciplines within the same establishment. The Government is convinced that these requirements cannot be met where the courses amount to a small percentage of a college's work. It will be necessary, therefore, to select a small number of colleges in which higher level work will take place. All of this emphasises the need for strategic planning on a Province-wide basis.

5.10   The Government has decided, therefore, to set up a review group whose remit will be to advise it about the planning and funding of further education. The terms of reference of the group will be:

• To examine the present pattern of further education provision on a whole-Northern Ireland basis, with the objective of achieving provision which maximises efficiency, effectiveness and access;

• To devise a funding methodology designed to provide incentives to colleges to increase participation and make more cost-effective provision; and

• To make recommendations on the range of higher education courses which should be provided in the further education sector and their geographical distribution.

IV.18   Review Group on Further Education, DENI, June 1992.

Following the receipt of responses to the Signposts document, Lord Belstead, the minister responsible for education, set up a Review group to advise on the planning and funding of the further education sector in Northern Ireland under the chairmanship of Mr. Noel Stewart of Coopers and Lybrand in September 1991. The Review Group's report presented the most fundamental realignment of further education since the 1964 White Paper.

PLANNING PROVISION

1.1   ... Recognising, however, the contribution that all colleges are making to the social and economic development of local communities through the provision of courses for, in particular, young trainees, the unemployed, adults lacking basic skills and those with learning difficulties, it was considered that any programme of rationalisation should not include closure of existing college sites at this time. In any case, the Review Group was of the opinion that to close sites would be counter-productive to the Government's aim of increasing participation until such time as adequate facilities were available elsewhere.

1.13   The Review Group has concluded that there should be fewer management units and that the necessary restructuring should be achieved by grouping together some of the colleges. This should provide more educationally viable institutions while at the same time retaining access for local communities to programmes at NVQ levels 1 and 2, or equivalent, and to adult and community education. It will also mean that some existing colleges will no longer operate as free-standing institutions with their own governing bodies.

RECOMMENDATION 5

The Review Group recommends that the number of free-standing further education colleges should be reduced to 13.

RECOMMENDATION 6

The Review Group recommends that 9 of the 13 colleges should be formed by grouping some existing colleges together.

1.20   The Review Group is of the opinion that full-time higher education should be provided by only a few colleges to enable the development of a higher education ethos which would be acknowledged by all interests. This is not to say that part-time higher education should be similarly restricted. In the Review Group's view, any limitations on the development of part-time higher education in non-designated colleges should only be those which apply to all colleges for the purpose of co-ordinating higher education overall.

1.21   In light of the above, the Review Group considers that only 5 of the 13 colleges should be designated for the development of full-time higher education courses, and that these should be:

Belfast, North-East, North-West,
Southern and Upper Bann.

The Review Group considered that full-time higher education should not be provided in colleges within easy commuting distance of the Belfast Institute i.e. at Newtownabbey, Lisburn and North Down and Ards and that, because of its monotechnic nature and specialist resources, the Catering College at Portrush needs the academic strength of a college providing full-time higher education to support its work.

RECOMMENDATION 10

The Review Group recommends that there should be a centrally determined strategic plan for the further education sector in Northern Ireland and for the co-ordination of higher education provision within this sector.

RECOMMENDATION 11

The Review Group recommends that the strategic plan for the further education sector should be drawn up by a new central independent planning body.

FUNDING

RECOMMENDATION 13

The Review Group recommends that there should be a new independent body with responsibility for both planning and funding for the further education sector by 1995.

RECOMMENDATION 23

The Review Group recommends that there should be a major and immediate increase in the level of recurrent and capital funding in the further education sector and that, in particular, capital programmes should be given a much higher priority to reflect the sector's own needs.

HIGHER EDUCATION

3.10   The Review Group considers that the ability of designated institutions to attract students (and their capacity to retain them) who might otherwise travel outside Northern Ireland for their full-time higher level courses, will remain dependent not only on an extended range of provision but also on the standard and perceived status of both the courses and the institution themselves. For this reason the Review Group is of the opinion that it is imperative that future planning of full-time higher education should be based, not just within the designated institutions alone, but on the lead campus only of these institutions so as to develop an appropriate atmosphere and image and to optimise the use of resources. The Review Group also considers that the only exception to this rule should be the Portrush campus for catering-type courses and that any full-time higher education courses at institutions which have not been so designated should be phased out and, if necessary, relocated elsewhere.

RECOMMENDATION 24

The Review Group recommends that full-time higher education provision within the further education sector should be located only on the lead campus of the 5 designated institutions, with the one exception of the Portrush campus.

V

TEACHER EDUCATION 1922-1992

V.1   Final Report of the Departmental Committee on the Educational Services in Northern Ireland, Cmd.15.

Apart from St Mary's College in Belfast, a Roman Catholic college catering only for female students, no other teacher education facilities for those wishing to pursue a career in primary education existed in the region. Catholic male students and all Protestant student-teachers usually trained in colleges in the southern provinces. For various reasons, attempts to maintain permanent links with training colleges in the South did not meet with success and alternative provisions had to be made. A Ministry of Education committee was established in May 1922 to consider new arrangements. The following extract, published in the Lynn Committee's Report on the Educational Services in Northern Ireland (par.28), contains the Committee's review of the existing situation and details the principal recommendations made for future structures and courses to be provided in the region:

"Owing to the non-existence of any training colleges in Northern Ireland in connection with the Ministry of Education it became necessary for the Ministry to take steps to provide training facilities for candidates for the position of primary school teacher in this area not later than the beginning of the present month. This course was all the more necessary seeing that it would soon be discontinued in the Dublin colleges — a state of things which has in great measure now come to pass, the Marlborough Street undenominational college, under a provisional arrangement with the Ministry, continues to train students from Northern Ireland on a programme of studies officially approved.

"In order to make arrangements for the new training institution the Minister of Education appointed a Committee, of which the Right Honourable H.M. Pollock, Minister of Finance, is Chairman, and this Committee, after careful consultation with representatives of the Queen's University, the Municipal College of Technology and other parties, has drawn up a tentative scheme of training, which is to be put into operation for a period of two years. At the end of that time the scheme may be continued, modified or extended as seems most desirable.

"The chief features of this scheme are the following:— The period of training will be two years except for students who have already had a year's training in colleges hitherto recognised. The question whether in certain cases a third or fourth year of training should be provided is left open for consideration.

"The students now entering on training are divided into two Classes, A and B. Class A are those accepted by the University as eligible for courses in the Faculty of Arts, and the remainder of the students make up Class B.

"The University is willing to accept as eligible for degree work all students who passed the King's Scholarship examination in the First Division and such students of the Second Division as are adjudged by the Training Committee to be fit to enter on such a course of study. The Committee decided that students who passed at the Scholarship examination in the Second Division with 65 per cent in the University subjects may be included in Class A. Of 136 First Year students admitted to training 53 are in Class A, and 83 in Class B.

"The University Class, or Class A, consists therefore, of 76 students for the session now beginning. The remainder of the 202 students, 126 in number, are in Class B. There are 49 men students and 153 women students.

"The course of students for the B.A. pass degree at the Queen's University comprises eight courses spread over a minimum period of three academic years, not more than four courses being taken in any single year. The eight courses must comprise study in five separate subjects of which English Literature and an ancient or a modern language are compulsory subjects. There are second and third year courses in certain subjects.

"The University training students (Class A) will be allowed to take two courses in their first year of training, and a further two in their second year. At the end of the two years' training course they will have completed four courses out of the eight required for the B.A. pass degree. In the session now commencing the students will take English Literature and Mathematics, but women will be permitted to take History instead of Mathematics as their second subject.

"No definite regulations have been laid down for the completion of the degree course in the case of these students, but it is contemplated that after leaving the training college, University students will be allowed to absent themselves from their schools on providing a substitute in order to attend at the University in two subsequent years. Whether any further pecuniary assistance should be given to the more brilliant students to enable them to attain their degree is a matter for consideration.

"As many of the students of Class A may not be up to matriculation standard in the ancient or modern language required for the B.A. degree, it is proposed to provide preliminary classes in French or Latin for these students so as to enable them to take the degree course in one or other of these subjects at a later stage.

"The subjects of training college study not included in the B.A. course will be taught partly by University professors and teachers, partly by teachers in the Technical College and partly by teachers appointed by the Training Committee. Owing to the kind co-operation of the Senate, students of both Classes (A and B) will receive some of their instruction from teachers of University standing, and a great deal of the teaching will for the present be conducted in the University Lecture-rooms lent for the purpose. The Belfast Technical Instruction Committee has also given the use of rooms at the Technical College and in addition Drawing and other practical subjects will be taught there to all the students.

"The professional training of all students will be carried on in the Education Department of the University, the teaching staff of which will be strengthened for the purpose by the appointment of a Master of Method and at least two training assistants.

A well conducted National school in the vicinity of the University will be used as a demonstration school, and some ten or twelve of the best schools of the City will be utilised for practising purposes by the students.

"The residence and grounds of Stranmillis House have been obtained by the Ministry for the purpose of the erection of hostels and other accommodation for the students. A large house in Lisburn Road has been rented for the men students, and it is proposed to provide temporary buildings as hostels for the women students at Stranmillis. Pending the erection of these hostels, which will not be ready before January, women students whose parents are not resident in Belfast or the neighbourhood are living in lodgings, for which a money allowance is made by the Training Committee. An experienced lady warden has been appointed to look after the women students, and to give them advice and assistance in the prosecution of their studies.

"All students pay an annual fee of £22.10s — the University fees, salaries of professors and teachers, and cost of board and lodging being defrayed by the Training Committee. The average cost of each student's training is estimated to be from £90 to £100 per annum including all overhead charges."

V.2   Statement by the Northern Bishops of the Catholic Church, 12 October, 1923.

Stranmillis College did not prove acceptable to the Catholic bishops in Northern Ireland as an institution in which Catholic male student-teachers could be trained. The Ministry of Education refused to sanction the courses in southern colleges because of their new emphasis on Irish and none of the Catholic colleges were prepared to offer alternative courses which might have been sanctioned. The Catholic bishops denounced the Ministry's proposals for a non-denominational college and their refusal to recognise qualifications obtained in the Catholic colleges in the South. They pressed for teacher training arrangements which would be directly under Church control. Eventually an agreement was reached whereby places were made available for Catholic male students in St Mary's College, Strawberry Hill, London. The following extract is taken from the bishops' statement in 1923 in which the new arrangements for teacher education were attacked as one part of what was alleged to be an aggressive campaign against the Catholic minority in Northern Ireland:

"As if to trample upon the feelings of those who have been opposed to the Partition of Ireland, an Oath of Allegiance not only to the King but to the Northern Government has been prescribed for all who hold offices of emolument under the Government or local bodies, and for other besides.

Teachers in the North of Ireland are under the galling necessity of taking that Oath to retain their salaries whilst nothing of the sort is demanded in any other part of the British Empire ... An education measure has been passed under which Catholic schools are starved unless they go under a control that is animated by the dominant spirit towards Catholics; and whereas Protestant young men from the North are freely allowed to go to train as teachers in Kildare Street, Dublin, Catholic candidates, if they intend to become teachers in Northern Ireland are not permitted to go to the college in Drumcondra, for which the Catholics of the North in common with their co-religionists throughout Ireland made such heavy sacrifice to provide the proper training for their young teachers. Instead of that Catholic young men are being inveigled into courses of training in Belfast which ... we cannot consider a tolerable preparation for the high office of a teacher in a Catholic school ... It is doubtful whether in modern times any parallel can be found for the way in which the Catholic minority in the North of Ireland is being systematically wronged under the laws of the Northern Parliament ..."

V.3 The Recruitment and Training of Teachers, 1947, Cmd.254.

This report constituted an important milestone in the development and provision of teacher education courses in Northern Ireland, not least for the fact that it recommended that the existing two-year period of training for primary and secondary teachers should be increased to three, and subsequently four years of study. By this time, 1947, it was a widely held view that the two year period of training then in vogue was inadequate, and that an extra year would produce more able and better trained teachers. This perception had already received attention in the 1944 White Paper on *Educational Reconstruction in Northern Ireland.*

Referred to as the 1947 Gibbon Report, because its chairman was Colonel W.D. Gibbon, the report's recommendations also covered the areas of course content, as well as training in the specialist areas of religious and physical education. The importance of practical subjects in the primary school was emphasised, as were the historical study of pioneers in education, the study of health education and school hygiene, and that of what was referred to as "practical sociological work," though the latter only in the final year of the course. The study of English should remain a central feature of the course programme.

Among other recommendations were: (i) the provision of a concurrent training college and university course for intending secondary school teachers; (ii) relaxation of the existing ruling that student teachers should undertake their training only in Northern Ireland — by allowing them to undertake training in recognised schools in Northern Ireland or Great Britain; (iii) extension of the period of teaching practice; the provision of a one-year course in professional training for graduates, though honours graduates were to be exempted from attending an institutional course; and (iv) opportunities for students in training to specialise in the study of a subject of their own choice, throughout their period of study.

CHAPTER XVI

SUMMARY OF RECOMMENDATIONS

****

GENERAL POLICY (CHAPTER V)

****

4.   All teachers in primary and secondary schools should receive professional training, but honours graduates should not necessarily be required to attend an institutional course.

5.   The course of preparation for teachers in primary and secondary schools should in no case occupy less than three years of post-school study and as soon as conditions permit this minimum should be extended to four years.

****

7.   Students in training colleges should be given the opportunity of studying intensively a subject of their own choice throughout their course.

****

PRIMARY SCHOOL TEACHERS (CHAPTER VI)

Length and content of course
11.   The present two-year training college course should immediately be extended to three years.

****

15. Suitable provision should be made throughout the course for Religious Education and Physical Education.

16. The study of English should occupy the foremost place in the curriculum throughout the primary training course.

Teaching practice
17. There should be a growing emphasis on teaching practice throughout the course leading up to a continuous period of full-time teaching practice of at least two months in the final year.

18. As many students as possible should have opportunities for teaching practice in country schools and those who intend to seek their first posts in country schools should spend their continuous period of teaching practice in such a school.

Principles of Education

****

21. The course in Principles of Education should also include instruction in the use of objective intelligence and other tests of ability and aptitude, together with some account of the growth of the educational system and of the work of prominent educational pioneers.

Selection of subjects, etc.
22. The importance of practical subjects for primary school teachers should be fully recognised and the study of at least one practical subject should be maintained throughout the course.

****

24.   The choice of the special subject for advanced personal study should be left as wide as possible.

****

26.   More attention should be paid to the study of Health Education and School Hygiene.

27.   There should be opportunities for practical sociological work in the final year of the course.

Training Graduates
28.   The professional training of graduates who wish to be qualified to teach in primary schools should be undertaken by the training colleges.

29.   A one-year course of professional training for graduates should be provided.

30.   There should also be a concurrent four-year training college and university course for intending primary school teachers.

SECONDARY SCHOOL TEACHERS (CHAPTER VII)

Non-Graduate Teachers
31.   A three-year course for non-graduate teachers of general subjects in secondary schools should be introduced immediately in the training colleges.

32.   This three-year course should be extended as soon as possible to one of four years' duration and, from the outset, a fourth year of training should be insisted on for the "general subjects" non-graduate teacher who wishes to become a semi-specialist in a practical subject.

33.   English should be a basic subject throughout the three-year course and adequate provision should be made for Religious and Physical Education.

****

Concurrent Course
41.   There should be a concurrent training college and university course for intending secondary school teachers.

****

43.   Throughout the concurrent course adequate provision should be made at the training college for both Religious and Physical Education.

44.   There should be a growing emphasis on professional training throughout this course and in the final year provision should be made for a continuous term of teaching practice.

****

TECHNICAL SCHOOL TEACHERS (CHAPTER IX)

Part-time Teachers
69.   The Ministry should organise short courses of professional training for the benefit of part-time teachers of evening classes in technical schools.

****

Persons entering the teaching profession from
Commerce or Industry
71.   The recognition as full-time teachers in technical schools of persons with adequate experience in commerce or industry, but with no part-time teaching experience, should be provisional until they have passed a teaching test.

RECRUITMENT AND SUPPLY (CHAPTER XII)

Conditions

****

87.   The present training agreement binding students to serve in recognised schools in Northern Ireland for two years should be abandoned and should be replaced by a statement of intention to teach in a grant-aided school or educational institution in Northern Ireland or Great Britain.

****

ADVANTAGES AND DISADVANTAGES OF RESIDENTIAL COLLEGES (CHAPTER XIV)

93.   All students should have the advantage of a residential training college life.

94.   The maximum freedom consonant with essential discipline should be allowed to students.

95.   Hostels should be so constructed as to ensure privacy and quiet for students and staff.

****

V.4 Higher Education in Northern Ireland — Report of the Committee appointed by the Minister of Finance, 1965. Cmd.475.

Not until the nineteen-sixties did significant developments again affect teacher education. The Lockwood Committee which was appointed to review higher education stressed the need to integrate teacher education into the university system. The Committee's most significant recommendation in this respect was that the New University of Ulster to be established at Coleraine should develop teacher education courses for both the primary and the secondary sectors. The result was the inclusion of an Education Centre at the New University which, in addition to catering for both these sectors, also provided the first denominationally integrated courses for students intent on primary training.

234. The existence of training colleges is an accident of history. The work done in them should have been undertaken by the universities in the first place; but for a variety of reasons, mainly social and financial, they grew and developed as they did. Their association with the universities became more difficult as public interest in schooling increased and as universities became more self-conscious and concerned for standards in disciplines which they regarded as truly academic. But what logical reason is there for differentiating in principle between the methods of educating a student teacher and a student doctor or a student engineer? "One thing that may be said with certainty is that, if the country had to plan a system of higher education from the outset, the pattern of training colleges would be very different from the one that we have." The situation in Northern Ireland, where there is only a handful of training colleges, will, we hope, be more amenable to change than the complex situation in Great Britain.

235. Teachers must have a good and imaginative education: professional training is now also accepted as highly desirable. But there is no unanimity about the balance between personal education and professional training for any particular kind of teacher. Obviously the sixth form grammar school teacher must have a competent knowledge of his particular subject and the primary school teacher must know how to handle young children. But it does not follow that the sixth form teacher requires no tutoring in the transmission of knowledge and in the understanding of

adolescents, or that a child in a primary school cannot discriminate between an inspiring teacher who has the gift of invention and a mechanical but professionally qualified dullard. One of the problems confronting us in our attempt to confer an appropriate status on all preparation for teaching is that professional training has too often become an object of interest in itself instead of being a designedly practical exercise directed towards actual classroom work.

236.   Many graduates become teachers by accident or by default. On the other hand, students who go to the training colleges are typed as teachers from the moment they leave school, and those who later find teaching unattractive have no real escape since they are not formally qualified for any other employment. There is a strong argument in favour of risking the loss of some who could become a liability in the classroom in the hope of gaining a profession more content in the sense that it knows it is not irrevocably bound to blackboard and chalk. Already the seed of the idea has been sown by the abolition of the student teacher's undertaking to teach for at least two years in a grant-aided school or institution in Northern Ireland upon the successful completion of the training course. Furthermore, a training system designed more as a part of normal higher education should facilitate the attraction to the teaching profession of persons in other employment who later in life feel an urge to teach; and should make it possible for teachers to refresh themselves by periods of experience in business and commerce in the knowledge that the way back to teaching will be open and that opportunities will be available for their re-assimilation on return.

AN EDUCATION CENTRE WITHIN THE NEW UNIVERSITY

237.   We therefore favour the provision of the necessary additional facilities for teacher education within the

framework of the new university.   As an interim expedient, teacher education at the new university should be organised in what we propose should be called an Education Centre, controlled and operated through a body established by the governing body of the new university in association with the Ministry of Education.   This Centre must be built on the main university campus (this is of paramount importance) and it should be responsible for all aspects of the professional pursuit of education. These should range from the provision of broadly based courses for young people who wish to make their careers in primary schools (and whose attainment at entry may be below the standard normally accepted for university matriculation) to courses in education and psychology related to education for those who wish to include these subjects in the compass of an ordinary academic degree, or to take them in supplementation of a degree.   The Education Centre should organise teaching practice in schools as the training colleges do at present, and should be responsible for the pursuit of research in education; and, in particular, of research into the possibility of evolving a course for intending primary school teachers which could lead to a degree, and in consequence to the ultimate absorption of the Centre completely within the university.   It should also provide facilities for improving the quality of university lecturing and for research into methods of educational communication at all levels, whether by improved lecture and classroom techniques or by the better use of educational aids and demonstration material.   It should be ready to experiment with many types of courses.   Examples are courses for graduates, undergraduates and non-graduates, which could be full-time or part-time, initial or refresher courses for older students — adults with a vocation for teaching discovered later in life and married women who wish to return to teaching after bringing up their families; and in-service courses for teachers on a varied pattern and of varied duration during both term and vacation.   The aim in placing the Education Centre on the main university campus is to ensure that practical training for teaching will enjoy the same advantages and status as practical training for other professions which the university provides. The provision of facilities for about 1,000 students in the Education Centre will significantly increase the total number of students on the campus of the new university from the 5,000/6,000 estimated in Paragraph 159.

238. We visualise four main categories of student associated with the proposed Education Centre:—

(a) Those who enrol at the new university with the main purpose of obtaining a degree and who may later decide to teach.

(b) Those who enrol at the new university with the object of entering the teaching profession and who have satisfied the matriculation requirements.

(c) Those who enrol with the object of teaching but who have not satisfied the matriculation requirements.

(d) Those who enrol for part-time professional training or for refresher or re-assimilation or in-service courses.

We shall suggest possible lines for the development of courses for these four categories, but each suggestion will need to be examined in detail by the Academic Planning Board of the new university in consultation with appropriate teacher training interests. These must include the Ministry of Education which has been charged by Parliament with the responsibility of making of teachers whose preparation is adequate to the discharge of the responsibilities which will be laid upon them. The acceptance of a teacher for service in grant-aided schools is a matter for the Ministry of Education, and must remain so.

RELIGIOUS EDUCATION

246.   Before we turn to the situation in Belfast we wish to comment briefly on religious education. There are very few people who would not subscribe to the importance of religious education in the upbringing and education of children. Under the Education Act of 1947 religious education is compulsory in all grant-aided schools, subject to the right of withdrawal of individual pupils. In county schools, subject to the exercise of conscience by teachers and to right of access for denominational instruction, it has to be undenominational. In voluntary schools it is of such kind as the managers of the schools determine. We appreciate that religious education presents complex and difficult problems but we hope that the Education Centre will provide fully satisfactory arrangements for all sections of the community.

QUEEN'S UNIVERSITY AND THE TRAINING COLLEGES

247.   The preceding paragraphs are a sketch-plan; the working drawings have still to be prepared. The period ahead for the preparation of these working drawings is short, and the Academic Planning Board of the new university should consider as soon as possible the implications of these proposals for the development of teacher education and initiate the negotiations which will be necessary if they are to be followed up quickly and effectively. During the next few years, moreover, Queen's University and the training colleges in Belfast must give further study to the parts which they can respectively play in future development. In the long run it would be hard to justify significantly different teacher education systems operating in one small area like Northern

Ireland such as would occur if students attending the Education Centre of the new university were eligible to receive privileges denied to their contemporaries in Belfast. We welcome the willingness of Queen's University to enter into a new relationship with the training colleges and to afford facilities which will enable training college students who have reached the University's matriculation standard to read for University degrees within their colleges. Nevertheless, we think that it would be unwise to separate non-degree students who follow the training college course successfully into those eligible to receive University certificates and those not so eligible by reference only to standard of attainment at the point of admission to the course. We hope that after further examination of the situation the University will see its way to enter into a full partnership with the training colleges and to give university acknowledgement to all who successfully complete training college courses by awarding them the University Diploma in Education. The existing University arrangement for the award of the Diploma in Social Studies to non-matriculated students sets a pattern which should be followed.

GENERAL TRAINING COLLEGE MANAGEMENT

248. To facilitate the introduction of a degree course or degree courses for students attending the general training colleges who have the minimum matriculation requirement, the governing bodies of the colleges will, we hope, be willing to supplement their membership by an appropriate University representation. We make no general recommendation on the extent or nature of the representation and we think that it need not necessarily be the same in each case. We think it also very desirable that the Principal and some members of the staff should be granted full membership of the governing bodies of the colleges.

249.   The management of Stranmillis College presents a problem of its own in view of its position as a Government foundation.   Subject, however, to reservations which we make in Paragraph 251, we think that it would be advantageous for the Ministry of Education to transfer the management of the College completely to a fully responsible governing body containing strong University representation. This would involve the assumption of direct responsibility by the governors for the academic, financial and administrative affairs of the College, subject to the external application of financial control to the degree necessary to safeguard the expenditure of public funds.   The Ministry would also cease to control the admission of individual students.   An interim development along these lines — some steps have very recently been taken — would probably make it easier for Queen's University to move into the position of close association and co-operation which we would welcome.

250.   The Ministry would, we hope, give the same measure of independence to the voluntary colleges as an association between them and Queen's University develops.   The Ministry should in the meantime continue to pay grants direct to the colleges and should encourage them, and Stranmillis College, to plan well ahead by estimating their grant requirements on a triennial basis rather than by annual assessments.

251.   The ultimate objective in Belfast, as within the organisation proposed for the new university, should be the assumption by Queen's University of a responsibility for producing teachers for all kinds of schools.   We have indicated that the new university should arrange for an appropriate association between its Education Centre and the Ministry of Education in view of the responsibility of that Ministry to Parliament to ensure an adequate supply of

teachers for service in grant-aided schools.   A similar
association between Queen's University, the training colleges
and the Ministry is desirable in Belfast.   Meanwhile the
Ministry must retain sufficient control of the situation to
ensure that it can discharge its statutory responsibilities and
must continue to determine the minimum educational
standards for admission to courses in the training colleges,
the number of places to be provided, and the types of school
towards which the provision should be directed.   The
colleges must, moreover, continue to have the co-operation of
the Ministry's Inspectorate in matters affecting curricula and
in determining examination standards.

COURSES AT THE GENERAL TRAINING COLLEGES
AND AT QUEEN'S UNIVERSITY

252.   The courses provided in the general training colleges
should be adjusted to conform with the pattern which we
have indicated for the Education Centre at the new university
and with our recommended pattern of university
undergraduate and postgraduate courses.   The four-year
Course B should, for example, be merged with the three-year
Course A and provision made for post-certificate or post-
diploma courses in specialist or semi-specialist work, to be
taken either immediately upon completion of the three-year
course or after an interval of some years' experience in the
teaching service.   We agree with the Advisory Council for
Education that there is need for a reappraisal of the respective
functions of the Queen's University Department of Education
and the training colleges.   We suggest that postgraduate
students seeking a practical training course should incline
more to the training colleges and that the university
Department of Education should direct its energies
increasingly to research.   We would, however, welcome the
undertaking of research by training college staffs.

THE SPECIALIST TRAINING COLLEGES

253.   In Chapter IX we consider future administrative arrangements for the Belfast College of Domestic Science and the teacher training department of the Belfast College of Art. The position of the Ulster College of Physical Education is different.   We propose no change in its management or organisation for the time being at least but its position should be reconsidered at a later stage when the arrangements which we propose for the general training colleges and the other specialist training colleges have come effectively into operation.   All three specialist institutions wish to retain responsibility for the giving of professional training to their own students and meantime at any rate the present arrangements should be retained.   However, we hope that it will be possible for these institutions also to develop an association with Queen's University which would lead to the award of a University Diploma to their students as well as to students of the general training colleges.

COLLEGES OF EDUCATION

254.   We agree with the Robbins Committee, and the Advisory Council for Education, that the general training colleges should be renamed "Colleges of Education." We wish to see every encouragement offered to their ultimate diversification in order to include preparation for related professions such as the welfare and social services.   But we doubt the practicability of diversification within the next few years in view of the urgency of the demand for teachers.   Our concept of an Education Centre at the new university will introduce non-graduate students to a more liberal atmosphere by involving them closely with undergraduate students in a wide range of academic disciplines.

V.5 The Education, Initial Training and Probation of Teachers in Northern Ireland Schools and Institutions of Further Education, 1973.

In 1971 a Committee chaired by Professor Lelievre of Magee College was appointed to report on the 'education, initial training and probation of teachers in Northern Ireland schools and institutions of further education.' The Committee's appointment was at a time of continuing growth in pupil rolls: the extension of compulsory education to sixteen in 1972 was expected to further increase demand for teachers, while rapid developments in continuing and further education were making new demands for enhanced teaching skills. The brief of the Committee included determining: ' (i) what should be the content and organisation of courses provided; (ii) the role of colleges of education, universities, the Ulster College and institutions of further education in the development of teacher training ...' The Committee's proposals in answer to these questions are outlined in the following extract from its report:

PROPOSALS FOR THE FUTURE

(a)   General considerations
7.14   This outlines the present position.   Turning to the future we note that statistical forecasts of the supply of teachers in Northern Ireland indicated some time ago that we were moving towards a period in which there could be a small surplus of teachers. However those forecasts, although based on all the information available at the time when they were made, have to some extent, been overtaken by events. Some enlargement of provision for nursery education is already in progress and a major expansion may be expected. If our own recommendations concerning the induction year, inservice education and training for service in further education are accepted, in whole or in part, they will add to the demand for teacher education. The attainment of some other educational objectives, not the direct concern of our

committee, such as an improvement of teacher-pupil ratio, would have the same effect.

Mention has already been made of the reorganisation of training institutions in Britain, and it has been recognised that while the effect of this on Northern Ireland cannot yet be foreseen with certainty, the possibility exists that access to colleges in Britain may become more difficult for our students. Indeed we have already had some indication of this. We cannot estimate with precision our future requirement of teachers nor the rate at which the demand will increase, but for a variety of reasons, some of which we have stated above, we are convinced that our provision must be a growing one. It is against that background that we make our proposals for an organisational structure.

7.15 We have made three basic assumptions: first, that Northern Ireland is of a size that can be effectively comprised within one unit, secondly that institutions should continue to enjoy the measure of autonomy and initiative that is traditional in higher education and thirdly that both common sense and the public interest require that there should be machinery for effective discussion, co-operation and rationalisation of effort between the various institutions concerned with the education and training of teachers.

(b)   The Queen's University and colleges of the Institute of Education
7.16 It is clear that the largest source of supply of teachers for the foreseeable future will continue to be the Queen's University and its associated colleges of education, and if overall rationalisation of provision and a measure of flexibility between courses is to be attained, one of the highest priorities is the achievement of such objectives within the Belfast complex. Unless there is a satisfactory structure

here, it will prove very difficult to realise many of the Committee's general recommendations.

7.17   From the evidence we have received there would appear to be a number of weaknesses in the existing structure, leading to unnecessary duplication of activities and confusing disparities in the status of courses.   Thus the one-year full-time course for postgraduate students in the colleges leads to the award of the Graduate Certificate in Education whereas a similar course in the university Department of Education leads to a Diploma in Education.   Other postgraduate courses and research leading to the award of the higher degrees in Education are administered by the Faculty of Arts of the Queen's University, even though there is no provision for the undergraduate study of Education in that faculty, while first degrees (B.Ed.) are administered by the Faculty of Education. There also appears to be considerable overlap between the provision of courses under the auspices of the Institute of Education and the courses leading to the award of the B.Ed. degree arranged by the Faculty of Education.   Indeed under the new regulations for the B.Ed. the Faculty and the Institute are both involved in the first two years of the course, with duplication of boards of study, examination arrangements and general administration.   Satisfactory working of the system depends increasingly on personal co-operation and compromise rather than on the integral nature of the system itself.   Relations between the colleges and university departments present similar difficulties, which arise from the administrative structure and are alleviated by co-operation at the personal level.   The colleges as independent institutions with their own governing bodies work through the Institute, with its Professional Board and Governing Body, for regulations covering some of their courses: for others they work through the Faculty of Education.   The Academic Council of the university, on which the colleges are not directly represented, can make decisions that affect them. There have been problems in regard to the introduction of new courses, and the recognition of college lecturers as university teachers for the purpose of degree courses can involve difficulties. As far as the colleges themselves are concerned, the evident wishes of governing bodies, staffs and students have achieved some rationalisation of course provision and some sharing of certain facilities and of the services of staff. Co-operation is far from complete, however, and links with appropriate subject departments in the university can often be tenuous.

****

7.19 In the White Paper the Secretary of State for Education and Science indicates various possible futures for colleges of education in England and Wales. Some will be encouraged either singly or jointly to develop into "major institutions of higher education concentrating in the arts and human sciences with particular reference to their application in teaching and other professions;" others will be encouraged "to combine forces with neighbouring polytechnic and other colleges of further education to fill a somewhat similar role;" others will seek complete integration with the university sector of higher education, their staff, students and courses being entirely absorbed into the university institution concerned; while others may need to change their functions entirely or close down.

7.20 The situation in Northern Ireland, however, is not the same as that in England and Wales, to which the White Paper's proposals were directed. We have already said that we expect growth, not a situation in which the demand for teachers is outstripped by the supply, with a sudden reduction in the activities of St. Mary's, St. Joseph's and Stranmillis as colleges of education. Whatever other arguments there may be there is no need for the purpose of their survival for the three colleges to develop into major institutions of diversified higher education in a province of a million and half people with two universities and a polytechnic already established. For the foreseeable future the need for the colleges is assured and they may have to be strengthened and expanded over the next decade. In saying this we do not imply that the organisation of the colleges and their relationships with each other and with the Queen's University will necessarily remain unchanged and we now give further consideration to this matter.

7.21   We have envisaged a number of ways in which the colleges might in future operate and we consider that there are three main possibilities. The first is that the three colleges combine into a major integrated institution concerned either partly or wholly with the education of teachers outside the university sector of higher education, being completely responsible for the organisation of their own courses and obtaining validation for such degrees as they offer from C.N.A.A. The second possibility is that the colleges merge either separately or collectively with any of the other institutions of higher education. The third possibility is that the colleges either maintain their separate administrative existence as institutions or from a major integrated institution, diversified or not, but in either case continue to be associated with the Queen's University within a new form of academic structure.

7.22   The most important, though not necessarily overriding, considerations adduced in our discussion of those three possibilities are set out below.

(i)   If the colleges remain physically separated from each other, liaison between them in practical working terms will be limited.

(ii)   Physical separation of the colleges from either the Queen's University or the Ulster College similarly limits liaison between the colleges and the university or polytechnic as the case may be.

(iii)   Any proposal to build a unified college or group of colleges on one site involves considerable expenditure of public funds as well as legal and administrative difficulties for the governing bodies.

(iv)   Absorption of the colleges into either the Queen's University or into both Queen's and the New University creates problems in regard to sites and buildings, finance, university recruitment quotas, faculty balance, admission procedures and staffing.

(v)   Any proposal to build a unified college or group of colleges except on the site of a university or polytechnic encounters the danger that the institution would be set up in physical and professional isolation.

(vi)   It has been indicated to us in evidence that St. Mary's and St. Joseph's Colleges do not wish to lose completely their identities as institutions serving the needs of schools under Roman Catholic management.

7.23   For educational, social and community reasons we wish to encourage the colleges to work as closely together as possible.   We have not found any scheme that meets all the points raised in the preceding section, but in the short term at any rate, from the various discussions we have had, and on the basis of written and oral evidence submitted to us, we have concluded that the needs of the province would be most realistically and efficiently served by a continuation and development of the association between the three colleges of education and the Queen's University. Continued participation in this arrangement should not in our view prevent any of the three colleges considering alternative forms of association. Meanwhile since we have referred earlier to certain weaknesses, as we see them, in the existing arrangements, we wish to offer suggestions for structural improvement. These should be regarded as forming part of the general administrative and consultative framework we are advocating for the province as a whole.

7.24   Within the Queen's University system we suggest that greater co-operation and improved rationalisation of course arrangements could be achieved by establishing a School of Education.   This body would assume all those functions and responsibilities at present discharged separately by the Department of Education, the Institute of Education, the Faculty of Education, the recognised colleges of education and the Department of Extra-Mural Studies. Such a school could operate as a faculty does within the administrative structure of the university, making regular reports to the Academic Council and Senate and seeking approval and validation of various degrees and awards it proposed.   It could operate internally through various constituent divisions as several university based schools of education already do in England — a research and advanced studies division (concerned with research projects, the arrangement of courses leading to higher degrees, the publication of research etc.); a graduate certificate division (concerned with the training of teachers who undertake professional studies for a year following graduation in another field of study); an undergraduate division (concerned with undergraduate degree and certificate courses); a further professional training division (concerned with the provision of inservice professional courses and liaison with teachers' centres); an adult education division (concerned with extra mural courses of a general kind, arrangement of subject conferences, field study courses etc). Each division could be headed by a person of professorial status who might become Director (Dean) of the School of Education by rotation. However the Committee does not wish to advocate detailed arrangements. We commend the proposal of a school of education to the authorities of the Queen's University as a means of improving provision for the education and training of teachers and promotion of research in education.

7.25 Many of us, from considerations arising from section 4.10, would wish to go further than this in seeking for the colleges closer association with or even complete integration within the Queen's University but nearly all of us feel that it would not be proper to come to a firm conclusion when there have not been discussions between the different autonomous bodies concerned about the practical problems and other difficulties involved. Because we regard the matter as highly important, and because it so directly affects the colleges, we do not see it as one that should await the formation of our proposed council (7.31). We therefore recommend that the Ministry should initiate and take part in consultations between the authorities of the university and the colleges about these matters.

(c) *The Ulster College*
7.26 Although geographically the Ulster College could be regarded as part of the Belfast complex, its nature and external affiliations mean that co-ordination of its work in the field of teacher education and training can best be achieved through direct participation in the province-wide structure we

later propose, rather than by joint involvement with the Queen's University in a Belfast area council or committee.

Both in written and in oral evidence the Ulster College saw the work of its Faculty of Education as primarily concerned with certain specialist teachers for secondary and further education and for special care teaching. At theoretical level the training of teachers in specialisms such as art, domestic science or physical education separately from other teachers has been the subject of discussion in our Committee: in practice we are satisfied that since the programme of studies contains elements common to the various specialisms and since there is sharing of some courses or lecturers with non-teacher students, disadvantages that might be inherent in a complete segregation by specialist interest are considerably diminished. The present practice of complementing specialist training by appropriate studies in other subjects of a more general nature contributes to the same end. At a time when more teachers are needed, this provision of specialist teachers does not appear to present problems of rationalisation.

(d)   Londonderry Technical College
7.27   In our visit to the Londonderry Technical College discussions with staff and with students who were following the course for teachers of commercial subjects included three matters, all outside the sole control of the college. The first was the wish, expressed from within the college, to have an external validation for the course; the second was the extent of the difficulty lecturing staff might have in keeping continuous contact with others working in teacher education; the third was a corresponding difficulty at student level. In addition our Committee is bound to keep before it the general principle that teacher education should be clearly seen to be part of higher education, which means that it is carried out by

universities and their recognised or constituent colleges and by polytechnics.

We understand that at the present time the Senate of The New University of Ulster has agreed in principle and subject to certain conditions to enter into an association with the Technical College with a view to validating the award for the commercial subjects teachers course. Now that initial staffing appointments have been made in the education division of the Institute of Continuing Education, which is situated in Magee University College, mutually advantageous contact between education staffs at both Londonderry colleges is possible and the Education Centre at Coleraine will also be involved. Opportunities for students to associate with others in the higher education sector do exist since Education Centre students are supervised in part from the university college while carrying out teaching practice in Londonderry. The teachers' centre in Magee University College provides both staff and students of the technical college with opportunities for further professional contacts. Plans have been made for the future development of the Technical College and it has been envisaged that the College will achieve a status comparable to that of a polytechnic.

If all the projects and possibilities mentioned earlier materialise, the course could contribute to, and benefit from, the general development of the Londonderry Technical College.   If these necessary conditions are not fulfilled, however, we think it right to say that the Ulster College should be asked to absorb the course, with proper safeguards for staff and students.   In saying this we bear in mind that five of the specialist teachers' courses now provided by the Ulster College were formerly situated in five different institutions and if the commercial subjects teachers' course were transferred, the same process of rationalisation would be operating as with the other courses now concentrated in the polytechnic.

(e)   The New University of Ulster
7.28   Within The New University of Ulster the Education Centre acts as a school of education for the university and has essentially the same powers and functions as the other schools, although it is not so designated.   A question of liaison arises in connection with the Education Centre. During the session 1972-1973 The New University of Ulster established in Londonderry, as one of the academic functions of Magee University College, an Institute of Continuing Education.   One of the constituents of the Institute is an education division, which includes, or plans to include, among its activities the inservice education of teachers through courses leading to named awards and through other courses, conferences and seminars.   It will also be concerned with the advancement of educational research.   Some problems of overlap in provision could arise between the Education Centre and the Institute of Continuing Education but we note that there is cross-representation between them and that both work with the university's development committee.   The effectiveness of these arrangements can be judged when they have been longer in operation.

(f)   Postgraduate certificate courses
7.29   It is our expectation that in Northern Ireland the demand for places on postgraduate certificate courses will increase.   Our concern is that there should be discussions between all the institutions which intend to provide postgraduate certificate or diploma courses to establish complementary areas of special interest. In that way it would be possible to achieve a reasonable coverage for the province as a whole and an advantageous concentration of emphasis within each institution.

(g)   The machinery of co-ordination

7.30   So far in this chapter we have concentrated our attention mainly on problems of organisation as they affect particular universities and colleges at the present time. Elsewhere we have referred to the setting up of a permanent body concerned with teacher education and we conclude by outlining the nature and functions of the proposed body and its supporting structure.

We recommend that there should be a Northern Ireland Council for the Education of Teachers, the duties of which would be to hold in constant review provision for the general and professional education of teachers throughout the province and to advise the Ministry on such matters; to act as a forum for discussion of problems, new developments, and long-term needs and objectives of teacher education, and to promote research into such matters; to advise and help on the co-ordination of activities of the providing institutions in this field; to ensure high standards of recruitment to the profession; to advise on the provision of facilities for continuous inservice education of teachers; and to act as a channel of communication on all such matters by publication and by organisation of conferences in this field.

7.31   Since functions of the Council would include helping in co-ordinating the efforts of individual institutions and examining their proposals for development, it seems to us equitable that all providing institutions should be directly represented on it.   It is equally clear that there should be representation adequate to cover teachers in schools and in colleges of further education.   The employing authorities of both voluntary and controlled schools must also share in the Council's work.   We specify these participants, recognising that there are numerous other bodies or organisations that would have various degrees of interest in the functions of the

Council. The most practical way of recruiting from such other sources appears to be direct nomination by the Minister. We have not investigated the question whether, since one of the Council's duties would be to advise the Minister, participation in its work by officers of the Ministry would present difficulties, but as a Committee we have found the presence of an assessor most helpful and the same or a similar arrangement could assist the Council. It seems to us that arrangements for the financing and servicing of this Council could probably best be made in the light of experience gained with the Northern Ireland Examinations Council.

7.32   The Council might find it advantageous to set up an academic committee whose functions could include the following: advising the Council in all matters concerning the provision of courses in initial and inservice education of all categories of teachers; advising on the standards of such courses and assessing their equivalence within Northern Ireland and elsewhere in the United Kingdom; advising on the induction period; recommending fields of research in the education and training of teachers and liaison for this and other purposes with the Northern Ireland Council for Educational Research; and maintaining links between the providing institutions. We envisage that it would also set up working parties as necessary to study particular questions.

7.33   In the introduction to our report we referred to the Ministry's working party on a Teachers' Registration Council. We feel that we have discharged our specific obligations in indicating the body which we believe should be set up to deal with "the education, initial training and probation of teachers'" and with the needs that the concept of career-long education may reveal. The relation of our proposed Council to other bodies clearly remains a matter for discussion.

7.34   Each providing institution would contribute to the work of the Council for the Education of Teachers and its associated committees and each would receive reports on their deliberations. The interchange of ideas and information can be assisted in another way. The Board of the Education Centre of The New University of Ulster includes nominees of other institutions as full members. While we recognise that in some cases the provisions of charter, statutes or other instruments of government may make formal cross-representation of this sort difficult or impossible, we commend for general consideration the principle of inviting nominees of other institutions to join committees or boards at a level at which effective participating is possible. We have been assured that the practice has been found helpful by the Education Centre.

7.35   The organisational structures we have proposed are designed to increase the practical effectiveness of our system of teacher education and training. It is our particular hope that the setting up of a Northern Ireland Council for the Education of Teachers will also create conditions in which insight, enquiry and discussion are facilitated and vitality of thought encouraged. Our system will then be informed by those ideals of continuous renewal and self-fulfilment which are placed before the individual teacher at the outset of his career.

V.6   Interim Report of the Higher Education Review Group, Department of Education, 1980.

Because of rapidly declining school rolls towards the end of the nineteen-seventies, the demand for teachers envisaged by Lelievre Committee was not sustained. To meet the new situation the Department of Education appointed the Higher Education Review Group (The Chilver Committee) to make recommendations as to how course provision might be rationalised. The Review Group's interim report in 1980 caused considerable controversy when it recommended that rationalisation would best be achieved by the amalgamation of the Catholic male college, St Joseph's, with its female counterpart St Mary's following which a Belfast Centre for Teacher Education would be established on the site of Stranmillis College. The Centre would consist of Stranmillis, St. Mary's and the Department of Education at Queen's University. The recommendation was immediately denounced by the Catholic Church authorities as an attempt to remove the Catholic presence in teacher education. So strong was that opposition that the government decided not to proceed with the Review Group's main recommendations. The following extract from the Group's report on teacher education summarises these recommendations:

CHAPTER 1

SUMMARY OF MAIN CONCLUSIONS AND RECOMMENDATIONS

GENERAL

1.1   The reduced level of intakes to teacher education courses that is to be expected in the foreseeable future requires a consolidation of the present arrangements for teacher education. To continue with the present structure, in which there is a number of institutions of teacher education, will make these institutions increasingly non-viable in their academic work and increasingly uneconomic in their use of resources. Consolidation of the present provision would strengthen academic viability, permit better and wider opportunities for students, and enable scarce resources to be used more efficiently.

1.2   Although the future teacher education system will be a smaller one, the requirements imposed on it in terms of numbers of students and styles of teacher education courses must be expected to vary over the years ahead. It is important, therefore, that the teacher education system is a flexible one, capable of responding reasonably quickly to changing demands, without undue expense and upheaval. To this end, a number of teacher education bases and styles should be maintained, compatible with economy in the use of academic and financial resources.

1.3   The future structure of the teacher education system should reflect the status of teacher education as a full partner in higher education generally, and should encourage the academic and social mixing of teacher education students with their fellow-students in other disciplines.

1.4   The nature of the Northern Ireland school system gives rise to distinctive requirements for religious education in controlled and voluntary schools. The teacher education system should meet these distinctive needs and the Churches should continue to have an involvement in teacher education.

PROPOSALS FOR SPECIFIC INSTITUTIONS

1.5   St. Mary's College and St. Joseph's College should amalgamate to form a single voluntary college. The amalgamated college should join with the Queen's University of Belfast (Q.U.B.) and Stranmillis College to form the Belfast Centre for Teacher Education. Each of the three partners in the Belfast Centre for Teacher Education could maintain a separate legal and administrative existence. The Belfast Centre would facilitate co-operation and mutual academic support between each of the three partners which is essential if the colleges of education are to be academically viable and are to make efficient use of resources at the lower enrolment levels now envisaged.

1.6   The three elements in the Belfast Centre for Teacher Education should operate from a common site, close to the main campus of Q.U.B. The most suitable site would be that occupied at present by Stranmillis College. The detailed organisation of the Belfast Centre and the arrangements amongst the three partners can take a number of alternative forms. The detailed administrative structure should be decided by the interests directly involved; the arrangements should encourage academic and practical co-ordination and the academic and social mixing of students, while retaining safeguards for the distinctive educational ethos of each of the colleges of education.

1.7   There should be a teacher education base in the North-West retaining the features of the present teacher education courses at the New University of Ulster (N.U.U.) and operating in close association with a strong institution of higher education.

1.8   Teacher education at the Ulster Polytechnic should be concerned mainly with the specialist areas of physical education, home economics, art, music, craft design and technology, and further education.

1.9   Although "free trade," whereby students can undertake their teacher education outside Northern Ireland, is desirable in principle and should be resumed at the earliest possible time, it should not be re-introduced for the present.

V.7   A Refutation of the Chilver Committee's Recommendations,
***The Irish News*, 25 June, 1980**

Rev. Dr Brian Brady of St Joseph's College, Belfast, published a detailed refutation of the Chilver Committee's recommendations in the course of which he outlined the principles upon which the Church based its opposition to those recommendations. In the course of this refutation Dr Brady linked the Group's recommendations to what he claimed had been a concerted attack on Catholic education in general. In the following extract Dr. Brady argues his defence of the Catholic presence in teacher education in human rights terms:

The effect of the Chilver recommendations, if the Catholic community were to tolerate their implementation, would be an infringement of their rights and a serious lessening of the present partial protection of those rights. The rights at stake in the post-Chilver debate about the future of the Catholic colleges of education are, the right to freedom of opinion and expression, the right to association, the right to education itself and the right to freedom of thought, conscience and religion.

****

Any attempt to close or substantially alter the organisation and/or character of the Catholic colleges would be an infringement of the right of freedom of opinion and expression. In Article 19 of the Universal Declaration on Human Rights of the United Nations the implications of that right are spelled out as :

"Freedom to hold opinions without interference and to seek, receive and impart information and ideas through any media and regardless of frontiers."

It might, at first sight, seem that this right is adequately protected by having a free press and free radio and television services. One may be tempted to think that it is a right which is only violated by oppressive censorship in a totalitarian state — the banning of political tracts and religious books as well as the jamming of broadcasts and telecasts are obvious examples of such violations.

A school or college is also a medium through which information and ideas are imparted. The scholastic community is engaged in the process of seeking and receiving that information and those ideas. The Catholic colleges of education are a medium for imparting and receiving certain ideas and information not available elsewhere.

They are also involved in opinion-making according to the principles of the Catholic faith. In Northern Ireland, students who freely seek such ideas and information at the level of higher education will not find them elsewhere. The proposal to interfere with the present status of the Catholic colleges is an infringement of the right to freedom of thought, opinion and expression.

Another fundamental human right germane to the debate about the future of the Catholic colleges of education is the right to freedom of peaceful assembly and association. The statement of that right by the United Nations is clear and unambiguous. "No one may be compelled to belong to an association" (Art.20).

Schools and colleges are associations engaged in the activities of teaching and learning. The Catholic colleges of education are associations involved in teaching and learning according to the Catholic value-system. Other institutions of teacher education are associations providing teaching and learning with different sorts of values.

To compel students, who freely opt for the Catholic colleges to go elsewhere for their training as teachers is compulsion to join an association. The restriction of intake into the Catholic colleges has already substantially eroded the right of many Catholic students not to be compelled to join an association. There are Catholic students presently in other teacher-education institutions in Northern Ireland who had to be refused admission to the Catholic colleges because of the government imposed ceiling on numbers.

The present Chilver proposals will force Catholic students still further into associations which they do not desire. They amount to a violation of the right not to be compelled to join an association.

The human right which is most obviously ad rem in the debate about the future of the Catholic colleges of education is the right to education itself. It is worthy noting that the relevant Article 26 is the longest and most detailed statement of the entire 29 articles of the Universal Declaration-some indication of the importance of this right.

There are a number of difficulties in analysing our educational situation in Northern Ireland in terms of Article 26. This article is an attempt to ensure basic education for all people in the world even in the most underdeveloped countries. It sets out minimal requirements rather than proposing an optimum ideal. This is evident from its first paragraph:

> "Everyone has the right to education. Education shall be free, at least in the elementary and fundamental stages. Elementary education shall be compulsory. Technical and professional education shall be made available and higher education shall be equally accessible to all on the basis of merit."

In Northern Ireland our education system more than adequately fulfills the requirements of that paragraph. We have free education at all levels. Secondary, as well as elementary education is compulsory. Higher education at the colleges of education, universities and the polytechnic is equally accessible to all on the basis of merit and also free.

The closure of the Catholic colleges of education would not make higher education, as such, inaccessible to Catholic students. Hence one must take the succeeding paragraphs of Article 26 into account when considering the right to have these colleges. In paragraph 2 it is stated:

> "Education shall be directed to the full development of the human personality and to the strengthening of respect for human rights and fundamental freedoms. It shall promote understanding, tolerance and friendships among all nations, racial or religious groups and shall further the activities of the United Nations for the maintenance of peace."

The Catholic community holds that education only fully develops the human personalities of its members when it includes education in the Catholic faith and promotes the values of that faith in all its disciplines.

That is the reason why Catholics support and send their children to Catholic schools; that is the reason why they desire Catholic education for those who teach in those schools; that is the reason why they will fight to maintain the Catholic colleges of education.

It is a fight for the defence of the educational right to have institutions which will develop most fully the personalities of the teachers who teach their children. (Irish News, 25 June 1980)

V.8   Teacher Education in Northern Ireland — The Future Structure, 1992.

Following its decision not to implement the Higher Education Review group's main recommendations the Department of Education proposed that rationalisation focus on the kind of courses provided by the different institutions. For the future, the colleges of education would have as their main emphasis the provision of teachers for primary education, while the two universities would concentrate more on the secondary sector:

STRUCTURE

BACKGROUND

1.   Since the publication of the Interim Report of the Higher Education Review Group in May 1989, and particularly over the past year, there have been extensive discussions with all the major providers of teacher training in Northern Ireland about the restructuring of the teacher training system which is necessary in order to deal with the considerable over-capacity of the present system in relation to the current and prospective levels of intakes into teacher training courses.   There has been a protracted period of uncertainty about the future roles of the various institutions, and this has been detrimental to the academic and the economic viability of these institutions.   The purpose of this statement is to set out the conclusions which government has reached as to future roles, and which will be the basis on which the 1983 intakes to teacher training courses must now be determined.

2.   The re-organisation suggested by the Review Group would have involved the three colleges of education in Belfast coming together on a single site, with the Queen's University of Belfast, so as to be able to pool their academic

and physical resources. This would have allowed these institutions to maintain a wide range of academically strong courses at an economic cost. However, the necessary consensus in favour of physical grouping together of the separate institutions was not forthcoming and it is, therefore, necessary to adopt an alternative approach to rationalisation.

FUTURE TRENDS

3. It has also been necessary to take full account of the factors that were set out in the Working Paper on Future Trends in Teacher Training, which was issued in November by the Department of Education for Northern Ireland. The Working Paper pointed out that although there is likely to be some increase in the overall level of intakes to teacher training there is no prospect in the next decade of a return to the levels of peak demand experienced between 1970 and 1975, when intakes were twice their current level, and to which the existing structure is geared. The need for restructuring in order to remove the excessive over-capacity in the present system therefore remains. The Working Paper also pointed out that the predominant demand for newly-qualified teachers over the next decade will be from the primary schools sector; that there will be a sharp decline in the number of newly-qualified teachers entering secondary schools; and that the relatively low level of demand for secondary school teachers would make it impossible to sustain the present full range of B.Ed. Honours courses in secondary school subjects.

4. The net effect of demographic and other factors on the possible demand for newly-qualified teachers in the primary and secondary school sectors is shown in the following graph:

POSSIBLE DEMAND FOR NEWLY-QUALIFIED TEACHERS, IN THE
PRIMARY AND SECONDARY SECTOR

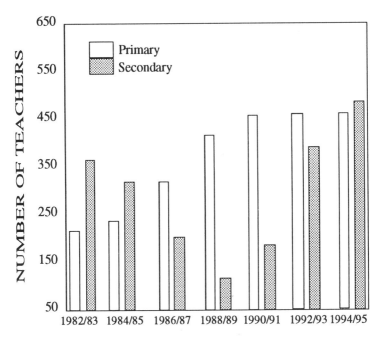

The Working Paper explained that these trends had important implications for the teacher training system, and need to be taken fully into account in any restructuring. In particular, the Working Paper concluded that in future it would be necessary for initial training courses to be more clearly geared to the particular needs of either primary or secondary schools[1]; and that there would be an increasing role for

---

[1] Qualified teacher status carries with it recognition for teaching in any type of school, and nothing in this statement implies any change in the existing teacher recognition arrangements. References such as "training courses for primary schools" as used in this statement are simply a short-hand for "initial teacher training courses geared particularly to the needs of teachers tho expect to teach in primary schools" and should be read accordingly.

PGCE[2] courses especially in relation to secondary schools but also, although to a much lesser degree, in relation to primary schools, so that in future about 70% of newly-qualified teachers entering secondary schools and about 20% of those entering primary schools could be expected to have PGCE qualifications.   The balance of the provision would come from B.Ed.[3] courses which would then be the main entry route for prospective teachers in primary schools and the subsidiary route in relation to secondary schools.

5.   Changes are also taking place in the organisation of the higher education system as a whole.   When the merger of the New University of Ulster and the Ulster Polytechnic is complete, and when — as the Trustees of the two voluntary colleges have proposed — these two colleges have been amalgamated, there will only be four separate major institutions offering teacher training instead of six at present. This also needs to be allowed for in the restructuring of teacher training.

OBJECTIVES

6.   In considering the future structure of the teacher training system in Northern Ireland there are four main objectives to be achieved.:

(a)   To secure a sufficient supply of suitable teachers for schools of all types and of all denominations, and to maintain a reasonable balance between supply of and demand for newly-qualified teachers.

---

[2]
One year Postgraduate Certificate in Education courses, which provide a teaching qualification for graduates, and which in Northern Ireland are at present provided both by the Queen's University of Belfast and by the Colleges of Education.

[3]
Three and four year degree courses which combine academic subject studies with a professional teaching qualification.

(b)   To combine academic strength with cost-effectiveness in the providing institutions.

(c)   To maintain a strong role in teacher training for the universities[4] (which have an important academic contribution to make and which in social terms are the only teacher training institutions which are attended by students of all denominations) as well as for the colleges.

(d)   To promote a flexible system which can respond effectively to changes in the numbers of students and in the demands of schools.

THE FUTURE ROLE OF THE COLLEGES OF EDUCATION

7.   A major issue in the discussions which have taken place has been the suggestion advanced by the Trustees of the voluntary Roman Catholic teacher training colleges that they should properly be allocated at least 40% of the total Northern Ireland teacher training intakes in each year, instead of 25% which has been typical of their share in recent years. A corresponding claim has been advanced by Stranmillis College, which is non-denominational, but which is attended almost exclusively by Protestant students. However, government does not believe that the objectives set out above would be best met by having such a major and permanent concentration of the teacher training provision in the colleges of education. In addition to the general desirability of retaining a major role for the universities in teacher training it is also relevant that the future system will need to be capable

---

[4] References to "universities" cover both the Queen's University of Belfast and the new university institution which will replace both the New University of Ulster and the Ulster Polytechnic.

of a high degree of flexibility, and it is particularly difficult for colleges which are providing only teacher training courses to adjust to the sort of fluctuations in both the level and the nature of demand that is now foreseen. It is, therefore, not possible to accept the suggestion that such a high and permanently fixed proportion of the total provision should be placed in the colleges, at the expense of the universities.

8. Nonetheless there are good reasons to wish to strengthen the colleges and to give them a more stable role. The important contribution which they make is being undermined in their present situation, in which too few students are being spread over too many courses and institutions. It is the view of government that the necessary strengthening can best be achieved by some increase in the size of their intake and by a greater degree of specialisation in the range of courses which they provide. The amalgamation of the two voluntary colleges, which has been proposed by their Trustees, is also a useful step towards a more streamlined system, and as such is welcomed by government.

9. In recent years the teacher training provision in Northern Ireland has been made in roughly equal measure by the colleges of education, which have accounted for about half of the total intakes, and by the universities and the Polytechnic which have also provided about a half of the total places. For the future the detailed allocation of places to each institution will continue to be determined on an annual basis, and will reflect the latest assessment of schools needs and the contribution which each institution can best make towards meeting those needs. However, there is no doubt that for the foreseeable future these factors will point in the direction of giving the colleges a larger proportion of the teacher training intakes than has been the case in recent years. The number of students going to the colleges will therefore

increase, and in some years the colleges' intakes could amount to as much as two-thirds of the total Northern Ireland teacher training provision.

10.   The consideration of the future role of the colleges has been greatly helped by recent discussions with the authorities of both the Roman Catholic colleges and of Stranmillis, in which they have each made clear their genuine desire to work out ways of closer practical co-operation with one another. They have explained that it is their intention to promote greater sharing of resources, and to give greater opportunities for staff and students from the separate colleges to meet and work together.   They hope that these inter-denominational contacts will spill over into the schools sector and will encourage similar contacts and co-operation there. It has also been stressed by the college authorities that they see such co-operation not just as something that is forced on them by practical considerations, but as something which is desirable in itself and indeed a duty in itself.

11.   The attitude which the colleges are taking to these matters is warmly welcomed by government. Closer co-operation between the colleges will help create a more cost-effective system, and it also has the potential to make a very valuable contribution to better mutual understanding between the communities in Northern Ireland. While it remains a pity that it has not been possible to reach agreement on the physical grouping of the colleges which would have made such co-operation both easier and more effective, nonetheless the constructive attitude which is being displayed is greatly appreciated. The practical working out of this co-operation will be watched with great interest, and government will give it every possible help and encouragement. It is one of the principal factors that have led to the conclusion that the roles of the institutions should now be so defined as to increase the

colleges' share of the Northern Ireland teacher training provision.

V.9   Review of Initial Teacher Training in Northern Ireland, Belfast : Department of Education, 1991.

In 1991 following announcements that teacher education in Britain was to undergo significant change, in particular to achieve closer co-operation between the institutions providing teacher education courses and schools, the Department of Education in Northern Ireland published guidelines for a comprehensive review of such courses. The wider context for this review was the Education Reform Order (Northern Ireland) 1989. A particular stress in these guidelines is the need to ensure that new teachers have acquired a basic set of professional competences. Referring to a preliminary consultation process the document setting out the terms for the review of Initial Teacher Training (ITT) stated that:

COMPETENCES

1.2   There was general agreement that the changing requirements of schools, arising in large measure from Education Reform, had significant implications for the competences required by the beginning teacher. A basic requirement was a sound knowledge and understanding of the Northern Ireland Curriculum (NIC) and how it is to be assessed. With this foundation, beginning teachers should be able to :

- plan their own schemes and lessons;
- teach to the level of achievement required by the NIC;
- be aware of the importance of teaching and assessing the six educational themes in a thoroughly integrated manner.

They should be able to:

* manage their pupils individually, in groups and as a whole class;
* differentiate work according to ability;
* plan a sequence of work with discernible progression in the NICs five areas of study;
* use a range of teaching methods, communicate clearly and use an appropriate range of resources.

Finally they should be able to evaluate the effectiveness of their teaching, assess and record pupils' progress as required by the NIC, recognise the special educational needs of individual pupils and know when and how to seek help for those with learning difficulties.

1.3   These and other attributes discussed undoubtedly matched the criteria of the Council for the Accreditation of Teacher Education (CATE). However, it was acknowledged that the challenges now lay in attempting to define these attributes as specific teacher competences, and to match them to credible and realistic attainment targets. A consensus emerged that, despite the difficulties, the time was now right to attempt to define and quantify those competences which might reasonably be expected at the culmination of the major phases of training (initial, induction, early in-service). This could sharpen the focus of training and give it greater overall coherence.

****

1.12   Closely linked to any review, of course, was the question of co-operation between ITT providers and the possible implications of this for ITT structures. It was agreed that changes in courses, especially if they resulted in an increase in the amount of school-based training, would have far-reaching implications for the interaction and relationship between ITT institutions and schools. Respective functions would have to be redefined, with the method of selecting schools, the division of training between schools and institutions, and the function and training of mentors requiring particular attention.

**V.10   Department of Education Northern Ireland (1993)
          Review of Initial Teacher Training (ITT) in Northern
          Ireland — Report of the Development Group
          (Working Group IV).**

In June 1993 the Working Groups established following the publication of the above review document reported. One of these groups, the Development Group, had been charged with reviewing the reports of the other three and with bringing forward an overall set of proposals. These proposals confirm two features of the review document, i.e. that courses in the future should be competency based and that schools should play a key partnership role in the training of teachers alongside the universities and the colleges of education. An important feature of the approach advocated by the Development Group is the stress placed on integrating initial training, induction and the early stages of in-service training. The following extract is taken from the Development Group's report:

A SCHEME FOR THE BASIC EDUCATION OF TEACHERS IN NORTHERN IRELAND

3.1   Key features of the recommended scheme are that the basic education of teachers integrates and co-ordinates ITT, induction and early INSET: by school-based theory and practice involving schools and HEIs in full partnerships developing students' competences at Stage 1 (ITT) and, schools in partnership with HEIs and ELBs as appropriate, further developing these competences at Stage II (induction) and as necessary during early INSET (Stage (III).

STAGE I : INITIAL TRAINING

3.2   It is proposed that initial training should continue to be associated with undergraduate [B.Ed. and B.A.(Ed)] awards and postgraduate (PGCE) awards both associated with the primary and post-primary phases.

3.3   The structure of undergraduate and postgraduate initial training courses should conform to the requirements of national accreditation but in developing school-based ITT courses partnerships of schools and HEIs are recommended to consider:

3.3.1 Developing undergraduate courses of training for intending primary school teachers in which there is a broad range of Subject Studies across the whole Northern Ireland Curriculum while allowing, within these courses, for more specialised programmes of subject study to underpin initial training preparation for curriculum leadership;

3.3.2 ensuring that all undergraduate courses, or postgraduate courses of training for intending primary school teachers include a study of language, literacy and numeracy, together with their professional applications, as a co-ordinating study and that this encompasses a thorough preparation in the teaching of reading by a range of appropriate methods;

3.3.3 ensuring that all undergraduate courses, or postgraduate courses, offering subject specialist teaching in the post-primary school include the use of language in the teaching of the specialism, and, where appropriate, the use of mathematics in the teaching of the specialism.

3.4   The Group endorsed the recommendation of Group III that all undergraduate Primary and Secondary students should complete a free standing modern language component at a level appropriate to their entry qualification.

STAGE II : INDUCTION

3.5   The Group considered that a two year programme of Induction should be developed, accredited and delivered as a coherent whole to complete, as Stage II, the basic education of a teacher begun during Initial Training at Stage I.

3.6   The resources of the newly qualified teacher's school, supported by those of the HEIs and ELBs, would be deployed to enable the teacher to achieve specified competences (Appendix II) including delivery of the Northern Ireland curriculum.   The programmes at Stage II would be accredited by the Northern Ireland Co-ordinating Committee for Teacher Education.

3.7   The Group expected that the development of Stage II would be evolutionary and recommended that the co-ordinating committee keep its proposals for Stage II under review:

3.7.1 with the aim of sustaining their co-ordination and rigour as a key element in professional support for a successful start in working life as a teacher, and, also;

3.7.2 with the aim of developing the possibility of articulating the scheme for professional accreditation at Stage II with the structure of higher education awards available to serving teachers in Northern Ireland thereby providing a link to long-term professional development (Stage III).

3.8 Recognising that evolutionary development of the scheme would apply also to Stage I, the composition and terms of reference for the co-ordinating committee (4.4 and 4.5 below) recommended by Group IV aim to enable the co-ordinating committee to liaise with the school-HEI partnerships in order to maintain the co-ordination and integration of the scheme as a whole and to facilitate discussion of concerns which apply to schools, HEIs, ELBs and other employing authorities across Northern Ireland generally.

FULL-TIME AND PART-TIME TEACHERS

3.9 While the majority of students and teachers may well be those who embark upon initial training full-time and gain a full-time post upon completing training there will always be a proportion of newly qualified teachers who gain part-time posts and/or whose full or part-time employment is interrupted or delayed.

3.10 A scheme of induction based upon the attainment of specified competences and accredited to achieve professional recognition (Stage II) should prove appropriately flexible to meet individual needs. However, the Group is concerned that distinctive support is required by this group of newly qualified teachers and recommends that the co-ordinating committee accredit ELBs to set up a structure of human and multi-media support, including drawing on the strengths of Stage I partnerships of schools and HEIs, for those teachers who register with the ELBs. This support should include a period of work in schools in order to meet the needs of a school-based programme. Where appropriate to individual schools and teachers this period could be up to full-time. The funding of this support is set out in Chapter 6.

SELECTION OF INSTITUTIONS AND SCHOOLS FOR ACCESS TO THE SCHEME

3.11   It is expected that all HEIs currently involved in ITT will wish to seek accreditation as partners in school-based training with schools.

3.12   The involvement of schools who wish to take part in initial training will accord with national criteria and proposals are made in Chapter 6 for resources to assist in the formation of initial training partnerships and in the funding of Stage I partnerships.

3.13   Any school employing a teacher who has successfully completed Stage I will have laid the foundations of Stage II and ultimately all schools are likely to be involved in the development of Stage II as they appoint newly qualified teachers.   Proposals are made in Chapter 6 for resources to assist schools, employing authorities, and HEIs in forming appropriate partnerships to assist schools in framing appropriate staff development plans.

IMPACT OF THE NEW SCHEME ON CURRENT COURSES OF INITIAL TRAINING

3.14   The new Scheme recommended in this report requires HEIs to develop and validate new or revised courses of initial training in partnership with schools; this is essential for accreditation by CATE.

3.15   The resource implications of these developments and the contractual obligations to existing students make it at least difficult, if not impossible, to adapt courses already in progress to meet the new criteria of competences, yet graduates of such courses will, in many cases, be required to enter into Stage II programmes of competence attainment.

3.16   The Group recommends that HEIs be given support and resources (see Chapter 6) during the development period of the new Scheme (see Chapter 5) to undertake a competences audit of existing courses, where necessary, so that appropriate transcripts can be supplied to employers enabling them to offer appropriate professional development during a time of change.

VI

UNIVERSITY EDUCATION

VI.1   Queen's University of Belfast Act (Northern Ireland) 1928, 18 and 19 Geo.5, C.21.

Following the Irish Universities Act of 1908 university education in Northern Ireland entered a period of development quite separate from that in the rest of Ireland.   By this Act the Queen's College in Belfast became The Queen's University of Belfast; its separation from university education in the rest of Ireland making it an educational precursor of the political division between North and South which was to be effected some twelve years later.

For the next sixty years Queen's was to remain the only university in Northern Ireland.   Following the Government of Ireland Act in 1920 the university became the responsibility of the government of Northern Ireland as far as funding was concerned and, therefore, also as far as its general development was to be concerned. However, apart from a number of legislative provisions effecting the university's financial situation and the rather curious arrangement whereby the Faculty of Agriculture was established and separately maintained by the Northern Ireland Department of Agriculture, by the terms of the Queen's University of Belfast Act (Northern Ireland), 1928, no major change affected the structure of university education in Northern Ireland until the Lockwood Committee on Higher Education in Northern Ireland reported in 1965.

[18 & 19 GEO 5.] QUEEN'S UNIVERSITY OF BELFAST ACT
[CH.21.] (NORTHERN IRELAND, 1928)

****

2. — (b)   There shall be paid, in respect of each
financial year, out of moneys provided by Parliament to the
governing body of the University, for defraying the cost for
such year of the subordinate staff and fees of examiners, and
of maintaining the buildings (including the insurance,
lighting, heating and water supply thereof) and equipment in
connection with the Agricultural Faculty of the University,
such sums as are determined by the Ministry of Agriculture,
after consultation with the Ministry of Finance, to be
reasonable and necessary for those purposes and such
accounts shall be kept and estimates and certificates
furnished, in respect of all sums expended or proposed to be
expended under this provision, as the said Ministries may
determine.

****

VI.2   Report of Committee on the Possible Development of Magee University College, 1950, Cmd.275.

Magee College in Derry was founded in 1865 as the Magee
Presbyterian College and in 1879 became a teaching college of the
Royal University of Ireland. Controlled by the General Assembly
of the Presbyterian Church in Ireland Magee was essentially a
theological college for intending ministers of that church.   The
college was a one faculty institution in which theology and related
studies were predominant, although some arts subjects were also
taught.   It was the latter which attracted small numbers of lay
students to the college. Following the Irish Universities Act of 1908
Magee entered into an association with the University of Dublin

(Trinity College) whereby students at Magee would commence degree studies in Derry and complete them in Dublin. This arrangement lasted until 1968. Following the establishment of Northern Ireland an attempt to link Magee with Queen's as a condition for government assistance came to nothing. Much later, in 1951, a link similar to that with Trinity College was established with Queen's. However, it virtually failed in practice since very few students chose to avail themselves of it.

The Acheson Committee was established in 1949 to examine the possibilities for developing the role of Magee as a second centre for university education in Northern Ireland. The committee's recommendations were extremely cautious with respect to any development at Magee. It rejected proposals put forward by the college authorities for departments of science and social studies since, in the committee's opinion, facilities at Queen's were sufficient to cope with any expansion in these areas.

Instead, the committee recommended a limited number of developments conditional, primarily, on the college separating its theological studies from its other academic work. Subsequent legislation, Magee University College, Londonderry (Northern Ireland) Act, 1953, gave effect to this recommendation by dividing the college into two institutions, Mageè Theological College and Magee University College. The academic developments recommended included strengthening the provision for the arts subjects already on offer.

The following were among the main recommendations of the Acheson Committee (pp.32-33):

SUMMARY OF MAIN CONCLUSIONS AND RECOMMENDATIONS

1.　　That the increase of university students within the next decade is not likely to be so great as to make Queen's University unduly large if no other institution of university standing is available in Northern Ireland (Paragraph 90).

2. That there is no justification for the immediate development by means of government grants of a true university college in Londonderry (Paragraph 102).

3. So far as science is concerned the resources of the province should be concentrated on the Science Faculty at Queen's University and that a science department should not be established at the college (Paragraphs 92 and 94).

4. That courses of social studies should not be established in the College (Paragraph 100).

5. That the government should offer further financial assistance for a limited development of the existing Arts Department in the College. The increase in grant to be for an initial period not exceeding seven years and subject to the following conditions (Paragraph 109):

    (a) The transformation of the College into a truly denominational institution (Par.110) by:-

        (i) the closing of the Theological Department (Par.111) and
        (ii) the establishment of a representative denominational Governing Body (Par.112);

    (b) The provision of a full range of courses in both honours and pass subjects up to a degree stage (Par.116);

    (c) The provision of separate classes for the pass and honours students for a full academic year which will necessitate additions to the teaching staff (Par.118);

(d)   The approval of the qualifications of the new members by the University to which the College is associated;

(e)   The institution of a proper contributory superannuation scheme for the staff with a compulsory retirement age of 65 (Par.120);

(f)   As assurance from the local authorities concerned that they are prepared to make suitable annual grants to the College (Par.121);

6.   That the College should be linked to a parent university, that it is not practicable for Magee to be linked to Queen's and Trinity College, Dublin simultaneously, and that there is no reason on academic grounds for breaking the link with Trinity (Par.116).

VI.3   Higher Technological Studies Act, 1954.

This Act influenced significantly the provision for and teaching of engineering-technology based courses at the Queen's University Belfast.

The Act established a Joint Authority for Higher Technological Studies, comprised of an equal number of representatives from the aforementioned university and from the Belfast Corporation.

The Act both recognised the importance of engineering and technology as academic disciplines and of the need to provide facilities appropriate to the future status and development of each in the higher education context.

1954 CHAPTER 29.

An Act to make provision for the furtherance of certain higher technological studies and for related purposes. (21st December, 1954.)

****

3. For the purposes of carrying the principal agreement and any supplemental agreements into effect, the University, the Corporation and the Joint Authority for Higher Technological Studies which is to be established pursuant to paragraph 2 of the principal agreement (in this Act called "the Joint Authority") shall, respectively, have all such powers as may be necessary for or incidental to the due performance and discharge by them or any of their obligations and functions under the principal agreement or under any supplemental agreement.

****

FIRST SCHEDULE

DRAFT AGREEMENT BETWEEN THE UNIVERSITY AND THE CORPORATION WITH RESPECT TO THE JOINT AUTHORITY FOR HIGHER TECHNOLOGICAL STUDIES

ESTABLISHMENT OF JOINT AUTHORITY

For the purpose of co-operating in the furtherance of higher technological studies in Northern Ireland the parties will establish a joint authority to be known as the Joint Authority for Higher Technological studies.

3.   The Joint Authority shall consist of eight members of whom four shall be appointed in writing by each party. The members appointed on the establishment of the Joint Authority shall hold office until the 31st day of December 1955 and, subject to paragraph 5 hereof, members subsequently appointed shall hold office for twelve months beginning on the 1st day of January following their appointment. Any member appointed by either party may be appointed for a second or subsequent term. An appointment made by either party may be revoked by that party at its discretion. In the case of any member appointed to the joint Authority who was at the time of such appointment a member of the Senate of the University or a member of the Corporation or any Committee thereof, such person shall cease to hold office on ceasing to be a member of the Senate, Corporation or Committee as the case may be and shall be replaced by another member appointed by the appropriate party.

****

POWERS AND DUTIES OF JOINT AUTHORITY

9.   It shall be the duty of the Joint Authority, subject to the provisions of this agreement —

(a)   to maintain and repair the fabric of any premises for the time being occupied by it;

(b)   to purchase and maintain equipment for teaching and research in any such premises;

(c)   to facilitate the provision therein of courses in higher technological studies provided by either party;

(d) to permit the use of any premises for the time being occupied by it —

    (i) by University teachers and Corporation teachers for the purposes of higher technological studies; and

    (ii) by students duly enrolled for courses in higher technological studies provided by either party; and

    (iii) for such other purposes as shall conduce to the furtherance of higher technological studies.

(e) to engage and employ in connection with the equipment, maintenance and use of any such premises as aforesaid and the teaching and research carried on therein such technical, clerical, domestic or other staff as appear to it to be necessary;

(f) to do all such other acts or things as appear to it to be necessary or ancillary to the due performance of any of the above-mentioned functions;

(g) to present to each party an annual report upon the performance of its functions during the preceding financial year, including a duly audited account containing particulars of its receipts and expenditure.

****

PROVISION OF ACCOMMODATION FOR MECHANICAL AND ELECTRICAL ENGINEERING STUDIES

11. — (1) The University will as soon as practicable and subject to the necessary funds being available erect a building designed for studies in mechanical and electrical engineering

and will initially equip that building with appropriate furniture and technical equipment.

(2)   When and so soon as the architect employed by the University to supervise such erection certifies that the building has been completed, the University will as from the date so certified be deemed to have leased, and the Joint Authority will as from that date be deemed to have taken on lease, that building, together with all appurtenances thereto belonging and all rights easements and privileges reasonably necessary to enable the same to be used for the purposes of this agreement, upon the terms and subject to the conditions set out in the next succeeding paragraph hereof.

(3)   The University may build or adapt other premises for the purposes of this agreement, and, with the consent of the Corporation, may hand them over to the Authority, upon such terms and subject to such conditions as may be agreed between the parties.

12. — (1) The term of the said lease shall be nine hundred and ninety-nine years from the date certified as aforesaid, determinable —

(a)   at any time by agreement between the parties;

(b)   by the Committee referred to in paragraph 21 of this agreement if satisfied on the application of either party that by reason of a change of circumstances it is reasonable to terminate the lease;

and the rent shall be £600 per year payable half-yearly.

(2)   The Joint Authority shall covenant to maintain and deliver up the premises in repair, to insure and keep insured the premises, to permit representatives of the lessors to inspect the premises, to pay to the University the rent reserved and to pay all taxes and other lawful outgoings in respect of the said premises.

(3)   The Joint Authority shall covenant to observe and perform the conditions specified in the Indenture of Lease made the 10th day of April, 1952, between Robert John Nelson, Frederick Hugh Crawford and the University and registered in the Registry of Deeds, Belfast on the 30th day of April 1902, Book 17, No.60.

TEACHING STAFF

13.   Teaching and research in higher technological studies in the Mechanical and Electrical Engineering Building shall be given and conducted by University teachers and Corporation teachers.

14.   A University teacher shall in respect of his teaching in connection with degrees or other awards of other universities and with Higher National Certificates be regarded for the purposes of paragraph 16 hereof as a part-time Corporation teacher.

15.   University teachers shall be appointed by the University, in accordance with the provisions of the Charter, Statutes and Regulations of the University, on the recommendation of a joint committee consisting of the Curators of the University, as defined in the said Charter and Statutes, together with the four members appointed by the Corporation to the Joint Authority or such other persons not exceeding four in number as the Corporation may appoint for the purpose of this paragraph.

16. — (1) The Corporation shall make payments to the University in respect of the work done by University teachers as part-time Corporation teachers.

(2) The amount of such payments to be made in respect of each University teacher shall be equivalent to such portion of his emoluments as bears to the whole thereof the same proportion as the time spent by him on part-time Corporation teaching bears to the total time spent by him on University teaching and Corporation teaching together.

(3) The sum due to the University under this paragraph shall in respect of each financial year be determined by the Joint Authority whose decision shall be final and binding on the parties.

17.   For the purposes of the last preceding paragraph, the emoluments of a University teacher means the salary paid to him as a University teacher in respect of his teaching duties in the University and National Insurance contributions paid by the University as his employer, together with any superannuation payments and any allowance or bonus paid to him in accordance with the regulations of the University for the time being in force, but does not include any payment made to him in respect of any part-time teaching or administrative duties.

FINANCES OF THE JOINT AUTHORITY

19.   The Joint Authority shall out of the moneys at its disposal defray the following expenses, that is to say —

(a)   the cost of the maintenance and repair of the fabric of the Mechanical and Electrical Engineering Building and any other premises for the time being occupied by it;

(b)   the cost of purchasing and maintaining equipment for teaching and research in any such premises;

(c)   the salaries and wages of such technical, clerical, domestic or other staff as may from time to time be employed in or about any such premises;

(d)   such other expenses as appear to it to be reasonable necessary —

    (i)   in connection with the use of any such premises;

    (ii)   to the due performance of its functions;

under this agreement.

SECOND SCHEDULE

DESCRIPTION OF SITE OF MECHANICAL AND ELECTRICAL ENGINEERING BUILDING

All and singular the premises comprised in and demised by an Indenture of Lease made the 10th day of April, 1952, between Robert John Nelson of 35 Edgecumbe Gardens in the County of the City of Belfast Company Director of the first part (therein called "the Lessor") Frederick Hugh Crawford of "Cloreen" 30 Malone Road Belfast aforesaid Lieutenant Colonel in His Majesty's Army (Retired) of the second part and the Queen's University of Belfast (therein called "the Lessees") of the third part and registered in the Registry of Deeds Belfast on the 30th day of April 1952 Book 17 No.60 which premises are in the said Indenture of lease described as "All That piece or parcel of land situate on the East side of Malone Road and North West side of Chlorine Gardens in the Parish and County of the City or

County Borough of Belfast containing One acre three roods and twelve perches or thereabouts statute measure Bounded on the South West partly by property of the Trustees of Fisherwick Presbyterian Church and partly by property of the Lessor on the West by Cloreen Park on the North West by property of the Lessor's undertenant on the North by property of the said Frederick Hugh Crawford and about to be acquired by the Lessees on the North East by premises situate in the Stranmillis Road on the South East and South by premises in Chlorine Gardens which said piece or parcel of land is more particularly delineated and described and edged red on the Map hereon endorsed."

VI.4   Higher Education in Northern Ireland, Report of the Committee appointed by the Minister of Finance, February 1965, Cmd.475.

The Lockwood Committee's report marked a major watershed in the development of university education in Northern Ireland. The committee was set up in 1963 in the context of considerable debate then taking place in Britain and in Ireland on the need to expand provision for third level education. The Lockwood committee's brief was to "review the facilities for university and higher technical education in Northern Ireland ..."

Central to the committee's approach to its brief was its examination of the need for a second university in Northern Ireland. The need for a second university was accepted by Lockwood and, consequently, attention was to focus on the committee's recommendation with respect to the university's location and its academic responsibilities.

On the latter the committee stressed that the second university should have an academic programme distinct from Queen's. Queen's would, in the committee's opinion, be distinguished in the future by a strong emphasis on technology and engineering, as well as by its work in traditional areas like medicine, law and the arts. As far as the new university would be concerned Lockwood laid particular stress on its recommendations regarding biological and allied sciences (paragraphs 189-192) and on agriculture which is suggested should be transferred from Queen's to the new university. (Pars. 204-210).

As to the location of a second university three towns were in competition, Derry, Armagh and Coleraine. Derry was considered by many to be the obvious choice. It already possessed a small third level institution, Magee University College, and as Northern Ireland's second city seemed to have an almost indisputable claim to the second university. Armagh's claims were based on the city's ecclesiastical traditions and on its close proximity to the new city of Craigavon, whereas Coleraine's claims were essentially of a practical kind. Coleraine had an extensive and readily available site as well as being close to two coastal resorts which provided it with considerable accommodation, especially for students.

On both issues the Lockwood Committee's recommendations were to be met with considerable opposition. On the question of agricultural studies forming part of the curriculum of the new university, opposition from Queen's University and the Department of Agriculture itself quickly rendered that recommendation a deadletter. It was the question of location, however, which caused the greater controversy.

Lockwood recommended Coleraine as the site for Northern Ireland's second university (par.221) and with that recommended that Magee University College lose its university role (par.226-228). Both decisions were regarded as a snub to the city of Derry. In the context of Northern Ireland's community divisions the recommendations were inevitably interpreted as a rejection of the claims of a Roman Catholic and nationalist city for university facilities in favour of the claims of an area predominantly Protestant in religion and unionist in politics.

These recommendations threw the development of Northern Ireland's second university into the maelstrom of local politics and were to cloud the early years of the new institution, eventually designated The New University of Ulster.

The following paragraphs in the Report deal with the academic programme recommended and with the choice of Coleraine and the consequent implications for Magee.

188.   Our proposal is for a second university of between 5,000 and 6,000 full-time undergraduate and postgraduate students by 1980.   About 3,000, however, would afford a minimum base for the interdisciplinary support which is especially necessary for science subjects.   The university organisations should have regard to the general principles bearing on undergraduate and postgraduate study ...   It is not our intention to recommend in detail how the curricula of a second university might develop (for that would be the task of an academic Planning Board) but there are a few general observations which we wish to make.

189.   We have visualised the study of biological sciences as providing the most significant academic foundation for the work of the new university.   Traditional subjects within this field include botany and zoology, physiology, biochemistry, biophysics, genetics and biostatistics.   We believe that these should be regarded less as isolated subjects and more as related parts within a study of biological sciences as a whole.   The application of knowledge deriving from the study of subjects such as these should have a particular relevance in Northern Ireland to agricultural science and technology, to food processing, to soil study, and, to an extent, to forestry.   In human and veterinary medicine also there is an obvious application, the latter having a particular relevance against the Northern Ireland economic background.   We have also been very conscious of the potentialities of marine biology not as an incidental study but as a source of new knowledge and of new economic wealth through a controlled harvesting of the seas.

190.   A breadth of study in the biological sciences would require support from the physical sciences — physics, chemistry, mathematics and statistics.   Environmental sciences such as geology, geography and oceanography would also be relevant.   So too would the social and

behavioural sciences, such as economics and management studies related in particular to agriculture and agricultural commerce; business administration mainly in terms of local conditions and problems; sociology and history; psychology and related subjects; and law and public administration directed particularly to the needs of central and local government in Northern Ireland. We would encourage the maximum possible association and inter-relationship between whatever subjects are finally adopted; "hybrid courses" involving the biological and physical sciences through the study of phenomena at the molecular level or the biological and social sciences, for example, in animal behaviour; and operational research specially directed at the general life and economy of a rural community. The need to develop more concentrated agricultural production in a fuller consciousness of the demands of the balance of nature could make applied economy, which so far has received little attention, one of the most profitable studies of the future. The way in which post-graduate work and research would develop would depend on circumstances, but the opportunities are many in the disciplines which we have listed.

191. The second university should also have a sound foundation for study of the humanities, not necessarily by duplication of the facilities available at Queen's University. We have depicted the scientific development of the new institution as a development with a practical objective. We would encourage a similar approach to arts subjects in so far as this is possible. We would also like to make one small point of detail: in the study of modern languages more emphasis might be placed on languages as a support for other subjects, and language laboratory facilities could be employed to assist with research in linguistics. We have, moreover, distinctive proposals for the education of intending teachers, to which we devote Chapter VIII.

192.   The educational spectrum we propose may therefore
be summarised as comprising in the main:

(a)   the biological and related pure and applied sciences;
(b)   environmental and social sciences;
(c)   the humanities;
(d)   teacher education.

We do not think that any hesitation or anxiety about the
prospects of graduate employment need be felt by intending
students of the biological sciences.   Apart from well-
established fields such as medicine and agriculture, the range
of biological sciences which we have indicated should
provide many opportunities for research and industrial
employment.

208.   Agricultural studies would not relate sufficiently
closely to the direction of development which we
recommended for Queen's University.   They would no longer
be appropriate in an urban university distinctly oriented
toward technology and the applied physical sciences and
hence would lack the necessary emphasis and priority.   On
the other hand they would have a very important and
significant place in a new university of the kind we suggest.
We are satisfied that within the new university organisation
there will be no lack of the supporting facilities in other
disciplines which university work in agriculture requires.
There are also other considerations.   The Faculty of
Agriculture at Queen's University has already outgrown its
accommodation and a new site has been offered to Queen's
University on the outskirts of Belfast.   In the interest of both
the university and the faculty, we cannot commend this
proposed arrangement.

209.   We readily and gladly pay tribute to the work of the past 40 years in agricultural education at undergraduate and postgraduate level, and in particular to the part played by the Ministry of Agriculture in this work.   While we appreciate the reasons which, 40 years ago, led to the unusual arrangement whereby the Faculty of Agriculture is staffed by civil servants and is financed directly by the Ministry of Agriculture, we see no convincing reason to justify its continuance.   We are strongly of the opinion that agricultural education at university level in Northern Ireland should in future be controlled and financed in the same manner as other disciplines, and we are satisfied that a faculty or school of agriculture should be established as an integral part of the organisation of the new university and that the arrangement with Queen's University should then be terminated.   This would not preclude the making of special co-operative arrangements between the new university and the Ministry of Agriculture in a relationship broadly similar to that which obtains between the Northern Ireland Hospitals Authority and Queen's University, or of the kind which we indicate in Chapter VIII should obtain between the new university and the Ministry of Education for the education and professional training of teachers.

210.   We are not, however, suggesting that agriculture should be the foundation element of the new university but rather that, along with fisheries, it should form one of the important fields of application of the biological sciences in which the new university should specialise, in broadly the same way as technology within Queen's University will be seen as the application of the physical sciences.   This would be an innovation wholly germane to the needs of Northern Ireland and would give agriculture the enhanced standing which is its rightful due in a country so dependent on it as is Northern Ireland.   Although the numbers of persons engaged

in agriculture will diminish with improved scientific and technological methods, those remaining in the agricultural industry will require more knowledge and skill if it is to maintain a competitive position in United Kingdom and world markets.   With agriculture so closely associated with the biological orientation which we propose for the new university, it is essential that the new university should not only offer undergraduate teaching but also should provide post-graduate courses and should engage in postgraduate research.   It has been represented to us by the Ministry of Agriculture that, in view of the interlocking of the work of the Faculty and the Ministry, it is not possible to separate the postgraduate work of the Faculty and the Ministry, it is not possible to separate the postgraduate work of the Faculty from that of the Ministry's research divisions.   It has also been represented to us that research work must be concentrated in Belfast mainly for reasons of proximity to the Ministry's administrative divisions and for ease of transport of product samples, infected carcasses and so on from all parts of Northern Ireland.   We have carefully considered these arguments but do not find them convincing.   We suggest that some of the research work at present carried out by the Ministry of Agriculture research divisions might well be carried out at or near the new university.   Such a development would be fully in line with the present trend of policy in Great Britain, which seeks to group research institutes near universities and which has been welcomed by the Bosanquet Committee.   We recognise inherent difficulties in implementing this suggestion but urge that it should be considered in relation to any further capital development in agricultural research.

****

LOCATION

221. The foundation of a new university is a difficult project and factors that are of special assistance in its initial development may reasonably count for more than longer term considerations only would suggest. It is impossible to give precise weighting to each relevant factor but in our concerted view the Coleraine area satisfies better than any of the other areas we have considered and we are of the opinion that the new university will have the opportunity of a good start and of ultimate success in that area. We recommend accordingly. This area alone can provide the residential facilities which must be available in the critical years immediately ahead and it has amenities which can be greatly developed. It has a background distinctively different from the background against which Queen's University is set, and for that reason is eminently suitable for the establishment of the different kind of university which we recommend ...

226. The implications of this recommendation for Magee University College are inescapable. We see no alternative to its discontinuance. This should not be taken to imply that in our opinion the College has failed to fulfil its purpose during the century of its existence. We appreciate fully what has been done by the Trustees and by the Faculty, particularly over the past few years, but in its present buildings and on its present site the College could not be regarded as the nucleus of a new university planned to expand to 5,000/6,000 students ...

In view of developments in university education in the early eighties it is important to note that the Lockwood Committee was also concerned with technical education. The Committee recommended the establishment of a regional college of technology, to be known as Ulster College which would offer courses in a range of disciplines to Higher National Diploma Level (par. 268). Ulster College would embrace a number of existing technical colleges offering advanced courses and was intended to stand at the pinnacle of the network of local and area technical colleges which already existed throughout Northern Ireland (pars. 273-275). Lockwood did not envisage that the Ulster College would provide degree level courses (par.272).

268.   The work of the proposed Regional College of Technology would consist basically of the advanced courses which otherwise would have continued to be provided at the Belfast College of Technology after the transfer of degree work to Queen's University. In addition, the functions of the Regional College should include the non-degree work intended for the School of Applied Science and Technology which was proposed to us in evidence ...

272.   It will be important to ensure that students who demonstrate by their performance in ordinary National Diploma and Ordinary National Certificate examinations that they have the ability to proceed to a university degree, should have an opportunity to embark on a full-time or sandwich degree course at this stage ... In view of the comprehensive role which we envisage for Queen's University in degree work in technology and applied science, we hope that the University will reconsider the conditions under which students with Ordinary or Higher National Diplomas and Certificates may be admitted to degree courses; and that they will be afforded treatment similar to that which is available from the technological universities in Great Britain. We hope that the University will also consider giving credit

within degree courses to able students with Higher National Diplomas and Certificates of high standard ...

274.   In dealing with the consequential effects of our higher educational proposals on further education we have, so far, considered only technical education. One of the most serious defects of further education in the United Kingdom in the past has been the separation of Colleges of Technology from Colleges of Commerce, Colleges of Domestic Science and Colleges of Music and Art. In Belfast the separation is a recent phenomenon brought about partly by the rapidly growing volume of work ... There is urgent need to reverse this process of dispersal and unrelatedness, though we realise that a reversal would not be without practical difficulties arising out of commitments to sites and building programmes.

275.   Ideally these colleges, together with the Regional College of Technology, should be on the same campus, thereby providing opportunities for the association of courses, the intermingling of staff and the sharing by students of common amenities and activities such as characterise a university. Quite apart from the general educational benefit which would flow from a re-amalgamation, a combined institution would be such as would command respect in Belfast and throughout Northern Ireland. But we recognise that complete re-amalgamation on a common site is not likely to be practicable in the immediate future. In any case, each of the spheres of further education into which the original Belfast College of Technology has been separated now requires opportunity for development with sufficient independence to enable it to satisfy the needs of the community within its own particular ambit. Yet a change in attitude and outlook could well be indicated by conferring a title such as "Ulster College" on a combined institution

without the customary suffixes "of Art" "of Domestic Science" or "of Technology." This combined institution would comprise the Regional College of Technology, the College of Domestic Science, the College of Art, and, as developed, Colleges of Commerce, Catering, Music and Drama. This, we think, is most important, both for the positive reason of giving status to the institutions providing these forms of education and also in order to avoid a severe sense of disappointment or of failure in a situation of comparison with the university world. A university is a university because at its level it is a multi-functional institution; it is the interplay of faculties one with another which gives a university its character. In its own way and at its level this should also be true of the Ulster College. It could have an inner corporate life of its own in which, for example, its arts and its technical resources would support each other in social activities. This, we are convinced, will prove to be the accepted pattern of development over the next decade or so for institutions providing high-level non-degree courses. We hope that in its sphere of non-degree work Northern Ireland will lead the way and that Ulster College, as a multi-functional institution, will be enabled to play an effective part in higher education alongside the multi-functional universities.

VI.5   Government Statement on the Report of the Committee under the Chairmanship of Sir John Lockwood, Cmd.480, 10 February, 1965.

The controversy which followed the recommendation of Coleraine as the location for the new university was a major one. Indeed so controversial was this recommendation and that affecting the future of Magee, that the government felt obliged to reject the proposals for the complete withdrawal of university courses from Magee. The government's response to the Lockwood Report was contained in a statement from which the following extracts are taken:

The Report on the facilities for university and other higher education is the most complete survey that has ever been undertaken in this country. Like the Robbins Report in Great Britain, it will enable the government to make far-reaching plans for higher education with a clear sense of purpose and direction.

The basic assumption of the Lockwood Committee is that courses of higher education should be available to all those who are qualified by ability and attainment to pursue them and who wish to do so. The government accepts this assumption and also the estimate made by the committee of the consequent requirement of 8,000/9,000 full-time places by 1973/74. The government agrees also that it appears likely that a further big expansion in university places will be needed by 1980 and is prepared to plan ahead with this in mind ...

The Lockwood Committee considers that immediate steps be taken to establish a new university so that it may be able to admit the first students by October 1968 and to provide for a build-up to 2,000/3,000 students by 1973 and a further large increase by 1980. The committee has recommended the Coleraine area as the most suitable location for the new university and the government accepts this recommendation subject only to the condition that a site approved by the University Grants Committee will be made available without delay ...

The government has considered the conclusion reached by the Lockwood Committee that the implications of the establishment of a second university in Northern Ireland are inescapable for Magee University College, and the view of the committee that there is no alternative to the discontinuance of the College as a university institution.

After much consideration, the government is not prepared, in present circumstances, to accept the committee's view in these respects. Accordingly the government proposes to investigate further whether the College can be incorporated in the new university and, in addition, proposes to promote, in Londonderry, an important centre of non-university education which will have the dual advantages of helping to satisfy the growing demands for such type of education and, with that end in view, of utilising the considerable resources of that part of the province ...

The government accepts the views of the committee on the importance of higher education outside the university sphere, and agrees that a substantial increase in facilities for further education at this level is essential in the long-term interests of Northern Ireland. The government also agrees that higher institutions of further education which provide a Northern Ireland service, such as the Belfast Colleges of Art and Domestic Science, should become central institutions: it accepts in principle the committee's proposal that an "Ulster College" should be established as an integrating body for the purpose, and that this should include a new Regional College of Technology in Belfast ...

VI.6   Debate in the Northern Ireland House of Commons on the Report of the Lockwood Committee, March 1965.

The government's decision to maintain a form of university education at Magee did not defuse controversy over the choice of Coleraine. As the controversy developed the parliament of Northern Ireland experienced one of the longest and most intense debates in its history on the government's motion to note the Lockwood Report and its own consequent statement. The debate was introduced by Prime Minister Terence O'Neill on a motion asking that the House of Commons note both the report and the government's response:

Because the Report is a document of such scope and imagination it is perhaps a pity that public attention has been concentrated almost entirely on a single issue — the location of a second university — there are other matters of great importance involved. Because the issue has been the focus of public debate I should like to make a few points clear. There have been allegations that the Committee's recommendation on this subject was in some way politically inspired. On behalf of all my colleagues as well as myself I must repudiate any such suggestion. Those who have advanced this fantastic theory must know little indeed of academic independence of mind if they are prepared to believe that men like Sir John Lockwood, Sir Peter Venables and Sir Willis Jackson can be used as pawns by this or any other government.

As the House knows, this is a time of considerable university expansion in Great Britain, and it has, therefore, been necessary to determine the location of a number of new universities in England and Scotland. Indeed, over the last five years, eight new universities have been founded in Great Britain. How was this done? The claims of alternative potential locations in particular areas were considered by an expert committee, the University Grants Committee. Having weighed these claims the University Grants Committee reported confidentially to the government. The government then announced their decision. The last word must rest with the government, since considerable expenditure of public money is involved, but in matters of this kind the government would accept the advice of the University Grants Committee. It would, indeed, be difficult to set aside such advice, coming as it does from a body with formidable expertise in this particular field ...

The argument of the Lockwood Report, for those who will study it objectively, is logical. In order, it examined the numbers for whom university places ought to be provided; the possibility of providing for those places by an extension of the existing university; and having decided that this would not be practicable, the sort of further institutions which would be complementary rather than competitive with Queen's. On these successive points the argument of the Report has undeniable authority. But some people have expressed the view that the exercise should have stopped there, that the committee should have left the question of location alone. The government could, it is true, have taken this decision without seeking any expert advice. Nowhere in Britain has the location of a new university been decided in this arbitrary way. The University Grants Committee could have been asked to review the situation, but it made it clear that it was entirely happy that the Lockwood Committee should deal with the location ...

Of course Londonderry had a claim to be the location of our second university. No one in the government has anything other than respect for the qualities of that ancient and historic city. But there were other claims too: those of Armagh, a place of devotion and learning through the ages ... ; of Lurgan-Portadown, the nucleus of a bold experiment in urban development; and of course Coleraine. These claims had to be weighed in an expert and impartial way. The issues were too important to be determined by other factors.

May I say this about the implications of the Lockwood Report for Londonderry? We have made it quite clear in the government statement issued with the Report that we are anxious to take the fullest possible account of the economic and other interests of the city. This does not mean that existing institutions can remain precisely as they are, within the new pattern of higher education. We want in conjunction with the Academic Planning Board of the new university, to see whether Magee University College can be incorporated in that university and that in any changes which will take place we will accept responsibility for assisting the Trustees in protecting the legitimate interests of the staff and students. In any case the Lockwood Report makes it perfectly clear that university education is only one aspect of higher education. It is in the field of non-university higher education that Londonderry may legitimately expect developments which would be of direct benefit to the local economy. Above all, let us not lose sight of one central fact. We are not discussing here a university of Coleraine, or a university of Londonderry, or a university of Armagh or any other area. We are discussing a university for Northern Ireland to serve all its sons and daughters ...

Moving an amendment that, in noting both documents, the House should agree that the second university be located in Derry, Mr. David Bleakley of the Northern Ireland Labour Party stated:

What is the shadow over Lockwood? What is the shadow we are talking about and which the Prime Minister really did not deal with this afternoon? The Prime Minister was a man who did not get going in his speech this afternoon, a man who stuck very carefully by his brief, a brief prepared by someone else and I believe his heart was not in what he was saying. What is the shadow over Lockwood? The shadow is the one of location. It is a shadow that may become permanent unless we face up to the implications in it.

No real discussion of the Lockwood Report is possible until this issue is finally settled and until it is settled correctly. It is far too fundamental a question for Parliament to allow it to be decided by any outside body no matter how eminent. This is a community decision and as Lockwood himself has said it is not all that important to put one university into a place like Britain where there are already thirty-one universities but it becomes a matter of greatest importance when one starts a new university in a community which has only one other university.

This is the importance of location; it is not just one of many institutions. It means that we are doubling the number of university institutions in a very tiny community and a university, as Lockwood has said, has an intimate connection with the community it serves; it has an effect, and a profound effect, and, therefore, the question of location is one of the utmost importance. In any case a small community like this would have been interested about location.

Mr. Austin Currie, a leading Nationalist Party M.P., said in the same debate:

Everyone welcomes this Report except, seemingly, one particular section which deals with the location of the new university in Coleraine. It strikes me that that one section is the poison which might destroy all of this Report, the Coleraine poison. I do not think that this matter should be a political one. I believe the majority of the people in this House, and certainly any thinking person outside of this House, would agree that the location of a new university should not be a political decision or a political matter. This decision is important not only to the people of this House and to the people living in the North of Ireland today; it is important to generations yet unborn. It is a decision which needs the complete support of the community. I would suggest that the future of any society, the future of any area in

Ireland, or indeed of the world, depends more and more on the quality of its education. This is likely to be of increased importance in the future. I would suggest that if we look on this debate properly we shall see it is of fundamental importance to generations which will come after us ... Yet I believe everyone would agree that this is a political debate. Anyone who has been reading the press comments since the Lockwood Report appeared would agree that the Report has been treated as a political document. I am not one of those people who would dare suggest that the newspapers have made it a political document. I would suggest to a certain extent that the Lockwood Committee made it a political document. But I am going to suggest even more strongly that the actions of the government have ensured that this would be nothing but a political debate. Yet it is a debate in which those other qualities which I emphasised earlier are so needed. But it is the type of debate in which those qualities are not likely to be exercised and certainly have not been exercised ...

The siting of the university in Coleraine is bound up with something which is exercising the minds of many people, particularly in counties Tyrone, Fermanagh and Derry — the isolation of the West, that part of the North on the other side of the River Bann. I am convinced that when people in Derry saw the committee's recommendations and the government's acceptance of them in the White Paper they felt the same sort of asphyxia as was felt in Tyrone and Fermanagh. It is an asphyxia one can understand because it follows the cutting of the railways, the decision to site the new city between Portadown and Lurgan, and for quite a few years no, or very few new, industries have been sited on the other side of the Bann. As I have said before, a few years ago the isolation of the west was a party slogan. That is no longer the case because even Unionists, and I would almost

say former Unionists, in Tyrone and Fermanagh are saying to
themselves "This is no longer a party slogan; this is something
which is actually happening; the West is being isolated."
They are also saying that the decision to site the university in
Coleraine is the straw which could break the camel's back. A
new curtain, I would not describe it as an iron curtain ... has
been erected and the people in Fermanagh, Tyrone and Derry
are sure it has been erected on the other side of the Bann.

VI.7   The future of Higher Education in Northern Ireland, Report of the Higher Education Review Group for Northern Ireland, Chairman Sir Henry Chilver, 1982.

The government persisted with its endorsement of Coleraine as the
location of the New University of Ulster and with its decision that
Magee should become part of that university and retain some
university level courses. The new university received its first
students in October 1968, but its development never reached the
levels of enrolment anticipated by Lockwood.   By contrast,
Northern Ireland's second new third-level institution, the Ulster
College, later the Polytechnic of Northern Ireland, did seem to be
meeting its targets and to be enjoying a more favourable reputation.
When the Ulster College became the Polytechnic of Northern
Ireland in 1972, its affiliation to the CNAA (Council for National
Academic Awards) in Britain, enabled it to offer degree bearing
courses and so add considerably to its status and its appeal.

The problems of growth encountered by the New University of
Ulster were among the reasons which led to the establishment, in
1978, of the Higher Education Review Group for Northern Ireland,
commonly known as the Chilver Committee.   The Group's brief
was to review the whole field of higher education, but it was clear
from the outset that the future of the New University would be its
primary focus, as the following paragraphs from its final report
indicate:

1.10   The New University of Ulster (NUU) has not achieved the role which was envisaged when it was set up in 1968.   On its present model of operations it faces such severe and increasing problems of academic and financial viability, that it was necessary for us to question whether or not it could make any long-term contribution to higher education provision in Northern Ireland.   The Review Group found it necessary, therefore, to give very full consideration to the future of NUU.

1.11   In the past, NUU has not in general been successful in attracting young undergraduate students.   Its total enrolments — contrary to the expectations of the Lockwood Committee — have grown little in the past decade, which was a period of considerable expansion of higher education generally; it receives a low proportion of first preference applicants through the Universities Central Council on Admissions (UCCA); and it has recruited only a small proportion of students with good A level qualifications.   It has been more successful in the provision which it has made for mature students.

1.12   We believe that NUU's difficulties stem mainly from the fact that there is no present or prospective need in Northern Ireland for two universities, each catering primarily for the traditional 3-year full-time degree course.   The current enrolments at NUU are already too low relative to the range of activities which NUU is attempting to offer, and we believe that a simple continuation of NUU's present model of operations would lead only to even more acute academic and financial problems.   Nor do we see any scope for helping NUU by transfer of courses to it from the Belfast institutions.

1.13 The arguments for closure or continuance of NUU are finely balanced. After the most careful consideration we believe that — on balance — NUU should be retained but only provided the University implements fundamental changes in its policies and activities in ways which lead to the development of a new style of institution. The new approach which we envisage would include an increasing concern with mature students, a greater emphasis on activities relevant to the needs of the Northern Ireland community, and the development of distance learning. It would also involve making greater use of Magee University College as a means of meeting the immediate needs of the Londonderry area. We envisage that of the existing degree programmes only those, including teacher education, which are well supported and which have particular intrinsic merits should be retained, and that the proportion of non-degree work — such as Dip.H.E. courses — should increase, as should the number of post-experience short courses, especially in vocational and technical subjects.

1.14 The resulting institution might well be somewhat smaller in terms of total enrolments than is the present NUU, but it would have a clear and distinctive role. We believe that it would be academically viable and that it could be funded at a level directly related to its actual enrolments, thus improving its cost-effectiveness.

1.15 Such a new approach would involve major changes of policy and staffing at NUU. We appreciate this will pose a considerable challenge, but we believe it is the only approach which will give a realistic prospect of a worthwhile and successful long-term role for NUU.

1.16   The Queen's University of Belfast (QUB) should develop largely along its present lines, but in some areas changes of policies are needed, while in others present policies should be strengthened. We do not envisage any significant increase in its total enrolments in the short term, and in the longer term they may well be lower. We place emphasis on the need to maintain the highest academic standards, even at the expense of numbers if necessary. It is important that QUB should keep in mind the need for innovation in its approach to its traditional subject areas. We recommend the development of more broadly-based courses and inter-disciplinary studies, and wish to see an increase in part-time courses. We also recommend the replacement of 4-year degree courses by 3-year courses wherever possible.

1.17   The Ulster Polytechnic (the Polytechnic) is a young institution which has displayed commendable energy and initiative in developing a wide range of courses. The Polytechnic should increase its commitment to vocational studies, and should consolidate its activities following the considerable growth which has already taken place.

1.18   We recommend that the Polytechnic should ensure that its contribution to the needs of Northern Ireland at sub-degree level is both comprehensive and excellent. This implies some redistribution of the Polytechnic's resources. We believe that in any case there should be a reduction in the number of students following general arts degree courses at the Polytechnic.

VI.8   Department of Education for Northern Ireland, Higher Education in Northern Ireland — Future Structure. Belfast, HMSO 1982.

The government's response amounted virtually to the complete rejection of the Group's recommendations for the New University. Instead the decision was made to merge the New University of Ulster with the Polytechnic and to constitute a single institution to be known as the University of Ulster with effect from October 1984. In making this proposal the government also rejected what many had believed was a more likely alternative, the merger of the New University with Queen's. Ironically, the proposed new institution promised a more significant role for Magee College than that which it had enjoyed as part of The New University.

The government's case is set out in the following extracts from its document which commented on the Chilver Committee's Report:

THE BASIS OF THE NEW INSTITUTION

4.1.   Although there would be superficial logic in merging two universities, rather than a university and a polytechnic, the facts of the situation lend themselves more easily to a merger with the polytechnic.

Thus —

(a)   QUB is already the largest higher education institution in Northern Ireland. It is a specific recommendation of the Review Group that QUB should not greatly increase in size, and to add NUU to it would produce a large and unwieldy institution.

(b)   As a mature and long-established institution, QUB has its own deep-rooted traditions and attitudes. These would not lend themselves readily to developing into a split-site institution with a major focus outside Belfast.

(c)   The Polytechnic has shown itself to be a flexible institution with a marked capacity for innovation. It is likely to be able to adapt to the changes which such a merger would entail.

(d)   The Polytechnic has already developed an interest in a regional role, and has initiated programmes which involve the use of out-centres to bring higher education opportunities to part-time students who live at a distance from Belfast. There is thus an existing basis for developing a policy of geographical out-reach.

4.2   The Government also believes that the existing talents of NUU and of the Polytechnic are complementary, and that a merged institution which combined the stronger features of each of the existing institutions would be of major benefit to Northern Ireland. The Review Group pays particular tribute to the Polytechnic's energy and innovation, and sees its practical and vocational courses as being particularly strong, but sees also a need for some academic consolidation. By contrast, the Report points out that NUU's range of courses is lacking in vocational and professional studies, but does not question its academic standing. The concept of a merger thus provides an opportunity for these distinctive strengths to be combined.

4.3   If Northern Ireland is to have only two major higher education institutions, it is also important that they should each have a clear and distinctive role. The role of QUB as a traditional university centre of scholarship is clearly endorsed in the Review Group's Report; while this is without detriment to the need for QUB also to maintain and develop vocational courses, it gives a particular academic emphasis to the totality of QUB's work. A new institution which incorporated the particular applied and technological emphasis of the Polytechnic would be a valuable counterpoint.

NATURE OF THE NEW INSTITUTION

4.4   If the merger is to be successful, it will be important to establish at the outset that this would not be a case of one institution taking over the other. Rather, what is required is a new institution which will subsume and replace both the existing institutions. This in itself will make it easier to incorporate the strengths of each existing institution while shedding weaknesses.

4.5   The government believes that it will be appropriate for the new institution to be a university, rather than a polytechnic. It is of course essential that the nature and range of the new institution's activities should not be preconditioned by any particular conception of roles, and the government does not intend the new institution to be curtailed in principle from offering any less wide a range of levels of study or courses than is at present available in NUU and the Polytechnic.

4.6   There are many different models of universities, both within the United Kingdom and wider afield. The government wishes the new institution to have the distinctively practical and applied emphasis which is referred to in Section 4.3. This does not preclude other purely academic activities, but it is essential that the main emphasis be quite distinct from that of QUB. It is also essential that the existing non-degree work of the Polytechnic should be incorporated and maintained within the new institution, and that appropriate provision should continue to be made for part-time studies.

4.7   The government envisages that the new institution will make a significant provision in the field of teacher education. While it would be premature at present to say what the precise distribution of courses and activities must be amongst the several campuses of the new institution, teacher education is clearly one activity that would be best centred, in whole or in part, in Coleraine rather than at Jordanstown. This would be in keeping with the Review Group's suggestion that there should be a major teacher education base outside the Belfast area.

4.8   Magee University College in Londonderry will also be a significant element within the new institution.   As the only campus of the new institution that will be located in the middle of a large concentration of population, and as serving an area remote from the educational facilities of the Belfast area, the government acknowledges the force of the Review Group's view that fuller use could, and should, be made of Magee in meeting the immediate requirements of the Londonderry area.. The nature of the new institution should lend itself well to making maximum use of the Magee campus in the provision of courses and activities which relate directly to the immediate requirements of the Londonderry area, which is the role envisaged for Magee in the Report.

VI.9   The Open University.

The Open University (OU), established in Britain in 1969, to provide university level courses through 'distance learning' has operated a regional centre in Belfast from 1971.   Since then it has made a small, but significant contribution to the provision of undergraduate, postgraduate and post-experience courses in Northern Ireland. The following extract is taken from Chapter II of the Chilver Committee's report which reviewed the work of the Open University in Northern Ireland:

11.1   The OU was established by Royal Charter in 1969, and first admitted students in 1971. Essentially the University is concerned with teaching part-time adult students at a distance.   The method is a combination of correspondence texts, television and radio broadcasts — produced in partnership with the BBC — other audio-visual techniques, and both correspondence and face-to-face tuition.   The study programme offered includes undergraduate and postgraduate courses; courses for associate students — that is to say, courses which may be taken outside a degree programme; and short courses — not at university level — for community education.

11.2   In Northern Ireland the OU functions in the same way as in other parts of the United Kingdom which, for administrative purposes the OU has divided into 13 regions, of which Northern Ireland is one.   The University's admissions policy is to maintain a relationship between the number of applicants admitted from each region and that region's population as a proportion of the total population of the United Kingdom.   In the case of Northern Ireland this has been taken to be 2.8%.

11.3   Within the Northern Ireland region the approach to the allocation of places has been, up to the present, on a first-come first-served basis.   Although there is an occupational quota, we were told that this has not been operated for several years and that, in any event, it had relatively little effect on intakes.

11.4   The OU has established nine study centres throughout Northern Ireland where students may meet each other and the part-time staff, where they may view broadcasts and have access to computer terminals.   While data on the area of domicile of students taking OU courses were not available to us, we were given to understand that the breakdown of new undergraduate students by study centre would provide a fair representation of the geographical distribution of students. Table 11.1 lists this breakdown for 1976 and 1981. It will be seen that the geographical distribution of new undergraduate students at the various study centres indicates a concentration of numbers in areas close to Belfast with 79% of students attending centres within 40 miles of Belfast.

11.5 The most remote counties from Belfast are Armagh, Fermanagh, Londonderry and Tyrone. The percentage distribution of population — 1971 census — by county compared with the geographical distribution of new undergraduate students is shown in Table 11.2. While, on the basis of population alone, there appears to be a fair representation of students from the more remote areas, we feel that the OU may not have taken sufficient account of the distances applicants live from the traditional higher education institutions. Hence our belief, stated in section 3.20 that the OU should consider placing emphasis on the admission of applicants who reside at a distance from the major higher education institutions, so as to compensate for this disadvantage. We recommend, therefore, that future admissions policy in Northern Ireland should take account of this.

GUIDE TO SOURCES

Volume I of *Irish Educational Documents* contains (pp364-83) a "Guide to Sources" which lists bibliographies, guides and primary material. We now include a guide to two other sources:

(a)   a list of journals in which articles of importance to the history of Irish education appear;

(b)   a select bibliography of secondary works relating to education in Northern Ireland.

(a) Articles of significance for the study of Irish education have appeared in the following journals. Where possible, their date of first publication is given:

An Múinteoir, Journal of the Irish National Teachers Organisation, Previously *An Múinteoir Náisiunta.*

ASTIR, Journal of the Association of Secondary Teachers, Ireland.

Catholic University Bulletin, (1903- 1914).

Church of Ireland Gazette (1900-), Formerly *Irish Ecclesiastical Gazette* (1856-).

Compass, Journal of the Irish Association for Curriculum Development (1972-).

Dublin Review (1836- 1968/9).

Hermathena : a Trinity College, Dublin, Review (1875-)

Irish Booklover.

Irish Ecclesiastical Record (1865- 1968).

Irish Education Decision- maker. (1990-).

Irish Educational Review (1908- 1914).

Irish Educational Studies, Conference Papers of the
  Educational Studies Association of Ireland (1981-),
  Previously *Proceedings of the Annual Conference
  of the Educational Studies Association of Ireland* (1977-1980).

Irish Journal of Education (1967-).

Irish Monthly (1873- 1954).

Irish Review (1911- 1914).

Irish University Review (1954-).

Journal of the Statistical and Social Enquiry Society of Ireland (1855-).

Journal of the Teachers Union of Ireland.

New Ireland Review (1894- 1911).

Nineteenth Century (1877- 1950).

Oideas: Iris na Roinne Oideachais, Journal of the Department of
  Education, Dublin (1968-).

Proceedings of the Irish Catholic Historical Committee, (1955-1968.)

Search : a Church of Ireland Journal (1978-), Previously
  New Divinity (1970-).

Social Studies (1972-), Previously *Christus Rex.*

Studia Hibernica (1960-).

Studies in Education (1983-).

Studies : an Irish quarterly review.

Ulster Folklife.

(b) A select bibliography of works relating to education in Northern Ireland

AKENSON, D.H.,
Education and Enmity: the control of schooling in Northern Ireland 1920-50 (Newton Abbot and New York, 1973).

BUCKLAND, P.,
The factory of grievances (Dublin, 1979).

CAMPBELL, J.J. ,
Catholic Schools: a survey of a Northern Ireland problem (Belfast, n.d.).

CORKEY, W.,
Episode in the history of Protestant Ulster 1923-1947 (Belfast, 1948).

CRAIG, A.R. and McNEILLY, N.,
Belfast Model Schools 1922-1957 (Belfast, n.d.).

ELLIS,T.H.,
Noisy Mansions, (Lisnaskea, 1983), Secondary Education in Northern Ireland post- 1947.

GILLIES, J.F. and WHITE, O.,
Technical education in Northern Ireland: an historical study (Ulster Polytechnic, Belfast, 1982).

HENDERSON, J.W.,
Methodist College, Belfast 1868-1938 (2 Vols., Belfast, 1939).

JAMIESON, J.,
The history of the Royal Belfast Academical Institution 1810- 1960 (Belfast, 1959).

LAWRENCE, R.J.,
The government of Northern Ireland: public finance and public services, 1921-64 (Oxford, 1965).

MARSHALL, R.,
   Stranmillis College, Belfast (Belfast, n.d.).

McALEER, J. and McALEAVY, O. M.,
   Further education in Northern Ireland: the context and development (Belfast, 1989).

McIVOR, J.A.,
   Popular education in the Irish Presbyterian Church (Dublin, 1969).

McNEILLY, N.,
   Exactly fifty years: the Belfast Education Authority and its work 1923- 1973 (Belfast, 1974).

MOODY, T.W. and BECKETT, J.C.,
   Queen's Belfast 1845- 1949: the history of a university (2 Vols., London, 1959).

ROBSON, R.B.,
   Autobiography of an Ulster Teacher (Belfast, 1937).

WALLACE, M.,
   Northern Ireland: 5O years of self- government (Newton Abbot, 1971).

APPENDIX I

Introduction to Ministry of Education Files 1921-1960s in the Public Record Office of Northern Ireland.

(Trevor Parkhill)

ESTABLISHMENT OF THE MINISTRY

The Ministry of Education was established under the provisions of the Government of Ireland Act, 1920 on 7 June 1921. The new Ministry took over all or some of the functions of four separate, semi-autonomous government agencies which had administered education in Ireland previous to partition. These were the Commissioners of National Education in Ireland, the Intermediate Education Board for Ireland, the Department of Agriculture and Technical Instruction, and the Commissioners of Education in Ireland.

1923 EDUCATION ACT

The first Minister of Education in the Northern Ireland Government was Charles, 7th Marquess of Londonderry. He appointed a committee, under the chairmanship of Sir Robert Lynn, to examine the existing educational system and to make recommendations for extensive reforms. The report of the Lynn Committee was to form the basis of the Education Act, 1923, which shaped the educational structure in Northern Ireland for some 25 years. Essentially, this Act delegated the daily administration of schools willing to come under government control to eight local education authorities based upon the existing county and county borough councils. These authorities would be responsible for the provision and maintenance of schools, as well as the award of scholarships to enable all pupils to attend secondary establishments though the finance for these schemes would come mainly from the Northern Ireland Exchequer. Schools built by the authorities were termed 'provided,' while those coming under government control were designated 'transferred.' Overall control was to rest with the Ministry of Education. This was most apparent in the elementary sector, whose syllabuses and teachers' salaries had long been regulated by the preceding National Education system. Schools retained the right to remain independent of government control if they so desired. Those that did were termed 'voluntary' schools. Voluntary schools could claim only 50% of annual overhead costs from the educational authorities, although those schools which placed their management into the hands of a statutory committee, one third of whose membership was nominated by the authority, were entitled to a greater degree of assistance. The composition of these committees was such that they acquired the popular label of 'four and two' boards.

The Act of 1923 did not meet with universal approval. The churches — Roman Catholic and Protestant — expressed reservations, particularly with regard to the reduced degree of control they would retain in former church schools under transferred or voluntary 'four and two' status. Furthermore, the churches asserted that the provisions regarding religious instruction were inadequate. The Marquess of Londonderry was, accordingly, criticised by church leaders and by other religious organisations. Subsequent amendments made in 1925 and 1930 relating to 'Bible Instruction' went some way to accommodating Protestant viewpoints; however the Catholic hierarchy remained very strongly of the opinion that it would not be in the interests of the church to place schools under government control.

WAR-TIME EDUCATION

The Second World War placed new burdens on the Ministry of Education. The schooling of evacuees had to be provided for, often in rural schools whose curricula did not cater for urban dwellers.   Teachers had to be trained in the instruction of young children in emergency procedures to be followed in the events of gas or bomb attack.   Indeed, a good deal of the syllabus had to be re-oriented towards the wartime situation.   The war effort, however, necessitated the complete cessation of school-building programmes, and severe restrictions on normal maintenance work. This, coupled with war damage and a steep rise in the birth rate immediately after the end of hostilities, placed immense pressure on the post-war educational structure in Northern Ireland.   The Ministry of Education recognised the inadequacy of many schools to meet those new demands.   Moreover, the passage in the Imperial Parliament of the Education Act of 1944, which overhauled much of the educational structure in Great Britain, placed a responsibility on the Ministry to introduce similar reforms.

1947 EDUCATION ACT

Legislation designed to provide an educational system for the post-war period came in the Education Act (NI), 1947 which repealed virtually all existing statutes.   All children were now to be given some form of secondary education.   The elementary schools, which had formerly catered for children from the age of 6 up to the age of 14, were re-styled primary schools, catering for the education of children from 5 until the age of 11.   At age 11-12, selection tests would be undertaken by each child, if parents so wished, to ascertain which type of secondary education was most suited to its abilities.   Initially, three types of secondary education were to be offered: secondary intermediate, technical intermediate, and secondary grammar.   However, as the technical sector remained comparatively small in practice the choice was restricted to two types.   Intermediate education was to be free, while scholarships were to be provided by the education authorities to allow more able children, from families with limited financial means, to attend grammar schools — in practice, scholarship holders were to become the majority.   Secondary education was to continue until age 15 and instruction for the Junior and Senior Certificate Examinations was also to be provided.

The distinction between county and voluntary schools remained, though the latter could now recoup 65% of their overhead costs, with additional benefits available to those voluntary schools willing to come into the 'four and two' sector, and also to voluntary grammar schools ('A' schools) which reserved 80% of places each year for scholarship holders (as compared with 'B' voluntary grammar schools which did not).   While the Catholic church authorities acknowledged that voluntary schools in Northern Ireland received more by way of subsidy than church schools in England and Wales, they remained reluctant to apply for county status, not wishing to place the distinctiveness of Catholic education in jeopardy.

DEVELOPMENTS IN 1960s

Although much of the Education Act (NI), 1947 was scheduled to come into force on 1 April 1948, it was to be some years before its provisions were fully implemented.   Unreorganised elementary schools, while declining in number, remained a feature of the Northern Ireland education structure until the mid-1960s.   The school-leaving age was not raised to 15 until 1957; compulsory schooling to the age of 16 did not come into effect until 1 September 1972.   Technical education establishments remained few in number, and the concept of technical education was eventually phased out after 1964, being replaced by more general secondary (intermediate) and grammar schooling.   Even in 1922, many schools were too small and in other ways inadequate for teaching purposes.   In effect, not only had the educational structure to be remodelled, but also an extensive programme of building and re-building schools had to be undertaken.   This was only largely achieved by the late 1960s.   Reform, therefore, had always to take account of the facilities available: the wide-ranging changes proposed by the 1947 Act could not be implemented in buildings or with equipment which had been designed for the education of children prior to 1918.

The last years of the Parliament of Northern Ireland witnessed further improvements in educational provision, primarily in administration. The maintenance of libraries and museums was transferred from the Ministry of Health and Local Government to the Ministry of Education on 1 May 1964, while the award of university scholarship grants previously made by the Ministry of Finance came under the remit of Education on 1 January 1965. However, the most radical restructuring proposal was that of transferring the daily supervision of schools from the eight local education authorities to five education and library boards. These boards would be financed entirely by taxation and be directly answerable to the Minister. Although this was accepted at the time, the changeover did not take place until 1 October 1973, after the indefinite prorogation of the Parliament of Northern Ireland. The voluntary school sector also was subject to reorganisation. The Education (Amendment) Act (NI), 1968 provided for the establishment of Maintained Schools to replace the voluntary sector: 'four and two' management was to be encouraged, while subsidy levels were raised to between 80 and 100% depending upon the nature of the costs.

DEPARTMENT OF EDUCATION (NI) FROM 1974

The Ministry of Education continued to function after the suspension of the Parliament of Northern Ireland on 30 March 1972. With the passage of the Northern Ireland Constitution Act, 1973, however, it was abolished and replaced, from 1 January 1974, by the present Department of Education for Northern Ireland.

ED 13 SERIES

ED 13 comprises two series of files, both of a varied nature, covering all aspects of the Ministry of Education's portfolio, though in those areas where the Ministry had a greater role — particularly in the elementary/primary education sector — the number of files is proportionally larger.

The 'G' series (listed under ED.13/1) is the larger of two series, containing some 2800 files dating (in some cases) from the mid-1880s to the 1960s, though the majority of papers relate to the years between 1922 and 1955. Since the Ministry of Education succeeded four other government bodies, files were transferred (mainly from Dublin) to the Government of Northern Ireland to ensure continuity of operations, thus some information pre-dates 1921. The content of the 'G' files reflects the variety of issues which the Ministry of Education was called on to deal with, ranging widely over educational policy and practice. In addition to papers relating to the extensive building programme, there are files on topics such as payment of school fees, status of teachers in model schools, instruction in the Irish language, the payment by the Free State of salaries of teachers in Northern Ireland schools who refused to recognise the newly created state, school attendance, appointments to committees, curriculum matters including religious instruction in schools, and particular instance papers involving disputes, both between schools and the Ministry of Education and between teachers and the respective education authorities.

There is a considerable quantity of material (from ED.13/1/1800-2220) which is concerned with the management of the education system during the war years 1939-1945. This includes files on the 1938 Education Act whose most significant recommendation, the raising of the school-leaving age to 15, was postponed until after the war. There are papers on the role of education in general and schools in particular — for first-aid and technical training, as evacuation centres and for the collection of scarce commodities — during the emergency until 1945.

The 'G' series continues for a number of years after the Second World War and contains papers relating to, for example, transport problems arising out of the changes brought about by the implementation of the 1947 Education Act. There is also material on the developing responsibilities of the Ministry of Education in the late 1940s including, for example, a series of files (/1/2030-2037) on the Council for the Encouragement of Music and the Arts, forerunner to the Arts Council.

ED.13/2, the General and Policy (Numerical) Series contains evidence of the extensive changes that became apparent in educational provision in the 1950s, with the full implementation of the 1947 Education Act. As was the case in the 'G' series in ED.13/1, the content of the c.130 files varies widely. The early files are concerned largely with development schemes for primary, secondary, technical and grammar schools, and with the advisory councils that were established in the mid-1950s. The papers of committees on teachers' salaries, local authorities' financial arrangements for education, and files relating to schemes of management for teacher training colleges, the selection of pupils for secondary level education and the provision of special education, especially for physically handicapped children, are representative of the increasingly complex professional matters with which the Ministry of Education had to deal. The developing cultural role of the Ministry may also be seen in this series. Files relating to the Ulster Museum, the Ulster Folk and Transport Museum and the Armagh Planetarium reflect the Ministry of Education's involvement in the provision of cultural institutions of international repute in Northern Ireland.

MINISTRY OF FINANCE TREASURY DIVISION FILES (FIN.18)

The Ministry of Finance was formally established on 7 June 1921 "to administer the financial business of the Government of Northern Ireland ... and will discharge functions corresponding to ... the Treasury of the Government of the United Kingdom ... It will also administer the business of the Government of Northern Ireland in connection with taxation and will discharge functions in relation to taxes which the Parliament of Northern Ireland has power to impose ..."

The importance attached to these treasury responsibilities meant that, of the seven divisions in the Ministry of Finance, itself the senior ministry, Treasury Division was to be pre-eminent. It was to carry out duties which had been formerly administered by the Imperial Treasury: it was also charged with certain administrative powers formerly exercised by the Irish Department in Dublin.

In broad terms, the files of Treasury Division fall into the following main categories:

1.   The control of all proposals for the drafting of estimated public expenditure.

2.   Financial relations between Imperial and Northern Ireland Exchequers, including the calculation of contributions paid and received by the N.I. Government.

3.   The Northern Ireland government's annual budget.

4.   Collection of tax revenue which the N.I. government had power to levy, death and stamp duties, etc.

5.   A range of administrative functions including teachers' pensions, coordination of parliamentary business, charitable donations and requests, Land Purchase annuities, the issue of public loans under the Loans Guarantee Act etc.

The core work of Treasury Division, that of managing public finance and treasury matters, was determined by the conditions of the Government of Ireland Act, 1920. This limited the Northern Ireland government's monetary and fiscal powers and, in the inter-war years, as revenue declined and expenditure rose, the work of the Division became increasingly difficult. In addition to its Treasury role, the Ministry of Finance was to be responsible for the services previously administered by the Paymaster General, the Commissioners of Public Works, the Register of Births, Deaths and Marriages, the Commissioner of Valuation and the Commissioners of Charitable Donations and Bequests.

The files in FIN.18 are concerned with Treasury Division's work in the discharge of all these responsibilities. There are a number of specific topics relating to the establishment of the new government and its wide-ranging political, economic and social responsibilities which can be identified. The subject areas with which the files are concerned are set out in the text which follows. Individual file numbers have been given where considered appropriate. Normally, however, a number of files scattered throughout the archives may relate to any one topic; and other files not immediately relating to the topic may in fact contain papers associated with it. The researcher will, therefore, find it profitable to consult the list of records in FIN.18 using this appendix as the general guide it is intended to be.

CHIEF SECRETARY'S OFFICE FILES

The earliest files in the archive in point of fact pre-date formation of the new administration in June 1921. They began as files of the Chief Secretary's Office, Belfast Branch, and are concerned with the establishment of the Northern Ireland government and its administrative structure, in addition to the transfer of official records from Dublin to Belfast. The first two files in the FIN 18/1 series are the forerunners of a series of files in this class which look at the financial arrangements of the new Northern Ireland government as set out in the Government of Ireland Act, 1920. Funds were transferable to it by order of the Joint Exchequer Board which had been created by the 1920 Act.

GOVERNMENT STAFFING AND ACCOMMODATION

The contribution of Sir Arthur Clark to the establishing of an effective administration, even before the details of the Government of Ireland Act had been settled, is evident in a number of areas, not least in his gathering together of a civil service staff capable of carrying out day-to-day duties while political uncertainty and civil unrest continued. He estimated that, exclusive of staff in labour exchanges and out-branches, accommodation for some 350 staff would be required initially (FIN.18/1/270).

The accommodation and equipment that was required in the establishment of the new administration feature is in the FIN.18 archive. In FIN.18/1 are details of its early locations, including the Presbyterian Assembly College, Belfast City Centre and Stormont Castle, and Government House, Hillsborough. There is also a file containing a case made out by Armagh Chamber of Commerce to have Parliament House sited in Armagh city (FIN.18/1/194). The transfer of records to the area covered by the six Ulster counties, and of books in the library and law room at Dublin Castle and the Irish Office in London, are also detailed.

IMPERIAL CONTRIBUTION

The Imperial Contribution was the annual amount paid by the Northern Ireland Government to the Westminster parliament for 'imperial services' (the army, navy, servicing the National Debt etc.). This was supposed to be a fixed charge on the revenue and was determined initially at nearly £8 million, though it had dwindled away to a token figure by the 1930s in acknowledgement of the Northern Ireland government's financially parlous position. Throughout the early series in the FIN.18 archive are a number of files containing papers created and gathered by the Ministry of Finance on this crucial topic, which links the economic difficulties faced by both governments with the political considerations of the maintenance of good relations between Westminster and Belfast.

JOINT EXCHEQUER BOARD

The income from most taxes, under the Government of Ireland Act, was 'reserved' to the parliament at Westminster and included income tax, customs duties and excise duties, all of which were imposed at uniform rates throughout the UK. The Joint Exchequer Board was responsible for allocating to Northern Ireland its share of the United Kingdom revenue. The Board was to consist of a chairman appointed by the Crown (Lord Colwyn), one from the Treasury in London and a representation of the Ministry of Finance, this latter position being filled by Sir Ernest Clark, Permanent Secretary of the Ministry. The Joint Exchequer Board determined the sum Northern Ireland should contribute towards reserved and excepted or imperial services and left the remainder of revenue to fund transferred services. It was also to settle any financial questions arising between the British and the Irish governments, including any matter "in connection with the Irish residuary share of reserved taxes, or Irish revenue to expenditures, or the cost of any reserved service which may be referred to them for determination."

The agenda and minutes of the JEB 1921-8 are available in FIN.18/6/64-69; and scattered throughout the FIN.18 archive is a number of files relating to the work of the Colwyn Committee which was set up to arbitrate in disagreements on financial provision for Northern Ireland.

COLWYN COMMITTEE

The Northern Ireland government had, from the outset, appealed against the financial provisions of the 1920 Act. The Conservative government in 1923 eventually agreed to refer the matter to arbitration and set up the Northern Ireland Arbitration Committee, more generally known as 'the Colwyn Committee' after its chairman, Lord Colwyn. The main responsibility for preparing the Northern Ireland case fell to Sir Ernest Clark, the Permanent Secretary of the Ministry. The implications which arose in trying to establish criteria for an equitable imperial contribution by Northern Ireland, and Clark's marshalling of the complicated economic evidence and statistics, some of it relating to Ireland's economic performance in the early days of the Act of Union of 1800, are outlined in the files relating to the Colwyn Committee.

SPECIAL CONSTABULARY

With the transfer of powers for law and order, the new government had at its disposal some 2,300 members of the RIC and some 20,000 'special' constabulary. The early files in FIN.18, particularly in FIN.18/1, provide evidence of the establishment of the Special Constabulary and its crucial security role in coping with military activities during the transitional period when the new Royal Ulster Constabulary replaced the Royal Irish Constabulary. The nature of the files in FIN.18/1-5 relating to the Special Constabulary, until its disbandment following the settlement of the boundary issue, include practical details on their equipment, pay,

conditions of service, pensions and compensation for injuries to
policy discussions and exchanges of papers involving the Prime
Minister, the Permanent Secretary of the Department of Finance,
and General Solly-Flood, military adviser to the government of
Northern Ireland.

ROYAL ULSTER CONSTABULARY

The role of the Ministry of Finance in controlling government
expenditure centrally is evident in the files in FIN.18/2-4 which
relate to the setting up and early years of the Royal Ulster
Constabulary under the Constabulary Act (N.I.) 1922 (FIN.18/2/12).
These include criteria for the enlistment of new members and
former officers in the Royal Irish Constabulary (FIN.18/2/257).
There is also a range of files on financial provision for the force as
a whole, in Estimates 1922-24 (FIN.18/2/203) and in a number of
files relating to pensions to be paid to widows of officers killed on
duty. In the later series of files is material relating to developments
in the RUC's role. These include the use of the force in the issuing
of gun and game licences, arrangements "for training officers of
coloured and other foreign forces" in Northern Ireland, and a
proposal to establish a village constable system, on the English
model, in selected venues in Northern Ireland.

PRISONS

The administration of prisons was principally the responsibility of
the Ministry of Home Affairs. There is, however, a number of
early files relating to the equipping and accommodation generally
of prisons in Northern Ireland (FIN.18/2/6 and 116-156). There
were other custodial centres in which the Ministry of Finance was
more closely involved, particularly in managing their finances.
The papers in FIN.18 include a series of files (some of which are
closed) relating to the special circumstances of the use of the ships
S.S. Argenta and the tender *Lull,* stationed in Belfast Lough, for the
internment in the early 1920s of identified nationalists. There are
also papers on file for internment camps at Ballykinler, Co. Down
and Larne, Co. Antrim; the proposed use of Malone Reformatory as

a joint state reformatory and borstal and the consequent consideration for determining a rate for contribution to its upkeep by county councils; the financial detail even extended to the Ministry setting a scale of fees for the infliction of floggings in Belfast Prison.

INDUSTRY

The establishment of the Northern Ireland government coincided with the deepening post-war recession which particularly affected Northern Ireland's staple industries, shipbuilding and linen.   To counter this decline in Britain, the Trade Facilities Bill became law in November 1922, by which the government guaranteed loans from clearing banks to industry.   In April 1922 this was introduced in Northern Ireland as the Loans Guarantee Act, to be supervised by the Ministry of Finance, as is recorded in the minutes of evidence of the Loans Guarantee Advisory Committee, 1923 (FIN.18/3/84).

Throughout the FIN.18 archive there is a significant number of files detailing the companies which applied to the Ministry for guarantee of loan.   A considerable proportion of the files relate to contracts for the construction of merchant and passenger ships by Harland and Wolff and Workman, Clark and Co., though the intervention by the government was not enough to prevent the latter from going into liquidation.   The files relating to ships contracted by Harland and Wolff to build for the Royal Mail Steam Packet Company contain some evidence of the battle of wills that went on between the Ministry and the RMG chairman Lord Kilsant, who had also succeeded Lord Pirrie as chairman of Harland and Wolff.   The Ministry of Finance had agreed to guarantee loans of over £4m; when Harland and Wolff could not repay them, and the Ministry tried to force Harland and Wolff to do so, Kilsant threatened to close the yard, with all its economic and social consequences. Nevertheless, the shipyard survived those turbulent times and the even more economically depressed 1930s, partly due to the orders it continued to receive from abroad, particularly the Scandinavian concern Burmeister and Wain.

Other enterprises applied to the Ministry to guarantee loans they
had taken out, including the Dunmurry Electric Light and Power
Company 1922-3, Grand Central Hotel Belfast, Londonderry Water
Scheme, Ballycastle Colliery and Tandragee Urban and Rural
Council for a local water supply installation. The Ministry of
Finance from 1922 also administered a series of public loans to
local enterprises and local authorities. Among these were, for
example, loans of £3,000 to Portadown UDC for the construction of
Pleasure Gardens and tennis courts (FIN.18/6) and of £46,700 for
new mains drainage scheme 1923-31 (FIN/6/47), to Donaghadee
UDC £9,500 for the erection of 28 houses etc, and to the
Londonderry Port Sanitary Authority, 1921-39 (FIN.18/4/51-2).

UNEMPLOYMENT

The rapid decline of shipbuilding and linen after 1920, a year which
saw the numbers employed in both industries at a peak, meant that
unemployment was already a serious problem when the new
administration took office. Throughout the FIN.18 archive is
evidence of how the government addressed the problem in its early
days, and the shape its policy took over the next few years.

Indeed, even before this, on October 1920 a deputation representing
trade union and labour organisations had met in Belfast with the
Chief Secretary of Ireland (FIN.18/1/68). Also in FIN.18/1 are
files containing papers on the causes and possible remedies for
government consideration of the scourge of unemployment. One
of the measures was the introduction of grants in aid of work
schemes. FIN.18/3/42-43 contain the papers of the Belfast
Unemployment Grants Committee for 1922 and 1923, and in
FIN.18/6/133 are papers relating to grants for specific schemes, in
this case the Belfast Harbour Commissioners.

Other papers in the archive reflect the extent of the serious
consideration given to finding even short-term solutions to the
problem. The financial burden of the abnormally high level of
unemployment in the early 1920s is outlined particularly clearly in

FIN.18/11/1-50. The Unemployment Insurance Fund, for which
the Northern Ireland government had assumed responsibility in
1921, proved an almost impossible monetary burden. The Ministry
of Finance wrote unsuccessfully to the Colwyn Committee in
September 1922 (FIN.11/12) to obtain an advance of nearly £1m to
maintain levels of unemployment relief on a par with those in
Britain. In the event, from 1925 the British government accepted
responsibility, under the Unemployment Reinsurance Agreement,
for any deficit in the unemployment funds. Experimental training
schemes for unemployed men were considered in 1925, in addition
to a general scheme for unemployment (FIN.18/4/61). In the
1930s, when the issue was just as problematic, ideas such as grants
to farmers for improvements to agricultural land as a means of
providing employment were considered (FIN.10/15/68).

AGRICULTURE

The difficult years experienced by agriculture throughout Ireland,
which were in contrast to the opportunities presented by the wide-
open market in Britain during the First World War, had financial
implications with which the Ministry of Finance, as well as the
Ministry of Agriculture, was concerned. In addition to the claims
by farmers for grants to recompense their post-war losses (which
were exacerbated by atrocious weather and poor growing
conditions in 1923 and 1924), there was the burden on the
Exchequer of the Land Purchase Act of 1925 which completed the
work of the late 19th and early 20th centuries in the transference of
ownership of agricultural land from landlords to tenant farmers.

The Pirrie Committee set up in 1922 to give consideration to the
plight of farmers recommended that a non-statutory grant of
£128,000 be paid in assistance to agriculture 1923-6. Other more
specific aid given to the farming community in Northern Ireland in
the early years of the new administration included loans for the
replacement of animals lost through diseases, for fencing, for
house-building for the improvement of livestock, and for the
development of flax-growing. A grant was paid even to the Ulster
Farmers' Union. Some of the policy relating to grants in aid was

developed in association with the Empire Marketing Board whose Chairman, Sir Stephen Tallents had, as Imperial Secretary, been the representative of the British Government in Northern Ireland during the formative period of the new administration.

The gradual reversal at Westminster in the later 1920s and early 1930s of the traditional policy of free trade in agricultural produce was mirrored and, in some cases, anticipated by the Northern Ireland government. For example, the 1928 Marketing of Eggs Bill, proposals on the marketing of potatoes, and a scheme (1928-32) which used the resources of the Agriculture Development Fund to extend poultry breeding foreshadowed the general encouragement offered to farmers in Britain, in the form of subsidies, for milk, cattle and bacon.

The files of Treasury Division also reflect the Ministry of Agriculture's activities in the proposed acquisition of lands for afforestation; in fertilising and feeding stuffs, for which a Bill was introduced in 1926; in fisheries, on which an advisory committee was established in 1926; in the agricultural cooperative movement and in the dairying industry. Of particular interest with regard to the latter are the papers in FIN.18/4/250 which relate the government's proactive role in experimenting with a scheme to produce butter of a uniform quality, in response to competition, from cream supplied to a central creamery by a number of auxiliary creameries.

TRANSPORT

There is in the FIN.18 archive evidence of developments in the three main forms of transport with which the new government had to cope; railways (which, of course, had long been established); cars and buses, still in their infancy, and aeroplanes, a brand new form of civil transport.

The inter-war period witnessed the former dominance of railways consistently giving way to the competing claims of road transport, at least for the carriage of passengers. Several railways were in receipt of grants in aid, including the Londonderry and Lough Swilly Railway and the Clogher Valley Railway Company, into which there was held an inquiry in the late 1920s. The growth of road transport was a source of income for the Northern Ireland government as it was one of the few forms of taxation not administered or centralised in London. The local revenue raised via vehicle taxation is described in FIN.18/3/78. There was also the consequent need for traffic regulations, specifically in the Motor Traffic Act, 1926 and the Motor Vehicles Regulations Bill, 1929. The Roads Advisory Committee, established in 1924, recommended that "as the driving of such (motor) vehicles at high rates of speed has a disastrous effect on the roads ... the police should be urged to take strong action ... it is proposed to supply the Royal Ulster Constabulary with stop-watches or seconds-recorders for the purpose of checking the speed of motor vehicles on public roads."

As far as air transport is concerned, as early as 1928 (FIN.18/8/28) there was a proposal to start an air service between Northern Ireland and Great Britain.

TRADE BOYCOTT

The boycott of goods made in and transported from Belfast, which had been the policy of the southern government, continued long after it was suppressed officially. FIN.18/1/102-4 relate details of the implementation of the boycott and government attempts to limit its effectiveness. There are also files relating the circumstances of cases of organised attacks on Roman Catholic traders in Belfast in 1921-2 (FIN.18/1/262).

EDUCATION

Education and the administration of educational establishments is perhaps the single most common theme in the FIN.18 series of files. This may be accounted for by the financial implications of the continuation of already established educational provision in national, model and technical schools following the partition of

Ireland. It was also a direct result of the 1923 Education Act which created a separate second tier of education in the form of intermediate secondary schools and sought to improve both the quality of school buildings and the average daily attendance at schools. The early years of the Northern Ireland government were, consequently, a period of thoroughgoing change in the educational provision available and this is evident in the papers of Treasury Division of the Ministry of Finance.

Teacher Training

The 1923 legislation not only expanded the educational system but also created a demand for more trained teachers. As far as Northern Ireland was concerned, this requirement presented particular difficulties. A paper on the Treasury Blue Notes file for education 1924-5 found that "the fact that only one of the seven Training Colleges recognised by the Commissioners of National Education was in Northern Ireland (St. Mary's Training College, Belfast, conducted by nuns of the Dominican Order) made it necessary for the Ministry of Education to take early steps to make provision under this head. The closing of Marlborough Street Training College (in Dublin) which had supplied to a large extent the needs of the north of Ireland, made this need still more urgent." A committee for the Training of Teachers was appointed in May 1922 and Stranmillis College was opened in October 1922. The question of enabling the training of male Roman Catholic teachers in St. Mary's Training College (whose students had, until then, been exclusively female), and the general issue of capitation grants for all training colleges, were all considered between 1923-1932.

Teachers

The involvement of the Ministry of Finance in the restructured educational system was largely associated with the pay, pensions and conditions of service of teachers. In particular, the question of providing a suitable pension system was incorporated in the Teachers' Superannuation Bill, 1925. In association with this central issue, Treasury Division attention was also brought to bear on a number of related questions. They included the settling of salary scales for teachers in the new secondary intermediate schools and the former national, now re-named public elementary, schools. There are also papers relating to the amendment of regulations of the employment and conditions of service of teachers in technical and preparatory schools. There were the tricky political problems of 'recalcitrant' national school teachers who did not recognise the newly-created state and whose salaries were paid (for some years) by the Free State government, and payments due to teachers who had been interned in the early days of the new government.

Independent and Special Schools

The Educational Endowments (Ireland) Act 1885 enabled schools not in the national school system to be governed and managed. Governors were elected for the management of the school, under the superintendence of the Judicial Commissioner constituted under the 1885 Act. There is a series of files throughout FIN.18 relating to the Ministry of Finance's involvement in the financial provision for these schools which were, on the whole, independent of the educational system administered by the Ministry of Education.

The files in FIN.18 contain papers on more specialised areas of education in whose financial provision the Ministry of Finance was involved. They include reformatory and industrial schools on which a departmental committee was established and whose papers (1922-3) are in Fin.18/3/16. There are also papers on the position under the Government of Ireland Act and Education Act (NI) 1923 of teachers in the former model schools. The early provision and maintenance of special schools for pupils with tuberculosis, specifically Graymount Open Air School, Belfast Municipal Sanatorium and Bangor Home of Rest, is related in FIN.18.2.

Local Education Authorities

The Education Act, 1923 contained provision for devolving the administration of the new arrangements for public elementary and secondary education to local county education authorities. A small number of files in FIN.18 contains papers relating to this important development for the administration of education in the province, particularly the transfer of schools to the County Borough of Belfast Education Committee.

CHARITY COMMISSIONERS FOR NORTHERN IRELAND

The practicalities of the transfer of services to the Belfast administration are evident in the many files dealing with charitable bequests. The Commissioners of Charitable Donations and Bequests had from their offices at 2, Kildare Place administered the conditions of many legacies. A large proportion of these were associated with churches and charities that had been set up prior to 1921. The two main responsibilities of the Commissioners, the distribution of income to the needy and the management of capital funds, now fell on Treasury Division of the Ministry of Finance.

FIRST NORTHERN IRELAND REVALUATION

There had been no general revaluation of property since the 1860s and the Northern Ireland government from the outset sought to bring up to date the income it could generate from the rateable valuation of lands and buildings. By 1926-7 it had obtained the agreement of the British government to proceed with a revaluation of property. This was carried out in 1935-6. Before that, the papers of the Valuation Committee of the Ministry of Finance, containing the agenda, minutes and discussion papers for meetings, also contain evidence of the controversial decision to de-rate agricultural land, itself an acknowledgement of the difficult period through which the farming industry went in the inter-war period (FIN.18/4/24; /4/266-7).

EMIGRATION

The increased interest in Northern Ireland in emigration in the 1920s was a predictable response to the increasingly difficult employment opportunities available to the working population. The United State's post-war policy on immigration made it increasingly difficult as an emigrant's destination, but this was compensated for to some degree by a range of schemes attracting emigrants to British Dominions. The two principal venues, Australia and Canada, were the subject of Imperial government schemes: the Ministry of Finance undertook to pay half the cost of meetings held throughout Northern Ireland at which intending emigrants heard further details of overseas settlement in Australia; there was also the Canadian Harvesters Scheme, in which the Prime Minister, Sir James Craig, took an interest, aimed at supplying the Canadian government with agricultural labour for harvesting wheat and other crops.

HOUSING

The provision of housing was a commitment which could have had even more serious financial implications for the Northern Ireland government. The Joint Exchequer Board, however, grant-aided the building of labourers' cottages, a scheme for the construction of which had been in operation since the end of the 19th century. Loans for these cottages were also available from the Land Purchase Commission. The provision of loans for soldiers and sailors was also a responsibility which fell to the new government.

PUBLIC RECORDS

One of the early pieces of legislation instituted by the Northern Ireland government was a Public Records Act, 1923. There are also files relating to the appointment of a Deputy Keeper of the Records and other staff in the Public Record Office of Northern Ireland. In FIN.18/1 and FIN.18/2 are files relating particularly to the transference of historical and administrative records from Dublin, including central registry records, Ordnance Survey records and papers relating to the Registry of Deeds.